W9-BDZ-345

In Memory of Her

Wherever the gospel is preached in the whole world,
what she has done will be told in memory of her.

Mark 14:9

Elisabeth Schüssler Fiorenza

IN MEMORY OF HER

A *Feminist Theological Reconstruction of Christian Origins*

CROSSROAD · NEW YORK

1983

The Crossroad Publishing Company
575 Lexington Avenue, New York, N.Y. 10022

Printed in the United States of America

Library of Congress Cataloging in Publication Data

Fiorenza, Elisabeth Schüssler, 1938—
  In memory of her.

  Includes bibliographical references.
  1. Christianity—Origin. 2. Women in Christianity—
History—Early church, ca. 30-600. 3. Bible.
N.T.—Criticism, interpretation, etc. I. Title.
BR129.F56 1983   270.1'088042   82-19896
ISBN 0-8245-0493-3

For Christina Marlene Schüssler Fiorenza

We are together, my child and I.
Mother and child, yes,
but *sisters* really,
against whatever denies us
all that we are.

                    Alice Walker

Contents

Acknowledgments

A book is never just the work of an author although it is her sole responsibility. This is especially true for a feminist theological work like this.

It is impossible to mention by name all the women who have contributed to my experience and thought, especially those with whom I have collaborated in building up the women's movement in the church and in developing feminist theology: the women of the national Women's Ordination Conference, Sisters Against Racism in Washington, D.C., the Feminist Theological Institute, New York, Women Scholars in Religion, Women Moving Church, the Women's Caucus of the AAR/SBL, WIT (Women in Theology) at Catholic University and Notre Dame, and the various task forces and workshops on the problems of women in church and theology. Discussions with my feminist colleagues in the academy have challenged and inspired me, while conversations with my friends have encouraged and sustained me in this undertaking. To all of you my heartfelt thanks.

Ms. Laurie Boddie, M.Div., acted as my research assistant during the summer of 1982, while Cheryl Reed, Sandy Dewulf, Karen Kretschner, and Janet Wright of the Notre Dame Word Processing Center typed the manuscript. I am grateful to them for their labors.

Some of the interpretations and arguments more fully developed in this book were presented in lectures and seminars at the following institutions: Chicago Divinity School, Perkins School of Theology, the Catholic University of America, Gettysburg Lutheran Theological Seminary, McGill University, Duke Divinity School, the University of Indiana, Seton Hill College, the College of St. Catherine, and Wichita State University. I have had the honor of discussing my work as Antoinette Brown lecturer at Vanderbilt Divinity School, J. Balmer Showers lecturer at Dayton United Theological Seminary, Colwell lecturer at the School of Theology in Claremont, Georgia Harkness lecturer at Garret-Evangelical Theological Seminary, Nelle Morton lecturer at Drew Divinity School, and as theologian in residence at the College of Wooster, Ohio. To have the opportunity for discussing with students and colleagues of these institutions difficult exegetical-hermeneutical problems regarding a feminist reconstruction of early Christian origins was of invaluable help in the development of my research and the crystallization of my thought.

Finally, I want to thank the men who have "nurtured" this book. Justus George Lawler's careful reading of the manuscript helped me to struggle through the writing process. Frank Oveis shepherded the manuscript through the different stages of editing and production with great care. Robert Craft and Frederick Holper checked the references and proofread the printed version. Mr. Holper not only attempted to catch my Germanisms in the different versions of the manuscript but as my teaching assistant for the past two years has also supported my work with intellectual enthusiasm for the theological-hermeneutical questions raised by feminist historical scholarship. Last but not least I am indebted beyond words to Francis Schüssler Fiorenza for his critical friendship and support.

Throughout the whole process Christina Schüssler Fiorenza has admonished me "to work hard" so that we would have more time to talk and play. I hope at some future point in her life she will realize that this book is part of our ongoing conversation and creative imagination.

NOVEMBER 12, 1982
BIRTHDAY OF ELIZABETH CADY STANTON

Introduction
In Search of
Women's Heritage

In the passion account of Mark's Gospel three disciples figure prominently: on the one hand, two of the twelve—Judas who betrays Jesus and Peter who denies him—and on the other, the unnamed woman who anoints Jesus. But while the stories of Judas and Peter are engraved in the memory of Christians, the story of the woman is virtually forgotten. Although Jesus pronounces in Mark: "And truly I say to you, wherever the gospel is preached in the whole world, what she has done will be told in memory of her" (14:9), the woman's prophetic sign-action did not become a part of the gospel knowledge of Christians. Even her name is lost to us. Wherever the gospel is proclaimed and the eucharist celebrated another story is told: the story of the apostle who betrayed Jesus. The name of the betrayer is remembered, but the name of the faithful disciple is forgotten because she was a woman.

Although the story of the anointing is told in all four Gospels,[1] it is obvious that the redactional retelling of the story seeks to make the story more palatable to a patriarchal Greco-Roman audience. Whereas the Fourth Gospel identifies the woman as Mary of Bethany who as faithful friend of Jesus shows her love by anointing him, Luke shifts the focus of the story from woman as disciple to woman as sinner. Whether Luke used Mark's text or transmits a different tradition is disputed. But this exegetical dispute does not matter much since we are used to reading the Markan story in the light of Luke. In the process the woman becomes a great sinner who is forgiven by Jesus.

Despite their differences, all four Gospels reflect the same basic story: a woman anoints Jesus. This incident causes objections which Jesus rejects by approving of the woman's action. If the original story had been just a story about the anointing of a guest's feet, it is unlikely that such a commonplace gesture would have been remembered and retold as the proclamation of the gospel. Therefore, it is much more likely that in the original story the woman anointed Jesus' head. Since the prophet in the Old Testament anointed the head of the Jewish king, the anointing of Jesus' head must have been understood immediately as the prophetic recognition of Jesus, the Anointed, the Messiah, the Christ. According to the tradition it was a woman who named Jesus by and through her prophetic sign-action. It was a politically dangerous story.[2]

In Mark's Gospel the story is sandwiched between the statement that the leaders of Jesus' people wanted to arrest him and the announcement of Jesus' betrayal by Judas for money. Mark thus depoliticizes the story of Jesus' passion: first, by shifting the blame for his death from the Romans to the Jewish establishment; and second, by theologically defining Jesus' messiahship as one of suffering and death. Whereas according to Mark the leading male disciples do not understand this suffering messiahship of Jesus, reject it, and finally abandon him, the women disciples who have followed Jesus from Galilee to Jerusalem suddenly emerge as the true disciples in the passion narrative. They are Jesus' true followers (akolouthein) who have understood that his ministry was not rule and kingly glory but diakonia, "service" (Mark 15:41). Thus the women emerge as the true Christian ministers and witnesses. The unnamed woman who names Jesus with a prophetic sign-action in Mark's Gospel is the paradigm for the true disciple. While Peter had confessed, without truly understanding it, "you are the anointed one," the woman anointing Jesus recognizes clearly that Jesus' messiahship means suffering and death.

Both Christian feminist theology and biblical interpretation are in the process of rediscovering that the Christian gospel cannot be proclaimed if the women disciples and what they have done are not remembered. They are in the process of reclaiming the supper at Bethany as women's Christian heritage in order to correct symbols and ritualizations of an all-male Last Supper that is a betrayal of true Christian discipleship and ministry.[3] Or, in the words of the artist Judy Chicago: "All the institutions of our culture tell us through words, deeds, and even worse silence that we are insignificant. But our heritage is our power."[4]

The explorations of this book have two goals: they attempt to reconstruct early Christian history as women's history in order not only to restore women's stories to early Christian history but also to reclaim this history as the history of women and men. I do this not only as a feminist historian but also as a feminist theologian. The Bible is not just a historical collection of writings but also Holy Scripture, gospel, for Christians today. As such it informs not only theology but also the commitment of many women today. Yet as long as the stories and history of women in the beginnings of early Christianity are not theologically conceptualized as an integral part of the proclamation of the gospel, biblical texts and traditions formulated and codified by men will remain oppressive to women.

Such a reconstruction of early Christian history as women's history and of biblical-historical theology as feminist theology presupposes historical and theological critical analysis as well as the development of a feminist biblical-historical hermeneutics. Since I am trained in New Testament exegesis, I will limit my explorations to the beginnings of Christianity but not include all of biblical history. Methodologically, however, it will be necessary to go beyond the limits of the New Testament canon since it is a product of the patristic church, that is, a theological document of the "historical winners." To forego such an undertaking because historical critical scholarship and hermeneutics are "male" but not feminist does an intellectual disservice to women. Since it reinforces male-female role stereotypes, such an assumption is not capable of naming the particular oppressive assumptions and androcentric components of such scholarship.

Reconstruction of early Christian history in a feminist perspective raises difficult hermeneutical, textual, and historical problems. Since feminism has developed different theoretical perspectives and models, this reconstruction must also include the formulation of a feminist heuristic framework or model that allows for the oppression as well as for the historical agency of women in early Christianity.

1. A fundamental methodological insight of historical criticism of the Bible was the realization that the *Sitz im Leben* or life setting of a text is as important for its understanding as its actual formulation. Biblical texts are not verbally inspired revelation nor doctrinal principles but historical formulations within the context of a religious community. Although this insight is challenged today by literary formalism as well as textual biblicism, it nevertheless remains basic to any historical reconstruction. Studies of the social world of Israel and early Christianity are in the process of developing heuristic models that comprehend more fully the social-historical context of the biblical texts.

Similarly, feminist theory insists that all texts are products of an androcentric patriarchal culture and history. The current feminist movement has therefore engendered an explosion of scholarly works in all areas of scientific inquiry and research.[5] Historians, philosophers, and anthropologists have emphasized that current scholarly theory and research are deficient because they neglect women's lives and contributions and construe humanity and human history as male. Feminist scholarship in all areas, therefore, seeks to construct heuristic models and concepts that allow us to perceive the human reality articulated insufficiently in androcentric texts and research.

The explorations of this book begin therefore with the hope of moving away from the pervasive apologetic that characterizes most treatments of women in the Bible, to a historical-critical reconstruction of women's history and women's contributions to early Christian beginnings. Moreover, I have assumed that the new questions raised by feminist scholarship will enhance our understanding of early Christian history. The attempt to "write women back into early Christian history" should not only restore early Christian history to women but also lead to a richer and more accurate perception of early Christian beginnings. If scholars employ philosophical, sociological, or psychological analyses for constructing new interpretative models of early Christian development, nothing should prevent us from utilizing feminist heuristic concepts as well, in order to reconstruct an early Christian history in which women are not hidden and invisible. While an androcentric model cannot do justice to those texts that positively mention women's leadership in early Christianity, a feminist model can positively integrate them.

Biblical scholars, however, do not perceive the question as a serious historical problem of great significance for the reconstruction of early Christian history and theology. As a "woman's issue" it is trivial or marginal to the academic enterprise. Seen as a "woman's problem" the issue belongs to books and symposia on "woman" but not in the program of exegetical conferences or in the pages of an exegetical *Festschrift*. Usually, anyone identified with the "feminist cause" is ideologically suspect and professionally discredited. As one of my colleagues remarked about a professor who had written a moderate article on women in the Old Testament: "It is shame, she may have ruined her scholarly career."

The tacit assumption underlying such expressed or unexpressed reservations is that scholars who do not reflect or articulate their political allegiances are "objective," free from bias, nonpartisan and scientific. Yet, anyone even slightly familiar with problems raised by the sociology of knowledge or by critical theory will have difficulty asserting such scholarly objectivity on scientific grounds. In a brilliant analysis of slavery in antiquity the eminent scholar Moses Finley has explored the ways in which current ideological and societal interests have deeply affected the historiography of ancient slavery. He sums up his explorations:

> Nevertheless, other contemporary ideological considerations are active in that seemingly remote field of historical study—active in the sense that they underlie, and even direct, what often appears to be a purely "factual," "objective" presentation. . . . I believe that a full, open account of how modern interest in ancient slavery has manifested itself is a necessary prerequisite to the substantive analysis of the institution itself, and I have therefore begun with that theme.[6]

Since historical knowledge is inferential (Collingwood), historians have to construct some frame of reference within which to discuss the available historical evidence. Such a frame of reference is always determined by their own philosophical perspective and values. Historians who pretend to record nothing but pure facts while refusing to acknowledge their own presuppositions and theoretical perspectives succeed only in concealing from themselves the ideologies upon which their historiography is based. All historiography is a selective view of the past. Historical interpretation is defined by contemporary questions and horizons of reality and conditioned by contemporary political interests and structures of domination. Historical "objectivity" can only be approached by reflecting critically on and naming one's theoretical presuppositions and political allegiances.

Interest in legitimization, as well as in opening up future possibilities, is a major motif in biblical interpretation. As James Robinson states:

> New Testament scholarship as an intellectual activity is a modern science reflecting as well as molding the modern understanding of reality, a reciprocity it shares with the humanities in general. . . . Every scholar or scientist who deals with a subject matter from the past does so in terms of his present grasp of reality and the results of his research in turn flow into the current body of knowledge from which the continual modification of our understanding of reality emerges.[7]

If this is the case—and I believe it is—then it must be asked whether the reluctance of scholars to investigate the present topic might be sustained by an unconscious or conscious refusal to modify our androcentric grasp of reality and religion rather than by a legitimate concern for the integrity of biblical-historical scholarship. The dictum of Simone de Beauvoir about scholarship on women in general applies also to studies of women in the Bible: "If the 'woman's question' seems trivial it is because masculine arrogance has made it a 'quarrel' and when quarrelling one no longer reasons well."[8]

2. While it is hard to dislodge the intellectual misgivings of my colleagues in the academy, I have found it even more difficult to sustain my biblical interests in the face of feminist objections. Questions and misgivings expressed by women in response to my lectures and publications have taught me how to phrase problems more clearly and how to keep in mind the structural obstacles to a feminist historiography or theology. Such exchanges have also compelled me to explore more deeply how a "feminist hermeneutics" can be formulated. The first part of this book—which might to many women seem strange and too academic at first glance—owes its conception to feminist rather than to academic theoretical questions.

When I attempt to explore the history of women who became Christians in the beginnings of Christianity this should not be misunderstood as an attempt to save the Bible from its feminist critics. I simply mean to raise the question: How can early Christian origins be reconstructed in such a way as to be understood as "women's affairs"? In other words, is early Christian history "our own" history or heritage? Were women as well as men the initiators of the Christian movement?

While theologians in the academy refuse to discuss publicly their own political allegiance and preconceived bias and function, many postbiblical feminists are prepared to relinquish their historical roots and their solidarity with women in biblical religion. Recognizing that androcentric Western language and patriarchal religion have "erased" women from history and made them "non-beings," such feminists argue that biblical religion (and theology) is sexist to the core. It is not retrievable for women, since it ignores women's experience, speaks of the godhead in male terms, legitimizes women's subordinate positions of powerlessness, and promotes male dominance and violence against women. Therefore, feminists must move beyond the boundaries of biblical religion and reject the patriarchal authority of biblical revelation. Revisionist interpretations of the Bible are at best a waste of time and at worst a legitimization of the prevailing sexism of biblical religion—therefore, a cooptation of women and the feminist movement. Feminist praxis is rooted in the religious experience of contemporary women but does not derive its inspiration from the Christian past.

Yet such a postbiblical feminist stance is in danger of becoming ahistorical and apolitical. It too quickly concedes that women have no authentic history within biblical religion and too easily relinquishes women's feminist biblical heritage. Nor can such a stance do justice to the positive experiences of contemporary women within biblical religion. It must either neglect the influence of biblical religion on women today or declare women's adherence to biblical religion as "false consciousness." Insofar as biblical religion is still influential today, a cultural and social feminist transformation of Western society must take into account the biblical story and the historical impact of the biblical tradition. Western women are not able to discard completely and forget our personal, cultural, or religious Christian history. We will either transform it into a new liberating future or continue to be subject to its tyranny whether we recognize its power or not.

Feminists cannot afford such an ahistorical or antihistorical stance because it is precisely the power of oppression that deprives people of their history. This is perceived by both black and Latin American theologians. In his book *Roots*, Alex Haley traces the history of his people from its slave days. He does so in the hope "that this story of our people can alleviate the legacies of the fact that preponderantly the histories are written by the winners."[9] In a similar mode Gustavo Gutierrez states:

> Human history has been written by a white hand, a male hand, from the dominating social class. The perspective of the defeated in history is different. Attempts have been made to wipe from their minds the memories of their struggles. This is to deprive them of a source of energy, of an historical will to rebellion.[10]

Among feminists, artist Judy Chicago has underlined the importance of women's heritage as a source for women's power. She created the *Dinner Party* as a symbolic history of women's past "pieced together" from the scanty information gleaned from cultural-religious channels. She observes:

> Sadly most of the 1038 women included in the Dinner Party are unfamiliar, their lives and achievements unknown to most of us. To make people feel worthless, society robs them of their pride: this has happened to women. All the institutions of our culture tell us—through words, deeds and even worse silence—that we are insignificant. But our heritage is our power.[11]

Thus to reclaim early Christian history as women's own past and to insist that women's history is an integral part of early Christian historiography imply the search for roots, for solidarity with our foresisters, and finally for the memory of their sufferings, struggles, and powers as women.

If history in general, and early Christian history in particular, is one way in which androcentric culture and religion have defined women, then it must become a major object for feminist analysis. Such an analysis of history and the Bible must critically reveal patriarchal history for what it is and, at the same time, reconstruct the history of women in early Christianity as a challenge to historical-religious patriarchy. Therefore, a feminist reconstruction of early Christian history has not only a theoretical but also a practical goal: it aims at both cultural-religious critique and at reconstruction of women's history as women's story within Christianity. It seeks not just to undermine the legitimization of patriarchal religious structures but also to empower women in their struggle against such oppressive structures. In other words, a feminist reconstruction of early Christian beginnings seeks to recover the Christian heritage of women because, in the words of Judy Chicago, "our heritage is our power."

Yet such a recovery of women's history in early Christianity must not only restore women to history, it must also restore the history of Christian beginnings to women. It claims the Christian past as women's own past, not just as a male past in which women participated only on the fringes or were not active at all. The New Testament sources provide sufficient indicators for such a history of early Christian beginnings, since they mention that women are both followers of Jesus and leading members of the early Christian communities. Moreover, in the second and third centuries Christianity was still defending itself against the accusation that it was a religion of women and uncultured people. The task, therefore, involves not so much rediscovering new sources as rereading the available sources in a different key. The goal is an increase in "historical imagination."

3. The debate between feminist "engaged" and androcentric academic "neutral" scholarship indicates a shift in interpretative paradigms.[12] Whereas traditional academic scholarship has identified humanness with maleness and understood women only as a peripheral category in the "human" interpretation of reality, the new field of women's studies not only attempts to make "women's" agency a key interpretative category but also seeks to transform androcentric scholarship and knowledge into truly human scholarship and knowledge, that is, inclusive of *all* people, men and women, upper and lower classes, aristocracy and "common people," different cultures and races, the powerful and the weak.

Thomas Kuhn's notion of scientific paradigms and heuristic interpretative models[13] can help us to understand this shift in interpretation and to map out a new feminist paradigm that has as its scientific
goal an inclusive "human" reconstruction of early Christian history.
According to Kuhn, a paradigm represents a coherent research tradition created and sustained by a scientific community. A paradigm
defines the type of problems to be researched, interpretations to be
given, and interpretative systems to be constructed. Thus a scientific
paradigm determines all aspects of scientific research: observations,
theories and interpretative models, research traditions and exem-
plars, as well as the philosophical-theoretical assumptions about the
nature of the world and its total world view. All data and recorded
observations are theory laden, no bare uninterpreted data and
sources exist. Equally there are no criteria and research models that
are not dependent on the scientific paradigm in which they were
developed.

The shift from an androcentric to a feminist interpretation of the
world implies a revolutionary shift in scientific paradigm, a shift with
far-reaching ramifications not only for the interpretation of the world
but also for its change. Since paradigms determine how scholars see
the world and how they conceive of theoretical problems, a shift from
an androcentric to a feminist paradigm implies a transformation of
the scientific imagination. It demands an intellectual conversion that
cannot be logically deduced but is rooted in a change of patriarchal-
social relationships. Such an intellectual conversion engenders a shift
in commitment that allows the community of scholars to see old
"data" in a completely new perspective. The debate between androcentric scholarship and feminist scholarship does more than indicate
the intellectual limitations of the scholars involved in the argument.
In fact, it shows a competition between rival paradigms that may exist
alongside each other in the phase of transition, but ultimately are
exclusive of each other.

According to Kuhn, such a transition can only be accomplished
when the emerging paradigm has produced its own institutional
structures and support-systems. While the androcentric paradigm of
scholarship is rooted in the patriarchal institutions of the academy,
the feminist paradigm has created its own institutional basis in the
alternative institutions of women's centers, academic institutes, and
study programs. Yet the patriarchial dependencies and hierarchical
institutions of the academy guarantee structural perpetuation of the
androcentric scientific paradigm. The issue is not just a problem of

feminist reconstruction of history and of a renaming of the world, but a fundamental change of both scholarship and the academy. Feminist studies are therefore primarily accountable to the women's movement for societal-ecclesial change rather than to the academy. Or in the words of Michelle Russel:

> The question is this: How will you refuse to let the academy separate the dead from the living, and then yourself declare allegiance to life? As teachers, scholars, and students, how available will you make your knowledge to others as tools for their own liberation? This is not a call for mindless activism, but rather for engaged scholarship.[14]

While a critical feminist reconstruction of women's early Christian history is in the interest of all women who are affected by the influence of biblical religion in Western societies, it nevertheless owes its special allegiance to Christian women of the present and of the past. In my opinion, feminist biblical scholarship and historical biblical scholarship share as their common hermeneutical perspective a critical commitment to the Christian community and its traditions. Although historical-critical analysis of the Bible has developed over and against a doctrinal understanding of Scripture and has challenged clerical control of theology, it nevertheless has as its hermeneutical presupposition a theological engagement insofar as it operates theoretically within the boundaries of the canon as well as institutionally within Christian schools of theology. The Bible is not just a document of past history but functions as Scripture in present day religious communities. Therefore, like women's studies, exegetical-biblical studies are by definition already "engaged." Insofar as biblical studies are canonical studies they are conditioned by and related to their *Sitz im Leben* in the Christian past and present. Like feminist studies, historical-critical interpretations of the Bible cannot abstract from the presuppositions, commitments, beliefs, or cultural and institutional structures influencing the questions they raise and the models they choose for interpreting their data. Historical biblical studies, like historical studies in general, are a selective view of the past whose scope and meaning is limited not only by the extant sources and materials but also by the interests and perspectives of the present.

Similarly feminist theology as a critical theology of liberation[15] has developed over and against symbolic androcentrism and patriarchal domination within biblical religion, while at the same time seeking to recover the biblical heritage of women for the sake of empowering women in the struggle for liberation. Feminist historical analyses, therefore, share both the impetus of historical biblical studies and an explicit commitment to a contemporary group of people, women, who, either religiously or culturally, are impacted by the traditions of the Bible. Critical-historical analysis and a clearly specified commitment serve as the common ground between academic biblical scholarship and a feminist critical theology of liberation. The explorations of this book, therefore, begin with the hope that this common ground might engender a hermeneutical perspective and method for reconstructing early Christian history in such a way that it overcomes the chasm between historical-critical studies and the contemporary church of women.

In order to theoretically move away from the pervasive biblical apologetics that has dominated the studies of women in the Bible, it is necessary to explore the roots and ramifications of this apologetics. The first section, therefore, will explore the impetus and implications that the discussion engendered by *The Woman's Bible* has had for the study of women in the Bible. This section also raises the theoretical problem of moving from androcentric biblical texts to their sociohistorical contexts and attempts to chart the way from an androcentric-historical to a feminist-historical reconstruction. It therefore discusses the theoretical models developed for the reconstruction of early Christianity and analyzes their implications for the role of women in early Christian beginnings with a view to developing a feminist theoretical model for such a reconstruction. Only after such extensive hermeneutical explorations in the first section of the book will it be possible in a second step to trace the development of early Christian origins as the liberation struggle of Christian women within the patriarchal society of the Greco-Roman world.

While the reconstructive part of this book heavily relies on a traditional historical-critical method of analysis sharpened by a "hermeneutics of suspicion," it was much more difficult to find an adequate approach for the hermeneutical and methodological explorations of the first section. In order to highlight the difficult questions involved I have settled on the mode of dialogue, discussion, and further elaboration of alternative biblical-theological and feminist-historical interpretations. In exploring different approaches and models, I was not so much interested in summarizing or delineating opposing intellectual positions and camps. Rather, I sought to find building blocks and road marks for constructing a feminist heuristic model. Such a critical theoretical exploration was necessary in order to avoid either manufacturing the past by pressing it into a timeless feminist mold, or writing another collection of so-called data and facts on "Women in the Bible." What Paula Blanchard says in her conclusion to Margaret Fuller's biography could equally be said about the explorations of this first section of the book.

> Her achievement cannot be measured except in terms of the handicap under which she gained it. . . . But in carving a niche for herself on the enormous wall of resistance that faced her, she left a foothold for others.[16]

Friends who have read the manuscript have pointed out that the theoretical hermeneutical explorations of the book's first section might discourage those readers who are not attuned to such discussions. They have therefore suggested that I place the first part at the end of the book and begin with the historical-exegetical explorations. Although such an editorial move might at first glance be reasonable, it would invite readers to swim before they have learned to probe the currents, eddies, and cliffs of the androcentric stream. I would suggest that readers who are lost in the theoretical-critical complexities of a feminist hermeneutics read the second and third parts' constructive historical exploration; then, at their leisure, return to the probing of the first part, in order to check whether they have unconsciously pressed the text into their own preconceived theological or androcentric molds of perception.

Feminist analysis and consciousness raising enables one to see the world and human lives, as well as the Bible and tradition, in a different light and with different "glasses." It has as its goal a new feminist engagement and way of life, a process traditionally called conversion. The discussions of the first part of the book seek to provide new lenses that enable one to read the biblical sources in a new feminist light, in order to engage in the struggle for women's liberation inspired by the Christian feminist vision of the discipleship of equals.

NOTES

1. For an extensive discussion of the exegetical literature, see Robert Holst, "The Anointing of Jesus: Another Application of the Form-Critical Method," *JBL* 95 (1976) 435–46.

2. Cf. J. K. Elliott, "The Anointing of Jesus, *Exp Tim* 85 (1974) 105–7.

3. Cf. also Elizabeth E. Platt, "The Ministry of Mary of Bethany," *Theology Today* 34 (1977) 29–39.

4. Judy Chicago, *The Dinner Party: A Symbol of Our Heritage* (New York: Doubleday, Anchor Books, 1979) 246–49.

5. *Signs: Journal of Women in Culture and Society,* which was founded in 1975, has regular reviews of scholarship in various areas. Of equal importance are the *Women's*

Studies International Quarterly and *Feminist Studies*. See also Dale Spender, ed., *Men's Studies Modified: The Impact of Feminism on the Academic Disciplines* (Oxford/New York: Pergamon Press, 1981).

6. Moses I. Finley, *Ancient Slavery and Modern Ideology* (New York: Viking Press, 1980), pp. 9f.

7. James M. Robinson and Helmut Koester, *Trajectories through Early Christianity* (Philadelphia: Fortress, 1971), pp. 1f.

8. See the introduction in Simone de Beauvoir, *The Second Sex* (New York: Knopf, 1953), pp. 18ff.

9. Alex Haley, *Roots: The Saga of An American Family* (New York: Doubleday, 1976), pp. 687f.

10. Gustavo Guiterrez, "Where Hunger Is, God Is Not," *The Witness* (April 1976) 6.

11. Judy Chicago, *The Dinner Party*, pp. 241–51.

12. For a discussion of this shift, cf. Elizabeth Janeway, "Who Is Sylvia? On the Loss of Sexual Paradigms," *Signs* 5 (1980) 573–89.

13. See Thomas S. Kuhn, *The Structure of Scientific Revolutions* (Chicago: University of Chicago Press, 1962); Ian G. Barbour, *Myth Models, and Paradigms* (New York: Harper & Row, 1974).

14. Michelle Russell, "An Open Letter to the Academy," *Quest* 3 (1977) 77f.

15. See my articles "Feminist Theology as a Critical Theology of Liberation," *Theological Studies* 36 (1975) 605–26; "Towards a Liberating and Liberated Theology," *Concilium* 15 (1979) 22–32; "To Comfort or to Challenge: Theological Reflections," in M. Dwyer, ed., *New Woman, New Church, New Priestly Ministry* (Rochester, N.Y.: Women's Ordination Conference, 1980), pp. 43–60.

16. Paula Blanchard, *Margaret Fuller: From Transcendentalism to Revolution* (New York: Dell, 1979), p. 342.

Part I

SEEING-NAMING-RECONSTITUTING

Chapter 1

Toward a Feminist
Critical Hermeneutics

To discuss the relationship between biblical-historical interpretation and feminist reconstruction of women's history in biblical
times is to enter an intellectual and emotional minefield. One has to
trace and lay bare the contradictions and tensions between historical
exegesis and systematic-theological tenets, the reactions and emo-
tions elicited by the prospect of "historical-critical" exegesis of the
Bible, the relationship between academic work and political-societal
forces and conditions, between so-called value-neutral scientific investigation and "advocacy" scholarship. To attempt this unraveling
of a complex theoretical and, at the same time, unconscious emotional situation entails by necessity simplifications and typifications of
a complex and very difficult set of theoretical problems.

To raise this complex set of historical, theoretical, and theological
questions from a feminist theological perspective[1] is to expose oneself
to double intellectual jeopardy. While women as a group share a
common experience and while feminists are committed to the struggle for the liberation of women, the individual perception and interpretation of women's experience of oppression, as well as the concrete formulation of the values and goals for women's liberation, vary
considerably. When paradigm as a disciplinary matrix determines the
acceptable theoretical models, permissible analogies, heuristic concepts that assign weight and priority to agreed on beliefs as well as
organize diverse information, "facts," and "data" in a coherent interpretative framework, then it is obviously important to explore the
theoretical models and heuristic concepts proposed by feminist scholarship. Such models are not factual descriptions and literal pictures
but imaginative theoretical constructs that help us to understand the

world and reality. Their main function is the correlation of a set of observations and the symbolic selection and accentuation of certain aspects of reality. Such interpretative models are heuristic devices for the interpreting of human and Christian historical reality. They provide a framework within which a variety of approaches can be integrated. Such heuristic concepts developed within the feminist paradigm are, for instance, woman, femininity, androcentrism, or patriarchy. All these analytical categories are not clearly differentiated and are often used interchangeably. Yet it is necessary to explore their heuristic interpretative usefulness in reconstructing women's history in early Christianity. If, however, such a reconstruction has as its goal not only to restore women to history and history to women but also to transform and reconceptualize early Christian history, then it is also necessary to explore their interplay with biblical-historical theoretical approaches before an integrative heuristic model can be formulated.

Models of Biblical Interpretation (Theology)

The formulation of a feminist historical hermeneutics[2] must not only trace the overall cultural shift from an androcentric to a feminist paradigm of reality construction and change, but must also discuss the theoretical models of biblical hermeneutics and their implications for the feminist cultural paradigm. Since the Bible as Holy Scripture is not only a historical book but also claims significance and authority for Christians today, theological scholarship has developed different theoretical approaches and models in order to do justice to this theoretical tension between the theological and historical claims of the Bible. The same theoretical tension is also given in a feminist historical reconstruction insofar as it is not antiquarian but committed to contemporary women and their struggle for liberation. It is necessary therefore to review the various theoretical models developed by biblical historical scholarship.[3]

The first model, which I will call the *doctrinal approach,* understands the Bible in terms of divine revelation and canonical authority. However, it conceives of biblical revelation and authority in a-historical, dogmatic terms. In its most consistent forms it insists on the verbal inspiration and literal-historical inerrancy of the Bible. The biblical text is not simply a historical expression of revelation but revelation itself. It does not just communicate God's word but *is* the Word of God. As such it functions as *norma normans non normata* or first principle. Its mode of procedure is to provide through proof-texts the ultimate theological authority or rationalization for a position already taken. The general formula is: Scripture says, therefore. . . . The Bible teaches, therefore. . . . As Holy Scripture the Bible functions as an absolute oracle revealing timeless truth and definite answers to the questions and problems of all times.

The second model, that of *positivist historical exegesis,* was developed in confrontation with the dogmatic claims of Scripture and the doctrinal authority of the church. Its attack on the revelatory authority of Scripture is linked with an understanding of exegesis and historiography that is positivist, factual, objective, and value-free. Modeled after the rationalist understanding of the natural sciences, positivist historical interpretation seeks to achieve a purely objective reading of the texts and a scientific presentation of the historical "facts." According to James Barr, biblical fundamentalism combines this model with the first model by identifying theological truth and revelation with historical facticity.[4]

Although historical-critical scholarship has moved away from such an objectivist-factual understanding of biblical texts, it still adheres to the dogma of value-neutral, detached interpretation. It often avoids articulating the implications and significance of its research because it does not want to be accused of pressing the biblical texts and "data" into a preestablished ideological mold. Although this scholarly detachment is historically understandable it is theoretically impossible.

That latter insight was developed by the third model, that of *dialogical-hermeneutical interpretation.*[5] This model takes seriously the historical methods developed by the second model, while at the same time reflecting on the interaction between text and community, or text and interpreter. The methodological explorations of form and redaction criticism have demonstrated how much biblical writings are theological responses to pastoral-practical situations, while hermeneutical discussions have elaborated upon the involvement of the scholar in the interpretation of texts. However form- and redaction-critical studies have been criticized for conceptualizing the situation of the early Christian communities too much in terms of a confessional struggle. Therefore, the studies of the social world of the Bible stress that it does not suffice to reconstruct the ecclesial setting. Christian community and life are always intertwined with cultural, political, and societal contexts.

Hermeneutical discussion is concerned with establishing the meaning of biblical texts.[6] Although the interpreter always approaches a historical text with specific contemporary experiences and questions, the scholar must attempt to become as free from preconceived understanding of the texts as possible, even though it is impossible to detach oneself completely from any preunderstanding. It is the subject matter of the text, or the text as such, and not preconceived ideas or a presupposed situation that should determine the interpretation of biblical texts.

At this point it becomes clear that in this third model dialogical interpretation is the governing factor. While form and redaction criticism elaborate how the early Christian communities and writers were in constant dialogue and argument with their "living tradition" and the problems of their communities, the hermeneutic circle continues the dialogic endeavor in the contemporary act of interpretation. Therefore, this hermenutical model can be combined with the neo-orthodox theological enterprise. Or as Schillebeeckx points out:

> The apparent point of departure is the presupposition that what is handed down in tradition, and especially the christian tradition, is always meaningful, and that this meaning only has to be deciphered hermeneutically and made present and actual.[7]

The fourth and last model of biblical interpretation is that of *liberation theology*. The various forms of liberation theology have challenged the so-called objectivity and value-neutrality of academic theology. The basic insight of all liberation theologies, including feminist theology, is the recognition that all theology, willingly or not, is by definition always engaged for or against the oppressed.[8] Intellectual neutrality is not possible in a world of exploitation and oppression. If this is the case, then theology cannot talk about human existence in general or about biblical theology in particular without critically identifying those whose human existence is meant and about whose God the biblical symbols and texts speak.

At this point it becomes necessary to inquire after the commitment of academic historical, theological scholarship. After freeing itself from the doctrinal infringements of ecclesiastical authority, it is in danger of falling prey to the interest of academic institutions that justify the status quo of the dominant political power structures. It tends to serve the interest of the dominant classes in society and church rather than to preserve its allegiance to God's people, especially the poor and exploited women and men of all nations and races. Rather than seek its own theological integrity, biblical theological scholarship often unwittingly serves the political interests of the academy which not only makes males normative subjects of scholarship but also serves theoretically to legitimize societal structures of oppression.

The Woman's Bible

No one who is even remotely aware of the history of feminist biblical interpretation can deny that the scholarly discussion of "Women in the Bible" can be abstracted from its apologetic-political setting and function of legitimization. Whether the Bible is used in the trial of Anne Hutchinson (1637) or in the Vatican statement against the ordination of women (1977),[9] its function is the same, namely, the legitimization of societal and ecclesiastical patriarchy and of women's "divinely ordained place" in it. From the outset of the women's movement and even today, the Bible has played a key role in the argument against women's emancipation. When the Massachusetts Congregationalist clergy argued that the New Testament defines women's duties and sphere, Sarah Moore Grimké countered that the distinction between masculine and feminine virtues is one of the "antichristian 'traditions of men.'"[10] In 1854 at the Women's Rights Convention in Philadelphia the Reverend H. Grew maintained "that it was clearly the will of God that man should be superior in power and authority to women." In response, Mrs. Cutler from Illinois "skillfully turned every text he had quoted directly against the reverend gentleman, to the great amusement of the audience."[11] Yet the argument was not resolved in the last century.

The debate surrounding *The Woman's Bible*, which appeared in 1895 and 1898, may serve to highlight both the political conditions and hermeneutical implications of feminist biblical interpretation and the radical critical impact of feminist theology for the interpretative task. In her introduction to *The Woman's Bible*, Elizabeth Cady Stanton, the initiator of the project, outlined two critical insights for a feminist theological hermeneutics: (1) The Bible is not a "neutral" book, but a political weapon against women's struggle for liberation. (2) This is so because the Bible bears the imprint of men who never saw or talked with God.

1. Elizabeth Cady Stanton conceived of biblical interpretation as a political act. The following episode characterizes her own personal conviction of the negative impact of Christian religion on women's situation. She refused to attend a prayer meeting of suffragists that was opened by the singing of the hymn "Guide Us, O Thou Great Jehovah," by Isabella Beecher Hooker. Her reason was that Jehovah had "never taken any active part in the suffrage movement."[12] Because of her experience that Yahweh was not on the side of the oppressed, she realized the great political influence of the Bible. She, therefore, proposed to prepare a revision of the Bible which would

collect and interpret (with the help of "higher criticism") all statements referring to women in the Bible. She conceded, however, that she was not very successful in soliciting the help of women scholars because they were

> afraid that their high reputation and scholarly attainments might be compromised by taking part in an enterprise that for a time may prove very unpopular. Hence we may not be able to get help from that class.[13]

And indeed, the project of *The Woman's Bible* proved to be very unpopular because of its political implications. Not only did some of the suffragists argue that such a project was either not necessary or politically unwise, but the National American Woman's Suffrage Association formally rejected it as a political mistake. In the second volume, which appeared in 1898, Cady Stanton sums up this opposition: "Both friend and foe object to the title." She then replies with biting wit to the accusation of a clergyman that *The Woman's Bible* is "the work of women and the devil":

> This is a grave mistake. His Satanic Majesty was not to join the Revising Committee which consists of women alone. Moreover, he has been so busy of late years attending Synods, General Assemblies and Conferences, to prevent the recognition of women delegates, that he has no time to study the languages and "higher criticism."[14]

Fundamentalist attacks, feminist polemics, and biblical apologetics still characterize many discussions of women in the Bible. However, this polemical quarrel surrounding the topic does not disqualify the topic but indicates how much impact the Bible still has on the struggle of women for liberation. While postbiblical feminists argue, for example, that the Pauline injunctions are a sign that Christian theology and faith were already sexist at a very early stage and that a revisionist feminist interpretation is therefore doomed to failure, Christian apologists respond by defending Paul as "liberationist"—Paul's writings correctly understood and interpreted support women's equality and dignity. Not the Pauline message but its patriarchal or feminist misrepresentation preaches the subjugation of women. The gist of the controversy is summed up in titles like "Paul the Apostle: Chauvinist or Liberationist?" Others argue that the demand for the subordination of women must be understood as a demand for "revolutionary subordination." Such subordination is a specific Christian form of life determining all Christian relationships. Christians therefore must uphold the revealed truth of such subordination in the face of the modern heresy of egalitarianism so that women in the twenty-first century can live their revealed subordination.[15] In order to rescue biblical texts from their feminist critics scholars do not hesitate even to put down women.

> Supporters of women's lib have certainly not themselves gone to the New Testament, armed with the scholar's tools to evaluate the Apostle's words; they have rather accepted the portrait painted of Paul by the popular establishment church, in both its liberal and conservative dress.[16]

Much of the debate centers around the subordination injunctions in the Pauline literature. In order to defend Paul, exegetes claim that the apostle had to formulate the injunctions for subordination in order to protect women from the consequences of their own actions and to correct their misbehavior:

> Why should St. Paul so concern himself with unveiled women speaking in the assemblies? Obviously because they were upsetting or giving scandal to some of the other members. . . . It is quite possible, then, that in insisting on the veil and silence (if 14:34, 35 are originally Paul) he was protecting not only (patriarchal) marriage but also those spirited women whose celebration of their freedom could have cost them dearly.[17]

Other interpreters attempt to defend Paul by "blaming the victim" when they stress that the pneumatic excesses of women and slaves provoked the injunctions for submission. These do not reestablish the patriarchal societal order within the church but insist on the order of creation.

> Part of the challenge of this material to the modern interpreter is to examine whether maintenance of sexual differentiation is actually as opposed to the stress on equality as we have come to think under the pressure of current liberation movements.[18]

Previously, theologians established the inferior role of women with reference to their inferior nature. In the face of the feminist critique, contemporary scholars attempt to salvage the Pauline statements with the help of the "equal but different" argument, which is understood as the expression of "orthodox" anthropology. Paul, so it is argued, corrected the enthusiastic "illusion" of the women prophets in Corinth who might have adhered to "gnostic androgyny."

Another scholarly defense of Paul subtly downgrades the "feminist" question as "ahistorical" and thus inappropriate.

> It is really not my intention to put Paul on trial before a panel of NT scholars to debate whether he is 30%, 75% or 100% a feminist. After all these are criteria that have emerged from our present situation. To attempt simply to judge Paul by such standards seems to me anachronistic and a waste of time.[19]

In order to excuse Paul this defense of Paul is unwilling to raise the historical question as to whether Paul's argument is directed against Christian women who did not accept the patriarchal order and theology of their time. Moreover, the statement implies that feminism as the struggle for women's liberation from patriarchy is just a very modern invention, overlooking the discoveries made by students of antiquity regarding the relative emancipation of women in the Greco-Roman world.

Even Frank and Evelyn Stagg feel the need to take sides with Paul by implicitly criticizing the feminist movement for its critique of patriarchal marriage:

> Probably the major danger today in our awakening concern for the freedom and rights of woman is precisely where Paul encountered it—the threat to morals and to structures. Freedom is more easily claimed and proclaimed than exercised responsibly. . . . With a partial recovery today of this perspective on woman is its obvious threat to structures, in particular the family.[20]

This sample of the "defense of Paul" in modern exegesis indicates not only the androcentric character of scholarly interpretation of Scripture but also its patriarchal function. In order to maintain the authority of the Pauline texts supporting women's subordination, exegetes are prepared to justify Paul at any cost.

Such scholarly apologetics overlook the fact, however, that the task of the historian is not the theological justification of Paul but the rediscovery of the life and practice of the early Christian communities. In reconstructing the Christian past scholars no longer can remain ignorant of the political implications of their theoretical models and explanations. To introduce "sexual differentiation" as an interpretative category requires a knowledge of the feminist critique of such a category.[21] Otherwise scholars will not be able to convince feminists that their interest in the Christian past is historical-critical and does not just serve theological apologetics.

Feminists in turn tend to evade the quarrel on women in the Bible either because of lack of scholarly interest or a deep alienation from biblical religion. They suspect the feminism of a revisionist biblical interpretation and do not recognize its political implications. Yet the political reasons which Cady Stanton gave for a corrective feminist interpretation of the Bible are still valid today, as the great influence of the Moral Majority documents.[22] Cady Stanton outlined three arguments why a scholarly and feminist interpretation of the Bible is politically necessary.

i. Throughout history and especially today the Bible is used to keep women in subjection and to hinder their emancipation.
ii. Not only men but especially women are the most faithful believers in the Bible as the word of God. Not only for men but also for women the Bible has a numinous authority.
iii. No reform is possible in one area of society if it is not advanced also in all other areas. One cannot reform the law and other cultural institutions without also reforming biblical religion which claims the Bible as Holy Scripture. Since "all reforms are interdependent," a critical feminist interpretation is a necessary political endeavor, although it might not be opportune. If feminists think they can neglect the revision of the Bible because there are more pressing political issues, then they do not recognize the political impact of Scripture upon the churches and society, and also upon the lives of women.

2. Cady Stanton's edition of *The Woman's Bible* was opposed not only because it was politically inopportune but also because of its radical hermeneutic perspective which expanded and replaced the main apologetic argument of other suffragists that the true message of the Bible was obstructed by the translations and interpretations of men. Sarah Moore Grimké had "entered her protest against the false translations of some passages by the MEN who did that work, and against the perverted interpretations of the MEN who undertook to write commentaries thereon. I am inclined to think when we are admitted to the honor of studying Greek and Hebrew we shall produce some various readings of the Bible, a little different from those we have now."[23] And Mrs. Cutler had announced: "The time has come for woman to read and interpret Scripture for herself," while Lucretia Mott argued, "We have been so long pinning our faith on other people's sleeves that we ought to begin examining these things daily ourselves, to see whether they are so; and we should find in

comparing text with text that a very different construction might be put on them."[24] Frances Willard continues this line of reasoning when she argues against the radical hermeneutics of *The Woman's Bible* that it is not the biblical message but only its contemporary androcentric interpretation that preaches the subjugation of women:

> I think that men have read their own selfish theories into the book, that theologians have not in the past sufficiently recognized the progressive quality of its revelation nor adequately discriminated between its records of history and its principles of ethics and religion.[25]

Cady Stanton would agree that the scholarly interpretations of the Bible are male inspired and need to be "depatriarchalized." Yet it was exactly her critical insight that the Bible is not just misunderstood or badly interpreted, but that it can be used in the political struggle against women's suffrage because it *is* patriarchal and androcentric. Over and against the doctrinal understanding of verbal inspiration of the Bible as the direct word of God, she stresses that the Bible is written by men and reflects the male interests of its authors. "The only point in which I differ from all ecclesiastical teaching is that I do not believe that any man ever saw or talked with God."[26] While the churches claimed that the degrading ideas about women and the patriarchal injunctions for their submission stem from God, she maintains that all these degrading texts emanated from the heads of men. By treating the Bible as a human work and not as a fetish, and by denying divine inspiration to the negative biblical statements about women, she claims her committee has shown more reverence for God then have the clergy or the church. Scholars do not draw out the implications of historical-scientific interpretation for the understanding of the biblical teachings on women because of their theological interests in maintaining patriarchal interpretations of Christian faith:

> The "Woman's Bible" comes to the ordinary reader like a real benediction. It tells her the good Lord did not write the Book; that the garden scene is a fable; that she is in no way responsible for the laws of the Universe. The Christian scholars and scientists will not tell her this, for they see she is the key to the situation. Take the snake, the fruit tree and the woman from the tableau, and we have no fall, no frowning Judge, no Inferno, no everlasting punishment,—hence no need of a Savior. Thus the bottom falls out of the whole Christian theology. Here is the reason why in all the Biblical researches and higher criticism, the scholars never touch the position of women.[27]

Yet despite her radical critique Cady Stanton maintains that some of the Bible's religious and ethical principles are still valid today. For example, the love commandment and the golden rule are such teachings. Therefore, she concludes that the Bible cannot be accepted or rejected as a whole, since its teachings and lessons differ greatly from each other. Neither a total rejection nor a total acceptance of the Bible is called for. Instead, every biblical passage on women must be carefully analyzed and evaluated for its androcentric implications.

In conclusion: In the face of the biblical opponents of the women's movement in the last century, Elizabeth Cady Stanton advocated an investigation of all the biblical passages on woman in terms of "higher" exegetical criticism. Her results and methods therefore correspond with the state of biblical-historical studies of her time. In her autobiography Cady Stanton explains that she initiated the project because she had heard so many "conflicting opinions about the Bible, some saying it taught woman's emancipation, and some her subjection." Since she wanted to know what the "actual" teachings of the Bible were, *The Woman's Bible* took the form of a scientific commentary on the biblical passages speaking about woman. This exegetical-topical approach has dominated and still dominates scholarly research and popular discussion of "Woman in the Bible."[28] This discussion clearly remained within the parameters set by the first two interpretative models, the doctrinal and historical factual model, although the impetus and force of the discussion reflects the political dimensions of the liberation model.

The major result of the discussion, however, is Cady Stanton's insight that the biblical text is androcentric and that men have put their stamp on biblical revelation. The Bible is not just interpreted from a male perspective, as some feminists argued. Rather, it is man-made because it is written by men and is the expression of a patriarchal culture. Cady Stanton and her coauthors thus confirm the general tenet of historical-critical scholarship that divine revelation is articulated in historically limited and culturally conditioned human language. But feminist interpretation particularizes and relativizes the Bible even more by specifying that biblical language is *male* language and that the cultural conditions and perspectives of the Bible are that of patriarchy. In doing so it resorts to the third model of biblical interpretation which stresses the interaction between text and situation. This hermeneutic-contextual model has not only established the canon of Scripture as the pluriform root model of Christian communities, but also has shown that the Bible includes often contradictory responses and that therefore not all biblical statements have equal truth claim and authority. In order to sift out such truth this model of interpretation must resort, however, to the doctrinal model by appealing to the teaching authority of the church or to the "canon" within the canon.   Sachkritik

The Neo-Orthodox Model of Feminist Interpretation

The historical-critical understanding of the canon as a collection of very different, often contradictory writings and cultural expressions has not only underlined the context and conditions of revelation but also engendered the need for formulating criteria for the theological evaluation and appropriation of diverse biblical teachings and traditions.[29] Since Christian faith and tradition are always intertwined with their cultural, political, and societal contexts and language, it does not suffice merely to interpret and understand the biblical text. One must also define theologically what constitutes the true word of God and the heart of the Christian message.

The theological search for the "canon within the canon" has attempted to formulate the criterion for appropriating the Bible along philosophical-dogmatic (cf. the "principles of religion" mentioned by Willard) and historical-textual lines. Some theologians distinguish between revelatory essence and historical accident, timeless truth and culturally conditioned language, constant tradition and changing traditions. When such a canon within the canon is formulated along the lines of the textual-hermeneutic approach, scholars juxtapose Jesus and Paul, Pauline theology and early Catholicism, the historical Jesus and the kerygmatic Christ, the Jesus of history and the earliest traditions about Jesus, Hebrew and Greek thought, Christian message and Jewish-Greco-Roman influence.

Since for much of Protestant theology—which has developed the neo-orthodox canon within the canon discussion—the heart of the Christian message is the Pauline gospel, much discussion of the New Testament teaching about women focuses on the interpretation of Pauline texts, especially the Pauline subordination passages which present a special problem. Much of the scholarly discussion concentrates on these passages in order to maintain Paul's theological relevance for today. Widely accepted historical-critical means for solving the problem are explanations based on tradition criticism, source criticism, or text criticism. In this way the subordination passages in Colossians, Ephesians, 1 Peter, and the Pastorals can be classified as deutero-Pauline statements, and 1 Cor 11:2–16 and 14:33–36 can be seen as post-Pauline interpolations. As secondary textual additions they represent the theology of early Catholicism but do not reflect the genuine theology of Paul.

Since liberation theology seeks to enlist the Bible on the side of the oppressed, it is in danger of aligning itself too quickly with the methods and interests of the neo-orthodox doctrinal model, and in so doing fails to explore sufficiently the function of the Bible in the oppression of the poor or of women. This neo-orthodox hermeneutics can be described with Peter Berger as an attempt "to absorb the full impact of the relativizing perspective but nevertheless to posit an 'Archimedean point' in a sphere immune to relativization."[30]

Thus, Letty Russell's book on liberation theology in a feminist perspective illustrates this alignment with neo-orthodox theology in order to develop a feminist theological hermeneutics. She maintains that the conflict between feminism and biblical religion stems from a misunderstanding of biblical religion. With God's salvific action in the world as her starting point, she distinguishes among Tradition, tradition, and traditions.

> Tradition is not a block of content to be carefully guarded by authorized hierarchies, but a dynamic action of God's love which is to be passed on to others of all sexes and races.[31]

Tradition refers to the total traditioning-process, while *the* tradition refers to Christ as the content of the traditioning-process. Traditions in turn are the facts and patterns constituting church history. Since the biblical message was addressed to a patriarchal society, the *form* of the biblical promise is situation-variable and relative to its patriarchal culture. Patriarchal imagery and androcentric language are the form but not the *content* of the biblical message. Since the content of the tradition is Christ, feminist theology must make clear "that Christ's work was not first of all that of being a male but that of being the new human."[32]

Thus the distinction between form and content, theological essence and historical variable, language and divine action, makes it possible to develop a feminist biblical hermeneutics that can acknowledge the patriarchal language of the Bible without conceding its patriarchal content. However, it can do so only by declaring a theological statement (God's redemptive and liberating activity in Jesus Christ) as the essence of biblical revelation and by relegating the concrete biblical texts to historically relative form. For instance, the Pauline subordination statements are, according to Russell, situation-variable and therefore script but not Scripture, because Paul still "recognized that the Tradition was handed over into the hands of both men and women."[33] The methodological problem of course remains. How can one distinguish between script and Scripture, if the formal element is the culturally conditioned historical text, while the posited "Archimedean point" is an abstract theological principle and transhistorical symbol expressed in historically contingent and thus variable language? In other words, can content and language, form and essence be distinguished in such a way that the historically contingent form becomes the mere container for its transhistorical, theological content or essence?

Even more far-reaching for a feminist history of liberation is the distinction between the usable and unusable past. Russell recognizes that the oppressed either do not have a past or are invisible in the records of the historical victors. Yet, significantly enough, Russell does not distinguish between a past of victimization and violence on the one hand and experiences of liberation on the other. She does not need to do so because she considers only people's "bondage to themselves and to their historical situation," without discussing whether the Christian tradition might have legitimized and perpetuated this bondage. Therefore, in discussing feminist theology's "threat to tradition" she can state:

> Liberation theology is a threat to these traditions because they
> need to be challenged when they perpetuate a past that is unusa-
> ble to a particular group of Christians.[34]

Curiously enough, although Russell's analysis is proposed as a liberationist analysis, it does not consider the political structures of the past and present that perpetuate violence against women. Therefore it cannot explore the function of the Bible in the historical oppression of Western women. Moreover, the historical agents of her story of the past are not women but God giving over Christ to all peoples. An absolute theological principle has become the hermeneutical key for biblical interpretation.

Similarly, in a recent debate with the women's spirituality movement Rosemary Radford Ruether has joined Letty Russell in the search for a "usable" past. If I understand her correctly, she seems to move from her previously dominant interpretative model of cultural-ecclesial-sexual dualism to a critical hermeneutics of culture. Although Ruether does not fully develop this biblical hermeneutics, it is possible to trace the main elements of her interpretative proposal. Unfortunately she develops this proposal over and against the separatist interpretations of Wicca. This polemic obscures the hermeneutical feminist issues at stake. It unnecessarily supports a misreading of her own cultural hermeneutics as another sophisticated apologetics of the Christian tradition.

In suggesting a methodology for the feminist critique of culture Ruether points to two presuppositions. On the one hand, she acknowledges that all inherited culture has been male biased and sexist. On the other hand, she maintains that all significant works of culture have not only legitimized sexism but also done *something else.* "They have been responding to the fears of death, estrangement, and oppression and the hopes for life, reconciliation and liberation of humanity."[35] Although they have articulated this response in male terms, women can discover this critical element in male culture and transform it so that it says "things it never said before."

Proceeding from this rather generalized principle of cultural critique, Ruether identifies the prophetic-messianic traditions of the Bible as such critical or liberating traditions. She claims that the Bible is written from the perspective of the people and not for the legitimization of worldly power. The biblical God vindicates the oppressed, and the God-language of the Bible tends to "destabilize" the existing social order. Although in apocalypticism this social-prophetic criticism with its vision of salvation "gradually loses its base in social hope altogether and becomes otherworldly,"[36] this critical prophetic tradition is also found in the New Testament. Ruether, however, is forced to concede that this critical prophetic tradition did not explicitly apply itself to the women's question either in the history of Israel or in Christianity. Nevertheless, she argues that women today can apply it to the feminist quest. "In sum, it is not some particular statements about women's liberation, but rather the critical pattern of prophetic thought, that is the usable tradition for feminism in the Bible."[37]

At this point the neo-orthodox implications of Ruether's hermeneutical proposal become apparent. Not only does she draw a rather idealized picture of the biblical and prophetic traditions but also she overlooks the oppressive androcentric elements of these traditions. Because she does not analyze the classical prophetic tradition as a historical phenomenon, but uses it rather as an abstract critical interpretative pattern, she does not consider its patriarchal polemics and repression of the cult of the Goddess. Rather, she simply postulates that as a social-critical tradition the prophetic traditions can be used in the interest of feminism. Without question this is the case, but we are not told how and in what way feminist theology can transform this social-critical androcentric tradition into a feminist liberating tradition and use it to its own ends.

What makes a social-critical tradition feminist? Can we simply assume that social-critical traditions are feminist traditions? Feminist
critics of the prophetic Israelite tradition have pointed to its devaluation and suppression of Goddess worship among Israelite women (cf.
Jer 44:15–19) as well as to its transference of the patriarchal marriage
pattern to the covenant relationship between Yahweh and Israel, in
which Israel is seen not only as the dependent virgin and wife but
also as the unfaithful harlot.[38] Postbiblical feminist objections against
the prophetic tradition—that it eliminates the divine female symbol
as well as perpetuates the patriarchal subordination of women—must
be dealt with critically from a historical perspective before feminist
theologians can claim the prophetic traditions as "liberating" for
women. A feminist biblical hermeneutics must take seriously the his-
torical-patriarchal elements of the prophetic traditions in order to set
free their liberating social-critical impulses for the struggle for
women. It must retrieve them in and through a feminist critical analysis rather than elevate them to an abstract interpretative principle or
criterion. Feminist theology, however, cannot assume without any
question that the revelatory "surplus" of the social-critical prophet
tradition is a feminist liberating one. In order to delineate the emancipatory impulses of this tradition it is necessary to explore its oppressive components.

Moreover, a biblical feminist hermeneutics should not be developed over and against postbiblical feminist objections to the Bible but
must learn from them in order to come to a fuller understanding of
the liberating biblical impulses for women's struggle against patriarchal biblical sexism. In a brilliant essay, "Why Women Need the
Goddess," Carol Christ has elaborated on the Goddess as the symbol
of women's power, freedom, and independence.

> The simplest and most basic meaning of the symbol of Goddess is
> the acknowledgment of the legitimacy of female power as a be-
> neficent and independent power. A woman who echoes Ntosake
> Shange's dramatic statement, "I found God in myself and I loved
> her fiercely" is saying "Female power is strong and creative."
> She is saying that the divine principle, the saving and sustaining
> power, is in herself, that she will no longer look to men or male
> figures as saviors.[39]

While I agree with Ruether that the quest for women's power, independence, and freedom cannot be solely nor even primarily formulated in terms of personal-individualist and biological female power
but has to be social-political, I concur with Carol Christ that at the

heart of the spiritual feminist quest is the quest for women's power, freedom, and independence. Is it possible to read the Bible in such a way that it becomes a historical source and theological symbol for such power, independence, and freedom? In answering this question we cannot, in my opinion, resort to an "Archimedean point"—be it Tradition with capital T or "prophetic-messianic traditions" as the revelatory or hermeneutic key for the scores of relative oppressive traditions and texts of the Bible. In the last analysis, reduction of the Bible to the prophetic-messianic tradition on the one hand and the concomitant reduction of this tradition to an abstract dehistoricized critical key on the other hand indicates that Ruether's hermeneutical proposal is more neo-orthodox than she perceives it to be. It serves more to rescue biblical religion from its feminist critics than to develop a feminist historical hermeneutics that could incorporate Wicca's feminist spiritual quest for women's power.[40]

Although Phyllis Trible focuses on the biblical text and rejects any attempt to separate text and tradition, form and content methodologically, she nevertheless shares with Russell and Ruether an understanding of the hermeneutic process that is rooted in neo-orthodox theology. While Russell and Ruether focus on the tradition, Phyllis Trible insists on the structure of the biblical text. While Russell and Ruether employ the metaphor of the "usable past," and therefore reify the biblical tradition, Trible personifies the text. Her key metaphor is repeated in the beginning and conclusion of her work: "The Bible is a pilgrim wandering through history to merge past and present."[41] But as opposed to Russell, Trible advocates an explicit feminist hermeneutics: "Moving across cultures and centuries, then, the Bible informed a feminist perspective, and correspondingly, a feminist perspective enlightened the Bible."[42] Whereas according to Letty Russell's hermeneutical proposal, God acts through Christ throughout the centuries, and this salvific mission is within the culturally variable form of traditions, for Trible the voice of God is ultimately identical with the biblical text. In order to find out the intention of God the biblical exegete must "listen" to and interpret the text as accurately as possible. Therefore, she chooses as her interpretative method rhetorical criticism that concentrates on the movement of the text rather than on extrinsic historical factors. Thus the exegete becomes a partner in the pilgrimage of the text through the centuries. Such an understanding of interpretation as a "participation in the movement of the text"[43] allows her to get hold of the theological meaning of the text, because "proper analysis of form yields proper articulation of meaning."[44]

Though in her article on "Depatriarchalizing in Biblical Traditions" her indebtedness to the neo-orthodox distinction between biblical faith and biblical relgion serves as her explicit hermeneutical principle, her book itself is much more cautious. Her article concludes: "In various ways they [the discussed texts and themes] demonstrate a depatriarchalizing principle at work in the Bible. Departriarchalizing is not an operation which the exegete performs on the text. It is a hermeneutic operating within Scripture itself. We expose it; we do not impose it."[45] The conclusion of her book restates this hermeneutical position. However, when pointing out that the Bible itself proclaims "that faith has lost female imagery and motifs" and summing up her results, she is forced to concede:

> Moreover, it uncovered neglected traditions to reveal *countervoices* within a patriarchal document. It did not, however, eliminate the male dominated character of scripture; such a task would have been both impossible and dishonest. [emphasis added][46]

Trible recognizes feminism as a clue between the text and the world, the text and its historical context. She defines feminism explicitly not as "a narrow focus on women" but rather as a "critique of culture in light of misogyny."[47] However, she does not engage in such a feminist critique of Scripture's misogynist stamp and character as a document of patriarchal culture because her method allows her to abstract the text from its cultural-historical context. If "historical background, archeological data, compositional history, authorial intention, sociological setting or theological motivation" are extrinsic to interpretation and only a "supplement" to the textual understanding of the biblical interpreter, then feminist analysis as a cultural critique can really not inform her work. Patriarchal culture and patriarchal religion need not be addressed because they are extrinsic to the *meaning* of the biblical text for today. Trible therefore never raises the question of whether the female imagery and traditions about women are really feminist "countervoices" or whether they are only remnants of the patriarchal repression of the Goddess and of women's religious powers. Since she focuses on the text and its interpretations, she also does not raise the political implications of biblical interpretation.

Of course, for such a biblical interpretation, executed in terms of the New Literary Criticism, androcentric language must be a major problem and obstacle.[48] Nevertheless, Trible skirts this problem and addresses it only in a footnote. Although her method is based on the tenet that "form and content are inseparable" and that the text is "an organic unity," she nevertheless claims that the grammatical gender of the masculine pronouns for God decides "neither sexuality nor theology"; at the same time, she concedes that "masculine pronouns reinforce a male image of God, an image that obscures, even obliterates, female metaphors for deity." At this point her combination of a feminist hermeneutics as "cultural critique in the light of misogynism" with a neo-orthodox hermeneutics that "encompasses explication, understanding, and application from past to present" breaks down.

> As yet, however, I do not know how to resolve the dilemma posed by grammatical gender for deity in the scriptures themselves, since translation must answer to both grammatical accuracy and interpretative validity.[49]

This last concession indicates that a feminist hermeneutics of Scripture must incorporate not only a cultural but also a theological critique. It also suggests that a method divorcing the language and text of the Bible from its socio-cultural patriarchal conditions cannot provide a model for the reconstruction of women's history as members of biblical religion. Moreover, a biblical theology that does not seriously confront "the patriarchal stamp" of the Bible and its religious-political legitimization of the patriarchal oppression of women is in danger of using a feminist perspective to rehabilitate the authority of the Bible, rather than to rehabilitate women's biblical history and theological heritage.

The Feminist Sociology of Knowledge Model

While the feminist neo-orthodox model attempts to isolate the liberating Tradition from the androcentric-patriarchal texts of the Bible, to distill the feminist kerygmatic essence from its culturally conditioned androcentric expressions, and to separate social-critical prophetic traditions from the patriarchal oppressive biblical traditions, the "androcentric" feminist model[50] seeks, with the help of the sociology of knowledge,[51] to move from the reading of androcentric texts to the construction of a life-center that generates new cultural texts, traditions, and mythologies. According to the androcentric theoretical model this *Lebenszentrum* (life-center) of the biblical texts and traditions are men. If all cultural texts and constructs of reality are androcentric, then it is not possible to isolate a feminist textual or cultural tradition. Rather, it becomes necessary to create a new feminist life-center that will generate new constructions of reality and new visions of life.

Although Mary Daly is neither a biblical nor historical scholar, her work must be analyzed here, since it represents the most consistent combination of the feminist critique of the androcentric model (which she labels phallocentric) with a sociology of knowledge analysis. Although she frequently uses patriarchy as her key analytical concept, her concern with "authentic being" indicates that she operates within the boundaries of the existentialist androcentric model formulated by Simone de Beauvoir.[52] While Daly would reject any attempt to use feminist analytical method and categories without also sharing in the feminist perspective, she comes close to Trible in her understanding of language, although she would insist that the patriarchal matrix of all language must be considered. Ultimately, this understanding that androcentric language as the medium of patriarchal interpretation *is* the message must lead her to the rejection not only of all biblical but of all cultural androcentric texts. A systemic analysis of the patriarchal documents of biblical religion can only produce a reconstruction of the biblical projection of reality as androcentric and patriarchal.

In her post-Christian introduction to the new edition of her book, *The Church and the Second Sex*, she categorically states: The medium *is* the message. In that book she had adopted Simone de Beauvoir's model of androcentrism in order to construct a revisionist feminist Catholic theology. In her post-Christian introduction to the new edition she combines this theoretical model of androcentrism with a sociology of knowledge analysis. It is the existential feminist "leap into freedom" that constitutes her new theoretical life-center. Therefore, she no longer can acknowledge the history of the revisionist Mary Daly as part of her own self-identity but relegates it to prehistory.

In *The Church and the Second Sex*, Daly made a hermeneutical move similar to that made by neo-orthodox feminist hermeneutics. For example, after attempting various apologetic explanations and justifications of the Pauline injunctions for women's subordination, she concludes her argument:

> It is not surprising that Paul did not see the full implications of this transcendence. There is an unresolved tension between the personalist Christian message and the restrictions and compromises imposed by the historical situation. . . . Those who have benefited from the insights of a later age have the task of distinguishing elements which are sociological in origin from the life-fostering, personalist elements which pertain essentially to the Christian message.[53]

In her post-Christian introduction, Daly rejects this interpretative move to distinguish between the essence of the biblical message and the accidents of cultural-sociological expression, between the core of Christian truth and "the ideas arising from social conditioning." In an imaginary conversation Daly remonstrates with Daly:

> "Professor Daly," I would say, "don't you realize that where myths are concerned the medium *is* the message? Don't you see that efforts of biblical scholars to re-interpret texts, even though they may be correct within a certain restricted perspective, cannot change the overwhelmingly patriarchal character of the biblical tradition. Moreover, this 'modern' historical accuracy about details has often been associated with an apologetic zeal that overlooks patriarchal religion's function of legitimating patriarchy."[54]

This statement indicates her theoretical indebtedness to a sociology of knowledge approach insofar as she understands the function of religion as legitimization of the patriarchal order, that is, as "world maintenance." Such a maintenance of the status quo in religious legitimization "interprets the order of the universe" and "relates the disorder that is the antithesis of all socially constructed *nomoi* to that yawning abyss of chaos that is the oldest antagonist of the sacred."[55] In such a methodological approach language, as interpretation and legitimization, is the key concept in the social construction of reality. The maintenance of the existing patriarchal order by religion, as well as the new construction of world by feminism, happens in and through language and interpretation.

This methodological approach enables Daly to restate more fully Elizabeth Cady Stanton's insight that the Bible is a product of men and of patriarchal society. The androcentric or phallocentric language system of the Christian tradition is not accidental to biblical religion but serves to maintain the sacred patriarchal order. A systemic feminist analysis like that provided by Neusner confirms this contention.[56] Women in turn have had the "power of naming" stolen from them. "The courage to be logical—the courage to name—would require that we admit to ourselves that males are the originators, controllers, and legitimators of patriarchy."[57] Therefore, feminist interpretation of Christian texts and traditions cannot use a method of "correlation" but rather requires a "method of liberation."

Such a method of liberation, according to Daly, involves not only a "castrating" of patriarchal language and symbols but also a "breakthrough to new semantic fields."[58] Her book *Gyn/Ecology* is concerned less with the critical analysis of patriarchal theological symbols than with demonstrating how androcentric language and scholarship have "erased" women from consciousness. Through semantic, etymological, and structural analysis she not only seeks to "invent" a new language for women in "feminist Time/Space" but also to uncover Goddess-murder and gynocide as the "systematic erasure of women." She discusses such disparate atrocities as Indian suttee, African genital mutilation, European witchhunt, American gynecology, and Chinese footbinding as sado-ritual reenactments of the Goddess-murder. Phallocentric language is the manifestation of such sado-rituals:

> The fact that patriarchal scholarship is an extension and continuation of Sado-Ritual is manifested often unwittingly and witlessly—by its language. This language betrays, or rather loyally and faithfully displays, the fact that "authorities" are apologists for atrocities.[59]

Yet a careful reading of the book suggests the opposite conclusion. Daly's history of women's oppression in patriarchy is conceptualized in terms of androcentric language and scholarship because in history women were despised, deprived, exploited, tortured, and killed but not "erased." It is the androcentric language and sociology of knowledge model that *erases* the history of patriarchal atrocities as women's history, in which women were suffering, collaborating, and struggling for liberation.

As aliens oppressed in a patriarchal world, feminist women are called "to name—that is to create—our own world." Since language and naming is so central for Daly's feminist approach, such a re-creation of the world happens first of all within the consciousness and language of individuals, within the Self:

> The reign of healing is within the Self, within the Selves seen by the Self and seeing the Self. The remedy is not to turn back but to become in a healing environment, the Self, and to become the healing environment.[60]

For Daly, feminist consciousness implies such a "qualitative leap" that the Daly of the post-Christian introduction can characterize the author of *The Church and the Second Sex* as someone "who was not an astronaut before it was possible to become one." However, it must be pointed out that in the ensuing ten years between the two editions of the book no such qualitative leap in social-political transformation of patriarchal society or religion has been realized. Such a qualitative leap has only taken place in the consciousness of some individuals.

Her hermeneutical-methodological approach, therefore, allows Daly to explore the feminist construction of world in language and in the consciousness of individuals, yet it does not focus on concrete social-political structures of oppression. Her "structuralist" analysis of sado-ritual and its violence highlights universal structures of patriarchal oppression but dehistoricizes the oppression itself, since her analysis can not conceptualize the concrete, historical oppression of women in different societies, cultures, and religions. Such a hermeneutical method, moreover, has no room for an often mixed, confused, inarticulate, and only partially feminist historical consciousness and agency of women living within the boundaries of patriarchal culture and religion. The androcentric sociology of knowledge approach *theoretically* does not allow for an emancipatory solidarity with women whose Selves are damaged by patriarchy and whose "journey into freedom" was, and is, a journey *within* the boundaries and oppressive mechanisms of patriarchal culture and religion.

At this point it becomes clear that the heuristic model of androcentrism does not allow us to restore history to women or to reconceptualize history as *human* history. While androcentrism maintains that women are the "Other," Mary Daly's "spinning" and journeying lead us to the "Otherworld," to the "Other Side" which we cannot know "until we arrive there."[61] She therefore denounces patriarchal scholarship as the "warped mirror image of creative Hagography" because it merely researches and re-covers women's history. But she affirms:

> On the boundaries of the male-centered universities, however, there is a flowering of woman-centered thinking. Gynocentric Method requires not only the murder of misogynistic methods (intellectual and affective exorcism) but also ecstasy, which I have called *ludic cerebration*.[62]

Daly thus accepts the androcentric theoretical construct of the world but stands it on its head by making the periphery the life-center of a feminist construction of the world. Such a shift can be made in language, ritual, and theory but is socially located on the "boundaries of the male-centered universities" and of all other social-political-cultural institutions.

While *Beyond God the Father* proposed a social group, namely, "sisterhood as anti-church," as the generator and life-center of feminist reality construction, Daly's historical experience of tokenism and intellectual-psychic colonialization of women now leads her to a careful reformulation of "sisterhood." Sisterhood becomes "sacred space," the bonding of the "Selves" who have "escaped," the friendship of "Self-centering" women opposing patriarchy. The cosmic covenant

> is where being is discovered in confrontation with nothingness.
> . . . Those who discover the covenant *find* themselves in new
> space. The old territory, then, is not encroached upon: one does
> not bother to invade non-being.[63]

This is said with respect to patriarchal space. But this statement implies that women who belong to the "territory of non-being" and have not made the "qualitative leap" are thereby excluded from sisterhood defined as sacred space. Thus the assumption of "sacred feminist space" over and against "secular space" defined as the "territory of non-being" engenders a dichotomy between women who find themselves in such sacred space and those who do not. This understanding of sisterhood—not as the bonding of the oppressed but as the gathering of the ideologically "pure," the network of Spinsters and Amazons, of the "elect" and the "holy"—has far-reaching consequences for Daly's understanding of history as well as for feminist political, ecclesial, and societal change.

Since women are non-beings in patriarchal culture and erased from its consciousness and language, only those women who have moved into the sacred new feminist Time/Space participate in history and in the making of history. These "women constitute an ontological locus of history . . . in this very process women are the bearers of history."[64] Only those who have the "courage to be" and to make the existential leap are historical subjects. While this theoretical understanding is able to construct a feminist life-world at the fringes of patriarchal culture, it is not able to restore history to women, since it understands patriarchal history as the "territory of non-being" but not as the arena of women's struggle. Daly must therefore methodologically exclude the history of women within early Christianity as well as reject a reconstruction of early Christian beginnings in a feminist perspective.

A Feminist Critical Hermeneutics of Liberation

I have sought to trace the major developments in feminist biblical hermeneutics engendered by *The Woman's Bible*. I have done so not to detract from the accomplishments of feminist hermeneutics but to test how much they will allow us to reclaim the Bible and early Christian history as women's beginnings and power.[65] While the feminist historical hermeneutics of *The Woman's Bible* has established the androcentric character of biblical texts and interpretations, it has not brought into focus the history of women as participants in patriarchal biblical history, society, and religion nor set free the liberating impulses of the biblical traditions.

The interpretative issues engendered by *The Woman's Bible* still determine the parameters of feminist biblical hermeneutics as well as the exegetical-historical explorations of "Woman in the Bible." Since the debate over *The Woman's Bible* was sparked by controversy and attacks against the women's movement in the last century, the discussion centers primarily around the revelatory authority of the Bible for today. Where the opponents of women's equality argue that the Bible demands the subordination of women, the defenders of the Bible maintain that such a reading of the Bible is a misunderstanding. While Cady Stanton pointed to the androcentric character of the Bible in order to prove that its misogynist texts are not the word of God but that of males, post-Christian feminists radicalize her position and reject not only the Bible but also those women who remain members of patriarchal biblical religion. Russell, Ruether, and Trible in turn argue with Cady Stanton that the Bible is not totally androcentric but also contains some absolute ethical principles and feminist liberating traditions. In order to do so, they adopt a feminist neo-orthodox model that is in danger of reducing the ambiguity of historical struggle to theological essences and abstract, timeless principles.

Although Cady Stanton had formulated the political character and necessity of a feminist biblical interpretation, the ensuing debate did not center on women as makers and participants in history, but on the authority of biblical revelation. The subsequent studies of "Woman in the Bible" were primarily interested in exploring the patriarchal biblical teachings on womanhood and woman's sphere and in defending or claiming the revelatory authority of the Bible for or against the feminist cause. A review of the ordination of women debate could amply substantiate this observation. Thus it appears that the feminist debate engendered by *The Woman's Bible* centers on questions of the theological rejection/legitimization of the Bible rather than on historical feminist reconstruction. It seems to me methodologically necessary, therefore, to bracket the issue of theological legitimization until women can come into focus as historical agents and victims and until biblical history can be restored to women. In order to do so, we have to see whether Cady Stanton's insight—that not only biblical interpretations but the biblical texts themselves were androcentric—can serve to recover a feminist biblical heritage.

The Woman's Bible has not only provoked feminist apologetic of the Bible's authority but also demonstrated that biblical interpretation in Western society is a historical-political task that may not be neglected by feminists. Ruether's argument that it would be feminist romanticism not to reappropriate and transform patriarchal culture and androcentric texts is an important one. Yet the question remains: How and on what grounds is such a reappropriation possible and what makes such a reappropriation feminist? Since feminism as a liberation philosophy and movement has diverse goals, strategies, and approaches, the answer to this problem, I would argue, may not be definitional-exclusive but only inclusive-constructive.

Post-biblical feminists like Mary Daly press the hermeneutical consequence of the androcentric interpretative model by insisting that the androcentric biblical text *is* the message and not just a container for it. Therefore, they do not allow for a neo-orthodox distinction between androcentric text and feminist revelation, or patriarchal traditions and liberating Tradition. Yet remaining within the perimeters of the androcentric hermeneutic model, they need also to find an Archimedean point in the sea of historical relativity of interpretations and visions in order to be able to claim a feminist absolute. While in *Beyond God the Father* this Archimedean point and hermeneutic key was sisterhood as anti-church, in *Gyn/Ecology* it is no longer "the bonding of oppressed women struggling for liberation" but the gathering of the feminist "Selves" who have "escaped" patriarchy. Yet Daly's bonding of the feminist "elect and holy" is rather a disembodied and dehistoricized vision that reminds one of the neo-Platonic Catholic hope for the communion of the saints as the communion of disembodied souls. This vision must reject not only biblical texts and religion but also abandon all other expressions of patriarchal culture and history as androcentric and totally oppressive of women.

However, relinquishing our biblical heritage merely reinforces the androcentric reality construction of Western culture according to which male existence and history is the paradigm of human existence and human history. Western androcentric linguistic and scientific structures define women as secondary to men and thus as insignificant in the making of human culture, religion, and history. In such an androcentric world view women are historically and culturally marginal. As an oppressed people they do not have a written history; they remain invisible in the reality constructions of those in power. However, it must not be overlooked that the marginality and invisibility of women in biblical history is produced by androcentric texts and linguistic reconstructions of history insofar as androcentric texts tend to erase women as active participants in history. Regardless of how androcentric texts may erase women from historiography, they do not prove the actual absence of women from the center of patriarchal history and biblical revelation.

Therefore, feminists cannot afford to disown androcentric biblical texts and patriarchal history as their own revelatory texts and history. They cannot afford

> to jettison all claims to the product and record of so many centuries of collective life. To the extent that men have spoken they have done so on the basis of the privileged access to history and rule, not on the basis of intrinsic personal or sexual merit. Their social representation and social institutions belong however to *our* collective past. The lords of creation do not exist independently of those they oppress.[66]

Androcentric texts and linguistic reality constructions must not be mistaken as trustworthy evidence of human history, culture, and religion. The text *may* be the message, but the message *is not* coterminal with human reality and history. A feminist critical hermeneutics must therefore move from androcentric texts to their social-historical contexts. It not only has to claim the contemporary community of women struggling for liberation as its locus of revelation, it also must reclaim its foresisters as victims *and* subjects participating in patriarchal culture. It must do so not by creating a gynocentric life-center on the fringes of androcentric culture and history, but by reclaiming such androcentric human and biblical history as women's own history. It is not the feminist philosopher or theologian but the feminist poet who has given us an image for such a feminist hermeneutical undertaking of "reconstituting" the historical world of Christian beginnings.[67]

Such a feminist reconstitution of the world requires a feminist hermeneutics that shares in the critical methods and impulses of historical scholarship on the one hand and in the theological goals of liberation theologies on the other hand. It not only challenges androcentric reality constructions in language but seeks to move from androcentric texts to patriarchal-historical contexts. While androcentrism characterizes a mind-set, patriarchy represents a social-cultural system in which a few men have power over other men, women, children, slaves, and colonialized people. Feminist theology as a critical theology of liberation therefore seeks to develop not only a textual-biblical hermeneutics but also a historical-biblical hermeneutics of liberation. It challenges biblical studies as "objective" textual interpretations and value-neutral historical reconstructions fundamentally.[68]

The historical-theological insight that the New Testament is not only a source of revelatory truth but also a resource for patriarchal subordination and domination demands a new paradigm for biblical hermeneutics and theology. This paradigm must not only shed its objectivist pretense of disinterestedness but also its doctrinal neo-orthodox essence-accidents model of interpretation. All early Christian texts are formulated in an androcentric language and conditioned by their patriarchal milieux and histories. Biblical revelation and truth are given only in those texts and interpretative models that transcend critically their patriarchal frameworks and allow for a vision of Christian women as historical and theological subjects and actors.

Such a vision of Christian origins, however, cannot be formulated by abstracting the essence of revelation from its accidental, patriarchal formations and cultural expressions, since such an abstract universal essence does not allow for a critical understanding of the particular roots and mechanisms of women's oppression and struggle for liberation in patriarchal culture and religion. Nor can such a vision be gained by analyzing merely the biblical passages on women, because such a topical analysis would take the androcentric dynamics and reality constructions of patriarchal texts at face value. A feminist revision of Christian origins and biblical history must be achieved in and through a critical analysis of patriarchal-androcentric texts and sources by recognizing as a methodological principle that being human and being Christian is essentially a social, historical, and cultural process. Therefore, being a Christian woman grows out of the concrete social and historical structures and processes of women's oppression as well as their struggle for liberation and transcendence.

A critical reconstruction of women's historical oppression within patriarchal biblical religion and community, as well as an analysis of its theological, conceptual justifications must, therefore, be based on an alternative feminist biblical vision of the historical-cultural-religious interaction between women and men within Christian community and history. Such a historical reconstruction and theological revisioning[69] is inspired not only by scholarly theoretical goals but also by practical interests in the liberation of women from internalized biblical patriarchal structures and doctrines. It is concerned not only with analyzing the historical oppression of women in biblical religion but also with changing the social reality of the Christian churches in which the religious oppression and eradication of women takes its specific historical patriarchal forms. In the last analysis, such a project is not just geared toward the liberation of women but also toward the emancipation of the Christian community from patriarchal structures and androcentric mind-sets so that the gospel can become again a "power for the salvation" of women as well as men. Such a revisioning of Christian community and belief systems is not only a religious but also an important political-cultural task, since biblical patriarchal religion still contributes to the oppression and exploitation of *all* women in our society. It would therefore be feminist romanticism to relegate biblical religion and its power of influence to the sphere of "non-being."

If feminist identity is not based on the experience of biological sex or essential gender differences but on the common historical experience of women as unconsciously collaborating or struggling participants in patriarchal culture and history,[70] then the reconstruction of early Christian origins in a feminist perspective is not just a historical but also a feminist theological task. Theological meaning cannot be derived either from the revelatory surplus of androcentric texts or of true feminist consciousness, but can only be found in and through androcentric texts and patriarchal history. It becomes necessary therefore to explore all the historical dimensions of androcentric biblical texts as well as of early Christian history and theology.

Rather than *abandon* the memory of our foresisters' sufferings and hopes in our common patriarchal Christian past, Christian feminists *reclaim* their sufferings and struggles in and through the subversive power of the "remembered past." If the enslavement and colonialization of people becomes total when their history is destroyed because solidarity with the faith and suffering of the dead is made impossible, then a feminist biblical hermeneutics has the task of becoming a "dangerous memory" that reclaims the religious suffering and engagement of the dead. Such a "subversive memory" not only keeps alive the suffering and hopes of Christian women in the past but also allows for a universal solidarity of sisterhood with all women of the past, present, and future who follow the same vision.

The continuing challenge of the victims of religious patriarchy is not met by the denial of their self-understanding and religious vision as mistaken or ideological self-deception, but only in and through an engaged solidarity and remembrance of their hopes and despair. Or in the words of J. B. Metz:

> Christian faith declares itself as the *memoria passionis, mortis, et resurrectionis Jesu Christi.* At the midpoint of this faith is a specific

> *memoria passionis* on which is grounded the promise of future
> freedom for all . . . [Such faith] is not a complete leap into the
> eschatological existence of the "new human" but rather a reflec-
> tion about concrete human suffering which is the point at which
> the proclamation of the new and essentially human way of life
> announced in the resurrection of Jesus can begin. . . . In this
> sense, the Christian *memoria* insists that the history of human
> suffering is not merely part of the pre-history of freedom but
> remains an inner aspect of the history of freedom.[71]

Such a remembrance of women's suffering and their history of patriarchal oppression must be kept alive as an inner moment in a feminist
Christian history and biblical theology. However, such a feminist
memoria of the suffering of Jesus Christ and of the innocent victims of
patriarchal oppression must be careful not to ascribe this suffering
and colonialization of women to the positive will of God, the heavenly patriarch, and to claim divine revelation and the agency of the
Holy Spirit as the theological justification of such suffering. Insofar
as androcentric biblical texts lend themselves to the perpetuation and
legitimization of such patriarchal oppression and forgetfulness of,
silence about, or eradication of the memory of women's suffering,
they must be demythologized as androcentric codifications of patriarchal power and ideology that cannot claim to be the revelatory Word
of God.

I would therefore suggest that the revelatory canon for theological
evaluation of biblical androcentric traditions and their subsequent
interpretations cannot be derived from the Bible itself but can only be
formulated in and through women's struggle for liberation from all
patriarchal oppression. It cannot be universal but must be specific
since it is extrapolated from a particular experience of oppression and
liberation. The "advocacy stance for the oppressed" must be sustained at the point of feminist critical evaluation of biblical texts and
traditions and their authority claims. The personally and politically
reflected experience of oppression and liberation must become the
criterion of appropriateness for biblical interpretation and evaluation
of biblical authority claims.

A feminist hermeneutical understanding that is oriented not simply
toward an actualizing continuation of biblical Tradition or of a particular biblical tradition but toward a critical evaluation of it must uncover and reject those elements within *all* biblical traditions and texts
that perpetuate, in the name of God, violence, alienation, and patriarchal subordination, and eradicate women from historical-theological

consciousness. At the same time, such a feminist critical hermeneutics must recover *all* those elements within biblical texts and traditions that articulate the liberating experiences and visions of the people of God.

A feminist theological hermeneutics having as its canon the liberation of women from oppressive patriarchal texts, structures, institutions, and values maintains that—if the Bible is not to continue as a tool for the patriarchal oppression of women—only those traditions and texts that critically break through patriarchal culture and "plausibility structures" have the theological authority of revelation. The "advocacy stance" of liberation theologies cannot accord revelatory authority to any oppressive and destructive biblical text or tradition. Nor did they have any such claim at any point in history. Such a critical measure must be applied to *all* biblical texts, their historical contexts, and theological interpretations, and not just to the texts on women.

This critical measure should also be applied to their subsequent history of interpretation in order to determine *how much* and *why* these traditions and interpretations have contributed to the patriarchal deformation of Christian faith and community, as well as to the oppression of women and all other subjected people. In the same vein, such a feminist critical hermeneutics must test whether and how much some biblical traditions contain emancipatory elements that have transcended critically their cultural patriarchal contexts and have contributed to the liberation of people, especially of women, although these texts and traditions were embedded in a patriarchal culture and preached by a patriarchal church. These texts of the New Testament, however, should not be misunderstood as abstract, timeless theological ideas or norms, but should be understood as faith responses to concrete historical situations.

Feminist theology therefore challenges biblical theological scholarship to develop a paradigm for biblical revelation that does not understand the New Testament as an archetype but as a prototype. Both archetype and prototype denote original models. However, an archetype is an ideal form that establishes an unchanging timeless pattern, whereas a prototype is not a binding timeless pattern or principle. A prototype, therefore, is critically open to the possibility of its own transformation. "Thinking in terms of prototype historicizes myth."[72] A hermeneutical understanding of Scripture as prototype not only has room for but requires the transformation of its own models of Christian faith and community. It therefore demands a critical exploration of the historical-social-theological dynamics operative in the formulation and canonization of the New Testament as Scripture, as well as an integration of biblical history and theology.

Such an understanding of Scripture not as a mythic archetype but as a historical prototype provides the Christian community with a sense of its ongoing history as well as of its theological identity. Insofar as it does not define the Bible as a fixed mythical pattern it is able to acknowledge positively the dynamic process of biblical adaptation, challenge, or renewal of social-ecclesial and conceptual structures under the changing conditions of the church's social-historical situations. In and through "structural transformation" (Jean Piaget) the Bible and the biblical community are able to respond to new social needs and theological insights, as well as to allow and to extrapolate new social-ecclesial structures, while preserving the liberating biblical vision by engendering new structural formations that belong to this vision. As the root model of Christian community and faith, the Bible functions as an active formation within the Christian churches and as a residual formation within Western culture.[73] Women living within the cultural and ecclesial trajectory of the Bible are not completely free to neglect its world of vision and to overlook its structural formations. "One's freedom does, however, consist in knowing the direction of the trajectory along which one is being borne, assessing alternate movements, and then taking relevant steps to redirect one's course toward a better outcome."[74]

Such a theological understanding of the Bible as prototype cannot identify biblical revelation with the androcentric text, but maintains that such revelation is found in the life and ministry of Jesus as well as in the discipleship community of equals called forth by him. Biblical texts and their subsequent interpretations are formulated in interaction with their patriarchal cultures and social-ecclesial structures. They therefore express such revelation experience in androcentric language and patriarchal codifications. Insofar as the model proposed here locates revelation not in texts but in Christian experience and community, it can point to the actual practice of the churches which define explicitly or implicitly biblical authority and the canon of revelation with reference to their own acknowledged or unacknowledged centers of ecclesial power. While the Roman Catholic Church has made explicit such a hermeneutical procedure, other Christian churches implicitly and practically follow it.

Similarly, liberation theologies insist that revelation and biblical authority are found in the lives of the poor and the oppressed whose cause God, as their advocate and liberator, has adopted. A feminist critical hermeneutics of liberation shares the "advocacy stance" of liberation theologies but, at the same time, it elaborates not only women's oppression but also women's power as the locus of revelation. As the root model of Christian life and community the Bible reflects biblical women's strength as well as their victimization. Therefore, the Bible is source for women's religious power as well as for their religious oppression throughout the history of Christianity to the present. A Christian feminist theology of liberation must cease its attempts to rescue the Bible from its feminist critics and assert that the source of our power is also the source of our oppression.

A feminist critical hermeneutics of liberation, therefore, must analyze carefully the theological and structural patriarchalization of the New Testament and "patristic" churches without too quickly resorting to biblical apologetics or to an a-historical disinterest. It must become conscious of the interrelationships between ecclesial-cultural patriarchy and theological texts and traditions. It can elucidate how a misogynist theology is always engendered by the patriarchal church in order to relegate women to marginal status and displace them as ecclesial and theological subjects. Such a hermeneutics, therefore, seeks to develop a critical method of analysis that allows women to move beyond the androcentric biblical text to its social-historical contexts. At the same time, such a hermeneutics must search for theoretical models of historical reconstruction that place women not just on the periphery but in the center of Christian life and theology. Insofar as androcentric biblical texts not only reflect their patriarchal cultural environment but also continue to allow a glimpse of the early Christian movements as a discipleship of equals, the reality of women's engagement and leadership in these movements precedes the androcentric injunctions for women's role and behavior. Women who belonged to a submerged group in antiquity could develop leadership in the emerging Christian movement which, as a discipleship of equals, stood in tension and conflict with the patriarchal ethos of the Greco-Roman world.

A feminist critical hermeneutics of the Bible must develop theoretical interpretative models that can integrate the so-called countercultural, heretical, and egalitarian traditions and texts into its overall reconstruction of scriptural theology and history. Although the canon preserves only remnants of the nonpatriarchal early Christian ethos, these remnants still allow us to recognize that the patriarchalization process is not inherent in Christian revelation and community but progressed slowly and with difficulty. Therefore, a feminist biblical hermeneutics can reclaim early Christian theology and history as women's own theology and history. Women had the power and authority of the gospel. They were central and leading individuals in the early Christian movement.

Women as church have a continuous history and tradition that can claim Jesus and the praxis of the earliest church as its biblical root model or prototype, one that is open to feminist transformation. A feminist Christian theology, in my opinion, has as primary task keeping alive "the *memoria passionis*" of Christian women as well as reclaiming women's religious-theological heritage. However, this theological heritage is misrepresented when it is understood solely as the history of oppression. It also must be reconstituted as a history of liberation and of religious agency. The history and theology of women's oppression perpetuated by patriarchal biblical texts and by a clerical patriarchy must not be allowed to cancel out the history and theology of the struggle, life, and leadership of Christian women who spoke and acted in the power of the Spirit.

NOTES

1. For reviews of the different approaches and perspectives in feminist theology, cf. Anne Barstow Driver, "Review Essay: Religion," *Signs* 2 (1976) 434–42; Carol P. Christ, "The New Feminist Theology: A Review of the Literature," *Religious Studies Review* 3 (1977) 203–12; idem, "Women's Studies in Religion," *Bulletin of the Council on the Study of Religion* 10 (1979) 3–5; and especially the introductions in Carol P. Christ and Judith Plaskow, eds., *Womanspirit Rising: A Feminist Reader in Religion* (San Francisco: Harper & Row, 1979), especially pp. 1–17. See also Catharina J. M. Halkes, *Gott hat nicht nur starke Söhne: Grundzüge einer feministischen Theologie* (Gütersloh: Mohn, 1980); and a more detached account, especially of American feminist theology, by Elisabeth Gössmann, *Die streitbaren Schwestern: Was will die feministische Theologie?* (Freiburg: Herder, 1981).

2. For a more thorough discussion, cf. my article "Toward a Feminist Biblical Hermeneutics: Biblical Interpretation and Liberation Theology," in Brian Mahan and L. Dale Richesin, eds., *The Challenge of Liberation Theology: A First World Response* (Maryknoll, N.Y.: Orbis Books, 1981), pp. 91–112.

3. For a more extensive discussion and documentation, cf. my article "For the Sake of Our Salvation . . . Biblical Interpretation as Theological Task," in Daniel Durken, ed., *Sin, Salvation, and the Spirit* (Collegeville, Minn.: Liturgical Press, 1979), pp. 21–39.

4. James Barr, *Fundamentalism* (Philadelphia: Westminster, 1978), p. 49.

5. See especially James Barr, "The Bible as Document of Believing Communities," in Hans Dieter Betz, ed., *The Bible as a Document of the University* (Chico, Calif.: Scholars Press, 1981), pp. 25–47.

6. For an excellent review and discussion, cf. Anthony C. Thistelton, *The Two Horizons: New Testament Hermeneutics and Philosophical Description with Special Reference to Heidegger, Bultmann, Gadamer and Wittgenstein* (Grand Rapids: Eerdmans, 1980); Paul J. Achtemeier, *The Inspiration of Scripture: Problems and Proposals* (Philadelphia: Westminster, 1980); and the review by Francis Schüssler Fiorenza in *CBQ* 43 (1981) 635–37.

7. Edward Schillebeeckx, *The Understanding of Faith* (New York: Seabury, 1974), p. 130.

8. See especially Frederick Herzog, "Liberation Hermeneutics as Ideology Critique, "*Interpretation* 27 (1974) 387–403; Juan Luis Segundo, *The Liberation of Theology* (Maryknoll, N.Y.: Orbis Books, 1976); Jose Miguez Bonino, *Doing Theology in a Revolutionary Situation* (Philadelphia: Fortress, 1975); and Lee Cormie, "The Hermeneutical Privilege of the Oppressed: Liberation Theologies, Biblical Faith, and Marxist Sociology of Knowledge," *Proceedings of the Catholic Theological Society of America* 32 (1978) 155–81.

9. See especially Leonard Swidler and Arlene Swidler, eds., *Women Priests: A Catholic Commentary on the Vatican Declaration* (New York: Paulist Press, 1977); Carroll Stuhlmueller, ed., *Women and Priesthood: Future Directions* (Collegeville, Minn: Liturgical Press, 1978); Maureen Dwyer, ed., *New Woman, New Church, New Priestly Ministry* (Rochester, N.Y.: Women's Ordination Conference, 1980). For the ecumenical discussion, cf. Constance F. Parvey, ed., *Ordination of Women in Ecumenical Perspective* (Faith and Order Paper 105; Geneva: World Council of Churches, 1980).

10. Aileen S. Kraditor, ed. *Up from the Pedestal: Landmark Writings in the American Women's Struggle for Equality* (Chicago: Quadrangle Books, 1968), pp. 51, 55.

11. Ibid., pp. 108f.

12. See Barbara Welter, "Something Remains to Dare: Introduction to the Women's Bible," in Elizabeth Cady Stanton, ed., *The Original Feminist Attack on the Bible: The Woman's Bible* (facsimile ed. New York: Arno, 1974), p. xxii.

13. Cady Stanton, *The Woman's Bible*, 1.9. Cf. Elaine C. Huber, "They Weren't Prepared to Hear: A Closer Look at the Woman's Bible," *Andover Newton Quarterly* 16 (1976) 271–76.

14. Cady Stanton, *The Woman's Bible*, 2.7f. For the cultural-religious context, cf. James Smylie, "The Woman's Bible and the Spiritual Crisis," *Soundings* 59 (1976) 305–28, and the contributions of Anne McGrew Bennett, Linda K. Pritchard, Mary K. Wakeman, Barbara Yoshioka, Clare Denton, Ebba Johnson, and Gayle Kimball to the symposium on "The Women's Bible: Reviews and Perspectives," *Women and Religion: 1973 Proceedings* (Tallahassee: American Academy of Religion, 1973), pp. 39–78.

15. Cf. John Howard Yoder, *The Politics of Jesus: Vicit Agnus Noster* (Grand Rapids: Eerdmans, 1972), p. 176n. 2, rejecting Krister Stendahl, *The Bible and the Role of Women: A Case Study in Hermeneutics* (Philadelphia: Fortress Press, 1966).

16. Robin Scroggs, "Paul and the Eschatological Woman," *JAAR* 40 (1972) 283–303:283.

17. Robert Kress, *Whither Womankind? The Humanity of Women* (St. Meinrad, Ind.: Abbey Press, 1975), pp. 92f.

18. Robert Jewett, "The Sexual Liberation of the Apostle Paul," *JAAR* Supplements 47/1 (1979) 55–87:68.

19. Elaine Pagels, "Paul and Women: A Response to Recent Discussion," *JAAR* 42 (1974) 538–49:547.

20. Evelyn Stagg and Frank Stagg, *Woman in the World of Jesus* (Philadelphia: Westminster, 1978), pp. 256f.

21. See especially Michelle Zimbalist Rosaldo, "The Use and Abuse of Anthropology: Reflections on Feminism and Cross Cultural Understandings," *Signs* 5 (1980) 389–417; Marilyn J. Boxer, "For and about Women: The Theory and Practice of Women's Studies in the United States," *Signs* 7 (1982) 696–700; Michèle Barrett, *Women's Oppression Today: Problems in Marxist Feminist Analysis* (London: Verso Editions, 1980), pp. 42–151; Judith Shapiro. "Anthropology and the Study of Gender," *Soundings* 64 (1981) 446–65.

22. See especially Charlene Spretnak, "The Christian Right's 'Holy War' against Feminism," in idem, *The Politics of Women's Spirituality* (New York: Doubleday, Anchor Books, 1982), pp. 470–96.

23. Kraditor, *Up from the Pedestal*, p. 54.

24. Ibid., pp. 109.

25. Cady Stanton, *The Woman's Bible*, 2.200.

26. Ibid., 1.12.

27. Kraditor, *Up from the Pedestal*, p. 119.

28. For such a topical approach, see Leonard Swidler, *Biblical Affirmations of Woman* (Philadelphia: Westminster, 1979); Karl Hermann Schelkle, *Der Geist und die Braut: Frauen in der Bibel* (Düsseldorf: Patmos, 1977); Erhard S. Gerstenberger and Wolfgang Schrage, *Frau and Mann* (Biblische Konfrontationen 1013; Stuttgart: Kohlhammer, 1980).

29. See the review of this discussion by John Charlot, *New Testament Disunity: Its Significance for Christianity Today* (New York: Dutton, 1970).

30. Peter L. Berger, *The Sacred Canopy: Elements of a Sociological Theory of Religion* (Garden City, N.Y.: Doubleday, 1967), p. 183.

31. Letty Russell, *Human Liberation in a Feminist Perspective* (Philadelphia: Westminster, 1974), p. 79.

32. Ibid., p. 138.

33. Ibid., pp. 87f.

34. Ibid., p. 78.

35. Rosemary Ruether, "A Religion for Women: Sources and Strategies," *Christianity and Crisis* 39 (1979) 307–11:309. See also idem., "Goddesses and Witches: Liberation and Countercultural Feminism," *Christian Century* 97 (1980) 842–47.

36. Ruether "A Religion for Women," p. 309.

37. Ibid., p. 310. See also her statement in "The Feminist Critique in Religious Studies," *Soundings* 64 (1981) 388–402: 400, that "liberationists would use the prophetic tradition as the *norm* to critique the sexism of the religious tradition. Biblical sexism is not denied, but it loses its authority. It must be denounced as a failure to measure up to the full vision of human liberation of the prophetic and gospel messages" (emphasis added). For a more fully developed account of this principle, see her "Feminism and Patriarchal Religion: Principles of Ideological Critique of the Bible," *JSOT* 22 (1982) 54–66.

38. See Merlin Stone, *When God Was a Woman* (New York: Dial Press, 1976), pp. 173–79; J. B. Segal, "The Jewish Attitude Towards Women," *Journal for Jewish Studies* 30 (1979) 121–37: esp. 127–31; E. Schüssler Fiorenza, "Interpreting Patriarchal Traditions," Letty Russell, ed., *The Liberating Word: A Guide to Nonsexist Interpretation of the Bible* (Philadelphia: Westminster, 1976), pp. 39–61:46f.

39. Carol P. Christ, "Why Women Need the Goddess: Phenomenological, Psychological, and Political Reflections," in Christ and Plaskow, *Womanspirit Rising*, pp. 273–87:277.

40. For a similar methodological principle, see Carter Heyward, Rosemary Ruether, and Mary Daly, "Theologians Speaking and Sparking, Building and Burning," *Christianity and Crisis* 39 (1979) 66–72:71.

41. Phyllis Trible, *God and the Rhetoric of Sexuality* (Philadelphia: Fortress, 1978), p. 1.

42. Ibid., p. 202.

43. Ibid., p. 4.

44. Ibid., p. 8.

45. Phyllis Trible, "Depatriarchalization in Biblical Interpretation," *JAAR* 41 (1973) 30–49:49.

46. Trible, *God and the Rhetoric*, p. 203.

47. Ibid., p. 7.

48. See also Polly Ashton Smith, "Contrasts in Language Theory and Feminist Interpretation," *USQR* 35 (1979/80) 89–98: esp. 91–94.

49. Trible, *God and the Rhetoric*, p. 23, n. 5.

50. Although Mary Daly maintains that this model is gynocentric, one must not overlook the fact that it does not have the power to break the androcentric patriarchal model, which situates women on the margins and boundaries but does not allow them to claim the center of patriarchal culture and religion.

51. Peter L. Berger and Thomas Luckmann, *The Social Construction of Reality: A Treatise in the Sociology of Knowledge* (New York: Doubleday, Anchor Books, 1966); Julia A. Sherman and Evelyn Torton Beck, *The Prism of Sex: Essays in the Sociology of Knowledge* (Madison: University of Wisconsin Press, 1977).

52. For a feminist discussion of Simone de Beauvoir's work, see: Mary Lowenthal Felstinger, "Seeing the Second Sex Through the Second Wave"; Michele Le Doeuff, "Simone de Beauvoir and Existentialism"; Sandra Dijkstra, "Simone de Beauvoir and Betty Friedan: The Politics of Omission"; and Jo-Ann P. Fuchs, "Female Eroticism in *The Second Sex*"—all in *Feminist Studies* 6 (1980) 247–313.

53. Mary Daly, *The Church and the Second Sex: With a New Feminist Postchristian Introduction by the Author* (New York: Harper & Row, Colophon Books, 1975), p. 84. Cf. also her statement "The equal dignity and rights of all human beings as persons is of *the essence* of the Christian message" (p. 83; emphasis added).

54. Ibid., pp. 21f.

55. Berger, *Sacred Canopy*, p. 39.

56. See pp. 00–00 of this book.

57. Mary Daly, *Gyn/Ecology: The Metaethics of Radical Feminism* (Boston: Beacon Press, 1978), p. 28.

58. Mary Daly, *Beyond God the Father: Toward a Philosophy of Women's Liberation* (Boston: Beacon Press, 1973), pp. 8f.

59. Daly, *Gyn/Ecology*, p. 112.

60. Ibid., p. 338.

61. Ibid., p. 1.

62. Ibid., p. 23. Sarah Bentley ("Method in the Work of Mary Daly" [Seminar paper, UTS New York, 1975]), has therefore rightly pointed out that what Daly "is espousing is that women live apart from patriarchal culture in every way possible, and especially in our *minds*" (emphasis added).

63. Daly, *Beyond God the Father*, p. 169.

64. Ibid., p. 35.

65. Marjorie Procter-Smith has pointed out that some feminists might consider my mode of critical discussion "male." It should by now be clear that I do not believe that there are "male" and "female" modes of research or "masculine" and "feminine" methods. However, in order to prevent such a misunderstanding, I would like to insist again that I am interested not in a devaluation but in a further development of feminist hermeneutics. Feminist theology needs critical clarification and discussion in order to come more fully into its own.

66. E. Fox-Genovese, "For Feminist Interpretation," *USQR* 35 (1979/80) 5–14:9.

67. Judith McDaniel, *Reconstituting the World: The Poetry and Vision of Adrienne Rich* (Argyle, N.Y.: Spinsters Ink., 1978): Joanne Feit Diehl, " 'Cartographies of Silence': Rich's Common Language and the Woman Poet," *Feminist Studies* 6 (1980) 530–46.

68. Mary E. Payer, "Is Traditional Scholarship Value Free? Toward a Critical Theory," in *The Scholar and the Feminist: A Conference Sponsored by The Barnard College Women's Center* (New York: The Women's Center, Barnard College, 1977), pp. 25–48; Hans Schöpfer, "Die Methodendifferenzierung durch 'hermeneutische Mediation' im gesellschaftstheologischen Engagement," *Freiburger Zeitschrift für Philosophie und Theologie* 26 (1979) 54–95.

69. Cf. Janet Wolf, *The Social Production of Art* (New York: St. Martin's Press, 1981), especially chap. 5: "Interpretation as Re-creation."

70. For a similar approach, see Beverly Wildung Harrison, "The Power of Anger in the Work of Love: Christian Ethics for Women and Other Strangers," *USQR* 36 (1981) 41–67:44ff.; cf. also Padma Ramachandran, *Report of the International Workshop on Feminist Ideology and Structures in the First Half of the Decade for Women*, 24–30 June 1979 (Bangkok: Asian and Pacific Center for Women and Development), 16 pp.

71. Johann Baptist Metz, *Faith in History and Society: Toward a Practical Fundamental Theology*, trans. David Smith (New York: Crossroad, 1980) pp. 111f.

72. Rachel Blau Du Plessis, "The Critique of Consciousness and Myth in Levertov, Rich, and Rukeyser," *Feminist Studies* 3 (1975) 199–221:219.

73. For such a conceptuality, cf. Raymond Williams, *Marxism and Literature* (Oxford: Oxford University Press, 1977), pp. 109–27, 199–205.

74. James M. Robinson and Helmut Koester, *Trajectories through Early Christianity* (Philadelphia: Fortress, 1971), pp. 4f.

Chapter 2

Toward a Feminist
Critical Method

I f the locus of revelation is not the androcentric text but the life and
ministry of Jesus and the movement of women and men called
forth by him, then we must develop critical-historical methods for
feminist readings of the biblical texts. If the silence about women's
historical and theological experience and contribution in the early
Christian movement is generated by historical texts and theological
redactions, then we must find ways to break the silence of the text
and derive meaning from androcentric historiography and theology.
Rather than understand the text as an adequate reflection of the reality about which it speaks, we must search for clues and allusions that
indicate the reality about which the text is silent. Rather than take
androcentric texts as informative "data" and accurate "reports," we
must read their "silences"[1] as evidence and indication of that reality
about which they do not speak. Rather than reject the argument from
silence as a valid historical argument, we must learn to read the
silences of androcentric texts in such a way that they can provide
"clues" to the egalitarian reality of the early Christian movement.

Androcentric texts are parts of an overall puzzle and design that
must be fitted together in creative critical interpretation. It is crucial,
therefore, that we challenge the blueprints of androcentric design,
assuming instead a feminist pattern for the historical mosaic, one that
allows us to place women as well as men into the center of early
Christian history. Such a feminist critical method could be likened to
the work of a detective insofar as it does not rely solely on historical
"facts" nor invents its evidence, but is engaged in an imaginative
reconstruction of historical reality. Or to use again the metaphor provided by the poet Adrienne Rich: in order to wrench meaning from

androcentric texts and history we have to "mine" "the earth-deposits of our history" in order to "bring the essential vein to light," to find the "bottle amber perfect," "the tonic for living on this earth, the winters of this climate."[2] Such a feminist hermeneutical method and process for unearthing biblical feminist history and revelation, for entering an old text from a new critical direction, is not just a chapter in cultural history but an act of feminist transformation. Such a transformation depends, however, on a critical reappropriation of the past.

> Women, looking to the most prestigious texts of the Western tradition, confront misogyny, idealization, objectification, silence. The absence of female consciousness from that tradition challenges a feminist interpretation to look beyond and through the texts. The absence anchors one term of a double meaning. The silences, all the more difficult to restore because of the circuitous interpretation they call for, offer clues to the willed suppression of women. But to translate silence into meaning requires a critical distance from the tradition as well as an *immersion* in it. [emphasis added][3]

However, a feminist critical analysis of biblical texts on women will not suffice. The topical, thematic approach to the analysis of women in the Bible usually adopted in discussing biblical texts already has adopted a theoretical approach and an analytical perspective that marginalize women, since only women (but not men) become the object of historical-critical inquiry and theological discussion. What is therefore necessary is not just a feminist analysis of biblical texts but also a metacritique of the androcentric frameworks adopted by biblical scholarship without any critical reflection on their systemic presuppositions and implications.

The systemic androcentrism of Western culture is evident in the fact that nobody questions whether men have been historical subjects and revelatory agents in the church. The historical role of women, and not that of men, is problematic because maleness is the norm, while femaleness constitutes a deviation from this norm. Whenever we speak of man as the scientific and historical subject we mean the male. For the Western understanding and linguistic expression of reality, male existence is the standard of human existence. "Humanity is male and man defines woman not in herself but relative to him. She is not regarded as autonomous being. He is the subject, the absolute; she is the other."[4] Therefore, our societal and scientific structures define women as derivative and secondary to men. This androcentric definition of being human has determined not only the scholarly perception of men but also of women. In such an androcentric world view woman must remain historically marginal. The androcentric scholarly paradigm can thematize the role of women as a societal, historical, philosophical, and theological problem but cannot question its own horizon,[5] which relegates the "women question" to the periphery of scholarly concerns, a trivial issue not worthy of serious attention. The historical-theological marginality of women is therefore generated not only by the original biblical sources but also in and through the androcentric interpretations and patriarchal reconstructions of biblical scholarship. A feminist analysis, therefore, must pay attention not only to the androcentrism of historical texts but also to that of contemporary scholarly reconstructions of these texts and their social contexts.

Androcentric Translations and Interpretations

The issue of androcentric language has received much attention in the past several years.[6] The biblical texts as they are read by individuals or heard in the liturgy of the church perpetuate the male bias and exclusiveness of our own culture and language.[7] Without question biblical language is androcentric, but is it deliberately exclusive of women? At a time when androcentric language patterns and linguistic praxis have come to consciousness and are much debated, such unconsciously androcentric language becomes exclusive, male-biased language.[8] Biblical translators, therefore, must confront the issue of historically appropriate and philologically correct translation.

Prodded by the Task Force on Inclusive Biblical Translation of the National Council of Churches Division of Education and Ministry, the Revised Standard Version (RSV) translation committee has confronted the issue of masculine biased language and decided to eliminate the word *man* where it is lacking in the original text and was inserted by later translators. For instance, in Luke 17:34 the King James translators introduced the word *men* contrary to the Greek texts so that the verse reads: "I tell you in that night there shall be two men in one bed. . . ." Another example: The committee has proposed to change Rom 2:6 from "He will render to every man according to his works" to "He will repay according to each one's works." Moreover, in all those passages where the Hebrew or the Greek use the generic expression for human being, the committee will translate it with generic expressions such as everyone, all people, human beings, persons, etc.

However, much more difficult is the case of generic pronouns. For example, in Psalm 8 the committee is prepared to replace *man* and *son of man* with *human being* and *mortal* respectively but has not replaced the masculine singular that occurs six times. Despite the two significant modifications made here, women are even more excluded than before, because human being and mortal are now masculine. Even more detrimental would be a refusal to change in the Pauline letters *brothers* to *brothers and sisters* or to abandon masculine pronouns for God. Such androcentric translations can not be justified simply with reference to "literal" translation requirements because every translation is always an interpretation as well. Bruce Metzger's criticism of nineteenth-century suffragist Julia E. Smith's all too literal "wooden" translation applies also to the RSV committee's refusal to change its masculine-biased God-language.

> Miss Smith illustrates dramatically a fact which some persons do not appreciate, namely that most words have more than one meaning and in translation the more specific meaning of a word in a particular context has to be determined from that context.[9]

In a social-cultural context where masculine biased God-language is no longer understood as generic language but as sexist-exclusive language, the translator must ask whether the biblical text insists on the natural masculine gender of God or whether such a genderization and sexualization of God is against the intention of the biblical text and its theological contexts.

While the appropriate translation of masculine metaphors and androcentric language remains a difficult task, another aspect of androcentric biblical language is not just important for contemporary translations and God-language but has hitherto-unexplored ramifications for our understanding of biblical texts as historical sources. A *historically adequate* translation must take into account the interpretative implications of androcentric language which functioned as inclusive language in a patriarchal culture. Such androcentric inclusive language mentions women only when their presence has become in any way a problem or when they are "exceptional," but it does not mention women in so-called normal situations. For instance, even today the minutes of an exegetic conference will still read, "Professor so and so, . . . he said, . . ." although women scholars might have been present at the conference. Only if a woman is exceptional or makes a presentation might the minutes identify her as a woman. Moreover, before consciousness about the issue of androcentric language, even women scholars or writers referred to themselves with the masculine pronoun. In other words, androcentric language is inclusive of women but does not mention them explicitly. Such androcentric inclusive language functions in biblical texts the same way as it functions today—it mentions women only when women's behavior presents a problem or when women are exceptional individuals.[10]

Scholars understand and interpret such androcentric language in a twofold way: as generic and as gender specific. Although many exegetes would refuse to translate the Pauline address "brothers" with "brothers and sisters," they nevertheless assume that the Christian communities to whom Paul writes consisted of "brothers and sisters." Since they do not usually claim that early Christianity was a male cult like the Mithras cult, exegetes understand grammatically masculine terms such as *elect, saints, brothers,* or *sons* as generic language designating men and women. They do not apply only to male Christians as over and against female Christians; rather, such male designations apply to all members of the Christian community. Grammatically masculine language with respect to community membership is not understood in a gender specific but in an inclusive generic way. However, whenever scholars discuss leadership titles—for example, apostles, prophets, or teachers—they *eo ipso* assume that these terms apply only to men despite clear instances in the New Testament where such grammatically masculine titles are applied to women also. Thus Rom 16:1 characterizes Phoebe with the grammatically masculine form of the Greek term *diakonos* and Tit 2:3 uses the grammatically masculine title *kalodidaskalos* for women.

If exegesis, therefore, would take seriously the issue of androcentric language as generic language, we would maintain that any interpretation and translation claiming to be historically adequate to the language character of its sources must understand and translate New Testament androcentric language on the whole as inclusive of women until proven otherwise. The passages of the New Testament that directly mention women do so because such women were exceptional or their actions had become a problem. These texts must not be taken to be all the available information on women in early Christianity. Thus we no longer can simply assume that only 1 Cor 11:2–16 speaks about women prophets, while the rest of chapters 11–14 refer to male charismatics and to male prophets. The opposite is the case. In 1 Cor 11–14 Paul speaks about the worship of all Christians, men and women, and he singles out women in 11:2–16 only because their behavior constituted a special problem. Therefore, a historically adequate translation and interpretation must not only take the inclusive function of androcentric language into account but also acknowledge the limitations of such language and reject the topical approach to woman in the New Testament as methodologically inadequate.

In addition, it must be recognized and made explicit that a *good* translation is not a literal transcription but a perceptive interpretation transferring meaning from one language context to another.[11] How much every translation is also an interpretation influenced by the contemporary perspective of the translators can be shown through a comparison of different contemporary Bible translations.[12] For example, 1 Cor 11:3 in a word by word literal translation reads:

> However, I want you [plural] to know that the head of every man is the Christ, however, a head of woman is the man, however, head of the Christ is the God.

the RSV translation reads:

> I want you to understand that the head of every man is Christ, the head of the woman is her husband, and the head of Christ is God.

The New English Bible renders the verse as follows:

> But I wish you to understand that while every man has Christ for his head, woman's head is man as Christ's head is God.

The Living Letters reads:

> But there is one matter I want to remind you about: that a wife is responsible to her husband, her husband is responsible to Christ and Christ is responsible to God.

And finally the Good News for Modern Man really brings out the good news for modern males:

> But I want you to understand that Christ is supreme over every man, the husband is supreme over his wife and God is supreme over Christ.

By dropping the definite article before Christ and God the translators have smoothed out the text theologically while, at the same time, interpreting it in terms of patriarchal hierarchy.

Finally, because contemporary translators share in the androcentric-patriarchal mind-set of Western culture, they cannot do justice to texts that speak positively about Christian women and integrate these texts into their constructive model of early Christian beginnings. Because they generally presuppose that men, and not women, developed missionary initiatives and exercised central leadership in early Christianity, texts that do not fit such an androcentric model are quickly interpreted in terms of an androcentric perspective. For example, most modern interpreters assume that Rom 16:7 speaks about two men, who had already become Christians before Paul and had great authority as apostles. However, there is no reason to understand Junia as a shortened form of the male name Junianus since Junia was a well-known female name. Even patristic exegesis understood it predominantly as the name of a woman. Andronicus and Junia were an influential missionary team who were acknowledged as apostles.[13]

Another example of androcentric interpretation is often found with reference to Rom 16:1–3. In this passage Phoebe is called the *diakonos* and *prostatis* of the church at Cenchreae, the seaport of Corinth. Exegetes attempt to downplay the importance of both titles here because they are used with reference to a woman. Whenever Paul calls himself, Apollos, Timothy, or Tychicos *diakonos*, scholars translate the term as "deacon," but because the expression here refers to a woman, exegetes translate it as "servant," "helper," or "deaconess." While Kürzinger, for instance, translates the title in Phil 1:1 as "deacon," in the case of Phoebe he explains that "she works in the service of the community." In a footnote he characterizes Phoebe as "one of the first pastoral assistants."[14] H. Lietzmann also understands the office of Phoebe by analogy to the later institute of the deaconesses which, in comparison to that of the deacons, had only a very limited function in the church. He characterizes Phoebe as an "apparently well-to-do and charitable lady, who because of her feminine virtues worked in the service of the poor and the sick and assisted in the baptism of women."[15] Origen had already labeled Phoebe as an assistant and servant of Paul. He concluded that women who do good works can be appointed as deaconesses.[16]

However, the text does not permit such a feminine stereotyping of Phoebe. As we can see from 1 Cor 3:5–9, Paul uses *diakonos* in parallel with *synergos* and with these titles characterizes Apollos and himself as missionaries with equal standing who have contributed to the upbuilding of the community in different ways.[17] Since Phoebe is named *diakonos* of the church at Cenchreae, she receives this title because her service and office were influential in the community. That Phoebe could claim great authority within the early Christian missionary endeavor is underlined by the second title *prostatis/patrona*. Therefore, when Paul calls Phoebe a *patrona*, he characterizes her by analogy with those persons who had influential positions as representative protectors and leaders in the Hellenistic religious associations.[18] G. Heinrici points out that in antiquity religious and private associations received legal protection and derived social-political influence from the patronage of eminent and rich members.[19]

Since exegetes of the New Testament take it for granted that the leadership of the early Christian communities was in the hands of men, they assume that those women mentioned in the Pauline letters were the helpmates and assistants of the apostles, especially of Paul. Such an androcentric interpretative model leaves no room for the alternative assumption that women were missionaries, apostles, or heads of communities independent of Paul and equal to him. Since Paul's position was often precarious and in no way accepted by all the members of the communities, it is even possible that some women's influence was more established than that of Paul's. Texts such as Rom 16:1–3 or 16:7 suggest that leading women in the early Christian missionary movement did not owe their position to Paul. It is more likely that Paul had no other choice but to cooperate with these women and to acknowledge their authority within the communities. Because scholars use androcentric heuristic models that cannot do justice to the position and influence of women like Phoebe, Prisca, or Junia, or adequately integrate them into their conception of early Christian leadership,[20] their reconstructions serve to legitimize the patriarchal practice of the contemporary church.

Androcentric Selection of Historical Traditions

One could reject such a critique of contemporary scholarly frameworks and maintain that the androcentric interpretation of early Christianity is conditioned and justified by our sources because they speak about women and their role in the early church only rarely and mostly in a polemic argument. Thus the historical marginality of women is not created merely by contemporary androcentric exegesis, or androcentric biblical texts, but by the fact that women actually were marginal in the fellowship of Jesus and that the early Christian church was male defined from its very beginnings. Jesus was a man, the apostles were men, the early Christian prophets, teachers, and missionaries were men. All New Testament writings claim to be written by male authors, and the theology of the first centuries is called the "theology of the Fathers." Women do not seem to be of any significance in the early church nor are they allowed any leadership or teaching functions. The Christian marginality of women has its roots in the patriarchal beginnings of the church and in the androcentrism of Christian revelation.

Such a theological conclusion presupposes, however, that the New Testament writings are objective factual reports of early Christian history and development. The rarity of women's mention in the sources would thus adequately reflect the actual history of their activity in the early church. Such a presupposition, however, neglects the methodological insights of form criticism, source criticism, and redaction criticism, which have pointed out that the early Christian writings are not at all objective, factual transcripts but pastorally engaged writings.[21] The early Christian authors have selected, redacted, and reformulated their traditional sources and materials with reference to their theological intentions and practical objectives. None of the early Christian writings and traditions is free from any of these tendencies. All early Christian writings, even the Gospels and Acts, intend to speak to actual problems and situations of the early church and to illuminate them theologically. We can assume, therefore, that this methodological insight applies equally to the traditions and sources about women in early Christianity. Since the early Christian communities and authors lived in a predominantly patriarchal world and participated in its mentality, it is likely that the scarcity of information about women is conditioned by the androcentric traditioning and redaction of the early Christian authors. This applies particularly to the Gospels and Acts since these were written toward the end of the first century. Many of the traditions and information about the activity of women in early Christianity are probably irretrievable because the androcentric selection or redaction process saw these as either unimportant or as threatening.

The contradictions in the sources indicate such an androcentric process of redaction, which "qualifies" information that could not be omitted. For instance, Acts mentions women, especially rich women who supported the early Christian missionary endeavor with their homes and wealth. However, this historical elaboration of Luke gives the impression that the leadership of the early Christian mission was totally in the hands of men.[22] We find short references to widows and prophetesses, but Luke does not tell us any stories about their activity or function. Luke's conception of history is harmonizing and therefore does not acknowledge a "women's problem" in the early church.

Such a problem does emerge, however, when one reads the Pauline letters.[23] The meaning of the Pauline texts that speak directly about women is still unclear, although numerous attempts at inter-pretation have been made. Exegetes are divided on the question of whether the influence of Paul was negative or positive with respect to the role of women in early Christianity. Paul presupposes in 1 Cor 11:2–16 that women speak as prophets in community worship but demands that in so doing they adapt to the prevailing custom. It is not clear, however, what the actual issue of discussion is between Paul and the Corinthians or how the individual arguments of Paul are to be evaluated and understood. The prohibitive interests of the in-junction in 1 Cor 14:33–36 are clear-cut, but exegetes are divided as to whether the famous *mulier taceat in ecclesia* is a later interpolation, since it seems to contradict 1 Cor. 11.

In Gal 3:28 Paul proclaims that all distinctions between Jews and Greeks, free and slave, male and female are obliterated, but he does not repeat in 1 Cor 12:13 that maleness and femaleness no longer have any significance in the body of Christ. Therefore, no exegetical consensus is achieved on whether Gal 3:28, like 1 Cor 12:13, applies to the Christian community, or to the eschatological future, or to the spiritual equality of all souls. The Pauline lists of greetings mention women as leading missionaries and respected heads of churches, but it is not univocal on how much they owe their leadership positions to Pauline approval and support. It is true that Paul values women as co-workers and expresses his gratitude to them, but he probably had no other choice than to do so because women like Junia or Prisca already occupied leadership functions and were on his level in the early Christian missionary movement.

That the sources are unclear and divided about women's role in early Christianity is also evident when one compares the information supplied by different New Testament writings. The Pauline letters indicate that women have been apostles, missionaries, patrons, co-workers, prophets, and leaders of communities. Luke, on the other hand, mentions women prophets and the conversion of rich women but does not tell us any instance of a woman missionary or leader of a church. He seems to know of such functions of women, as his refer-ences to Prisca or Lydia indicate, but this knowledge does not influ-ence his portrayal of early Christian history. Whereas all the Gospels know that Mary Magdalene was the first resurrection witness, the pre-Pauline tradition of 1 Cor 15:3–5 does not mention a single woman among the resurrection witnesses. The Fourth Gospel and its tradition ascribe to a woman a leading role in the mission of Samaria, while Acts knows only a Philip as the first missionary of this area. While Mark knows of the paradigmatic discipleship of women (*ako-*

louthein), Luke stresses that the women who followed Jesus supported him and his male disciples with their possessions.

The Lukan stress on Peter as the primary Easter witness must be situated within the early Christian discussion of whether Peter or Mary Magdalene is the first resurrection witness.[24] This discussion understands Peter to be in competition with Mary Magdalene insofar as he complains constantly that Christ has given so many revelations to a woman. The *Gospel of Thomas* reflects this competition between Peter and Mary Magdalene. The gnostic writing *Pistis Sophia* and the apocryphal *Gospel of Mary* further develop this motif. In the *Gospel of Mary* it is asked how can Peter be against Mary Magdalene on the grounds that she is a woman if Christ has made her worthy of his revelations? The *Apostolic Church Order* evidences that this discussion presupposes an actual ecclesial situation. While the *Gospel of Mary* argues for the authority of Mary Magdalene on the ground that Christ loved her more than all the other disciples, the *Apostolic Church Order* argues for the exclusion of women from the priesthood by letting Mary Magdalene herself reason that the weak, namely, the women, must be saved by the strong, namely, the men. This dispute about the resurrection witness of Mary Magdalene shows, however, that Mary, like Peter, had apostolic authority in some Christian communities even into the third and fourth centuries. It also makes clear that the androcentric interpretation of the egalitarian primitive Christian traditions serves as a patriarchal ecclesial praxis.

Finally, a textual-critical study of the transmission of New Testament texts and their variant readings shows that such an active elimination of women from the biblical text has taken place. For instance, in Col 4:15 the author extends greetings to the community at Laodicea (v. 13) and then to a person named *Nymphan*.[25] The accusative form of the name can refer to a man with the name Nymphas or to a woman whose name was Nympha. If one accepts the variant reading of Codex Vaticanus, some minuscules, and the Syriac translation—"and the church in her (*autēs*) house"—then the greetings refer to a woman who is the leader of a house church. If one reads with the Egyptian text "their" (*autōn*) house, then the greeting would either refer to Nymphas and his wife or Nympha(s) and his/her friends. The Western and Byzantine textual witnesses in turn consider the person to be a man because they read the masculine pronoun "his" (*autou*) house. The feminine reading is the more difficult reading and the masculine form can easily be explained as a correction of the female name since it was considered improbable or undesirable that a woman have such a leadership position.

circu/d?

The same antiwoman tendency can be found in the Western text of Acts.[26] Codex D adds in Acts 1:14 "and children," so that the women who were gathered with the apostles and Jesus' brethren become the "wives and families" of the apostles. Whereas Luke plays down the ecclesial leadership activity of women but underlines the support of prominent women for the Christian mission, Codex D eliminates them totally. In Acts 17:4 it rewrites "and not a few of the noble women" in such a way that these women become the wives of the noble men; in Acts 17:12 it also effaces the emphasis of the original text on the noble women. Likewise in Acts 17:34, which refers to a woman convert by the name of Damaris in Athens, D eliminates the woman's name completely, while in Acts 18:26 it mentions Aquila before Priscilla probably to make sure that Aquila is viewed as the primary teacher of Apollos, the eminent Christian missionary from Alexandria.

In conclusion: The inconsistencies in our New Testament sources indicate that the early Christian traditioning and redactional processes followed certain androcentric interests and perspectives. Therefore, the androcentric selection and transmission of early Christian traditions have manufactured the historical marginality of women, but they are not a reflection of the historical reality of women's leadership and participation in the early Christian movement. It is important to note that the redaction of the Gospels and of Acts happened at a time when the patriarchalization process of the early Church was well underway. Since for various reasons the New Testament authors were not interested in extolling women's as well as slaves' active participation in the Christian movement, we can assume methodologically that the early Christian writers transmit only a fraction of the possibly rich traditions of women's contributions to the early Christian movement.

Much of the information and traditions about the agency of women in the beginnings of Christianity are irretrievable because the patriarchal transmission and redaction process considered such stories and information either as insignificant or as a threat to the gradual patriarchalization of the Christian movement. Moreover, the inconsistencies between different New Testament writings also indicate such an androcentric transmission and redaction of early Christian materials about women. Most of women's early Christian heritage is probably lost and must be extracted from androcentric early Christian records. However, since the Gospels were written at a time when other New Testament authors clearly were attempting to adapt the role of women within the Christian community to that of patriarchal society and religion, it is all the more remarkable that not one story or statement is transmitted in which Jesus demands the cultural patriarchal adaptation and submission of women.[27]

Patriarchal Canonization and Function

While the androcentric transmission and redaction of early Christian traditions can be attributed partially to an early Christian cultural-political apologetics, the canonization of early Christian writings took place at a time when different parts of the church were engaged in a bitter struggle for or against women's leadership. This struggle was engendered by the gradual patriarchalization of early churches. The textual and historical marginalization of women is also a by-product of the "patristic" selection and canonization process of Scripture. Therefore, feminist studies in religion must question the patristic interpretative model that identifies heresy with women's leadership and orthodoxy with patriarchal church structures.

The classic understanding of heresy presupposes the temporal priority of orthodoxy.[28] According to Origen all heretics were first orthodox but then erred from the true faith. Heresy, then, is not only a freely chosen defection but also an intended mutilation of the true faith. The "orthodox" understanding of history knows that Jesus founded the church and gave his revelation to the apostles, who proclaimed his teaching to the whole world. By its witness the "orthodox" church preserves the continuity of revelation in Jesus Christ and establishes personal continuity with Jesus and the first apostles by maintaining the apostolic succession.

Since this understanding of Christian beginnings is shared by all groups of the early church, they all attempt to demonstrate that their group and teaching is in apostolic continuity with Jesus and the first disciples.[29] Montanists, gnostic groups of various persuasions, and the patristic church claim apostolic tradition and revelation in order to substantiate (and to legitimize) their own authenticity. Both parties, the opponents as well as the advocates of the ecclesial leadership of women, claim apostolic tradition and succession for such a leadership.[30] The advocates point to Mary Magdalene, Salome, or Martha as apostolic disciples. They stress the apostolic succession of prophetesses in the Old and New Testament and call attention to the women of apostolic times mentioned in Romans 16. They legitimize their egalitarian structures of community with reference to Gal 3:28. Others preserve the *Acts of Paul and Thecla* as a canonical book.

The patriarchal patristic opposition, on the one hand, appeals to the example of Jesus who did not commission women to preach or admit them to the Last Supper. They quote texts like Gen 2–3, 1 Cor

14, the deutero-Pauline household codes, and especially 1 Tim 2:9–15. Whereas egalitarian groups trace their apostolic authority to Mary Magdalene and emphasize that women as well as men have received the revelations of the resurrected Christ, patristic authors pit the authority of Peter against that of Mary Magdalene. While groups that acknowledge the leadership of women search the Old Testament Scriptures and the Christian writings for passages that mention women, patristic authors attempt to explain away or play down the role of women whenever they are mentioned.[31]

Origen, for instance, concedes that women had been prophets, but stresses that they did not speak publicly and especially not in the worship assembly of the church. Chrysostom confirms that in apostolic times women traveled as missionaries preaching the gospel, but he explains that they could do this only because in the beginnings of the church the "angelic condition" permitted it. Whereas the Montanists legitimize the prophetic activity of women with reference to the Scriptures, the extant church orders justify the institution of deaconesses which granted women only very limited and subordinate ecclesial functions in relation to the prophetesses of the Old Testament and the primitive church. While women who preached and baptized claimed the example of the apostle Thecla, Tertullian denounces the *Acts of Paul and Thecla* as a fraud. This example indicates that the process of the canonization of early Christian documents was affected by the polemics and struggle concerning the leadership of women in the church. Therefore, the canon reflects a patriarchal selection process and has functioned to bar women from ecclesial leadership.

The acid polemics of the Fathers against the ecclesial leadership of women and against their teaching and writing books indicate that the question of women's ecclesial office was still being debated in the second and third centuries c.e. It also demonstrates that the progressive patriarchalization of church office did not happen without opposition, but had to overcome various forms of early Christian theology and praxis that acknowledged the leadership claims of women.[32] We owe to these polemics the few surviving bits of historical, though prejudiced, information about women's leadership in various groups of the early church. Unfortunately, early Christian historiography does not understand them as the outcome of a bitter polemic but as historically adequate and theologically appropriate information.

The polemics of the patristic authors against women's ecclesial leadership and office ultimately resulted in the equation of women's leadership in the church with heresy. This progressive equation of women and heresy had as a consequence the theological defamation of Christian women. For example, the author of the book of Revelation inveighs against an early Christian prophetess whom he abuses with the name Jezebel.[33] This prophet apparently was the head of an early Christian prophetic school which had great influence and authority in the community of Thyatira. Since the author of Revelation stresses that despite his warnings and denunciations the prophetess still was active within the community, her authority seems to have at least equaled that of John whom, in turn, she might have perceived as a false prophet. Her influence must have been lasting, since Thyatira, in the middle of the second century, became a center of the Montanist movement in which prophetesses had significant leadership and influence.

The attacks of Tertullian indicate how prominent women's leadership still was toward the end of the second century. Tertullian is outraged about the insolence of those women who dared to "teach, to participate in theological disputes, to exorcise, to promise healings and to baptize." He argues that it is not permitted for women "to speak in the Church, to teach, to baptize, to sacrifice, to fulfill any other male function, or to claim any form of priestly functions."[34] He substantiates this exclusion of women from all ecclesial leadership roles with a theology that evidences a deep misogynist contempt and fear of women. He accuses woman of the temptation not only of man but also of the angels. According to him woman is the "devil's gateway" and the root of all sin.[35] Finally, Jerome attributes to women the origin not only of sin but of all heresy.

Such patristic polemics against women as the source of heresy must be seen in the gradual development of the concept of "orthodoxy" in early Christianity. This development became necessary because there was "never a single, pure, and authentic Christian position as later 'orthodoxy' would have us believe." Insofar as the writings collected and accepted in the New Testament canon were selected and codified by the patristic New Testament church, the canon is a record of the "historical winners." The selection of those writings which were apostolic and those which were not is an outcome of the struggle of the patristic church with Marcion, different gnostic groups, and Montanism. While it was debated for a time whether or not Paul was "gnostic," his genuine letters were finally accepted and redacted as apostolic. Moreover, "a representative of emerging classical orthodoxy may have edited or composed the letters of 1-2 Tim and Tit *in Paul's name* precisely in order to combat the allegedly Pauline Marcionites and to rescue Paul for 'orthodoxy.'"[36]

Considering this patriarchal context for the canonization process a hermeneutics of suspicion is called for. The information on women found in the surviving canonical texts and the writings of patristic orthodoxy are not value-neutral. Rather, they document that the progressive patriarchalization of church office did not happen without opposition but had to overcome an early Christian theology and tradition that acknowledged women's leadership claims. They do not give us historically adequate and theologically appropriate information. As the outcome of a bitter polemics they indicate the theological-patriarchal climate in which early Christian writings were selected and became "Holy Scripture." We must, therefore, broaden the sources and information we use as a historical and theological basis for the reconstruction of early Christian beginnings and for formulating the meaning of church. Early Christian history and theology must become "ecumenical," that is, inclusive of all Christian groups. *All* early Christian groups and texts must be tested *as to how much* they preserve and transmit the apostolic inclusivity and equality of early Christian beginnings and revelation.[37]

The canonization process of early Christian writings has preserved not only the patriarchalizing texts of the New Testament but also those earliest Christian traditions and texts that still permit us a glimpse of the egalitarian-inclusive practice and theology of early Christians. These texts are the tip of the iceberg indicating a possibly rich heritage now lost to us. Therefore, we must cease interpreting the women's passages in the New Testament in isolation from their historical-ecclesial-social contexts. What is necessary is a systemic interpretation and historical reconstruction able to make the submerged bulk of the iceberg visible. Moreover, it becomes necessary to understand not only canonical texts but also their subsequent history of interpretation and ecclesial-political function. While the so-called patriarchalizing texts always are used to bolster a patriarchal system and the subordination of women in the church or in society, the so-called egalitarian texts of the New Testament throughout the centuries have sparked a nonpatriarchal Christian vision and praxis. The canon thus does not function simply as perpetrator of women's secondary status in Christianity but also as a theological critique of this status.

Androcentric Projection

While I am not aware of any attempt to apply the analytic-heuristic concept of androcentrism to patristic texts, Jacob Neusner has done so in order to illuminate the Mishnaic system of "reality building."[38] His work shows at once the advantage of a systematic androcentric analysis over and against a topical androcentric analysis of "woman's passages"[39] and the drawbacks of such an approach for the reconstruction of women's history. Although Neusner accepts the feminist analytical model of androcentrism, he categorically rejects a feminist perspective because "we are not equipped to interpret the Talmud's world-view if we bring to it our own."[40] However, by doing so he fails to see that in turning to "anthropology for assistance in formulating questions and in gaining perspectives on the Talmudic corpus" he adopts implicitly a clearly contemporary perspective on history.

Neusner rightly rejects most of the studies on women in Judaism because they do not take systemic context seriously and therefore appear to substitute "lists of catalogues for questions and insight." He himself seeks to make sense of the Mishnah's choice of the theme of woman, and "what it wishes to say about that theme." In his reconstruction of the Mishnah's system Neusner primarily employs the analytical category of "woman as the other" or "woman as anomalous." This category was proposed by Simone de Beauvoir and utilized in the anthropological research of Zimbalist Rosaldo and S. Ortner.[41] This heuristic concept illuminates the Mishnaic tractate on women within the overall system of Mishnah in two respects.

1. This category can be used because the Mishnaic system is the construct of a few rabbinic men and expresses their view of women's place. The social referents of the Mishnaic treatment of women are not women but the circle of rabbis who produced the work. Moreover, it is not women per se, but the points of their transition from the hands of one man to that of another that are important. For what defines the woman's status is not whether she may have sexual relations, but "with whom she may have them," and what are the consequences for the natural and supranatural order. According to Neusner, therefore, the Mishnaic system on women is also devised to deal with the "transfer" of women and the property transactions involved therein. Here Neusner moves beyond the analytic category of androcentrism to that of patriarchy. Women are excluded from the sacred order whenever they are not under patriarchal control. Or more positively, women have access to the sacred only in and through the patriarchal family:

> So from the recognition of the anomalous character of women we find ourselves moving toward the most profound and fundamental affirmations of Mishnah about the works of sanctification: the foci and the means. Women are sanctified through the deeds of men. So too are earth and time, the fruit of the herd and of the field, the bed, chair, table, and earth—but in the nature of things, women most of all.[42]

Although Neusner repeatedly stresses how important it is to ask the right questions he does not analyze critically the androcentrism model, since he seems to take at face value its expression of "the nature of things." Because of the possible biological determinism underlying this category, Rosaldo critically revised her previously analysis of sexual assymetry and pointed out:

> What traditional social scientists have failed to grasp is not that sexual assymetries exist but that they are as fully social as the hunter's or the capitalist's role, and that they figure in the very facts, like racism and social class, that social science claims to understand.[43]

But if it is not in the "nature of things" that women are defined and legitimized in relation to, and as possession of, men, then Mishnah's definition of women's place in the sacred cosmos must be seen for what it is: a social-theological projection of men. Neusner makes it quite clear that Mishnah does not speak about the actual life of Jewish women in the second century but that it "is a man's document and imagines a man's world. Women have rights protected by men and Heaven alike. . . . Man is the center."[44] Therefore, Neusner insists again and again that Mishnah's system would be totally misunderstood if it were construed as historical information about Jewish women. Mishnah is not a description of Jewish life, but is prescriptive and imaginative. It speaks for and on behalf of the rabbinical circle that produced it in order to show "how the world should be." Only in later times will the Israelite world come to approximate and even to conform to Mishnah's vision of reality.

Thus, according to Neusner, the trajectory of the Priestly Code (Lev 1–15), the Holiness Code (Lev 17–26), the theological vision of Qumran, and the Mishnah express a cultic understanding of life that articulates an androcentric interpretation of the world and of God's intention. In this perspective women are excluded from the cult and the centers of holiness. They can become holy only by entering the sacred space of man. Women as women are therefore an anomaly and a threat to the sacred order. The Mishnaic system is thus developed in order to control the irregular and anomalous aspects of women's position not only on earth but also in heaven. The contemporaneous patristic cultification of Christian leadership and community needs to be seen in this context and in the same light.

2. According to Mishnah women can enter the sacred space only by being associated either with a father or husband, that is, by being integrated into the patriarchal order. Here it becomes evident that

"Mishnah is produced within and can only imagine a patriarchal society. Its legislation on women to begin with expresses the values of that society."[45] The most crucial moments in a patriarchal system of control are, however, those of transition. Therefore, for someone who seeks to understand this system the most important question to ask is: *why* did the handful of men who wrote the Mishnah feel compelled to project such a vision of the sacred order?

Interestingly enough, Neusner does not raise this question with respect to Mishnah's Division on Women. However, he does so with respect to the Division on Purities. In his opinion, the historical experience that all sacred space and Israelite boundaries were violated moved the rabbis to "construct boundaries which never again will be transgressed." In doing so the rabbis extended the cultic order of purity to all of Israelite life. "What one does because he is clean, is eat his ordinary meals as if he were a priest, and what he cannot do because he is unclean is join with those who eat like priests."[46] Yet such an extension of sacral space to everyday life had become necessary only because of the historical situation that had destroyed Israelite sacral boundaries.

Neusner does not contemplate a similar argument for the Mishnaic Division of Women, although he refers to a marriage contract of a prosperous woman found in the Cave Letters of Bar Kokhba.[47] He concludes from this that "any picture of the Israelite women of the second century as chattel and dumb animal hardly accords with the activities revealed in the legal documents of Babata."[48] Yet he never confronts this insight with his systemic analysis of women in the social world projected by the authors of the Mishnah. Insofar as Neuser fails to raise this question his analysis cannot but reconfirm the prejudice that Jewish culture and religion are patriarchal to the core. A systemic analysis of texts produced by men that confines its interpretation to these texts must necessarily remain within the boundaries of their androcentric perspective.

In order to move from androcentric text to the social-religious life of women, the historian must seek the social reality producing these texts. Could it be that the rabbis' "reality building" and androcentric projection in Mishnah were the response to a social-political current within the first and second century that allowed women to question and undermine the traditional hegemony of the patriarchal social order? Neusner's reference to Babata indicates that this might have been the case, but he does not explore this possibility.

In conclusion: In discussing Greco-Roman writers' statements on women, K. Thraede has pointed to several very important methodological rules for dealing with the information of androcentric texts.[49] First, these texts should never be seen in isolation but always in their immediate textual contexts. Second, these texts should also always be analyzed in their specific social-political context in order to establish their "function." Third, especially normative texts often maintain that something is a historical fact and a given reality although the opposite is the case. The last insight is supported by feminist scholars of American history who have analyzed the sermons and ethical instructions of the clergy on women's nature, place, and behavior in the last two centuries. They have shown that androcentric injunctions become more detailed and numerous with the growth of the women's movement in society. It would therefore be a methodological mistake to take androcentric-patriarchal texts at face value. Neusner's analysis has amply proven this. However, it has also shown that a systemic analysis of androcentric texts does not suffice. It has to be complemented by a feminist hermeneutics of suspicion that understands androcentric texts as ideological articulations of men expressing, as well as maintaining, patriarchal historical conditions.

Androcentric texts and documents do not mirror historical reality, report historical facts, or tell us how it actually was. As androcentric texts our early Christian sources are theological interpretations, argumentations, projections, and selections rooted in a patriarchal culture. Such texts must be evaluated *historically* in terms of their own time and culture and assessed *theologically* in terms of a feminist scale of values. A careful analysis of their androcentric tendencies and patriarchal functions, nevertheless, can provide clues for the historical discipleship of equals in the beginnings of Christianity. These clues can help us to construct a historical model of interpretation that does justice to the egalitarian as well as the patriarchalizing tendencies and developments in the early church.

Historical Imagination and Androcentric Texts

A last methodological issue needs to be raised here, one that is much discussed among women in the churches. Discovering that some early Christian writings are less androcentric, and that they contain more materials on women than others, scholars have postulated female authorship for such writings. Paul Achtemeier[50] has suggested that Mark might have been written by a woman; Leonard Swidler[51] has proposed that Luke's special source is the work of a woman; and Stevan Davies[52] has suggested that the apocryphal Acts were generated by a circle of widows. One of the earliest and most carefully worked out proposals was that of Adolf Harnack,[53] who argued that Priscilla and Aquila are the most likely authors of Hebrews. Such a suggestion has great historical probability and cannot be ruled out a priori. Yet the suggestion of female authorship does not overcome the androcentric character of the writings.

The suggestion of female authorship, however, has great imaginative-theological value because it opens up the possibility of attributing the authority of apostolic writings to women and of claiming theological authority for women. However, the authorship discussions in New Testament studies have shown that they center on issues of authority but have very little analytical value for historical reconstructions. Moreover, a look at writings attributed to women in antiquity or written by women today indicates that these works are not necessarily written differently and do not always espouse different values from those written by men. Women as well as men are socialized into the same androcentric mind-set and culture. Only if one would claim a clearly definable innate feminine quality of cognition could one establish "feminine" as essentially different from "masculine" authorship. Yet such an attempt would only perpetuate the prejudices and sexual assymetry created by the androcentric cultural mind-set. In short, it seems helpful to conjecture female authorship for early Christian canonical writings in order to challenge the androcentric dogmatism that ascribes apostolic authorship only to men. However, the conjecture of female authorship does not in and by itself suggest a feminist perspective of the author. All early Christian writings, whether written by women or by men, more or less share the androcentric mind-set and must be analyzed and tested critically as to how much they do so.

In order to break the hold of the androcentric text over our historical imagination, however, I have found it helpful to encourage students to write stories or letters from the perspective of leading women in early Christianity. Needless to say, such an exercise in historical imagination reflects our own knowledge and presuppositions about early Christian origins. Yet such an exercise helps to relativize the impact of androcentric texts and their unarticulated patriarchal mind-sets. The following "apocryphal" letter of the apostle Phoebe written by one of my students[54] can highlight the educational and imaginative value of retelling and rewriting biblical androcentric texts from a feminist critical perspective:

> Phoebe, an apostle of Christ Jesus by the will of God, called to preach the Good News, to all the saints, my sisters and my brothers, who are at Cenchreae:
> Grace to you and peace from God our Creator, Jesus our Wisdom, and the Spirit our Power.

I thank God each day as I think of you all, remembering how together we came to hear the Good News and how often we rejoiced that we have become one in Christ Jesus. May God, Mother and Father, Friend and Consoler, fill you with all love, all gentleness, all joy, and all faithfulness as you walk each day in the shelter of the Spirit.

Junia and Andronicus returned from my beloved Cenchreae but two days ago and brought your welcomed greetings. It saddens me to be so long away from you, but know it is only so that the work in Christ Jesus may prosper. My experiences here have been fruitful—there are so many stories about Jesus that we have not yet heard, and the churches here are so anxious to share teachings. What a far cry from our churches in Corinth! Has Paul's visit helped heal the bitterness in any way?

We met with him in Miletus on his way back to Jerusalem—thank you for your generous gifts to our brothers and sisters there—but he was not too friendly. My words with him after we had received his letter were not well received I fear! More of that later. We fear for his safety; the parting was one of many tears. Despite our differences, we did embrace and commend each other to God. Remember to pray daily that he will be strengthened in the service of Christ Jesus. On your behalf I sent greetings to Mary of Magdala and Simon Peter in Galilee, rejoicing with them in their work and exhorting them to make peace with each other. Each letter from Jerusalem brings further news of their disputes—indeed of scandal to all the saints. Peter so stubbornly refuses to listen to Mary, even though he himself so often tells how she brought him the first news of the Risen Lord. Mary's patience has been exemplary—Peter can be infuriating at times yet she always responds calmly. It can only come from her confidence born on that Easter Sunday morning. What a source of encouragement she is to all the saints, and what a privilege her community has in having such a leader.

The letters and messengers from Antioch are just as welcomed here as they are by you. There are so many stories and sayings of Jesus, and the disciples so love to retell them. Sometimes I wonder if we should not write them down lest some would become lost. It seems that Mary's people have collected sayings of our Teacher and use them in their preaching and prayer. We must consider doing that when I return. Two new stories have come from the disciples in Galilee. How necessary it is for the saints to share, and how valuable it is to have our missionaries and prophets move from church to church. Junia told me that Miriam the prophet had visited our church and led in the breaking of the bread while she was there. She remarked the coincidence—the reading you had settled for the day had been from the first Book of Kings, and Miriam noted how Huldah's word from Yahweh concerning the book of the Torah could well be her word concerning the fulfillment of the Torah in Christ Jesus.

But to return to the new stories—the first one concerns Jesus' meeting with a Gentile woman who requested that he cure her little daughter who was possessed. He refused, reiterating his claim to have come first to the Jews, but she persisted, turning his argument against him. Recognizing the wisdom of her words, Jesus then healed the little girl. I cannot remember any other story where someone convinced Jesus to change his mind. How fortunate for us Gentiles that he has come not only for the Jews! The second story is one I would like to discuss with Paul who lately seems so concerned with putting women back in "their proper places." He is so taken up with giving a good impression to the pagans that he is reverting to his rabbinic prejudices I think. As if the proper place of woman was in the home bearing children—"woman is the glory of man" indeed! Surely with his background he would know where Genesis puts woman: "in the image of God he created them; male and female he created them." What a strange man he is. In his letter to us he so firmly emphasized the equality of woman and man in marriage; in the same letter he raged on and on about hairstyles in the assembly.

To return to the story. After a woman in praising Jesus had said, "Blessed is the womb that bore you and the breasts that you sucked," Jesus answered, "Blessed rather are those who hear the word of God and keep it." If only more of our people would see that this doing the will of God is important, whether you are woman or man. That is what determines our equality and re- stores the "order" of creation.

And yet I cannot be too disheartened with Paul. He did refrain from writing to us about women keeping silence in the assem- bly. Yes, it's true! Some of the saints were encouraging him to do that. Do you remember his reading to us from his letter to the Roman church before he sent it? His words on the gifts—"Hav- ing gifts that differ according to the grace given to us, let us use them"—are so important if the churches are to grow in the knowledge of God. Surely that and not "the good order" will lead others to the truth. And, even more pointed, are these words from his letter to our Galatian neighbours: "For as many of you as were baptized into Christ have put on Christ. There is neither Jew nor Greek, there is neither slave nor free, there is neither male nor female; for you are all one in Christ Jesus." I do fear that some people hear, not these words of Paul which so clearly reflect the attitude and teaching of Jesus our Wisdom, but hear instead his returns to the past before he received the free- dom of the Spirit. I shudder to think that some time in the future a leader of one of the churches will say, "Gentiles, slaves, and women cannot become part of the ministry of the Word because Jesus did not entrust the apostolic charge to them." When I said that to Paul, he laughed uproariously and exclaimed, "Phoebe, you are a person with the strangest notions! If any of my letters do survive, only someone bewitched will fail to see the difference between my preaching of the Good News and my ramblings about cultural problems and situations. People from another age will easily disregard the cultural trappings and get to the heart of the message." If only that distinction were as clear to the rest of us as it is to Paul!

My beloved people, how much more I have to say to you, but it must wait until I return. I know from Junia and Andronicus that, in my absence, you have continued to devote yourselves to the breaking of the bread and prayers, remembering my teaching to you and encouraging each other in humility. Continue to go to the churches in Corinth, reminding them of the love they should have for one another. Perhaps, by your example, they will cease from factions and disagreements, and become, as we are all called to become, one body in Christ Jesus.

The saints from the church in Rome send greetings to you all. Prisca and Aquilla greet Apollos and tell him of their joy in hearing how faithfully he has spread the Good News. Junia and Andronicus greet you and thank you for the kindness you showed them in their stay with you. Greet Chloe for me and the church which meets in her house. Greet Stephanas through whom I first received the faith. Achaicus will bring this letter to you; welcome him home with heart-filled joy.

May my love be with you all in the Spirit.

NOTES

1. See Tillie Olsen, *Silences* (New York: Dell, 1979) and her dedication: "For our silenced people, century after century their beings consumed in the hard, everyday essential work of maintaining human life. Their art, which still they made—as their other contributions—anonymous, refused respect, recognition; lost."

2. Cf. Adrienne Rich, "Natural Resources," in idem, *The Dream of a Common Language: Poems 1974–1977* (New York: W. W. Norton, 1978), pp. 60–67.

3. Elizabeth Fox-Genovese, "For Feminist Interpretation," *USQR* 35 (1979/80) 10.

4. Simone de Beauvoir, *The Second Sex* (New York: Knopf, 1953), p. 10; cf. Elizabeth Janeway, *Man's World Woman's Place* (New York: Dell, 1971), who explores this androcentric mind-set as "social mythology." See also Margaret A. Simons and Jessica Benjamin, "Simone de Beauvoir: An Interview," *Feminist Studies* 5 (1979) 330–45, for a confrontation with contemporary American feminist thought.

5. See especially Dorothy Smith, "A Peculiar Eclipsing: Women's Exclusion from Man's Culture," *Women's Studies International Quarterly* 1 (1978) 281–96; Valerie Saiving, "Androcentrism in Religious Studies," *Journal of Religion* 56 (1976) 177–97; Elisabeth Schüssler Fiorenza, "Für eine befreite und befreiende Theologie," *Concilium* 14 (1978) 287–94; Dorothy C. Bass, "Women's Studies and Biblical Studies: An Historical Perspective," *JSOT* 22 (1982) 6–12.

6. See Robin Lakoff, *Language and Woman's Place* (New York: Harper & Row, 1975); Mary Ritchie Key, *Male/Female Language: With a Comprehensive Bibliography* (Metuchen, N.J.: Scarecrow Press, 1975); Nancy Henley and Barrie Thorne, *She Said/He Said* (Pittsburgh: KNOW, 1975); Wendy Martyna, "Beyond the 'He/Man' Approach: The Case for Non-Sexist Language," *Signs* 5 (1980) 482–93.

7. See for example J. Martin Bailey, "The Book That Draws People Together," *A. D. Magazine* (November 1977); Mary Collins, "Women and the Language of Public Prayer," (Document 13 prepared for the ICEL); Thomas J. Reese, "Liturgical Change:

What Next?" *America* 21 (1979); Joan Chittister, "Brotherly Love in Today's Church," *America* 19 (1977) 233–36; Dane Packard, *Worship: Inclusive Language Resources* (St. Louis: Office of Church Life and Leadership, UCC, 1977).

8. For such a distinction, see Casey Miller and Kate Swift, *Words and Women: New Language in New Times* (New York: Doubleday, Anchor Books, 1977), pp. 64–74; Katharine Doob Sakenfeld, "Old Testament Perspectives: Methodological Issues," *JSOT* 22 (1982) 13–20: esp. 17ff; Letty Russell, "Changing Language and the Church," in idem, *The Liberating Word: A Guide to Nonsexist Interpretation of the Bible* (Philadelphia: Westminster), pp. 82–98.

9. See the report by Bruce M. Metzger, "The Revised Standard Version," *Duke Divinity School Review* 44 (1979) 70–87:72.

10. Barbara A. Bate, "Generic Man, Invisible Woman: Language Thought and Social Change," *University of Michigan Papers in Women's Studies* 2 (1975) 2–13.

11. See e.g. E. A. Nida, *Language, Structure and Translation* (Stanford: Stanford University Press, 1975); C. R. Tabor, "Translation as Interpretation," *Interpretation* 32 (1978) 130–43; L. Williamson, Jr., "Translation and Interpretation: New Testament," ibid., pp. 158–70.

12. Cf. Daniel J. Harrington, *Interpreting the New Testament* (Wilmington, Del.: Glazier, 1979), pp. 25–41; B. and A. Mickelsen, "Does Male Dominance Tarnish Our Translations?" *Christianity Today* 23 (1979) 1312–18; Ruth Hoppin, "Games Bible Translators Play," photocopy (1972).

13. See my article "Die Rolle der Frau in der urchristlichen Bewegung," *Concilium* 12 (1976) 3–9, in which I pointed to M. J. Lagrange's decision in favor of a woman (*Saint Paul, Epître aux-Romains* [Paris, 1916], p. 366), although this textual reading was abandoned by Protestant exegesis. Bernadette Brooten explored this reference with respect to the history of interpretation in "Junia . . . Outstanding among the Apostles," in L. and A. Swidler, eds., *Woman Priests: A Catholic Commentary on the Vatican Declaration* (New York: Paulist Press, 1977), pp. 141–44.

14. *Das Neue Testament* (Aschaffenburg: Pattloch, 1956), p. 214.

15. H. Lietzmann, *Geschichte der alten Kirche*, vol. 1 (Berlin: de Gruyter, 1961), p. 149.

16. *Commentaria in Epistolam ad Romanos* 10.26 (*PG* 14.1281B), 10.39 (*PG* 14.1289A).

17. Mary A. Getty, "God's Fellow Worker and Apostleship," in Swidler and Swidler, *Women Priests*, pp. 176–82; Earl E. Ellis, "Paul and His Co-Workers," *New Testament Studies* 17 (1970/71) 439.

18. Ramsay MacMullen, *Roman Social Relations* (New Haven: Yale University Press, 1974), pp. 74ff, 124; Peter Garnsey, *Social Status and Legal Privilege in the Roman Empire* (Oxford: Clarendon Press, 1970) pp. 218, 273f.

19. G. Heinrici, "Die Christengemeinde Korinths und die religiösen Genossenschaften der Griechen," *Zeitschrift für Wissenschaftliche Theologie* 19 (1876) 465–526.

20. Hans Conzelmann, *Geschichte des Urchristentums* (Göttingen: Vandenhoeck & Ruprecht, 1971). Appendix 1 lists only Prisca among the leaders in the early church.

21. The centrality of community and "pastoral" situation is especially stressed in form and redaction criticism; cf. William G. Doty, *Contemporary New Testament Interpretation* (Englewood Cliffs, N.J.: Prentice Hall, 1972); Patrick Henry, *New Directions in New Testament Study* (Philadelphia: Westminster, 1979) and especially Norman Perrin, *What Is Redaction Criticism?* (Philadelphia: Fortress, 1970).

22. See my unpublished plenary address "Women's Discipleship and Leadership in the Lukan Writings" (delivered at the annual meeting of the Catholic Biblical Association, San Francisco, 1978), and its summary reception in Elisabeth M. Tetlow, *Women and Ministry in the New Testament* (New York: Paulist Press, 1980), pp. 101–9.

23. See my article "Women in the Pre-Pauline and Pauline Churches," *USQR* 33 (1978) 153–66.

24. See my contribution "Word, Spirit and Power: Women in Early Christian Communities," in Rosemary Ruether and Eleanor McLaughlin, eds., *Women of Spirit: Female Leadership and the Jewish Christian Traditions* (New York: Simon & Schuster, 1979), pp. 29–70: esp. 52ff.

25. See Eduard Lohse, *Colossians and Philemon* (Hermeneia; Philadelphia: Fortress, 1971), p. 174, especially n. 44.

26. William M. Ramsay (*The Church in the Roman Empire Before 170 A.D.* [New York: Putnam, 1892] pp. 161–165) ascribes this textual recension to Asia Minor. However, it seems that the text on which the D-text of Acts and the variant in Colossians is based originated in Antioch. See E. J. Epp, *The Theological Tendency of Codex Bezae Cantabrigensis in Acts* (Cambridge: Cambridge University Press, 1966), pp. 1–34, and especially M. Mees, "Papyrus Bodmer XIV (P^{75}) und die Lukaszitate bei Clemens von Alexandrien," *Vetera Christianorum* 4 (1967) 107–29.

27. See chap. 8 of this book.

28. For the problem of orthodoxy and heresy, see A. Hilgenfeld, *Die Ketzergeschichte des Urchristentums* (rev. ed.; Darmstadt: Wissenschaftliche Buchgesellschaft, 1963); W. Bauer, *Orthodoxy and Heresy in Earliest Christianity* (Philadelphia: Fortress, 1971); John G. Gager, *Kingdom and Community: The Social World of Early Christianity* (Englewood Cliffs, N.J.: Prentice-Hall, 1975), pp. 76–92.

29. See especially J. Pelikan, *The Emergence of the Catholic Tradition* (Chicago: University of Chicago Press, 1971), pp. 105ff.

30. This pattern is typical for all of church history. See e.g. the debate in the eighteenth century about Methodist women's ministry of the word; cf. Earl Kent Brown, "Women of the Word," in Hilah F. Thomas and Rosemary Skinner Keller, eds., *Women in New Worlds: Historical Perspectives on the Wesleyan Tradition* (Nashville: Abingdon 1981), pp. 69–87.

31. For extensive references, cf. my article "Word, Spirit and Power," notes; J. Kevin Coyle, "The Fathers on Women's Ordination," *Église et Théologie* 9 (1978) 51–101; Carolyn Osiek, "The Ministry and Ordination of Women According to the Early Church Fathers," in Carroll Stuhlmueller, ed., *Women and Priesthood: Future Directions* (Collegeville, Minn.: Liturgical Press, 1978), pp. 59–68; R. Gryson, *The Ministry of Women in the Early Church* (Collegeville, Minn.: Liturgical Press, 1976); Klaus Thraede, "Frau," in *RAC* 6 (1970) 197–267: esp. 238–53.

32. F. Heiler, *Die Frau in den Religionen der Menschheit* (Berlin: de Gruyter, 1977), p. 114. But at the same time he argues that, in the heretical communities, women in leadership positions were not "disciplined" enough.

33. Cf. my article "The Quest for the Johannine School: The Apocalypse and the Fourth Gospel," *NTS* 24 (1977) 402–27. It is generally assumed that the followers of Jezebel are identical with the Nicolaitans, a later gnostic group. Yet such an equation cannot be substantiated; cf. my article "Apocalyptic and Gnosis in the Book of Revelation and in Paul," *JBL* 92 (1973) 565–81; and my book *Invitation to the Book of Revelation* (Garden City, N.Y.: Doubleday, Image Books, 1981), pp. 63ff.

34. *De praescriptione haereticorum* 41.5; and *De baptismo* 17.4. See J. Kevin Coyle, "The Fathers on Women's Ordination," pp. 67ff.

35. Cf. Rosemary Radford Ruether, "Misogynism and Virginal Feminism in the Fathers of the Church," in idem, *Religion and Sexism: Images of Women in the Jewish and Christian Tradition* (New York: Simon & Schuster, 1974), pp. 150–83:157. Cf., however, F. Forrester Church, "Sex and Salvation in Tertullian," *Harvard Theological Review* 68 (1975) 83–101, for a partial rehabilitation.

36. Robert A. Kraft, "The Development of the Concept of 'Orthodoxy' in Early Christianity," in G. F. Hawthorne, ed., *Current Issues in Biblical and Patristic Interpretation* (Grand Rapids: Eerdmans, 1975), pp. 47–59.

37. Neither "orthodox" nor "heretical" writings can be assumed to be always positive for women. Thus it would be a mistake to assume that "gnostic writings" are "pro-women" and that their feminine imagery is liberating, as seems to be the tendency in the work of Elaine Pagels. All texts and traditions must be critically explored and evaluated, since they are all products of a patriarchal culture.

38. Jacob Neusner, *Method and Meaning in Ancient Judaism* (Brown Judaic Studies 10; Missoula, Mont.: Scholars Press, 1979), p. 96.

39. Cf. Neusner's acerbic polemics (ibid., pp. 88f) against Leonard Swidler's *Women in Judaism: The Status of Women in Formative Judaism* (Metuchen, N.J.: Scarecrow Press, 1976) and John T. Otwell's *And Sarah Laughed: The Status of Women in the Old Testament* (Philadelphia: Westminster, 1977).

40. Neusner, *Method and Meaning*, p. 28.

41. Michelle Zimbalist Rosaldo, "Woman, Culture and Society: A Theoretical Overview," in Michelle Zimbalist Rosaldo and Louise Lamphere, eds., *Woman, Culture and Society* (Stanford: Stanford University Press, 1974), pp. 17–42; and Sherry B. Ortner, "Is Female to Male as Nature Is to Culture?" ibid., pp. 67–88. But cf. Zimbalist Rosaldo's recent critical discussion of her own previous position in "The Use and Abuse of Anthropology: Reflections on Feminism and Cross-Cultural Understandings," *Signs* 5 (1980) 389–417.

42. Neusner, *Method and Meaning*, p. 100.

43. Rosaldo, "Use and Abuse," p. 417.

44. Neusner, *Method and Meaning*, p. 95.

45. Ibid., p. 94.

46. Ibid., p. 128.

47. Yigael Yadin, *Bar Kokhba: The Rediscovery of the Legendary Hero of the Second Jewish Revolt against Rome* (London: Weidenfeld and Nicolson, 1971), pp. 22–253.

48. Neusner, *Method and Meaning*, p. 93.

49. Klaus Thraede, "Ärger mit der Freiheit: Die Bedeutung von Frauen in Theorie und Praxis der alten Kirche," in Gerta Scharffenorth and Klaus Thraede, eds., *Freunde in Christus werden . . ." Die Beziehung von Mann und Frau als Frage an Theologie und Kirche* (Gelnhausen: Burckardthaus-Verlag, 1977), pp. 36f; and his criticism of Johannes Leipoldt, *Die Frau in der antiken Welt und im Urchristentum* (Gütersloh: Mohn, 1962).

50. P. J. Achtemeier, *Mark* (Proclamation Commentaries; Philadelphia: Fortress, 1975), p. 11.

51. Leonard Swidler, *Biblical Affirmations of Woman* (Philadelphia: Westminster, 1979), pp. 261f.

52. Stevan L. Davies, *The Revolt of the Widows: The Social World of the Apocryphal Acts* (Carbondale: Southern Illinois University Press, 1980), pp. 95–109.

53. Adolf von Harnack, "Probabilia über die Addresse und den Verfasser des Hebräerbriefes," *ZNW* 1 (1900) 16–41; and the popular account by Ruth Hoppin, *Priscilla: Author of the Epistle to the Hebrews* (New York: Exposition Press, 1969), pp. 15–116.

54. Sr. Elizabeth Davis, paper written for a course on "Women in Early Christianity," given at the University of Notre Dame, Summer 1978.

Chapter 3

Toward a Feminist Model
of Historical Reconstruction

I f a feminist reconstruction of history can no longer take patriarchal texts at face value but must critically interpret them in a feminist perspective, the notion of history as "what actually has happened" becomes problematic. Although scholars have widely abandoned this notion, it still dominates religious instruction, dogmatic books, and ecclesiastical statements. The psychological strength of fundamentalism is derived from such an understanding of the Bible as a historically accurate record of God's will.[1] Yet biblicist certainty is based not only upon an outdated theological understanding of biblical revelation but also on a historicist misunderstanding of what the Bible is all about. As a historical account of the ministry of Jesus or the life of the early churches, the biblical writings do not tell us how it actually was but how its religious significance was understood.

Our understanding of early Christian beginnings is usually monolithic. It is much determined by the Acts of the Apostles, which pictures a straightforward development from the primitive community in Jerusalem founded on Pentecost to the world-wide mission of Paul climaxing with his arrival in Rome, the political center of the Greco-Roman world. The Pauline epistles are understood not so much as historical sources reflecting a much more multifaceted early Christian situation fraught with tensions but as theological treatises expounding and defending the doctrine of justification by faith.

This biblicist-historicist understanding of early Christian beginnings still prevails in many textbooks and in the consciousness of many Christians and theologians. According to this understanding, Jesus instituted the church, ordained the twelve, and determined the institutional forms of the church. The apostles continued the mission and work of Jesus, and their message in turn is codified in the New Testament as Holy Scripture. All later developments are predicated on God's revelation in Scripture, and the true church has never deviated from the apostolic tradition.[2] However, such an ideological construct of early Christian beginnings is no longer scientifically acceptable and is theologically destructive of the self-identity of Christian women who, according to this portrayal of early Christian development, were members but not leaders within the church.

Historical-critical scholarship has proven this historicist and unilateral understanding of early Christian development to be a later theological construct. Exegetes, therefore, have sought to replace it with other heuristic models and theoretical frameworks that can make the diversity of thought and life in early Christianity more intelligible. But although most exegetes agree that Jesus did not leave a blueprint[3] for the organization of the church and that the apostolic age was far from being "one heart and one soul," their reconstruction of the actual development of early Christianity varies considerably. Questions regarding the historical importance of the twelve, the institution of the eucharistic meal and baptism, the relationship between charism and office, the difference between apocalyptic and gnostic "enthusiasm," the juxtaposition of Paulinism and early Catholicism, the issue of apostolic tradition and heresy, as well as the problem of the authority and significance of early Christian beginnings for Christians today— all are widely debated and have received different answers.

These scholarly discussions have shown that there is no single way of conceptualizing early Christian origins.[4] Yet insofar as such discussions are limited to the esoteric circle of scholarship, many women are still victims of a monolithic historiography and theology. Only by not relinquishing intellectual work and by insisting upon an open discussion of *all* the issues generally reserved for the expert—be it scholar or priest—will we be able to overcome the elitist character of academy and church.

Just like any good history, the history of early Christianity depends on the coherence of a "unifying vision."[5] In *History and Social Theory* Gordon Leff repeatedly states the criteria for such a good history: historical objectivity consists not in "pure" facts or data but in the dynamic interrelation between the information gleaned from the sources and the unifying vision of the interpreter. Historians gather all available evidence, account for its correct use, and order it within a reasonable framework. Nevertheless, historians argue from evidence as opposed to events accessible to our experience. In the attempt to make the past intelligible the historian must go beyond the events in an act of "intellectual re-creation." In doing so the historian shows at once why, for example, "Caesar's crossing of the Rubicon was significant for posterity and what it meant for Caesar and his contemporaries."[6] In order to do so the historian must have a theoretical frame of reference and must construct a model that is at once a comparative and an ideal construct.

> . . . the letters on a stone or a piece of parchment or the remains of a medieval village or a treatise by a schoolman do not of themselves provide more than the data on which the historian sets to work; and in order to make them into historical facts, i.e. what he [sic] assumes to have been the case—he [sic] has to employ a full critical and interpretative apparatus of selection, evaluation, interpolation and rejection—which rests upon inference as opposed to observation, and hence can never pass beyond a high degree of probability.[7]

Such an exploration of theoretical models and heuristic frameworks, however, must not lose sight of the question of women's active participation in early Christian beginnings. Therefore, all models need to be tested and evaluated as to how much they can account not only for the information of our sources on women's history but also for the way in which they are able to integrate this information in their overall framework so that it transforms androcentric historiography into our common history. An intellectual re-creation of early Christian beginnings seeking to make the past intelligible must depart from an androcentric historiography that cannot do justice to the information of our sources, namely, that women were participatory actors in the early Christian churches. Finally, such theoretical frameworks adequate to a feminist historiography must not only elucidate what it meant for women to become active members and leaders in early Christianity but also highlight the historical significance of women's active involvement in early Christian beginnings.

The recent scholarly interest in the social world of Christian beginnings is such a renewed attempt to find models of historical reconstruction. In searching for the social conditions and leading persons of the early Christian movement, these studies seek to move from the biblical texts to their social contexts. In doing so they continue the research for the *Sitz im Leben* of traditional forms and writings that has been a part of the history of traditions research conducted by New Testament scholarship in the last three quarters of this century.

After almost sixty years of focusing predominantly on theological-kerygmatic issues, scholarship in the last decade has resumed its search for the social context and matrix of early Christian traditions and teachings. Much of New Testament scholarship in the past half century has sought to identify the various groups and directions in early Christianity by their belief systems[8] and then to assess them according to the dualistic doctrinal model of orthodoxy and heresy. Thus, for example, it was recognized that Paul's writings or the Gospels could only be understood when their *Sitz im Leben* was fully explored, but redaction criticism tended to characterize this setting in terms of the belief systems of the Christian communities. It was argued, therefore, that Paul insisted on the creational order of women's participation in the community, whereas his "opponents" in Corinth were "Spirit-enthusiasts" or had a "gnosticizing" theology that denied the creational differences between men and women.

The study of the social world of early Christianity seeks to replace this dualistic model of opposing belief systems by reconstructing the social-sociological setting of early Christian sources and traditions. While the form- and redaction-critical approaches focus attention on the teachings of the early Christian traditions and writers and construe the social-cultural contexts of Judaism and Roman Hellenism as *backgrounds,* these studies seek to shift this focus to the life and behavior of the early Christians. In asking questions such as what was it like to become a Christian for a Jewish woman or for a Roman woman? what effects did it have on their social relations? how disruptive was it for a woman's family or her circle of friends? why did women join the early Christian group?,[9] the traditional conceptualization of early Christianity and its cultural "background" breaks down. A new theoretical framework becomes necessary, one that can grasp the dynamic interaction of early Christian beginnings and their cultural-sociological settings.

Students of the social world of early Christianity, therefore, are searching for new integrative heuristic models, not to establish a "master theory of early Christian evolution" but to achieve an "increment in historical imagination."[10] In a review of recent literature on the topic, John Gager has recommended distinguishing between the terms *social* as "designating society or the social order" and "the description of the relevant social data" on the one hand, and *sociological* as "a full range of explanatory theories and hypotheses . . . concerned with the explanations of social facts" on the other hand.[11] Yet on the practical level such a distinction breaks down in the reconstruction of early Christian history, as Gager's own review of Malherbe and Grant documents. In espousing the discussion of one's theoretical models for "explaining" social facts, one does not provide an objective description of social data but simply refrains from the articulation of one's own theoretical framework and interests.[12]

Early Christian Beginnings:
The Disinherited and the Marginal

The social studies of early Christian beginnings[13] widely utilize the sociological type or abstract model of "sect" in order to make the origins of early Christianity intelligible. They seem to have reached a consensus that the Jesus-movement in Palestine is best understood as a "sectarian" group.

Following W. Stark, Robin Scroggs has applied the sect typology most faithfully to the beginnings of early Christianity in order to show "that the community called into existence by Jesus fulfills the essential characteristics of the religious sect."[14] It can be shown that the Jesus group fulfills all seven characteristics of a sect.[15] It began as a protest (1) rejecting the view of reality taken for granted by the Jewish establishment (2). As an egalitarian and not hierarchically ordered community (3), it offered love and acceptance to all those who joined it, especially the outcast (4). As a voluntary association (5), the Jesus group demanded a total commitment (6). Since not all sects are adventist, its apocalyptic character shows that the Jesus movement had its major roots and support among the disinherited and suffering poor (7). Two methodological assumptions by Scroggs are important: first, he does not distinguish between the historical Jesus, the hearers of the historical Jesus, and the earliest community because, sociologically speaking, both groups are basically the same. Second, he develops his argument in terms of a peasant rather than an impoverished urban group, because most of the synoptic traditions reflect an agrarian setting. Scroggs therefore stresses that the term *sect* ought not to be misunderstood as counter-term to church but as counter-term to the wider society, the "world." In this sense the Jesus movement was a countercultural movement.

Whereas Scroggs's typology is somewhat generalized, S. R. Isenberg and John Gager have attempted independently to specify the sectarian character of the Jesus group as a millenarian movement. Isenberg has proposed that the Pharisees, the Essenes, and other groups in Greco-Roman Palestine were seeking access to religious power in different ways because they felt blocked off from its media, the Temple cult or the Torah.[16] Such millenarian groups—among them the Jesus movement—developed according to the following pattern: the feeling of deprivation, a concrete testing of their new beliefs about religious power, the appearance of a millenarian prophet during this process, and finally consolidation or dissolution. According to Isenberg, the Teacher of Righteousness at Qumran, as well as Jesus and Paul, were such millenarian prophets who claimed religious power outside the normal channels of power in Judaism.

Likewise, Gager claims that early Christian beginnings show all five traits of millenarian movements: the promise of heaven on earth in the immediate future; the reversal or overthrow of the present social order; a terrific release of emotional energy in ecstatic behavior; a brief life span of the movement; and most importantly, the central role of the charismatic leader or prophet. His emphasis on the millenarian prophet allows for a central role for Jesus as well as for the apocalyptic character of early Christian traditions. Therefore, Gager maintains that early Christianity was a movement of the disinherited and disprivileged. He reconciles this assumption with Pliny's remark that Christianity had attracted persons "of every social rank" by introducing the concept of "relative deprivation."[17] The category of disprivileged persons, therefore, also includes "alienated" or "disaffected" persons among whom could be intellectuals, women, foreigners, provincials or former slaves, who need not be economically poor. While Isenberg locates the millenarian character of the Jesus movement in the deprivation of and in the quest for religious power, Gager locates it in the quest for social power.

However, Gager does not distinguish between the Jesus movement in Palestine and the early Christian missionary communities in the urban centers of the Greco-Roman world.[18] But such a distinction does become the basis for the social reconstruction of Gerd Theissen.[19] Theissen's sociological model is functionalist and relies for its reconstruction of the Jesus movement primarily on conflict analysis. But whereas his analysis of the Jesus movement is "based on a sociological theory of conflict," for the reconstruction of early Christian beginnings in a Hellenistic urban society, he advocates "a sociological theory of integration." In the Hellenistic setting the chief stress was laid on the life of the local communities, whose leading members belonged to "more privileged classes." These communities existed in cities, and were not in opposition to the values of their society. "Love patriarchalism" best characterizes their religious-social atmosphere.

Jesus had "called into being a movement of wandering charismatics" but did not found local communities. These wandering charismatics shaped the Jesus traditions and their radical ethos. They are characterized by homelessness, lack of family, renunciation of possessions, and the relinquishment of defense. Like the wandering Cynic philosophers, the early Christian charismatics "seem to have led a vagabond existence" and to have chosen the role of outsiders. The organizational and economic base for this movement of itinerant preachers was provided by the local sympathizers who remained within the societal structures of Judaism.

> They were less obviously the embodiment of the new element which had emerged within earliest Christianity, and a variety of obligations and ties entangled them in the old situation. It was rather the homeless wandering charismatics who handed on what later was to take independent form as Christianity.[20]

Some critical issues must be raised. In Theissen's interpretation the followers of Jesus were not poor, disinherited, or alienated, as Scroggs and Gager have claimed. Rather, they *chose* to renounce their possessions, whereas the local sympathizers who did not do so are assigned a "secondary" Christian status. However, W. Stegemann's careful analysis of Theissen's textual basis has shown that the earliest followers of Jesus did not choose a different social status, "the outsider," but lived a different religious ethos.[21] The Cynic-image of the disciples of Jesus is later and especially prevalent in the interpretation of Luke. Their rejection of "family and possessions" was rewarded with a new kinship relationship, the community (Mark 10:30). It must not be overlooked that such a rejection of the family is, for Q, not an ascetic norm but a dire necessity because of the hatred that the confession of Jesus evoked (Matt 10:35).

Theissen himself had previously characterized the supporters of the itinerant charismatics as "those who themselves stood on the margin of society," while the transmitters of the Jesus traditions were seen as those "on the lower rung of society."[22] Yet in his book he characterizes them exclusively in terms of "their complementary relationship" to the charismatics,[23] in order to maintain his distinction between the ethical radicalism of the Jesus movement and the integrative love patriarchalism of the Christian communities in the Hellenistic world. However, it must be pointed out that this difference in early Christian ethos may well be produced by Theissen's chosen form of sociological analysis (conflict analysis for Palestine; integration for the Hellenistic centers). Early Christian apologetic literature as well as pagan attacks on Christians still seem to perceive the relationship of early Christianity with its society in terms of conflict, even during the second century.

In conclusion: The sociological studies of the Jesus movement converge in the sociological classification of the earliest Christian beginnings in Palestine as an "aggressive," "revolutionist," or millenarian type of sectarian movement. However, only Gager includes the earliest Christian missionary communities in the Greco-Roman world in this description, while Scroggs does not discuss them, and Theissen maintains that they are structurally very different from the itinerant radicals who have shaped the Jesus traditions. His claim that the Christian movement in the urban centers of the Greco-Roman world is integrative and not conflictual needs to be tested by a sociological analysis that applies the same conflict analysis to the evidence about these communities.

1. Meek's analyses of Pauline Christianity seem to point to a fundamental ambiguity in the Pauline letters: on the one hand, the Christian community is understood as an eschatological sect, with a strong sense of group boundaries, but on the other hand, it is an "open sect concerned not to offend those outside but to attract them to its message."[24] It is still open, therefore, whether the early Christian urban movement is a different type of sect, or whether it accentuates different aspects of the same type, or whether it is in transition from one type to the other. Its conflictual-protest character vis-à-vis the Greco-Roman "world" can, however, not be ruled out by definition.

2. The sociological location of the Jesus group owes its classifications to Weber and Troeltsch, although it modifies their classifications. In addition, one must keep in mind that sect or millenarian movement is a classification that describes typical but not particular relationships between society and religion. Moreover, Yinger has pointed especially to three weaknesses of the system developed by Troeltsch, and these must be kept in mind in the reconstruction of early Christian beginnings. He argues that a dichotomous typology does not allow for the many mixtures and shades of the real world. Church and sect should therefore not be understood as opposites but as end points on a continuum with intermediate points in between. Further, Troeltsch did not adequately discuss the conditions in which various types of religious organizations were most likely to occur. Finally, in order to describe the full range of the data three criteria need to be added: (i) the degree to which the religious group is inclusive of members of society; (ii) the extent to which the group accepts values and structures of society; and (iii) the context to which an organization integrates a number of units and creates a bureaucracy.[25]

3. All three analyses of the Jesus movement seem to underline the a-familial or antifamilial character of the earliest Christian groups. It

seems that this aspect provides a fruitful entry point for the analysis of women's role in this movement. However, although all scholars are concerned in one way or another with the question of what it was like to become or to be an (ordinary) Christian in the first century, none of them raises the question of what it was like for a woman in Palestine, or a Jewish woman in Corinth, or a gentile woman in Galatia to join the early Christian movement.

Consolidation and Institutionalization: Love Patriarchalism

Although sociologists and anthropologists vary widely in their classification and delineation of the sect type, they virtually agree that a brief life span is inherent in the sect type and millenarian movement. However, it is not quite clear why some millenarian movements disappear completely after the first upswell of enthusiasm whereas others persist and live on in different forms. Gager therefore states categorically that Christianity survived, but not as a millenarian cult,[26] and he asks, "What went wrong with early Christianity so that it not only survived the failure of its initial prophecies but did so in a spectacular fashion?"[27]

The hermeneutical implications of this sociological judgment are spelled out in his discussion of Gal 3:28. He reads this statement as "the prototype of millenarian ethics" and goes on to muse:

> In light of Paul's radical stance, as expressed in this and other passages, it may seem ironic that mainstream Christianity chose finally to exclude women from all important cultic roles and in the process often cited the authority of Paul. But to say that the churches failed to translate his program into reality is to belabor the obvious. For millenarian movements fail by definition, and those that survive do so under substantially new circumstances.[28]

He concedes that Christian groups like Montanism and Marcionism "carried forward the primitive ideal," yet he labels these "heresies." He seems to assume that their praxis did not (at least in this point) continue the millenarian ethos of the earliest Christian movement, although in a later chapter he rejects the traditional theological view of heresy as deviation from the orthodox Christian ethos.

In discussing the social constituency of early Christianity, however, Gager accepts the consensus among classicists on the social question which is contrary to his assumption of the short life expectancy of a sect. This consensus maintains that, on the one hand, "for more than two hundred years Christianity was essentially a movement among the disprivileged" and, on the other hand, "its appeal among these groups depended on social as much as ideological considerations."[29] Thus the social conditions and appeal of early Christianity as a sectarian protest against the existing social order did not change for more than two hundred years.

Switching from a millenarian to a Weberian analysis, Gager raises the question of the consolidation and success of Christianity. At the outset he states again that the development of early Christianity does not quite conform to that of a millenarian sectarian movement since its antinomian, charismatic tendencies persisted for such a long time. He notes that consolidation of office and structures took place only in the second half of the first century, and even then were actively resisted by a number of people. Only at the beginning of the second century do we find early Christian writers insisting on structured local office (see the Pastorals, Ignatius, *1 Clement*). However, he does not discuss whether these writings are descriptive of ecclesial office or whether they are prescriptive texts advocating one type of leadership over another. The primary leadership of prophets and its elimination needs to be explored here.

With Weber, Gager claims that the survival of any religious community lies in the "transition from no rules to new rules" and asks us to accept this as "a fundamental law." Therefore, we may not "lament the routinization of the primitive enthusiasm that characterizes all charismatic or millenarian movements in their second generation and sometimes even earlier."[30] Moreover, routinization of charism does not mean its elimination. Insofar as charismatic early Christian beginnings are codified in the body of Scripture, attempts to renew the institutional church can appeal to the biblical memory of its enthusiastic beginnings and thereby spawn new enthusiastic movements. Thus charismatic authority and the rise of institutional structures are "complementary not antithetical." Moreover, anti-Jewish polemics, pagan apologetics, and the struggle with heretics are additional consolidating factors in the churches' quest for identity. "Each of these represents an indispensable phase in the birth and growth of a successful religious movement."[31]

In his last chapter, however, Gager raises the question of success once more, albeit with a different approach. After discussing possible explanations of the growth and transformation of Christianity, Gager reviews the external and internal factors which contributed to this outcome. He cites a series of external factors that contributed to the rise of Christianity and one single overriding internal factor: "the radical sense of Christian community—open to all, insistent on absolute and exclusive loyalty, and concerned for every aspect of the believer's life. From the very beginning, the one distinctive gift of Christianity was this sense of community."[32]

Whether or not one agrees with this statement is not important. What is important is that Gager here contradicts his own Weberian analysis. The distinctive gift of Christianity was the vision of community expressed in Gal 3:28, not as a millenarian ideal but as a communal reality. Moreover, it must be asked whether it is legitimate to speak of Christianity in the singular or whether we have to speak of Christianities or Christian communities. Whether or not these early Christian groups were "church," denomination, established sects, sectarian movements, or charismatic sects—and which groups were what—needs to be explored much more carefully. Finally, it becomes necessary to distinguish between three basic types of sect: the aggressive or revolutionist, the avoidance or introversionist, and the acceptance or gnostic type, together with all their shades of interaction. While form criticism and redaction criticism have developed a pluralistic model for New Testament Christianity, the studies of the social world seem to have done so insufficiently. Instead, these studies too easily fall back into the theological dichotomy of orthodoxy and heresy, which in turn becomes equated with church and sect.

While Gager names the "sense of community" as the distinctive gift of Christianity, Theissen has identified this integrative power of Christianity as "love patriarchalism" in contradistinction to the conflict-producing ethical radicalism of the Jesus movement. In doing so he introduces an analytic concept adopted from Troeltsch (patriarchalism),[33] in order to explain the interaction of wealthy and powerful people with those of lower status within the Christian communities of the Hellenistic world. The theoretical model is the vision of the patriarchal *oikos* or *familia* with its structured hierarchies and differentiated roles.

The Christian religious ingredient is agapeic love which reduces frictions and leads to a "willing acceptance of given inequalities." It makes these inequalities "fruitful for the ethical values of personal relationships." In other words, the "gift" of Christianity to the Greco-Roman world is the internalization of the status inequalities and structural hierarchies typical of a patriarchal society. An analysis of 1 Corinthians, according to Theissen, shows that Paul is not interested in a reform or revolution of the social order but in its transformation and sublimation to a more fundamental plane. Troeltsch says:

> As stewards of God the great must care for the small, and as servants of God the little ones must submit to those who bear

authority; and since in so doing both meet in the service of God, inner religious equality is affirmed and the ethical possession is enlarged by the exercise of the tender virtues of responsibility for and of trustful surrender to each other. It is undeniable that this ideal is perceived dimly by Paul and only by means of this ideal does he desire to alter given conditions from within outwards, without touching their external aspect at all.[34]

It is important to note that Theissen does not derive his understanding of the integrative power of *Liebespatriarchalismus* either from a critical analysis of this heuristic concept and its social implications or from an analysis of the text, but rather superimposes this model on the text, especially on 1 Corinthians. Yet he asserts that because of this "tempered social conservatism" of love patriarchalism, Christianity was successful in the second and third centuries over and against Montanism and gnosticism because it was able to attract the masses.[35] Moreover, where antiquity sought to solve conflict-producing ethical radicalism with the philosophical vision of the equality of all free citizens, Christian love patriarchalism offered a different integrative pattern: the basic inner equality of all "in Christ" while the basic social differences and hierarchies in the political and ecclesial order were maintained.[36]

Theissen sums up his view of early Christian development:

> If one follows the transmission of Jesus' sayings in early Christianity, three social forms of early Christian faith are apparent: itinerant radicalism, love patriarchalism, and gnostic radicalism. In them the three types are seen whose development Troeltsch follows through the entire history of Christianity—sect, established church, and spiritualism. The ethos of itinerant radicalism repeatedly came to life in sect-type movements such as Montanism, Syrian itinerant asceticism, the mendicant monks of the middle ages and the left wing of the Reformation. Gnostic radicalism was expressed in recurring individualistic and mystic conventicles within and outside the church. But we have to thank Christian love patriarchalism for the lasting institution of the church. With success and wisdom it tempered early Christian radicalism sufficiently so that the Christian faith became a lifestyle that could be practiced collectively.[37]

He concedes that this love patriarchalism was enacted with more violence than love against those who did not comply; nevertheless, he declares it a social, historical necessity for the survival of Christianity. To state it crudely: the church is not built on prophets and apostles, who as charismatics belong to the "radical" tradition, but on love patriarchalism, that is, on the backs of women, slaves, and the lower classes. Not only is history *written* by the winners, it is also made by them.

Theissen's judgment is echoed by Elaine Pagels who locates the struggle between the gnostics and the orthodox, sociologically, as a struggle between "those restless inquiring people who marked out a solitary path of self-discovery and the institutional framework that gave to the great majority of people religious sanction and ethical direction for their daily lives." Although she differs from Theissen in her sociological heuristic model, she agrees with his evaluation:

> Had Christianity remained multiform, it might well have disappeared from history, along with dozens of rival religious cults of antiquity. I believe that we owe the survival of Christian tradition to the organizational and theological structure that the emerging church developed. Anyone as powerfully attracted to Christianity as I am will regard that as a major achievement.[38]

In conclusion: The dominant sociological model for the reconstruction of early Christian beginnings explains the process of gradual ecclesial patriarchalization which entails the historically necessary development from charism to office, from Paulinism to early Catholicism, from a millenarist radical ethos to a privileged Christian establishment, from the radical Jesus movement within Judaism to an integrative love patriarchalism within the Hellenistic urban communities, from the egalitarian charismatic structures of the beginning to the hierarchical order of the Constantinian church. Unlike the orthodoxy-heresy model, this interpretative framework does not justify the patriarchalization process of the early church on theological grounds but argues for it in terms of sociological and political factors.

Critical Evaluation

A critical evaluation of the sociological reconstructions of early Christian history needs to point to three methodological problems.

1. When reconstructing the Jesus movement scholars seem to develop the heuristic model of "sect or millenarian" movement over and against "the world" and total culture, while in their description of the consolidation of the early Christian movement the sect-church model seems to loom large. Such a theoretical shift may be justified but it is not critically reflected.

In a review of the results of Theissen's sociological reconstructions Leander Keck, therefore, has proposed to introduce the notion of "ethos" into the discussion. He defines ethos as a *"Gestaltic* term," gathering up into itself the practices and habits, assumptions, problems, values, and hopes of a community's lifestyle."[39] He suggests, therefore, that we have to reconceptualize our understanding of early Christianity's cultural "background" or "influences."[40] For example, most books on women in early Christianity discuss in a first chapter the cultural background or context of early Christian beginnings by pointing out the status and role of women in Greece, Hellenism, Rome, or Judaism. They do so in order to show that although the status of early Christian women was patriarchally conditioned, it was also much better than that of women in Greece or of Jewish women.

Thinking in terms of the ethos of a group, Keck suggests, would lead us not to ask for the influences of the cultural background on early Christian groups but to raise the question how much the early Christian preachers intruded into the ethos of people. The Hellenistic ethos was already in existence and the emerging Christian ethos was a foreign element. At this point, Keck appears to relinquish the distinction between ethos and culture that he had made in a previous article. However, it seems crucial to define the interaction between the ethos of emerging groups and that of the established culture. In other words, whereas Christians do not shed their cultural mind-set totally at their conversion, they must integrate it with the new self- and group-identity that is shaped by the ethos of the group.

In contrasting Jesus and Paul, Keck attempts to show how these two persons have shaped the ethos of two quite different Christian communities. Jesus sought to renew and reform an old community, while Paul was in the process of creating a new one. Therefore, "Jesus' message did not intrude into the ethos of his hearers in the same way as did Paul's Gospel." "Jesus was trying to purify an ethos, Paul was trying to shape a new one," which, after Paul, gradually became the characteristic Christian ethos.[41] As a prophet, Jesus reformed Judaism, while Paul was founding the Christian church.

Methodologically, however, Keck's proposal does not sufficiently distinguish between different Christian lifestyles, but speaks of *the* ethos of the early Christians. In doing so he leaves no room for the ethos of pre- or non-Pauline missionaries and communities nor for the different settings of the Jesus traditions. On the one hand, 2 Corinthians seems to indicate that Paul's opponents, the so-called superapostles, also lived their itinerant lifestyles in the cities; but on the other hand, the Jesus traditions were probably written down in urban centers for people of the city. In addition, Keck does not explore whether Jesus' reform of Judaism was so radical in its implications that it engendered the articulation of a new ethos.

One must ask whether the existence of itinerant women disciples of Jesus can be explained with reference to the rural situation of Palestine, whether such existence presupposes an abandoning of the cultic ethos delineated by Neusner, or whether it is due to an interplay of rural society and a noncultic ethos shaped by Jesus and his followers. To raise this question leads, furthermore, to a redefinition of the social shift that has taken place between Jesus and Paul. It seems that this shift should not be located in the opposition between country and city, between rural villages and urban centers, but should rather be identified as a shift in cultural horizons.

While the reform ethos of the Jesus movement is articulated in the context of Jewish society, culture, and religion, that of Paul is articulated in the context of Roman Hellenism and has missionary aims. The interaction between culture and subculture, dominant ethos and emerging ethos is therefore very different for Jesus and Paul. This interaction or interplay has produced different forms of Christian lifestyle (or ethos) not only within the Jewish but also within the Greco-Roman contexts. In using Keck's analytical category of ethos one must therefore be careful not to allow it to degenerate into the unifying theoretical concept of a life-center operative in the sociology of knowledge analysis. The term *lifestyle* seems less subject to such a misunderstanding since it can be conceived not only in terms of a plurality of integrative visions of the world but also in terms of the actual life-praxis of the early Christians. The cultural differences between, for example, Asia Minor, Syria, or Rome and their interaction with the emerging Christian movement have generated different communal lifestyles.

2. The assertion of "historical necessity" and "success" are categories of assessment derived from our own experience. Such an assessment equates sociological with theological evaluation. It seems that in these studies the sociological concept of "success" has become the Archimedean point of theological evaluations. The essential ingredient of such success is defined differently by different scholars but still monolithically. Implicitly they maintain that, from a sociological-political point of view, the gradual patriarchalization of the early Christian movement was unavoidable. If the Christian communities were to grow, develop, and historically survive, they had to adapt and take over the patriarchal institutional structures of their society.

It is implied that the institutionalization of the charismatic-egalitarian early Christian movement had to lead to the patriarchalization of ecclesial leadership functions—that is, to the exclusion of women from church office or to the reduction of their positions to subordinate, feminine, marginal ones. The more the early Christian movement became institutionalized the more Christian women had to be excluded from church leadership and office. They were relegated to powerless fringe groups or had to conform to the feminine stereotypes of the patriarchal culture. For example, the patristic office of widow and deaconess had to limit itself to the service of women, and finally disappeared from history. Moreover, these leadership functions could no longer be exercised by all women but only by those who had overcome their femaleness by choosing to remain virgins.

This assessment of the early Christian development seems to describe accurately the consequences and casualties of the gradual patriarchalization of the Christian church. However, it does not reflect on its own theological androcentric presuppositions, since it overlooks the fact that the history of early Christianity is written from the perspective of the historical winners. For the most part, official Christian history and theology reflect those segments of the church which have undergone this patriarchalization process and theologically legitimated it with the formulation of the canon. Insofar as the sociological-political model of assessment presents the elimination of women from ecclesial office and their marginalization in a patriarchal church as a historical necessity, it justifies the patriarchal institutionalization process as the only possible and historically viable sociological form of church.[42]

Both the androcentric theological model and the patriarchal sociological models for the reconstruction of early Christian life and community presuppose that the process of the patriarchalization of the church was historically unavoidable. They claim that early Christian theology and praxis, which acknowledged women as equal Christians and disciples, was either "heretical" or "charismatic," and hence theologically and historically nonviable. Neither model can conceive of a Christian church in which women are equal to men. Therefore, it is methodologically necessary to challenge these interpretative models for the reconstruction of early Christianity and to search for a new model which can integrate both egalitarian and patriarchal "heretical" and "orthodox" traditions into its own perspective. Since such an interpretative model presupposes and is based on the equality of all Christians, it could be called feminist.

3. The studies of the social world of early Christianity employ an a-familial or antifamilial lifestyle as the key analytical concept for the Jesus movement, and patriarchalism as the key analytical concept for the early Christian communities in the Greco-Roman world. Yet no

critical analysis or systematic reflection on these concepts has taken place. A feminist critical evaluation, therefore, must point out that the progressive patriarchalization of certain segments of the early Christian movement deserves further exploration. The historical sociological delineation of the gradual patriarchalization of early Christianity that had a different pace and form in various places or groups does not prove the historical necessity or theological rightness of such a development: it does not call for theological justification but for feminist theological evaluation.

Such a feminist critical evaluation of the patriarchalizing dynamics in early Christian history is made even more complex by the realization that early Christian history cannot a priori be equated with the dominant patriarchal culture, but rather is that of an emerging group not yet recognized by the dominant society and religion. A theoretical model for the reconstruction of women's early Christian history, therefore, must do justice to the fact that early Christian women *as women* were part of a submerged group, and *as Christians* they were part of an emergent group that was not yet recognized by the dominant patriarchal society and culture.

The Problem of Women's History

In the past decade women historians have articulated the theoretical problem of how to move from androcentric text to historical context and of how to write women into history.[43] Scholars of American history in particular have pointed out that the task of feminist historical interpretation is the placing of the lives of all women at the center of historical reconstructions, as women's responses to social changes affecting their lives, as well as at the center of women's efforts to transform and change societal structures and institutions:

> Feminist historians are asking what it was like to be a woman at various times in history and are exploring women's subjective responses to their environment. . . . In short, new approaches to women's history are attempting to integrate women into the mainstream of American historical development rather than isolating woman as a separate category.[44]

Women historians, therefore, point out that the literature on women in history is too often limited by narrowly focusing on woman as a topical or heuristic category rather than by exploring new conceptual frameworks that would allow women to be placed at the center of human social relations and political institutions. Feminist historians

question the androcentric scholarly evaluation of "historical significance," and they also point out that many historical sources on
women are not descriptive but prescriptive. Women are neglected in
the writing of history although the effects of their lives and actions are
a reality in history. Ideas of men *about* women, therefore, do not
reflect women's historical reality, since it can be shown that ideological polemics about women's place, role, or nature increase whenever
women's actual emancipation and active participation in history become stronger.

While theological-historical hermeneutics engendered by the debate around *The Woman's Bible* tends to locate feminist meaning of
Scripture and the biblical past either in the transcendental "something more" of androcentric tradition or in the sacred sphere of feminist Selves escaped from patriarchy, some feminist historians suspect
the whole androcentric-patriarchal interpretative model of history.
They reject it as an archaic and almost useless form of reference,
because it does not allow us to place women in the center of historical
examination. Nevertheless, neither Mary Beard's nor Gerda Lerner's
heuristic categories of "women as a civilizing force in history"[45] nor as
"the forgotten majority"[46] provide a satisfactory theoretical framework for the reconstruction of women's history.

Such a theoretical framework would not only have to "encompass a
view of women's historic role as located simultaneously in the center
of social relations and at the edge of them"[47] but also have to explore
patriarchy as the source of women's oppression as well as of women's
power. Such an interest of women in their own social history is very
much like colonialized peoples' interest in unearthing their own past.

> The search to understand collective conditions and the relations
> of race to the dominant society has enabled blacks to locate their
> strengths, their social importance, and the sources of their op-
> pression. Furthermore, this process has provided an analytical
> framework for recognizing their unity through historical experi-
> ence, rather than simply through their racial difference from the
> ruling caste.[48]

Like historians of other oppressed groups and peoples, feminist historians seek to comb androcentric records for feminist meaning by
reappropriating the patriarchal past for those who have suffered not
only its pain of oppression but also participated in its social transformation and development.

Feminist historians, therefore, seek a theoretical framework that
can maintain the dialectical tension of women's historical existence as

active participants in history as well as objects of patriarchal oppression. Since gender dimorphism is generated by such patriarchal oppression, it is not "natural" but social.[49] Therefore, feminist historians reject heuristic concepts such as "biological caste" or "women's experience as essentially different from that of men" because these categories render women passive objects of mere biological differences or male dominance. They seek instead for heuristic models that explore women's historical participation in social-public development and their efforts to comprehend and transform social structures.

Not "biological" sex differences, but patriarchal household and marriage relationships generate the social-political inferiority and oppression of women. Patriarchy is rooted in the patriarchal household and its property relationships rather than in innate biological differences between women and men. Wherever the "private sphere" of the patriarchal house is sharply delineated from that of the public order of the state, women are more dependent and exploited; while in those societies in which the boundaries between the household and the public domain are not so sharply drawn, women's positions and roles are more equal to those of men. While the public sphere is stratified by class differences, the domestic patriarchal sphere is determined by sexual role differences and dependencies.

Whereas some scholars of women's history and religion have postulated matriarchy as an *oppositional* structure to patriarchy, such matriarchal dominance structures, if they can be established at all, must be relegated to "prehistory" since recorded history is patriarchal history.[50] Rather than restrict women's historical agency and powers to such prehistorical times, some feminist historians seek to construct heuristic models that can help us to measure women's power and influence within patriarchal history. In order to do so they seek not only to restore women to history and history to women[51] but also to reconceptualize history and culture as the product and experience of both women and men.

Women's experience of solidarity and unity as a social group[52] is not based on their biological differences from men but on their common historical experience as an oppressed group struggling to become full historical subjects.[53] Such a theoretical framework allows women to locate their strength, historical agency, pain and struggle within their common historical experiences as women in patriarchal society and family. A reconstruction of women's history not based on the mere fact of biological sex as a timeless heuristic category, but on gender understood in social terms with reference to patriarchal relationships of inequality within the private and the public spheres, is also theoretically able to account for the variations of social status, class difference, and cultural identity.

Sociologist Elise Boulding has attempted to reconstruct the macro-history of women along the model of underlife and overlife structures. While the overlife structures encompass the public-political domain usually dominated by men, the underlife structures contain the private-domestic sphere generally considered the domain of women. The overlife structures are the dominant societal structures, into which the underlife structures sometimes can "erupt." Such possibilities of eruption are, for example, female-headed households, women's communication networks and groupings, and philosophical-religious associations. Women are free to move in the public domain when they belong to the aristocratic ruling families or to the working lower classes or to the destitute, while middle-class women are more restricted to the house. For example, Boulding mentions the following groups of women in classical Athens who were not confined to the women's quarters: older high-status women; poor and working women; slaves; foreign women, especially traders; and the "intellectuals" or *hetairai* who also were frequently foreign born.[54] She points out that religion or the church provided public space for women's social learning and interaction. According to her, this fact accounts for the important role women have played in the great religions. "If women and men share the same public spaces women will have a broader kind of training, more varied social reinforcements, and a wider range of role models than if the spaces of women are restricted."[55]

She argues against the assumption that hierarchical dominance relationships are "across-the-board-requirements" for social interaction. Another mode of relating is egalitarianism, "the most obvious *alternative* to dominance-submission relationships." However, such egalitarian relationships are based on "serial reciprocity" or "alternating dominance." That means that on a spectrum of relationships egalitarian relationships as "unstable" situations would constitute the midpoint, with dominance-submission and altruism at either end.[56] The essential condition of altruism as a social relationship and organization demands that the members of a group behave in such a way that their behavior benefits the group as a whole even at the expense of their own interests. While in marriage patriarchal dominance was historically prevalent, it was never absolute since it also always entailed the possibilities either of egalitarian or altruistic relationships. It seems that this distinction between different possibilities of social organization would enable scholars of Christian origins to assess more carefully institutional developments than the sect/institutional-ization pattern does.

While Boulding is more at home with general sociological models, the classics scholar Marilyn Arthur has attempted to develop a pattern that would specifically allow us to trace the historical shift in social relationships during antiquity.[57] She chides classical scholarship on women for neglect of theoretical frameworks that could bring the "facts" on women in antiquity into a coherent structure. She herself proposes an interpretative model with three elements—politics, economics, social relationships between the sexes—for charting social change in women's role and status. Arthur shows that in Greek as well as in Roman aristocratic society the household is coterminus with the public realm and rule, and that therefore aristocratic women in predemocratic Athens and in republican Rome had relative freedom and control of their rights. However, this relative advancement of women is limited to women of a certain class. In democratic Athens where the domestic and public realms pulled apart, the household was the basic form of production. The public-social order of the *polis* consisted of the male heads of such households, the only full citizens of the democratic state.

This hypothesis is confirmed by Moller Okin's philosophical analysis of the *Politics* of Aristotle which shows that the male-headed family, rather than the individual adult, is the primary unit of political analysis and theory.[58] In classical democracy the wives of middle-class propertied citizens were confined to the order of the household, to the production of legitimate sons, and to the supervision of slave labor and services. Athenian wives of the middle class did not directly belong to or participate in the public order. Noncitizen women who were free and fell outside the household and its property arrangement lived quite differently and could freely move in the public sphere. The rights, not of the individual woman but those of the independent household unit, were the primary principle of legislation and socialization.

In the Hellenistic period the empire gained importance to the detriment of the individual household and of the *polis*, in which women now gained some independence and influence. Citizenship no longer depended on membership in a family, and the laws no longer focused so strongly on wives as bearers of legitimate offspring. Women no longer were defined solely by their function as legitimizers of heirs to the household property but became property owners themselves. In the Hellenistic age women gained citizenship for outstanding public service and some of them held office.

The paradigm of the Hellenistic woman is Hipparchia, the wife of the Cynic philosopher Crates. She defended herself against a critic of her participation in public *symposia* and her philosophical lifestyle in general: "Do I seem to you to have been advised poorly about myself if I have devoted my time to my education instead of wasting it at the loom?"[59] While for classical Greek culture sexual dimorphism and the dichotomy between nature and the human sphere were characteristic, in the Hellenistic period woman was no longer feared as the enemy of civilization, and the "natural world" of marriage, sexual life, and privacy had become a common cultural concern. Women's participation in mystery religions, ecstatic cults, and philosophical schools during the Hellenistic age was freely accepted because these associations no longer viewed the natural world as the antithesis of culture and rationality. *(i.e., women)*

Marilyn Arthur maintains that the early Roman empire was structurally more similar to classical Greek democracy than to Hellenism because an entrepreneurial middle class had moved into the traditional aristocracy through interclass marriage. Moreover, the legislation of Augustus sought to strengthen the family by giving the state more control over it. Finally, for the first time Roman writers such as Tacitus or Juvenal saw women as a threat to culture and produced diatribes against them. However, Arthur herself has to concede that these obvious similarities to classical Greek democracy are upset by the influence of Hellenism on Roman society and the much greater economic and legal independence of Roman women despite the traditional concept of *paterfamilias* and legal guardianship. Far from strengthening patriarchal marriage and family the Augustan legislation undermined the patriarchal power of the *paterfamilias* even more, and gave women the possibility of de facto emancipation even from pro forma legal guardianship. Moreover, Roman women participated freely in public events and banquets.

A recent study by Ramsay McMullen has shown that women, although in lesser numbers, held public office just as men did, and that they functioned as rich *patronae* although they did not hold official political office.[60] It seems, therefore, that both the Augustan legislation and misogynist literature were attempts of middle-class men to curtail the public, legal, and economic freedom and rights of propertied women and to establish definite boundaries between the public male sphere and the private sphere of women. Yet such attempts must be understood as prescriptive rather them as descriptive of the actual situation and life in Roman Hellenism.

In the heuristic models of women's history as the history of their social-institutional interrelations with men, religion emerges as a "middle zone" between the public (male) sphere and the private (female) domain of the household. While for aristocratic society the social relations of class determine the boundaries between these two spheres, in democratic society gender roles and sexual differences define these boundaries, insofar as the property ownership of the male head of household determines the patriarchal family as the central unit of society. Although religion traditionally spanned both the public and the private spheres, women's participation was limited to the religion of the head of household, insofar as religious festivals and offices mirrored the dimorphism of the public and private spheres and the religious rights of women, slaves, and children were decided by the *paterfamilias*.

Insofar as the participation in mystery cults and philosophical schools depended on a personal decision for a certain "religious way of life" or a "personal" religion, in Hellenistic-Roman times religion became a third sphere between the public and private spheres. Hellenistic religious cults and associations were, therefore, always potentially subversive of the order of the patriarchal house and state. Thus in Roman Hellenistic literature we find many polemics against such cults because they corrupted the morals of women and allowed them to go out by themselves at night. However, for legally and economically independent women who were culturally and religiously marginal, these religious associations provided a means to overcome their status discrepancy.

In my opinion, this emancipatory function and not their sexual-social marginality as childless women or widows attracted women to the oriental cults, among them Judaism and Christianity.[61] While the a-sexual and a-familial ethos of early Christianity is often misunderstood as antisexual and antiwomen, it actually is an indication of a "role-revolt" which allowed women to "legitimately" move out of the confines of the patriarchal family and to center their life around the spiritual self-fulfillment and independence that gave them greater respect, mobility, and influence.

S. Johannsson has shown that the misogynist polemics of male writers, theologians, and historians must be understood as expressions of middle-class men whose psychic and economic reality were heavily determined by daily competition, and who therefore sought to maximize the "natural" difference between women and men in order not to be replaced by women. While in aristocratic society women of the upper classes were expected to substitute for men during times of war or death, middle-class men did not depend on the loyalty and resources of women of their class, but on using family resources with maximum effectiveness.[62] Since masculine identity for middle-class men of urban cultures is produced by intensive socialization and expensive education, "temperamental and occupational similarity between women and men threatened the economic, psychological, and social security of middle-class dominated families." While middle-class men *produce* symbolic and literary expressions of gender dimorphism and misogynism, peasant and working-class life

> is commonly shot through with *symbolic* manifestations of male superiority. . . . Men who experience daily humiliation and frustration because of their economic and social disadvantages find their most important form of solace in looking down on and abusing women. This psychological cushion against oppression makes class exploitation more bearable; perhaps as some feminists argue, it makes it more durable.[63]

However, it is the middle-class man who has produced the androcentric cultural, historical, and religious *texts* that marginalize women or stress their different "nature."

In conclusion: Feminist sociological models for the reconstruction of history using the patriarchal household and family structures as heuristic categories are helpful to explore the a-familial character and the love patriarchalism of the early Christian movement. Moreover, they combine such a heuristic concept with a class analysis that makes the social setting of androcentric texts and symbolizations intelligible. Finally, they show that the definitions of sexual role and gender dimorphism are the outcome of the social-economic interactions between men and women but that they are not ordained either by nature or by God.

If New Testament exegetes conceptualize early Christian history in terms of the patriarchal household and of love patriarchalism, then it becomes important to analyze not just women's role but, first, to consider the middle-class background of New Testament exegetes and, second, to analyze household structures and their religious meaning in Roman Hellenism. Moreover, such a social-structural understanding of women's role in early Christianity cannot construe the life and situation of Jewish, Greek, Asian, or Roman women as "backgrounds," but must instead show how much their conversion to Christianity intruded into the cultural patriarchal ethos and how much it supported emancipatory tendencies within the contexts of Roman Hellenism.

Insofar as the Christian movement rejected both sexual dimorphism and patriarchal domination as well broke down the rigid separation between the public and private religious spheres, it supported and advanced women's cultural-political emancipation. Insofar as it religiously justified such cultural sexual dimorphism and rigidified the lines between the public and private spheres of patriarchal society by relegating women to the house and assigning men public leadership within the church, it strengthened the patriarchal tendencies of middle-class men in Roman Hellenism. The remembrance of women's sufferings in religious patriarchy must be explored structurally in order to set free the emancipatory power of the Christian community which is theologically rooted neither in spiritual-sexual dimorphism nor in patriarchal ecclesial dominance, but in an egalitarian vision and in altruistic social relationships that may not be "genderized."[64]

Women who belonged to a submerged group in antiquity could develop leadership in the emerging Christian movement because it stood in conflict with the dominant patriarchal ethos of the Greco-Roman world. Therefore, the struggle and interaction of women in the Christian missionary movement can only be reconstructed as an integral part of the struggle between the emerging Christian movement and its alternative vision, on the one hand, and the dominant patriarchal ethos of the Greco-Roman world on the other. In this struggle women's leadership has become submerged again, transformed, or pushed to the fringes of the mainstream churches. Yet the egalitarian currents of early Christianity have never been eliminated. Neither fourth- nor twentieth-century patriarchal mainstream churches can be understood without this Christian "undercurrent."

The sociological-theological model for the reconstruction of the early Christian movement suggested here should, therefore, not be misread as that of a search for true pristine, orthodox beginnings, which have been corrupted either by early Catholicism or by "heresy," nor should it be seen as an argument for an institutional patriarchalization absolutely necessary for the historical survival of Christianity. The model used here is that of social interaction and religious transformation, of Christian "vision" and historical realization, of struggle for equality and against patriarchal domination.

NOTES

1. James Barr, "The Fundamentalist Understanding of Scripture," *Concilium* 138 (1980) 70–74.
2. See e.g. Manuel Miguens, *Church Ministries in New Testament Times* (Arlington, Va.: Christian Culture Press, 1976).
3. See especially Raymond E. Brown, *Biblical Reflections on Crises Facing the Church* (New York: Paulist Press, 1975) for the critical rejection of such a concept.

4. See especially the discussion in German scholarship: D. Lührmann, "Erwä-gungen zur Geschichte des Urchristentums," *EvTh* 32 (1972) 452–67; J. Blank, "Pro-bleme einer Geschichte des Urchristentums," *Una Sancta* 30 (1975) 261–86; H. Paulsen, "Zur Wissenschaft vom Urchristentum und der alten Kirche—ein methodischer Ver-such," *ZNW* 68 (1977) 200–230; N. Brox, "Fragen zur Denkform der Kirchengeschichts-wissenschaft," *Zeitschrift für Kirchengeschichte* 90 (1979) 1–22; and the work of H. M. Baumgartner, *Kontinuität und Geschichte: Zur Kritik und Metakritik der historischen Vernunft* (Frankfurt: Suhrkamp, 1972).

5. G. Heinz (*Das Problem der Kirchenentstehung in der deutschen protestantischen Theol-ogie des 20. Jahrhunderts* [Tübinger Theologische Studien 4: Mainz: Grünewald, 1974]) highlights the theological presuppositions undergirding the various reconstructions of early Christian beginnings.

6. Gordon Leff, *History and Social Theory* (New York: Doubleday, 1971), p. 111.

7. Ibid., p. 14.

8. For a review of the Pauline literature, cf. E. Earle Ellis, "Paul and His Opponents: Trends in Research," in J. Neusner, ed., *Christianity, Judaism and Other Greco-Roman Cults: Studies for Morton Smith* (Leiden: Brill, 1975), 1.264–98.

9. But these questions are usually not found in the different proposals for the social reconstruction of early Christian beginnings. This may also be due to the unconscious androcentrism of the sociological models and frameworks. See especially Dorothy Smith, "A Sociology for Women: The Line of Fault," in *The Prisms of Sex*, pp. 135–87; Meredith Gould, "The New Sociology," *Signs* 5 (1980) 459–67; Cynthia Fuchs Epstein, "Women in Sociological Analysis: New Scholarship Versus Old Paradigms," *Soundings* 64 (1981) 485–98.

10. Wayne A. Meeks, "The Social World of Early Christianity," *Bulletin of the Council on the Study of Religion* 6 (1975) 5.

11. John G. Gager, *Religious Studies Review* 5 (1979) 174–80:175.

12. See Dietfried Gewalt, "Neutestamentliche Exegese und Soziologie," *EvTh* 31 (1971) 87–99; and the hermeneutical essays in Fred R. Dallmayr and Thomas A. McCarthy, eds., *Understanding and Social Inquiry* (Notre Dame: University of Notre Dame Press, 1977).

13. See especially the review essays of J. Smith, "Social Description of Early Chris-tianity," *Religious Studies Review* 2 (1975) 19–25; D. J. Harrington, "Sociological Con-cepts and the Early Church: A Decade of Research," *Theological Studies* 41 (1980) 181–90; Robin Scroggs, "The Sociological Interpretation of the New Testament: The Present State of Research," *NTS* 26 (1980) 164–79; Cyrill S. Rodd, "On Applying a Sociological Theory to Biblical Studies," *JSOT* 19 (1981) 95–106.

14. R. Scroggs, "The Earliest Christian Communities as Sectarian Movement," in Neusner, *Christianity, Judaism and Other Cults*, 2. –23.

15. Cf. Kurt Rudolph, "Wesen und Struktur der Sekte: Bemerkungen zum Stand der Diskussion in Religionswissenschaft und-soziologie," *Kairos* 21 (1979) 241–54.

16. Sheldon R. Isenberg, "Millenarism in Greco-Roman Palestine," *Religion* 4 (1974) 26–46; and "Power through Temple and Torah in Greco-Roman Palestine," in Neusner, *Christianity, Judaism and Other Cults*, 2.24–52.

17. John G. Gager, *Kingdom and Community: The Social World of Early Christianity* (Englewood Cliffs, N.J.: Prentice-Hall, 1975), pp. 95f.

18. See also the review articles on Gager's work: D. Bartlett, "John G. Gager's 'Kingdom and Community': A Summary and Response," *Zygon* 13 (1978) 109–22; J. Smith, "Too Much Kingdom, Too Little Community," ibid., pp. 123–30; and D. Tracy, "A Theological Response to 'Kingdom and Community,'" ibid., pp. 131–35.

19. G. Theissen, *Sociology of Early Palestinian Christianity* (Philadelphia: Fortress, 1978); and the forthcoming collection of his essays on Corinth, *The Social Setting of Pauline Christianity: Essays on Corinth* (Philadelphia: Fortress, 1982).

20. Theissen, *Early Palestinian Christianity*, p. 8.

21. W. Stegemann, "Wanderradikalismus im Urchristentum? Historische und theologische Auseinandersetzung mit einer interessanten These," in W. Schottroff and

W. Stegemann, eds., *Der Gott der kleinen Leute: Sozialgeschichtliche Bibelauslegungen,* vol. 2., *Neues Testament* (Munich: Kaiser, 1979), pp. 94–120.

22. G. Theissen, "Itinerant Radicalism: The Tradition of Jesus Sayings from the Perspective of the Sociology of Literature," in N. K. Gottwald and A. C. Wire, eds., *The Bible and Liberation: Political and Social Hermeneutics* (Berkeley: Radical Religion Reader, 1976), pp. 84–93:89.

23. Theissen, *Early Palestinian Christianity,* p. 22.

24. Wayne A. Meeks, "Since Then You Would Need to Go Out of the World: Group Boundaries in Early Christianity," in T. J. Ryan, ed., *Critical History and Biblical Faith: New Testament Perspectives* (Villanova, Pa.: College Theology Society, 1979), pp. 4–29:22.

25. J. Milton Yinger, *The Scientific Study of Religion* (New York: Macmillan, 1970), pp. 251–81:257.

26. Gager, *Kingdom and Community,* p. 21.

27. Ibid., p. 37.

28. Ibid., p. 35.

29. Ibid., p. 96.

30. Ibid., p. 67.

31. Ibid., p. 87.

32. Ibid., p. 140.

33. Ernst Troeltsch, *The Social Teachings of the Christian Churches* (New York: Macmillan, 1931), 1.19.

34. Ibid., 1.78.

35. G. Theissen, "Soziale Schichtung in der korinthischen Gemeinde: Ein Beitrag zur Soziologie des hellenistischen Christentums," *ZNW* 64 (1974) 232–72:270.

36. Ibid., p. 272.

37. Theissen, "Itinerant Radicalism," p. 91.

38. Elaine Pagels, *The Gnostic Gospels* (New York: Random House, 1979), p. 142.

39. Leander E. Keck, "On the Ethos of Early Christians," *JAAR* 42 (1974) 435–52:440.

40. L. E. Keck, "Ethos and Ethics in the New Testament," in James Gaffney, ed., *Essays in Morality and Ethics* (New York: Paulist Press, 1980), pp. 29–49:33.

41. Ibid., pp. 36–37.

42. See also my article "' 'You are not to be called Father': Early Christian History in a Feminist Perspective," *Cross Currents* 39 (1979) 301–23: esp. 312–15.

43. See e.g. Lois W. Banner, "On Writing Women's History," in T. K. Raab and R. I. Rotberg, *The Family in History* (New York: Harper & Row, 1971): Berenice A. Carroll, ed., *Liberating Women's History: Theoretical and Critical Essays* (Urbana: University of Illinois Press, 1976); Natalie Zemon Davis, " 'Women's History' in Transition." *Feminist Studies* 3 (1976) 83–103; Sheila Rowbotham, *Hidden From History: Rediscovering Women in History from the 17th Century to the Present* (New York: Random House, 1976), especially the introduction to the American edition, pp. x–xxxiii; Kathryn K. Sklar, "Four Levels of Women's History," in D. G. McGuigan, ed., *New Research on Women,* vol. 3 (Ann Arbor: University of Michigan Press, 1977), pp. 7–10; Jane Lewis, "Women Lost and Found; The Impact of Feminism on History," in Dale Spender, ed., *Men's Studies Modified: The Impact of Feminism on the Academic Disciplines* (Oxford/New York: Pergamon Press, 1981), pp. 73–82.

44. A. D. Gordon, M. J. Buhle, and Nancy Schrom Dye, "The Problem of Women's History," in Carroll, *Liberating Women's History,* pp. 75–92:83f.

45. Mary R. Beard, *Woman as Force in History: A Study in Traditions and Realities* (New York: Macmillan, 1962).

46. Gerda Lerner, *The Majority Finds Its Past: Placing Women in History* (Oxford: Oxford University Press, 1979).

47. Ann J. Lane, ed., *Mary Ritter Beard: A Sourcebook* (New York: Schocken Books, 1977), p. 65; see also Berenice Carroll, "On Mary Beard's Woman as Force in History: A Critique," in Carroll, *Liberating Women's History,* pp. 26–41.

48. Carroll, *Liberating Women's History*, p. 85.

49. See especially Hilda Smith, "Feminism and the Methodology of Women's History," in Carroll, *Liberating Women's History*, pp. 369–84; Gayle Rubin, "The Traffic in Women: Notes on the 'Political Economy' of Sex," in R. R. Reiter, ed., *Toward an Anthropology of Women* (New York: Monthly Review Press, 1975), pp. 157–210:159; Michelle Zimbalist Rosaldo, "The Use and Abuse of Anthropology: Reflections on Feminism and Cross-Cultural Understandings," *Signs* 5 (1980) 389–417: esp. 400ff.

50. See e.g. Joan Bamberger, "The Myth of Matriarchy: Why Men Rule in Primitive Society," in M. Z. Rosaldo and L. Lamphere, eds., *Woman, Culture and Society* (Stanford: Stanford University Press, 1974), pp. 263–80; Leila Rupp, "Women, Power, and History," *Women* 6 (1978) 4–9; Rosemary Radford Ruether, *New Woman/New Earth: Sexist Ideologies and Human Liberation* (New York: Seabury, 1975). For the opinion that history and writing are integral to patriarchy because they reify people, see e.g. Elizabeth Fisher, *Woman's Creation: Sexual Evolution and the Shaping of Society* (New York: McGraw-Hill, 1980).

51. For this basic concept, see Joan Kelly-Gadol, "The Social Relations of the Sexes: Methodological Implications of Women's History," *Signs* 1 (1976) 809–23:809.

52. Glynis M. Breakwell ("Woman: Group and Identity," *Women's Studies International Quarterly* 2 [1979] 9–17) argues that women as a group are characterized by both marginality and power.

53. For "struggle" as the key concept of Virginia Woolf's work, see Berenice A. Carroll, " 'To Crush Him in Our Own Country': The Political Thought of Virginia Woolf," *Feminist Studies* 4 (1978) 99–131:110.

54. Elise Boulding, *The Underside of History* (Boulder, Colo.: Westview Press, 1976), p. 258.

55. Ibid., p. 26.

56. For a critique of altruism that is restricted to women in a patriarchal society, see J. Farr Tormey, "Exploitation, Oppression, and Self-Sacrifice," *Philosophical Forum* 5 (1975) 206–21; L. Blum, M. Homiak, J. Housman, and N. Scheman, "Altruism and Women's Oppression," Ibid., pp. 222–247.

57. Marilyn B. Arthur, "Women in the Ancient World," in *Conceptual Frameworks for Studying Women's History* (A Sarah Lawrence College Women's Studies Publication; New York, 1975), pp. 1–15.

58. Susan Moller Okin, *Women in Western Political Thought* (Princeton: Princeton University Press, 1979), pp. 15–96, on Plato and Aristotle; cf. also Marilyn B. Arthur, "Review Essay: Classics," *Signs* 2 (1976) 382–403.

59. Diogenes Laertius *Lives of Famous Philosophers* 6.98, as quoted by Marilyn B. Arthur, "Liberated Women: The Classical Era," in Renate Bridenthal and Claudia Koonz, eds., *Becoming Visible: Women in European History* (Boston: Houghton Mifflin, 1977), pp. 60–89:76.

60. Ramsay MacMullen, "Women in Public in the Roman Empire," *Historia* 29 (1981) 208–18.

61. For such a thesis, see Ross S. Kraemer, "The Conversion of Women to Ascetic Forms of Christianity," *Signs* 6 (1980) 298–307.

62. Sheila Ryan Johansson, " 'Herstory' as History: A New Field or Another Fad?" in Carroll, *Liberating Women's History*, pp. 400–30:413f.

63. Ibid., p. 415.

64. The one first-person narrative of a Christian woman that has survived testifies to this. Cf. Mary R. Lefkowitz, "The Motivations for St. Perpetua's Martyrdom," *JAAR* 44 (1976), reprinted in idem, *Heroines and Hysterics* (New York: St. Martin's Press, 1981), pp. 53–58; see also the introduction to and translation of *The Martyrdom of Perpetua*, by Rosemary Rader, in P. Wilson-Kastner et al., *A Lost Tradition: Women Writers of the Early Church* (Washington, D.C.: University Press of America, 1981), pp. 1–32.

Part II

IN MEMORY OF HER
Women's History as
the History of the
Discipleship of Equals

A feminist reconstruction of early Christian origins faces three problems from the outset. First, can two distinct forms of the early Christian movement be delineated or are these two distinct forms merely products of our literature? While the gospels transmit stories and traditions about Jesus, the Pauline literature contains almost no references to the life of Jesus of Nazareth but only makes available information about the missionary Christian communities and their beliefs. Second, how do we use historical criticism in order to move beyond the gospel texts to the historical reality of Jesus and his movement? Finally, how can we reconstruct the origins of the early Christian movement so that we recover the story of Christian women as the story of *Jewish* women since our sources make a recovery of our Jewish feminist roots difficult?

1. As we have noted, some scholars have sought to delineate the difference between the Jesus movement in Palestine and the Christian movement in the Greco-Roman cities—on the basis of the literary sources—as a difference between Jesus and Paul.[1] While Jesus preached the coming of the *basileia* in the very imminent future, Paul was the founder of Christianity. Others have suggested that we move beyond the literary texts in search of the distinctive character of both movements. They elaborate the difference, therefore, in terms of Jewish-Palestinian and Hellenistic environments, rural and urban settings, or radical discipleship of homeless itinerant preachers and integrative love patriarchalism. However, while all these distinctions highlight different aspects or facets of the problem, they do not comprehend it adequately.

Jesus *is* the initiator of the Jesus movement in Palestine, but Paul is *not* the initiator of the Christian missionary movement in the Greco-Roman world. The distinction between Jewish and Hellenistic cultures as well as that between rural and urban settings is important, but in the time of Jesus Palestine was Hellenized and strict Torah and Temple observance was practiced in the Dispersion. Moreover, the Jesus traditions are not restricted to rural Palestine but were formative in urban Christian communities. Jews initiated and carried out both movements, but at a very early stage proselytes, godfearers, and gentiles adopted the Palestinian Jesus traditions to speak to persons of their own cultural-religious worlds.

Therefore, the difference between both movements and historical formations cannot be defined in terms of "context" or "background" (Jewish Palestinian/Jewish Hellenist or rural/urban settings) or of "content" (Jesus/Paul), but rather in terms of function. Whereas the Jesus movement in Palestine was an alternative prophetic renewal movement within Israel, the Christian movement was a religious missionary movement within the Greco-Roman world, preaching an alternative religious vision and practicing a countercultural communal lifestyle. Both movements created tensions and conflicts with respect to the dominant cultural ethos. But where the Jesus movement could appeal to Israel's tradition as its very own religious tradition over and against certain practices within Israel, the Christian movement as a new religious group intruded as an alien element into the dominant cultural-religious ethos of the Greco-Roman worlds.

While the Jesus movement gathered after Easter in Galilee and Jerusalem in order to continue Jesus' ministry of renewal within Israel, and only very gradually expanded its boundaries to include neighboring non-Jews, the Christian movement emerged in Syrian Antioch and appears to have been strongly determined by the expulsion of the so-called Hellenists from the holy city. While the Jesus movement announced the inbreaking of God's *basileia* as good news to the impoverished and outcast among its own people, the Christian movement applied the "inclusiveness" of Jesus' vision and movement not only to members of Israel but also to the gentiles. It was thus constituted when it admitted gentiles as equal members to the community without requiring that they first become members of the Jewish covenant people. It was not in Galilee or even Jerusalem, but in Antioch "that the disciples were called for the first time Christians" (Acts 11:26), the religious associates of Christ. This naming process indicates that at a very early stage the Jesus movement was considered a distinct religious association and party.[2]

As a religious missionary movement the Christian movement intruded into the dominant patriarchal cultural-religious ethos of Roman Hellenism, while, as an alternative Jewish renewal movement, the Jesus movement was in tension with the dominant patriarchal ethos of its own culture. Both movements were first initiated and carried out by faithful Jews, men and women. Segments of the Jesus movement, however, soon stopped restricting themselves to Jews and admitted gentiles to full membership without requiring their conversion to Judaism. As an inner-Jewish renewal movement, the Jesus movement could presuppose a common cultural-religious milieu. The missionary movement, by contrast, had to address persons of very different cultural experiences, national origins, social status, and religious persuasions. While the religious matrices of both movements differed considerably, their overall cultural matrix was the same, since the cultural horizon of Palestinian Judaism was Roman Hellenism.

Therefore, the difference between the two movements cannot be traced to Jesus and Paul but only to the development of two distinct groups who moved in different environments and were propelled by different goals. As a consequence they appealed to different religious-political experiences, as well as to different theological legitimizations. Both movements were inspired by Jesus, the Christ, but both saw him in quite different lights. The Christian missionary movement had already developed *before* Paul and was joined by him. Paul has become its most important figure because his letters have survived oblivion, but he was neither its initiator nor its sole leader.

Therefore, it is more fruitful to see Paul in the context of this movement[3] than to construe the whole Christian missionary development before Paul's activity and during Paul's ministry solely in terms of Paul's leadership and unquestioned authority. Historical reconstruction in terms of Pauline texts usually has perceived other Christian formations and visions in terms of Paul's "opponents" who are then judged as "heterodox," that is, as theologically or historically "wrong," while Paul is seen as representing the "orthodox" apostolic position. Such a construction has no basis in history since Paul's letters show clearly that he and his mission were very controversial and far from acknowledged by all the segments of the early Christian movement. Moreover, the fact that Paul refers rarely to the life and ministry of Jesus of Nazareth, but instead stresses the death and resurrection of Christ, the Lord, does not prove that the Jesus traditions were not alive in the communities to whom he wrote. Finally, seeing Paul in the context of a Christian missionary movement initiated before Paul's "conversion" also allows us to conceptualize this movement in such a way that women can emerge as initiators and leaders of the movements and not just as Paul's helpers, benignly tolerated and utilized by the great apostle for his own missionary work.

2. The social world and vision of the Jesus movement as an inner-Jewish renewal movement is reflected in the Gospel accounts about Jesus of Nazareth. These accounts underwent a theological process of redaction and incorporated a lengthy traditioning process that was accomplished partially in the Christian missionary communities. Therefore, the Gospels may not be understood as actual transcripts of the life or work of the historical Jesus nor simply as textual tenets abstracted from their historical context and their social world. The New Testament writers were not concerned with preservation and antiquarian reading but with proclamation and interpretative persuasion. They did not simply want to set down what Jesus said and did; rather, they attempted to comprehend what Jesus meant to his first followers and what meaning his life had for their own time and communities. As a result, what we can learn from the gospel transmission and redaction process is that Jesus—as we can know him—must be remembered, discussed, interpreted, accepted, or rejected in order to comprehend the importance and impulse of his life. The Gospels center on the life-praxis of Jesus and speak of women only in passing. When they do so they tell us as much about the community to whom these stories or sayings were transmitted as about the historical women in the life of Jesus.

The Gospels, then, are paradigmatic remembrances, not comprehensive accounts of the historical Jesus but expressions of communities and individuals who attempted to say what the significance of Jesus was for their own situations.[4] Early Christian theology (as well as all subsequent theology) is the process of interpretative remembrance of Jesus, the Christ. This process is at the same time a critical appropriation of the memories and stories about Jesus circulating in oral or written form in the Christian community. Feminist Christian theology, therefore, must understand critically all the remembrances of those who throughout Christian history have entered into the discipleship of equals initiated by Jesus and who have called themselves followers of Jesus in the context of their own historical-societal situations and problems.

However, in order to appropriate theologically the impulse of Jesus and the early Christian faith perspective of the New Testament, we must not only attempt to understand it in its historical-linguistic-theological context, but we must also attempt to enter into a discussion with its perspective, hope, and wisdom. Thus to enter the discipleship of equals called forth by Jesus does not mean to imitate him or the Christians of New Testament times. Following Jesus is never a simple repetition or imitation, but an engagement in early Christian faith perspectives. It means not only sharing the vision of Jesus but also entering into Jesus' commitment and praxis as we know it from the remembrance of his first disciples. The Gospels are not transcripts but invitations to discipleship. They are theological interpretation-in-process.

Such an understanding of the New Testament has important methodological consequences. It does not seek to distill the "historical Jesus" from the remembering interpretations of his first followers, nor does it accept their interpretation uncritically and without question. Therefore, whenever I speak here of Jesus I speak of him as his life and ministry is available to historical-critical reading of the earliest interpretations of the first Christians. Among these earliest strata of interpretations New Testament scholarship has identified the sayings-source Q, reconstructed from the texts which Matthew and Luke have in common, pre-Q materials, pre-Markan materials, materials belonging to the special traditions used by Luke (SL) or Matthew (SM), and the earliest strata of tradition found in the Fourth Gospel. Although these texts are probably the earliest historically available accounts of the life and ministry of Jesus and of his followers' interaction with him, they nevertheless are interpreting and interpreted remembrances of Jesus. As the canonical collection of the memories about Jesus circulating in the earliest communities of disciples, they provide the paradigmatic informational and interpretational framework in which all later remembrance, discussion, appropriation, and redaction of Jesus moves and must move.

However, the gospel traditions about Jesus and his ministry are influenced not only by these earliest Christian remembrances of Jesus and the Jesus movement in Palestine, but also by very early proclamations of the resurrection and death of Jesus found in the pre-Pauline, Pauline, and post-Pauline writings. These later traditions evidence very little interest in the actual life and words of Jesus of Nazareth but are concerned primarily and almost exclusively with his glorious status as the resurrected Lord and with the significance of his death on the cross as a punctual event in a cosmic drama of mythological dimensions. In these Christian communities, the experience of the Spirit and of the resurrection as dawn of the new creation,[5] rather than the remembrance of Jesus of Nazareth, are decisive.

While the key integrative symbol of the Jesus movement in Palestine is the *basileia* of God, that of the Christian movement in the Greco-Roman cities is that of the new creation. Both agree, however, that the reality signified by these two symbols is experientially available here and now in the work of Jesus Christ and his discipleship of equals.[6] In the following, therefore, I shall trace the two very different faith experiences of the earliest followers of Jesus as they are transformed in interaction with each other and their specific social-historical situations. This is methodologically important, because the experience of the Jewish and Hellenistic women who became involved in this discipleship of equals is only available in and through this general early Christian experience and remembrance.

Notes to this section follow chapter 4 on page 154.

The Jesus Movement
as Renewal Movement
Within Judaism

To speak about the Jesus movement is to speak about a Jewish movement that is part of Jewish history in the first century C.E. It is therefore misleading to speak about "Jesus and his Jewish background" as though Jesus' Judaism was not integral to his life and ministry, or to describe the behavior of Jesus' disciples over and against Jewish practice as though the first followers of Jesus were not Jews themselves. Such statements reflect both rabbinic Jewish and Christian historical sources, virtually all of which were written in a period when the separation and schism between Judaism and early Christianity was an accomplished fact. Such historical reconstructions of Christianity over and against Judaism can be continuing resources for Christian anti-Judaism because they perceive Christian origins in light of the historical fact of Christianity's separation from and partial rejection of its Jewish roots and heritage.

Such an anti-Jewish sentiment and historical misperception is especially deeply ingrained in popular consciousness. In my classes, whenever students are supposed to elaborate the positive aspects of the Jesus movement they always resort not to Jewish faith and life but to general philosophical principles and theological universal arguments. However, when speaking about the "opponents" of Jesus and his movement they virtually never mention the Romans. Instead they always mention the "Jews"—without the slightest recognition that Jesus and his followers were Jews.

One of my friends spoke about Jesus, the Jew, to an adult education class in her parish. She encountered vehement objections to such a notion. Finally, after a lengthy discussion a participant expressed the religious sentiment underlying it: "If you are so insistent that Jesus was Jewish, then you are probably right. But the Blessed Mother for sure is not . . ." My friend told me this story after I had come exasperated from a college class, where I had been unable to convince a student that Saint Paul was a Jew. In a Protestant college class a Jewish friend attempted to show that the miracle stories of Jesus have the same literary form as those told by the rabbis. At the end when he tried to draw the conclusion from this form-critical exercise for understanding the Gospel stories, the students objected: the Jewish tales are just stories, but those in the Gospels have *really* happened. Everyone is aware of such anti-Jewish sentiments among Christians and easily could supply more such stereotypes.

Women in Judaism Before 70 C.E.: Perspectives

Feminist Jewish scholars such as Judith Plaskow have pointed out that Christian feminist literature and popular reasoning perpetuate these anti-Jewish notions when extolling Jesus, the feminist, over and against patriarchal Judaism, or when pointing to the extinction of goddess religion by Israelite patriarchal religion.[7] Plaskow has argued correctly that the rabbinic statements often adduced for the reconstruction of the time of Jesus should be appropriately read alongside the statements of the so-called Fathers, whose misogynism is widely acknowledged. She warns that Christian feminists' radical image of Jesus

> depends on an extremely negative depiction of the Jewish background, because the only way to depict him as a radical—that is as overthrowing tradition—is to depict the tradition as negatively as possible. Because despite the evidence that he in no way reinforced patriarchy, there's also no evidence that he did anything radical to overthrow it. So the only way you can make that argument is by depicting Judaism negatively.[8]

Christian feminists cannot take such a Jewish feminist warning seriously enough. At the same time it puts Christian feminists into a serious quandary. Can they—in order to avoid being labeled anti-Jewish—cease to analyze critically and denounce the patriarchal structures and traditions of Christian faith and community whenever it becomes obvious that they share in the dominant patriarchal Jewish structures of the first centuries? In other words, can feminists relinquish their search for the liberating elements of Christian vision and praxis that are formulated over and against the dominant patriarchal structures of Judaism? Would that not mean also an abandonment of feminist Jewish roots and of our Jewish foresisters who entered into the movement and vision of Jesus of Nazareth?

Because of the long anti-Semitic history of Christianity and the anti-Jewish presupposition of much Christian (including feminist) scholarship and popular preaching, one cannot insist too much on the historical insight that Jesus belongs first of all to Jewish history. Similarly, his first followers in the Jesus movement and in the missionary Christian movement were Jewish women as well as men. Christian feminist theology, therefore, can reappropriate the earliest Christian beginnings of the discipleship of equals only if and when it understands and explicates that Christian roots are Jewish and that the feminist Christian foundational story is that of Jewish women and their vision.

To rediscover "Jesus, the feminist," over and against these Jewish roots of the early Christian movement can only lead to a further deepening of anti-Judaism. Equally, to rediscover Jesus, the feminist, over and against Jewish but not over and against Christian patriarchy would only mean a further strengthening of Western religious patriarchy. To rediscover Jesus, the feminist, over and against Jewish life and beliefs would involve relinquishing the history of those Jewish foresisters who entered into the vision and movement of Jesus. The discipleship of equals called forth by Jesus was a *Jewish* discipleship.

But in seeking not to be anti-Jewish we cannot cease analyzing and identifying the dominant patriarchal structures of the Greco-Roman world into which Christianity emerged.[9] In doing so we must also examine the patriarchal structures of Judaism in order to see why Jewish women entered into the vision and movement of Jesus. To relinquish the critical impact of their story within the patriarchal context of their own culture would entail relinquishing women's Jewish and Christian heritage. Therefore, to reconstruct the Jesus movement as a Jewish movement within its dominant patriarchal cultural and religious structures is to delineate the feminist impulse within Judaism. The issue is not whether or not Jesus overturned patriarchy but whether Judaism had elements of a critical feminist impulse that came to the fore in the vision and ministry of Jesus. The reconstruction of the Jesus movement as the discipleship of equals is historically plausible only insofar as such critical elements are thinkable within the context of Jewish life and faith. The praxis and vision of Jesus and his movement is best understood as an inner-Jewish renewal movement that presented an *alternative* option to the dominant patriarchal structures rather than an oppositional formation rejecting the values and praxis of Judaism.

Rather than reading the texts on women in Judaism as accurate historical information about the status and role of women in actual life, I would suggest that we subject them to a feminist methodological approach. As yet no Jewish feminist critical reconstruction of first-century Judaism exists, nor are feminist critical analyses of Jewish literature between the Bible and the Mishnah available. Moreover, Jewish feminist theology is still in the process of developing a feminist understanding of Torah and tradition which, while declining to take theological statements of Jewish men at face value, nevertheless spells out its allegiance to Jewish women of faith.[10] In the meantime, feminist theology as a critical theology of liberation cannot cease to do the same for Christian Scriptures, traditions, and women's heritage. However, insofar as the Christian past is bound up intrinsically with its roots in prerabbinic Judaism, we must seek to reconstruct the historical experience of those Jewish women who stand at the beginnings of Christianity. Such a historical experience is, as we have seen, available only in and through Jewish or Christian *male* texts and historical sources.

The following methodological rules for a feminist hermeneutics of suspicion also apply, therefore, to the interpretation of texts speaking about women in Judaism.

Texts and historical sources—Jewish as well as Christian—must be read as androcentric texts. As such they are reflective of the experience, opinion, or control of the individual male writer but not of women's historical reality and experience. Such isolated statements should not be construed as the negative and positive tradition about women in Judaism. For example, it is methodologically not justified to declare, on the one hand, Rabbi Eliezer's infamous statement that "if a man teaches his daughter Torah it is as though he taught her lechery" as representing the normative negative tradition, while, on the other hand, explaining that the example of Beruria, who was held up as an example of how to study Torah, is "the exception that proves the rule."[11]

The glorification as well as the denigration or marginalization of women in Jewish texts is to be understood as a social construction of reality in patriarchal terms or as a projection of male reality. While J. Neusner has elucidated such an approach for the rabbinic literature, the same could be shown for wisdom and apocalyptic literature.[12] It must, however, not be overlooked that "intellectuals" who often belonged to the middle class were responsible for these literary expressions.

The formal canons of codified patriarchal law are generally more restrictive than the actual interaction and relationship of women and men and the social reality which they govern. Although in rabbinic Judaism women are categorized with children and slaves for legal religious purposes,[13] the biblical stories about women indicate that women were not perceived as minors or slaves in everyday life. Biblical women such as Ruth, Esther, Hannah, or the mother of the seven sons mentioned in 2 Maccabees are characterized with typical female roles and behavior, but they are not minors or imbeciles. Although the "praise of the good wife" in Prov 31:10–31 is given from a male point of view, her economic initiative and business acumen are taken for granted.

Women's actual social-religious status must be determined by the degree of their economic autonomy and social roles rather than by ideological or prescriptive statements.[14] As a rule, prescriptive injunctions for appropriate "feminine" behavior and submission increase whenever women's actual social-religious status and power within patriarchy increase. Moreover, women's independence and autonomy are generally limited not only by gender roles but also by social status and class membership. We can therefore assume that Jewish women shared the privileges and limitations placed on women in the dominant culture of their time. For example, in the Jewish colony at Elephantine women shared full equality with men; they were enlisted in the military units, were conspicuous among the contributors to the temple fund, and shared in all other rights given to women by Egyptian law.[15] Like the Seleucid or Ptolemaic princesses, Queen Alexandra[16] reigned for nine years in the fashion of Hellenistic queens, and the sister of the last Maccabean king, Antigonus, defended the fortress of Hyrcania against the military onslaught of Herod the Great.[17]

Furthermore, the historical-theological reconstruction of the Jesus movement as an emerging inner-Jewish renewal movement and its attractiveness to women not only faces difficult hermeneutical problems, it must also contend with a serious lack of sources, especially for the pre-70 period. Therefore, Jewish and Christian scholars are prone to reconstruct early Judaism and Christianity not only in terms of what has survived as "normative" in their own respective traditions but also as two distinct and oppositional religious formations. Since "rabbinic" Judaism[18] and patriarchal Christianity were the historical winners among the diverse inner-Jewish movements, such a reconstruction insinuates that only these represent pre-70 Judaism in general and the Jesus movement in particular.

Yet such reconstructions are questionable: in the period before the siege and destruction of Jerusalem, "normative" Judaism was not yet in existence, and the Jesus movement was still a renewal movement embedded in its Jewish social-religious matrix. A person could understand herself as a faithful member of Israel and a follower of Jesus at one and the same time. Moreover, the little information about pre-70 Judaism which survived in apocalyptic-esoteric sources and in the writings of Philo and Josephus, was selected, edited, and transmitted by early Christians. Finally, most of the Jewish-Christian sources are lost which affirmed the continuity between Judaism and Christianity, not only with respect to the Scriptures but also with respect to Jewish ethical and liturgical traditions.[19]

If, however, our general picture of pre-70 Judaism is blurred, and that of early Christian origins is equally vague, then the picture of the position and function of women in the multifaceted Jewish movements at the beginning of the common era must remain even more in historical darkness. Yet the available material still gives us some clues to such a picture. The following must therefore not be misunderstood to be even a partial reconstruction of women in pre-70 Judaism. It only points to some "shades" that allow us to see the overall colors in a somewhat different light.

The Dominant Ethos: The Kingdom and Holy Nation of Israel

Although Exod 19:6 is only very rarely quoted in the literature of the first century C.E.,[20] the common ethos or life praxis of Israel as the "kingdom of priests and holy nation" determined all groups of first-century Judaism.[21] All Jewish groups and factions of Greco-Roman Palestine were concerned with Israel's life and existence as God's holy people who were entrusted with the commandments of the covenant, a whole system of *mitzvot*, the revealed rules for salvation. Temple and Torah were therefore the key symbols of first century Judaism.

> Indeed the worldview of the Jew . . . depended on his [sic] understanding of Torah. But a fixed written scripture requires interpretation, and in that world the authority to interpret Torah meant power; it meant control of redemptive media. . . . But the terms of Torah serve as symbols in their sacrality . . . for the realities which they expressed were the realities of living men [sic] in living groups who experienced their present situations in the light of the realities of tradition.[22]

The foremost witness and testimony to Israel's enduring covenant with God was the sacred Temple in Jerusalem. Its rites and liturgies testified to Israel's loyalty to the commandments and stipulations of this covenant which made the whole land and nation of Israel a "kingdom of priests" which could not properly be governed by pagans. Although the Romans sought to avoid offenses against the religious beliefs and sacred rites of the Jews, their presence in and occupation of Palestine was the greatest offense to God's rule and empire established in the covenant with Israel. Therefore, the various Jewish movements and groups in Palestine were convinced that the imminent departure of the Romans was certain and God's intervention on behalf of Israel was immediate.

Exegetes generally agree that the central perspective and "vision" of Jesus is expressed by the tensive symbol *basileia* ("kingdom," "empire") of God.[23] Jesus and his movement shared this symbol, and the whole range of expectations evoked by it, with all the other groups in Palestine. Jews expected either the restoration of the Davidic national sovereignty of Israel and abolition of Roman colonialism or an apocalyptic universal kingdom of cosmological dimensions with the holy city and Temple as its center. Many groups hoped for both at the same time.

> An expectation of such an intervention in the not too distant future based on belief in a revelation of its imminence creates the apocalyptic consciousness. Clearly all Jews, perhaps most Jews, were not apocalypticists . . . but apocalypticism . . . was within the range of normal views of what could happen. It was an integral part of the social-psychic repertory.[24]

Such an apocalyptic hope for both national liberation and sovereignty, as well as for transformation of the whole creation by God's intervention, is articulated in the first-century apocalypse the *Assumption of Moses:*

> And then his [God's] kingdom shall appear
> throughout all his creation.
> And then Satan shall be no more
> and sorrow shall depart with him. . . .
> For the Most High will arise, the eternal God alone
> and he will appear to punish the gentiles.
> Then Thou, O Israel, shall be happy . . .
> and God will exalt thee
> and he will cause thee to approach the heavens of the
> stars. . .[25]

The Kiddush, a prayer used in Jewish synagogues at the beginning of our era, testifies how widespread was such a hope for God's immediate intervention:

> Magnified and sanctified be his great name
> in the world that he has created according to his will.
> May he establish his kingdom in your lifetime and in your day
> and in the lifetime of all the house of Israel,
> even speedily and at a near time.[26]

Similarly the followers of Jesus prayed:

> Father, hallowed be thy name.
> Thy kingdom come.

The different groups within Judaism answered the burning question of every Jew—What must I do to enter the kingdom of heaven?—quite differently, precisely because no single "orthodox" answer existed at the time.[27] The priestly establishment and aristocracy sought to preserve Israel's national existence as the people of God by preserving the Temple and the capital through collaboration with the Romans. The Essenes established separate communes in towns and cities throughout the country, held everything in common, employed a different ritual of purification, devoted themselves to agricultural labor, and were very strict in their interpretation of Torah. The community of Qumran, for example, withdrew into the desert to create a "holy people" to replace the Temple with its illegitimate rituals and priesthood until the Temple's sacredness would be restored and Israel would be liberated in the final "holy war." The *Sicarii* gathered for military rebellion the impoverished and disenfranchised, the people of the countryside plagued by high Roman and Jerusalem taxes, to liberate Jerusalem and Israel from Roman occupation and desecration. The Pharisees did not separate from the people but sought to realize their vision of a "holy people of priests" by transferring cultic purity and priestly holiness to everyday life. Their chief concerns were for the preservation of the cultic purity of the table community and especially for the observation of the dietary laws. In contrast to the common people they were meticulous in paying their Levitical and priestly tithes, in keeping the sabbath observance and purity laws. Some formed urban religious communities (*ḥavuroth*) whose members ate their food in rigorous levitical cleanness and kept company only with those who observed such strict observance of the priestly purity laws. Politically they were split, some participating in the revolutionary unrest, others advocating a politics of pacification.

The apocalyptic prophets who, according to Josephus, appeared in pre-70 Judaism sought to reenact the Exodus by leading people into the desert. John the Baptizer announced God's wrath and judgment and called the people to undergo a baptism of repentance. Apocalyptic scribes and wisdom teachers not only collected prophetic oracles and the sayings of the fathers but also wrote and collected whole new books of revelation and wisdom. The Sadducees, who were most influential among the upper classes, the landholders, and merchants, claimed to be the legitimate heirs of Israel's covenant and therefore insisted that since only the written Torah had the authority of revelation, it had to be strictly adhered to. They rejected as innovation the Pharisaic insistence on both written and oral Torah, and rejected all claims to revelatory authority alongside the written Torah as deception.

All these diverse Jewish renewal movements of the time[28] were strongly concerned with how to realize in every aspect of life the obligations and hopes of Israel as the kingly and priestly people of God. They sought to hasten God's intervention on behalf of Israel by scrupulously doing the will of God as revealed in Temple and Torah. Some stressed and strongly utilized the cultic priestly traditions, some claimed prophetic authority, some reenacted the Exodus, and still others integrated wisdom teachings with an apocalyptic perspective. Regardless of differences in lifestyle and theological outlook, however, all these groups were united in their concern for the political existence and holiness of the elected people of Israel. The proclamation of the *basileia* of God by Jesus and his movement shared this central theological concern for the renewal of the people of Israel as God's holy elect in the midst of the nations. However, the Jesus movement refused to define the holiness of God's elected people in cultic terms, redefining it instead as the wholeness intended in creation.

Regarding the role women had in these different groups and movements of the time, one finds no direct information, either in our sources or in the scholarly elaborations of these sources. Since the Sadducees and priestly aristocracy acknowledged only the written Torah as Scripture but not its oral traditions and subsequent interpretations, they presumably defined the role of women according to the written Torah. Probably this was the case, especially with respect to the cultic purity rules for worship and with reference to marriage legislation.

Our information about the group around John the Baptizer is scant. Matt 21:32 states that "tax collectors and harlots" believed John. However, the parallel in Luke 7:29f does not mention harlots as "having been baptized with the baptism of John."[29] The account of John's beheading in Mark 6:17–29 certainly has a historical basis but has been filled out with historically less reliable lurid details.[30] Herod was not a king, and he was totally dependent on Rome. Moreover, a young women with Salome's high social status would not have been a "dancing girl" at Herod's parties. Finally, the characterization of Herodias as "his brother Philip's wife" is ambiguous because Herod had two brothers named Philip.

The Qumranites in turn were inspired by the ethos of the holy war and true Temple, and therefore established a male military camp of priests with strict purity rules and social stratification for full members of the group. Whether or not they engaged in short-term marriages for the sake of the procreation of children, however, is debated. Women's and children's skeletons have been found, but it is not clear what role they had in the community. According to the *Manual of Discipline*, "All that present themselves are to be assembled together, women and children included. Then all the provisions of the Covenant are to be read out loud to them, and they are to be instructed about all its injunctions" (1QSa 1:4f).[31] The Damascus *Rule* also mentions "women and children" several times.[32] According to Josephus the Essenes declined to bring wives or slaves into the community because they believed "that the latter practice contributes to injustice and that the former opens the way to a source of dissension" (*Antiquities* XVIII.21).[33] Philo's presentation of the Essenic attitude toward marriage and women is colored by his own derogatory perspective:

> They eschew marriage because they clearly discern it to be the sole or principal danger to the maintenance of the communal life, as well as because they particularly practice continence. For no Essene takes a wife, because a wife is a selfish creature, excessively jealous and adept at beguiling the morals of her husband and seducing him by her continued impostures. . . . For he who is either fast bound in the love lures of his wife or under the stress of nature makes his children his first care ceases to be the same to the others and unconsciously has become a different man and passed from freedom into slavery. [*Hypothetica* 11.14–17]

That Philo's description is antimarriage rather than antiwoman, however, can be seen from his description of the ascetic Therapeutrides who are just as committed to their vocation and the study of the Scriptures as the men.[34]

Wisdom and apocalyptic literature also developed a negative understanding of women. They were the occasion of sin for angels as well as for men, especially for the wise. Middle-class intellectual men, thus, were warned to be very cautious and suspicious in their dealings with women. However, feminist analysis has shown that such an attitude of middle-class men is not typically "Jewish" but can be found in different ages and various societies. The negative statements of Philo and Josephus might have the same sociological roots.[35] Although the attitude the various groups of "revolutionaries" had toward women is unknown, according to Josephus the women of Jerusalem defended the city against the Roman army, and Romans considered Damascus unsafe because too many women of the city had converted to Judaism. Since these groups recruited their support from the common people and the impoverished of the countryside, their attitude toward women might not have been as strict as that of other groups.

We do not know for sure whether the Pharisees admitted women to their ranks and especially to the table community of the *havuroth*,[36] but then we know very little about these Pharisaic associations on the whole. As we have seen, according to Neusner, the system of Mishnah came to its conclusion only toward the end of the second century, while the system's generative ideas must have emerged some time before the turn of the first century. These generative ideas are basically congruent with those of the Damascus *Rule* and the *Manual of Discipline* in Qumran. According to Neusner this Mishnaic system is thoroughly androcentric, because "in the nature of things" women— like the earth, time, fruits, bed, chair, table, and pots—"are sanctified through the deeds of men."[37]

At the same time, the book of Judith, which was not accepted in the rabbinic canon, must have appealed to the theological imagination of various Jewish groups of the time. As a fictional account written sometime during the first century B.C.E.,[38] the book espouses not only wisdom, Exodus, pharisaic, and zealotic motifs but also calls upon God as the "God of the lowly, the helper of the oppressed, the protector of the forlorn, the savior of those without hope" (9:11). Its theology is consciously modeled after the Exodus narrative where by "the hand of Moses" Israel is liberated (Exod 9 and 14).[39] Its review of Israel's history serves as a remembrance of God's previous interventions in hopeless situations. Such a remembrance engenders the hope that God will again act on behalf of the covenant people. Just as according to Wis 11:1 *Sophia*-Wisdom "made their affairs prosper through the hand of the holy prophet" so the Lord will again take care of Israel "through the hands" of Judith (8:33; 9:10; 12:4; 13:14, 15; 16:6). Her scrupulous observation of the dietary prescriptions

(10:5) helps her to win the victory over the enemy. Judith's victorious act and faith are modeled after Moses, who liberated his people from Egypt's oppressive power, after Jael's victory over Sisera (Judg 4:21) and David's beheading of Goliath (1 Sam 17:51).

The heroic biography of Judith tells us several things about the position and role of women at the time when the book was written and read.[40] Judith had inherited her husband's considerable estate and had managed it through a woman steward (8:10). She was free to reject remarriage and, like the Therapeutrides, to dedicate her life to prayer, ascesis, and the celebration of the sabbath. She had the authority to summon the elders of the town and to rebuke them. She censured their theological misjudgment and misconduct in the face of the enemy: "Listen to me, rulers of the people of Bethulia! What you have said to the people today is not right" (8:11). No mention is made that she was veiled when leaving her house. To the contrary it is stressed that all who saw her were struck by her beauty:

> When they saw her, and noted how her face was altered and her clothing changed, they greatly admired her beauty. [10:7]

In a similar fashion Holofernes and all his servants said:

> There is not such a woman from one end of the earth to the other, either for beauty of face or wisdom of speech! [11:21]

At the news of her victory the high priest and the senate of Israel come from Jerusalem "to see" Judith and to greet her in blessing:

> You are the exaltation of Jerusalem, you are the great glory of Israel, you are the great pride of our nation! [15:9]

The victory march to Jerusalem is described as a "victory dance" of the women of Israel crowned with olive wreaths and following Judith. Like Miriam, Judith sings a "new song" leading all the women in the dance.

> And she went before all the people in the dance, leading all the women, while all the men of Israel followed, bearing their arms and wearing garlands and with songs on their lips. [15:13]

Judith continued to feast with the people in Jerusalem for three months, before returning home to her estate. She set her maid free, but remained unmarried, although "many desired to marry her." Like the patriarchs of old she lived as a famous woman to the advanced age of 105 years. Before her death she made a will and distributed her property to her husband's and her own kin and was mourned for seven days by the house of Israel. Such final acts of largesse and features of greatness were typical of the ending of heroic biography.

It would be a serious mistake, however, to read such heroic biography in moralistic terms. True, Judith is a woman who fights with a woman's weapons, yet far from being defined by her "femininity," she uses it to her own ends. Far from accepting such circumscription by feminine beauty and behavior, she uses it against those male enemies who reduce her to mere feminine beauty and in so doing seriously misjudge her real power. Intelligent wisdom, observant piety, shrewd observation, and faithful dedication to the liberation of her people are Judith's true definition and personal assets. Her guileful remarks, her enticing beauty, and her treacherous planning are highlighted in the story in an ironical fashion.

> And Holofernes said to her, "God has done well to send you before the people, to lend strength to our hands and to bring destruction upon those who have slighted my Lord. You are not only beautiful in appearance but wise in speech." [11:22–23]

The male enemies walk into her trap because they are beguiled by her attractiveness and femininity, but have not the faintest idea of her religious and national self-identity and strength. In taking her just as "woman"—and no more—they walk into the trap and their own destruction, which they want to avoid by all means:

> Who can despise these people, who have women like this among them? Surely not a man of them had better be left alive, for if we let them go they will be able to ensnare the whole world. [10:19]

Because the male enemies see women only as appendages and assets to men, they do not recognize that their true foes are not the men of Israel who are characterized as weak and timorous. Holofernes and his servants rightly assume that they will have a major part in the dramatic story, but, because of their masculine arrogance and stupidity, they do not recognize that their part is the "villain's role." Only when one sees the "feminist" irony of the story can one perceive Judith's greatness and appeal to the Jewish imagination of the time:

> Judith is no weakling. Her courage, her trust in God, and her wisdom—all lacking in her male counterparts—save the day for Israel. Her use of deceit and specifically of her sexuality may

> seem offensive and chauvinistic. For the author it is the opposite. Judith wisely chooses the weapon in her arsenal that is appropriate to her enemy's weakness. She plays his game, knowing that he will lose. In so doing she makes fools out of a whole army of men.[41]

However, Judith's dramatic victory is seen as the victory of all the people. It reveals the God of the oppressed and hopeless as the "God with us" (13:11). The risk, wisdom, and courage of a woman have saved the people of God, once more. The woman Judith does not become a victim and does not allow her people to accept the role of victim. In the name of God she struggles against the political power of oppression successfully. Wisdom has prevailed over brute power; the military helplessness of Israel over the military prowess of the oppressor; persistence and the faithful, intelligent courage of a woman over the timid resignation and the stupid boasting of powerful men. Anyone who read this story at the beginning of our era must have immediately understood it as a mirror image of Israel's situation under Roman occupation.[42] In such a hopeless situation the image of a wise and strong woman could incite Israel's imagination and engender hope and endurance in the religious-national struggle. This story of a woman could have appealed to the Essenes, the Pharisees, and to the revolutionary-prophetic groups. The first Christian writer to mention it is Clement of Rome, who points to the example of the "blessed Judith" in order to show that "many women, empowered by God's grace, have performed deeds worthy of men" (1 Clem 55.3.4). It seems greatly misleading, therefore, to picture Jewish women of the first century in particular, and Jewish theology in general, in predominantly negative terms. The book of Judith—whether written by a woman or by a man—gives us a clue to a quite different tradition and situation in first-century Judaism.[43]

The Basileia Vision of Jesus as the Praxis of Inclusive Wholeness

The book of Judith mediates the atmosphere in which Jesus preached and in which the discipleship of equals originated. Jesus and several of his first followers were at first disciples of John the Baptizer and received his baptism of repentance. Jesus, however, seems to have separated from the group around John because of a prophetic-visionary experience which convinced him that Satan's power was broken, the eschatological war was won (Luke 10:18).[44] Where John announces, "The axe is laid to the root of the trees" (Matt

3:10), Jesus proclaims: "the *basileia* of God is in the midst of you" (Luke 17:21). The difference between John and Jesus is not a "break" but a shift of emphasis. While John announces God's judgment and wrath preceding the *basileia* and eschatological restitution of Israel, Jesus stresses that, in his own ministry and movement, the eschatological salvation and wholeness of Israel as the elect people of God is already experientially available. His reply to John's question, "Are you the one who is to come? . . ." underlines this experiential aspect of the *basileia* by evoking a whole range of Isaianic images:

> Go and tell John what you have seen and heard: the blind receive their sight, the lame walk, lepers are cleansed, and the deaf hear, the dead are raised up, the poor have good news preached to them. [Luke 7:22 (Q)]

This section of Q about the relationship between John and Jesus not only emphasizes that Jesus restores the humanity of people but also stresses that different interpretations of the eschatological situation result in very different lifestyles. John's lifestyle is that of an apocalyptic ascetic while Jesus is seen by people as "a glutton and a drunkard, a friend of tax collectors and sinners" (Luke 7:34 [Q]).[45] The pre-Markan collection of controversy dialogues explicitly mentions that the disciples of John and the Pharisees were fasting while the disciples of Jesus did not do so (Mark 2:18ff). The oldest stratum of the story argues that guests at a wedding feast do not fast. The experience of the *basileia's* salvation in the presence and ministry of Jesus does not allow for traditional ascetic practices. Only at a later time does the Christian community reintroduce the practice of fasting, justifying it with reference to the absence of Jesus.[46]

It is the festive table-sharing at a wedding feast, and not the *askēsis* of the "holy man," that characterizes Jesus and his movement. Its central image is that of a festive meal. The parables speak of the *basileia* of God in ever-new images of a sumptuous, glorious banquet celebration. Just as the Essenes and Pharisaic associations, the Jesus movement gathered around the table and shared their food and drink. Yet while the Pharisees sought to realize Israel's calling as a "nation of priests" by carefully observing the ritual purity of the "holy table" and by eating their meals "like priests," Jesus and his movement did not observe these purity regulations and even shared their meals with "sinners." The central symbolic actualization of the *basileia* vision of Jesus is not the cultic meal but the festive table of a royal banquet or wedding feast. This difference in emphasis was

probably one of the major conflict points between the Jesus movement and the Pharisaic movement. None of the stories told by or
about Jesus evidences the concern for ritual purity and moral holiness
so typical of other groups in Greco-Roman Palestine. While Jesus
shares their vision of Israel as the "elect people and nation of
Yahweh" (Exod 19:5f), he does not share their understanding that the
"holiness" of Temple and Torah is the locus of God's power and
presence.

Although Jesus and his movement shared the belief of all groups in
Greco-Roman Palestine that Israel is God's elect people, and were
equally united with the other groups in the hope of God's intervention on behalf of Israel, they realized that God's *basileia* was already in
their midst. Exegetes agree that it is the mark of Jesus' preaching and
ministry that he proclaimed the *basileia* of God as future and present,
eschatological vision and experiential reality.[47] This characteristic tension between future and present, between wholeness and brokenness
is generally acknowledged, even though it is interpreted or resolved
differently. In my opinion, however, this tension can only be perceived and maintained when the reference point of the tensive symbol *basileia* is the general Jewish ethos of the time, and when the
history and community of Israel is its focus. The Jesus movement in
Palestine does not totally reject the validity of Temple and Torah as
symbols of Israel's election but offers an alternative interpretation of
them by focusing on the people itself as the locus of God's power and
presence. By stressing the present possibility for Israel's wholeness,
the Jesus movement integrates prophetic-apocalyptic and wisdom
theology insofar as it fuses eschatological hope with the belief that the
God of Israel is the creator of all human beings, even the maimed, the
unclean, and the sinners.[48] Human holiness must express human
wholeness, cultic practice must not be set over and against humaniz-
ing praxis. Wholeness spells holiness and holiness manifests itself
precisely in human wholeness. Everyday life must not be measured
by the sacred holiness of the Temple and Torah, but Temple and
Torah praxis must be measured and evaluated by whether or not they
are inclusive of every person in Israel and whether they engender the
wholeness of every human being. Everydayness, therefore, can become revelatory, and the presence and power of God's sacred wholeness can be experienced in *every* human being.[49]

Since the reality of the *basileia* for Jesus spells not primarily holiness
but wholeness, the salvation of God's *basileia* is present and experientially available whenever Jesus casts out demons (Luke 11:20), heals
the sick and the ritually unclean, tells stories about the lost who are

found, of the uninvited who are invited, or of the last who will be first. The power of God's *basileia* is realized in Jesus' table community with the poor, the sinners, the tax collectors, and prostitutes—with all those who "do not belong" to the "holy people," who are somehow deficient in the eyes of the righteous. It is like dough that has been leavened, but not yet transformed into bread, like the fetus in the womb, but not yet transformed in birth to a child.[50] The future can be experienced in the healings, the inclusive discipleship, and the parabolic words of Jesus, but Jesus still hopes and expects the future inbreaking of God's *basileia*, when death, suffering, and injustice finally will be overcome and patriarchal marriage will be no more (cf. Mark 12:18–27 and parallels). Jesus' *praxis* and *vision* of the *basileia* is the mediation of God's future into the structures and experiences of his own time and people.

However, this future is mediated and promised to *all* members of Israel. No one is exempted. Everyone is invited. Women as well as men, prostitutes as well as Pharisees. The parable of the "Great Supper" (cf. Matt 22:1–14; Luke 14:16–24 [Q]; *Gosp. Thom.* log. 64) jolts the hearer into recognizing that the *basileia* includes everyone. It warns that only those who were "first" invited and then rejected the invitation will be excluded. Not the holiness of the elect but the wholeness *of all* is the central vision of Jesus.[52] Therefore, his parables also take their images from the world of women. His healings and exorcisms make women whole. His announcement of "eschatological reversal"—many who are first will be last and those last will be first (Mark 10:31; Matt 19:30; 20:16; Luke 13:30)—applies also to women and to their impairment by patriarchal structures.

That the wholeness and well-being of everyone reveals God's presence and power comes to the fore especially in those *basileia* sayings that are considered most "authentic": the beatitudes and eschatological reversal sayings, the table community of Jesus with tax collectors and sinners, Jesus' "breaking of the sabbath law," and his authoritative reinterpretation of the Torah in the antitheses. It must be noted here that I am not seeking to "distill" the most "authentic" tradition of Jesus-sayings in such a way as to separate Jesus from his own people, Israel, and his first followers. The Jesus movement is not conceivable without Jesus, of course, but it is also inconceivable without Jesus' followers. Since I am interested in laying open the *tension* points of the Jesus movement with the dominant patriarchal culture in which it took shape, it is important to see who the people are for whom the *basileia* is claimed. Such tension points should not be misconstrued as anti-Judaism, however, since Jesus and his followers were Jews and claimed their election as the Israel of God. Of course the alternative *basileia* vision of Jesus and his movement created tensions but so did those of Amos and John the Baptizer, for that matter.

The earliest gospel strata assert again and again that Jesus claimed the *basileia* for *three* distinct groups of people: (1) the destitute poor; (2) the sick and crippled; and (3) tax collectors, sinners, and prostitutes.

1. Jesus announces that the *basileia* is given to the impoverished, while Q already claims the "beatitudes" for the Jesus community. That the first beatitude promises the *basileia* to the socially impoverished of Israel is underlined by the second and third: "Blessed are those that hunger, for they shall be satisfied.[53] Blessed are those who weep now, for they shall laugh." How dire the poverty of women was may be illustrated by the story of the poor widow who "gives her whole living" to the Temple treasury. "Her whole living" was "two copper coins which make a penny" (Mark 12:41–44).[54] Most of those who are poor, who do not know where they will get food to still their hunger, who cry and hear the crying of their children, then as now, are women and children dependent on women. It is not clear whether or not the "woe" sayings against the rich (some of whom are women), which parallel the beatitudes in Q, are original or were added later.[55] Nevertheless they underline the eschatological reversal brought about by the *basileia*. The pre-Markan reversal saying Mark 10:25 also emphasizes that such an eschatological warning was addressed to the rich very early: It stresses that it is *impossible* for someone who is rich to enter the *basileia* of God. This eschatological reversal is also announced in the pre-Lukan song of Mary, the Galilean:

> God has put down the mighty from their thrones,
> and exalted those of low degree;
> God has filled the hungry with good things,
> and has sent the rich empty away. [Luke 1:52f][56]

Thus the oldest traditions elaborate concretely Jesus' reply to John that "the poor have good news preached to them." Those who are dying of starvation and are desperate because they see no way out of their poverty into the future are promised the *basileia*. The promise of the *basileia* to the beggared and destitute affirms that God will make their cause God's own concern. God is on their side against all those who trample down their rights. The understanding that God is on the side of the impoverished has its roots in the covenant of God with Israel. Even though in antiquity—as today—poverty was seen as a personal failure (thus justifying despisal of the poor), in Israel poverty was understood as injustice. Since Yahweh is the owner of the land and has given it into the care of *all* the people, the poor of Israel are cheated out of their rightful inheritance. Therefore, the prophets never tire of announcing that God is on the side of the poor and will take up their cause (Deut 15:7–18; Amos 2:6–8). The promise of the *basileia* to the poor, among whom are also women, should therefore not be misconstrued as a future consolation prize but as proclamation of the poor's rights and of God's justice. In other words, the poor do have a share in God's future, while the rich and prosperous do not because they are consuming their inheritance now. Neither the magnificat of Mary nor the beatitudes speak of punishment for the rich but rather of eschatological reversal. This life and the life of the *basileia* are seen as a continuous whole.

The Q community added a fourth beatitude that refers all the beatitudes to the Christian community.[57] It pronounces blessing for those members of the Jesus movement who are persecuted, reviled, hated and excluded from their Jewish communities. Those who have been declared as no longer belonging to the elect people of Israel are told that they will share in the eschatological salvation. However it is clear at this stage that the members of the Jesus movement are still *socially* poor, destitute, and starving. Only Matthew's beatitudes expand the concept beyond social poverty to a religious attitude that can be shared by poor and rich.

2. The *basileia* of God is experientially available in the healing activity of Jesus. While there is much discussion as to whether miracles are scientifically possible and whether the miracle stories are historically "authentic," there is insufficient attention paid to the vision of being human that is realized by the power of God active in Jesus. The *basileia* vision of Jesus makes people whole, healthy, cleansed, and strong. It restores people's humanity and life. The salvation of the *basileia* is not confined to the soul but spells wholeness for the total person in her/his social relations.[58] The exorcisms of Jesus acknowledge that there are dehumanizing powers in this world that are not under our control. However, Jesus is not so much concerned with their polluting power as with their debilitating dehumanizing power. What we today call oppressive power structures and dehumanizing power systems, apocalyptic language calls "evil spirits," "Satan," "Beelzebul," demons. Therefore, if Jesus in the power of God casts out evil spirits and overcomes the evil powers that keep people in bondage, then the liberating power of God, "the *basileia* [,] has come (*ephthasen*) upon you" (Luke 11:20).[59] If the pre-Lukan tradition identifies Mary of Magdala as a woman "from whom he has cast out seven

demons" (cf. Mark 16:9 and Luke 8:2), then she is not thereby characterized as a "sinner," but as someone who has experienced the unlimited (seven) liberating power of the *basileia* in her own life.

Those who were maimed, crippled, and sick were either poor or
became impoverished through death and illness. The story of the
woman "who had a flow of blood for twelve years" (Mark 5:25–34)
shows this dramatically.[60] "She had spent all that she had" by con-
sulting "many physicians" but "she was not better but rather grew
worse." These few terse words narrate forcefully the economic im-
poverishment of the incurably ill. However, this woman's predicament was not just incurable illness but also permanent uncleanness.
She was not only unclean herself, but polluted everyone and everything with which she came in contact (Lev 15:19–31). For twelve years
this woman had been "polluted" and barred from the congregation of
the "holy people." No wonder she risked financial ruin and economic
destitution to become healthy, and therefore cultically clean, again.
Jesus calls her "daughter" of Israel and announces: Go in peace, that
is, be happy and whole (*shalom*). You are healed.

This story was probably interlinked with the story of the daughter
of Jairus, one of the rulers of the synagogue, not only because of the
catchword *twelve* but also because it proclaims the same understanding of wholeness and holiness. Jesus touches the dead girl and thus
becomes "unclean" (cf. Num 19:11–13). Yet the power of the *basileia*
does not rest in holiness and cultic purity. The girl gets up and walks,
she rises to womanhood (Jewish girls became marriageable at
twelve). The young woman who begins to menstruate, like the older
woman who experiences menstruation as a pathological condition,
are both "given" new life. The life-creating powers of women manifested in "the flow of blood" are neither "bad" nor cut off in death
but are "restored" so that women can "go and live in *shalom*," in the
eschatological well-being and happiness of God.[61]

The synoptic sabbath healings of Jesus present a special difficulty to
exegetes, because they seem to narrate occasions where Jesus "will-
fully" breaks the sabbath commandment of the Torah.[62] Exegetes are
at pains to explain that the pre-Markan (Mark 3:1–5) and pre-Lukan
(Luke 14:1–6) sabbath healings attempt to elucidate Jesus' general
theological principle that "to do good," "to heal," and "to save life"
overrules the sabbath Torah. Yet such a principle would have been
conceded by all the other Jewish interpreters of the law who agreed,
more or less, that one is allowed on the sabbath to "save the life" of
either humans or animals. Moreover, the healing stories do not support the general theological maxim implied in the question of the

controversy dialogue. The man with the withered hand as well as the man who had dropsy were not critically ill and easily could have waited one day longer to be healed. The offensiveness of the sabbath healings lies precisely in the fact that Jesus breaks the sabbath law even though it is not called for at all. To have him do so merely to teach his opponents a lesson appears to me to be later Christian interpretation.

I would suggest that Luke 13:10–17, the story about the "double bent woman," rather then Mark 3:1–5, represents the oldest tradition of the sabbath healings. Exegetes rule this assumption out on form-critical grounds when they argue that the controversy-dialogue in this story is not interwoven with the controversy of the scholastic teaching dialogue, but only later appended to it. Yet it is possible that the healing story (Luke 13:10–13) was originally independent and was expanded to a dialogue at a later stage. The dialogue does not argue that "in order to save life" Jesus broke the sabbath Torah—the woman was bent double for eighteen years—but it argues that he did so in order to make her whole and "free her from her infirmity." The reference point is not that one was allowed to save an animal in danger on the sabbath but that it was necessary to water ox and ass on the sabbath. To be sure, some Jews might have disputed such a "lax" interpretation of the sabbath Torah although it must have occurred. However, what is "disturbing" here is not a "lax" or "strict" interpretation of the law, but the fact that Jesus' response seems not to have heard the objection of the "ruler of the synagogue," whose precise point was that there were six days on which one could come to be healed, leaving no need to "come on the sabbath day to be healed." The dialogue startles and leads us to seek for another "clue" to understand the story. It forces us to ask, why did Israel observe the sabbath?

Sabbath observance was the ritual symbolization of Israel's election as a holy people since the exile. In the pre-Christian book of *Jubilees*, which also had great influence in Qumran, the sabbath is kept in heaven and on earth as a sign that the Jews are God's people and Yahweh is their God. Israel keeps sabbath by abstaining from all work, and so "to eat and to drink, and to bless Him who has created all things as he has blessed and sanctified unto Himself a peculiar people above all peoples" (*Jub* 2:20f). While his opponents insist on a complete "rest from work" on the sabbath day (cf. Luke 13:14), Jesus made it possible for the woman and the people to fulfill the *purpose* of the sabbath rest from work: the praise of God, the creator of the world and the liberator of this people. The woman who "was made straight" "praised God," while the common people (*ochlos*) were happy (*echairen*) about all the "glorious things that came into being through him. Therefore, the woman can truly be called "a daughter of Abraham" (cf. Luke 3:8 [Q]: children), a full member of the sanctified people of Israel.

A last aspect of this healing story is significant. The illness of the woman was caused by Satan. This daughter of Israel was in a bondage that deformed her whole bodily being for eighteen years. In helping her, Jesus freed her from Satan's power and restored God's creation. Jesus acted according to the *intention* of the sabbath Torah. Therefore, joy and praise are appropriate. Jesus' sabbath healing is not an offense against the sanctified people of Israel, but rather enables the daughter of Abraham, together with the community of angels, to celebrate God, the creator of all people and the liberator of the chosen people of Israel.

This interpretation is confirmed by the pre-Markan controversy dialogue Mark 2:23–28.[63] The statement that "the Human Being [Son of Man] is lord even of the sabbath" (2:28) probably is a later addition by the church that transmitted this story. The saying that "the sabbath was made for human persons but not humans for the sabbath" is most likely an original saying of Jesus that is the climax of the whole story. In this story it is not Jesus but his disciples who are accused of breaking the sabbath. It is not illness but hunger that leads them to do so. Jesus points to David and his followers who not only broke the sabbath law but ate sacred bread (although they were not priests). While the reference to Scripture reasons with the Pharisees, Jesus' word in v. 27 stresses the deepest intention of the sabbath law: it is created so that people can praise, in festive eating and drinking, the goodness of Israel's creator God. The disciples of Jesus, who, like the very poor, have no food but the ears of grain that they pluck and eat, do fulfill the intentions of the Torah. They keep the sabbath, that is, they eat to the praise of God, although they have almost nothing with which to do so. The story then tells what it means that the "sabbath came into being for human beings, and not humans for the sake of the sabbath." It would be misleading to insist on only one half of the sabbath commandment—the command not to work—while perverting the other—eating and drinking in honor of God—by letting people starve.[64]

3. While the sick and possessed are easily seen as belonging to the poor and starving to whom the *basileia* is promised, exegetes usually see the moral but not the social predicament of tax collectors, sinners, and prostitutes. They almost unanimously agree that the historical

Jesus and the earliest Jesus movement in Palestine associated with tax collectors, sinners, and prostitutes, although we have only scant traditions for this information.[65] Yet we can still trace redactional tendencies in the traditioning process and in the Gospels that seek to make this accusation against the Jesus movement more understandable and acceptable. Jesus' movement and praxis included everyone. Even prostitutes and tax collectors shared in its community gathered around the table. This historical praxis is still reflected in the Markan (2:15) and Lukan (15:2b) redactional overlay as well as in the Q tradition (Matt 11:19; Luke 7:34). It also comes to the fore in the provocative saying: "Truly I say to you, the tax collectors and harlots go into the *basileia* of God before you" (Matt 21:31 [SM]).

Usually the designations tax collectors, sinners, and prostitutes are understood in a moralizing sense. Yet sinner is not an inclusive concept for tax collectors and prostitutes. The tradition, especially in Luke, shows the tendency to identify the prostitute with sinner, but these two notions are not interchangable. It is also important to recognize that in a patriarchal society prostitution is the worst form of "pollution" (sin) for a woman, although prostitution is an essential function of patriarchy. Since prophetic times the notion "prostitute" had acquired religious theological overtones in Israel, insofar as the "harlot" was the paradigm of the "unfaithful people Israel" and of their "whoredom" with other gods in pagan idolatry. That the harlots will enter into the *basileia* ahead of the faithful and righteous Israelite is outrageous, to say the least.

The phrase "tax collectors, sinners, and prostitutes," however, characterizes not just a morally reprehensible group of people but even more a class so destitute that they must engage in "dishonorable" professions in order to survive.[66] Although because of Luke 19 we have an image of tax collectors as "rich," most of the tax collectors who did the actual work were impoverished, or were slaves employed by a "tax agency," and quickly dismissed if problems arose. Palestine was plagued by a very oppressive tax system: Roman tax agents gathered, as direct taxes, the produce and toll tax; servants of the high-priestly aristocracy of Jerusalem collected the tithes as their direct share in the harvest, leaving very little for the country priests and levites; indirect taxes, import and export taxes, and taxes on all produce and leases in Jerusalem were farmed out to the highest bidders. Since the custom and toll taxes could be collected, even when one was merely going from one village to the other, harassment by tax collectors was not only annoying but also very expensive, especially since tax collectors had to take in more than the official fee if they wanted to make a living. Levi was probably such a subordinate tax collector because he actually sat at the tollbooth (Mark 2:14). Throughout antiquity tax collectors were likened to robbers and thieves, and treated with contempt for their coarseness. Their harassment and extortion were notorious. In Judaism tax collectors were, in a special way, "unclean," and often hated as agents of Rome's colonial power.

As is the case today, so in antiquity most prostitutes were impoverished unskilled women.[67] Found mostly in the cities, they often lived in brothels or houses connected with a temple. Prostitutes usually were slaves, daughters who had been sold or rented out by their parents, wives who were rented out by their husbands, poor women, exposed girls, the divorced and widowed, single mothers, captives of war or piracy, women bought for soldiers—in short, women who could not derive a livelihood from their position in the patriarchal family or those who had to work for a living but could not engage in "middle"- or "upper"-class professions. In Palestine, torn by war, colonial taxation, and famine, the number of such women must have been great.

The notion of "sinner" can have a whole range of meanings. It can characterize people who did not keep the Torah, whether in the stricter Sadducaic or the wider Pharisaic senses; those who, in our terms, were criminals (in Israel, political and religious law were one and the same); or those who worked in disreputable jobs such as fruit-sellers, swineherders, garlic peddlers, bartenders, seamen, public announcers, tax collectors, pimps, prostitutes, servants, and other service occupations, all of which were deemed "polluting" or "unclean" by theologians and interpreters of the Torah. All categories of sinners were in one way or another marginal people who were badly paid and often abused. The few "rich" tax collectors or prostitutes were exceptions and, as such, proved the oppressive character of the societal-religious system.

The story of the woman who washed Jesus' feet (Luke 7:36–50) has a very complex tradition-history that is far from being adequately resolved.[68] It seems that already at a pre-Lukan stage of the tradition, some elements in the story of the "woman anointing Jesus' head" (Mark 14:3–11; John 12:1–8) had been taken over into the narrative. Such elements are probably the "alabaster flask of ointment" (7:37c), the anointing (7:38c), and the name of the Pharisee, Simon. Moreover, the parable might originally have been told independently, but if such was the case it must have been taken into the story at a very early stage. It seems, however, that the contrast between the Pharisee and the woman, as well as the emphasis on the forgiveness of sins, is the work of redaction, since later Christian authors emphasize the enmity between the Pharisees and Jesus' disciples. Luke especially stresses over and over again that "Jesus called sinners to repentance." Therefore, it was probably he who characterized the woman as "a woman of the city, a sinner," that is, a prostitute.

The original story is neither a story about a rich prostitute nor about a prostitute at all. The relationship between Jesus and the Pharisee is that between friends and colleagues, and Jesus is assumed to be "a prophet" as we see in the earliest Q christology. I would therefore suggest that the original story may have read as follows:

> One of the Pharisees asked Jesus to eat with him and Jesus went to the Pharisee's house and sat at table. And behold a woman having learned that he was sitting at table in the Pharisee's house, and standing behind him at his feet weeping, began to wet his feet with her tears and wiped them with the hair of her head, and kissed his feet. Now when the Pharisee who had invited him saw it he said to himself: "If this man were a prophet, he would have known what sort of a woman this is who is touching him; that she is a sinner." In response Jesus said to him: "I have something to say to you," and he answered, "What is it, Teacher?" "A certain creditor had two debtors; one owed five hundred denarii, and the other fifty. When they could not pay he remitted their debt, graciously. Now which of them will love him more?" And turning to the woman he said to her: "Your sins are forgiven. Go in peace (*shalom*)."

Some such story must have circulated very early among the Jesus disciples, probably claiming Jesus himself for its message. The story does not say what kind of sinner the woman was—she could have been a criminal, a ritually unclean or morally bad person, a prostitute, or simply the "wife of a notorious sinner." That the early Christian movement soon saw both this story and the story of the woman with a flow of blood as "baptismal" stories is evident from the formulaic statement "your faith has saved you" which alludes to early Christian baptismal tradition. That this statement is a later addition in both stories is obvious, however, since "the faith" of the women was not mentioned previously. The stories assert, then, that Jesus and his movement invited into their table community not only women but even notorious and well-known sinners. Sinners, prostitutes, beggars, tax collectors, the ritually polluted, the crippled, and the impoverished—in short, the scum of Palestinian society—constituted the majority of Jesus' followers. These are the last who have become the first, the starving who have been satisfied, the uninvited who have been invited. And many of these were women.

But how could Jesus have been a prophet of God, and his movement a prophetic movement in Israel making the *basileia* experientially available, when this inclusiveness ran counter to everything previously thought to be the will of God revealed in Torah and Temple? Was it not Beelzebul/Satan in the guise of God's prophet who was at work? That the praxis of Jesus and his disciples offended the religious sensibilities not only of their fellow Jews but also of later Christians is apparent when one examines the understanding of sin and forgiveness. While the earliest Jesus traditions eschew any understanding of the ministry and death of Jesus in cultic terms as atonement for sins, it was precisely this interpretation which soon took root in some segments of the early Christian movement. Yet such an interpretation of Jesus' death as atonement for sins is much later than is generally assumed in New Testament scholarship.[69] The notion of atoning sacrifice does not express the Jesus movement's understanding and experience of God but is a later interpretation of the violent death of Jesus in cultic terms. The God of Jesus is not a God who demands atonement and whose wrath needs to be placated by human sacrifice or ritual. C. Ochs has elaborated that the patriarchal God of Abraham and of Christians is judgmental and demands the sacrifice of the only son.[70] Although such an interpretation of the death of Jesus is soon found in early Christian theology, the death of Jesus was not a sacrifice and was not demanded by God but brought about by the Romans.

The Sophia-God of Jesus and the Discipleship of Women

The Jesus movement articulates a quite different understanding of God because it had experienced in the praxis of Jesus a God who called not Israel's righteous and pious but its religiously deficient and its social underdogs. In the ministry of Jesus God is experienced as all-inclusive love, letting the sun shine and the rain fall equally on the righteous and on sinners (Matt 5:45). This God is a God of graciousness and goodness who accepts everyone and brings about justice and well-being for everyone without exception.[71] The creator God accepts all members of Israel, and especially the impoverished, the crippled, the outcast, the sinners and prostitutes, as long as they are prepared to engage in the perspective and power of the *basileia*. Conversely, it is stressed: "No one is good but God alone" (Mark 10:18b; Luke 18:19b).

1. This inclusive graciousness and goodness of God is spelled out again and again in the parables.[72] It has already been shown that the parable of the creditor who freely remits the debts of those who cannot pay articulates this gracious goodness of God by stressing that women, even public sinners, can be admitted to the Jesus movement in the conviction that "they will love more." The double simile of the shepherd searching for the lost sheep and of the woman searching for her lost silver coin, in all likelihood was already taken over by Luke from Q in its present form.[73] The Q community used these similes to reply to the accusation that "Jesus receives sinners and eats with them" (Luke 15:2; cf. Mark 2:16b for a similar accusation), justifying it with the application that "in heaven there is joy over the sinner who repents." The original form of the double story was probably parable rather than simile, since it did not include this explicit "application" to the situation of the community. Like the original story, this application stresses the joy of "finding the lost" but no longer emphasizes the search. As Jesus might have told this parable, it would have jolted the hearer into recognition: this is how God acts—like the man searching for his lost sheep, like the woman tirelessly sweeping for her lost coin. Jesus thus images God as a woman searching for one of her ten coins, as a woman looking for money that is terribly important to her. In telling the parable of the woman desperately searching for her money, Jesus articulates God's own concern, a concern that determines Jesus' own praxis for table community with sinners and outcasts. The parable then challenges the hearer: do you agree with the attitude of God expressed in the woman's search for her lost "capital"?

The *basileia* parable of "the laborers in the vineyard" (Matt 20:1–16) articulates the equality of all rooted in the gracious goodness of God.[74] Its *Sitz im Leben* is similar to that of the parable of the lost sheep and the lost coin, namely, the Jesus movement's table sharing with outcasts. The social world of the parable is that of a first-century Palestinian landowner who, in order to save money, hired laborers day by day and hour by hour during the harvest. To a contemporary hearer of this parable the householder would clearly be God, and the vineyard, Israel. The contrast between the parable's world and the actual labor practices and exploitation of the poor laborers—daily or hourly—underlines the gracious goodness and justice of God. Those who are last receive a whole day's payment. Yet the story does not end here, for it also expresses the offense taken by some of the first hired. The householder had treated them justly in giving them the promised payment for the day's work. If the last had received less they would have been satisfied. But instead of arguing for "just wages" and labor practices for all, those first hired grumble because the householder "has made the last equal to themselves." Jesus' parable thus startles his hearers into the recognition that God's gracious goodness establishes equality among all of us, righteous and sinner, rich and poor, men and women, Pharisees and Jesus' disciples. It challenges the hearer to solidarity and equality with "the last" in Israel. The all-inclusive goodness of Israel's God calls forth human equality and solidarity. The tensive symbol *basileia* of God evokes in ever new images a realization of the gracious goodness of Israel's God and the equality and solidarity of the people of God. A very similar understanding of equality is expressed in one of the earliest statements of the contemporary women's liberation movement:

> We define the best interests of women as the best interests of the poorest, most insulted, most despised, most abused woman on earth. . . . Until Everywoman is free, no woman will be free.[75]

Radical feminism has rediscovered the "equality from below" espoused by the Jesus movement in Palestine without recognizing its religious roots.

The earliest Jesus traditions perceive this God of gracious goodness in a woman's *Gestalt* as divine *Sophia* (wisdom).[76] The very old saying, "Sophia is justified [or vindicated] by all her children" (Luke 7:35[Q]) probably had its setting in Jesus' table community with tax collectors, prostitutes, and sinners, as well. The Sophia-God of Jesus recognizes all Israelites as her children and she is proven "right" by all of them. The Q community qualifies this saying by stressing that the most eminent of the children of Sophia are John and Jesus. Only Matthew identifies Sophia with Jesus.[77] It is now Jesus-Sophia who becomes justified by her deeds.

Jewish wisdom theology developed in Egypt, but it also permeated apocalyptic literature and can be found in Qumran theology. From the third century B.C.E. on, Jewish wisdom theology celebrated God's gracious goodness in creating the world and electing Israel as the people among whom the divine presence dwells in the female *Gestalt* of divine *Sophia*. Although Jewish (and Christian) theology speaks about God in male language and images, it nevertheless insists that such language and images are not adequate "pictures" of the divine, and that human language and experience are not capable of beholding or expressing God's reality. The second commandment and the unspeakable holiness of God's name are very concrete expressions of this insistence. To fix God to a definite form and man-made image would mean idolatry. Classical prophetic theology, often in abusive language, polemicized against the pagan idols and thus rejected goddess worship, but it did not do so in defense of a male God and a patriarchal idol. By rejecting all other gods, prophetic theology insisted on the *oneness* of Israel's God and of God's creation. It therefore rejected the myth of the "divine couple," and thus repudiated masculinity and feminity as ultimate, absolute principles. But in doing so, it did not quite escape the patriarchal understanding of God, insofar as it transferred the image of the divine marriage to the relationship of Yahweh and Israel who is seen as his wife or bride.

Unlike classical prophecy, wisdom theology is not characterized by fear of the goddess in its apologetic "defense" of monotheism.[78] Rather, it is inspired by a positive attempt to speak in the language of its own culture and to integrate elements of its "goddess cult," especially of Isis worship, into Jewish monotheism. As such it does theology as "reflective mythology," that is, it uses elements of goddess-language in order to speak of the gracious goodness of Israel's God. A well-known prayer to Isis proclaims that all the different nations and peoples use divine names familiar to them. They call on the goddess, doing so because they know that Isis, being *one*, is all.

Divine Sophia is Israel's God in the language and *Gestalt* of the goddess.[79] Sophia is called sister, wife, mother, beloved, and teacher. She is the leader on the way, the preacher in Israel, the taskmaster and creator God. She seeks people, finds them on the road, invites them to dinner. She offers life, rest, knowledge, and salvation to those who accept her. She dwells in Israel and officiates in the sanctuary. She send prophets and apostles and makes those who accept her "friends of God." "She is but one but yet can do everything, herself unchanging. She makes all things new" (Wis 7:27). Wisdom sought a dwelling place among humanity, but found none. Therefore she has withdrawn again and "has taken her seat among the angels" (1 *Enoch* 42:1–2). Sophia is described as "all-powerful, intelligent, unique" (Wis 7:22). She is a people-loving spirit (*philanthrōpon pneuma*, 1:6) who shares the throne of God (9:10). She is an initiate (*mystis*) of God's knowledge, an associate in God's works, and emanation of the God of light, who lives in *symbiōsis* with God (8:3–4), an image of God's goodness (7:26). One can sense here how much the language struggles to describe Sophia as divine (without falling prey to ditheism). Goddess-language is employed to speak about the *one* God of

Israel whose gracious goodness is divine Sophia. Jewish wisdom theology, as distinct from gnostic theology, has successfully struggled against the danger of divine dimorphism. It did not, however, avoid anthropological dualism, as the negative characterization of women in wisdom and apocalyptic writings indicates. It thereby opened up the possibility for projecting such anthropological dualism into divine reality and for rejecting the creator God of Judaism.

While cosmological wisdom mythology has influenced the earliest christological expressions of the Christian missionary movement, its traces—though significant—are scant in the traditions of the Jesus movement. The earliest Palestinian theological remembrances and interpretations of Jesus' life and death understand him as Sophia's messenger and later as Sophia herself. The earliest Christian theology is sophialogy. It was possible to understand Jesus' ministry and death in terms of God-Sophia, because Jesus probably understood himself as the prophet and child of Sophia. As Sophia's messenger he calls "all who labor hard and are heavy laden" and promises them rest and *shalom*. He proclaims that the discipleship (the "yoke") of Sophia is easy and her load light to bear (Matt 11:28–30). Such a sophialogical context also makes more comprehensible the difficult saying of Q (Matt 12:32; Luke 12:10) that blasphemy against Jesus, the paradigmatic Human Being, will be forgiven, but not blasphemy against the Holy Spirit. A statement against Jesus can be forgiven, but a statement against the "child" or messenger of Sophia-Spirit cannot, because it means a rejection of the gracious goodness of God.

This theological reflection understood John and Jesus as the prophets and apostles who stand in the succession of Sophia's messengers. Like these others, they are persecuted and killed: "Therefore also the Wisdom of God said: 'I will send them prophets and apostles, some of whom they will kill and persecute'" (Luke 11:49 [Q?]). In a moving passage Sophia laments the murder of her envoys, her prophets, who are sent in every generation to proclaim the gracious goodness and justice of God to the people of Israel:

> O Jerusalem, Jerusalem, you slay the prophets and stone those who are sent to you. How often have I wanted to gather your children as a mother bird collects her young under her wings, but you refused me. [Luke 13:34 (Q)][80]

This saying likens the ministry of Sophia-Jesus to that of a hen gathering her very own brood under her wings. But the gentleness and care of Sophia is rejected.

To sum up, the Palestinian Jesus movement understands the ministry and mission of Jesus as that of the prophet and child of Sophia sent to announce that God is the God of the poor and heavy laden, of the outcasts and those who suffer injustice. As child of Sophia he stands in a long line and succession of prophets sent to gather the children of Israel to their gracious Sophia-God. Jesus' execution, like John's, results from his mission and commitment as prophet and emissary of the Sophia-God who holds open a future for the poor and outcast and offers God's gracious goodness to *all* children of Israel without exception. The Sophia-God of Jesus does not need atonement or sacrifices. Jesus' death is not willed by God but is the result of his all-inclusive praxis as Sophia's prophet. This understanding of the suffering and execution of Jesus in terms of prophetic sophialogy is expressed in the difficult saying which integrates the wisdom and *basileia* traditions of the Jesus movement: "The *basileia* of God suffers violence from the days of John the Baptist until now and is hindered by men of violence" (Matt 11:12). The suffering and death of Jesus, like that of John and all the other prophets sent to Israel before him, are not required in order to atone for the sins of the people in the face of an absolute God, but are the result of violence against the envoys of Sophia who proclaim God's unlimited goodness and the equality and election of *all* her children in Israel.

2. This reality of God-Sophia spelled out in the preaching, healings, exorcisms, and inclusive table community of Jesus called forth a circle of disciples who were to continue what Jesus did. Sophia, the God of Jesus, wills the wholeness and humanity of everyone and therefore enables the Jesus movement to become a "discipleship of equals." They are called to one and the same praxis of inclusiveness and equality lived by Jesus-Sophia. Like Jesus, they are sent to announce to everyone in Israel the presence of the *basileia*, as God's gracious future, among the impoverished, the starving, the tax collectors, sinners, and prostitutes. Like Jesus, his disciples are sent to make the *basileia* experientially available in their healings and exorcisms, by restoring the humanity and wholeness of Sophia-God's children. The majority of them were not rich, like the Cynic philosophers who could reject property and cultural positions in order "to become free from possessions." Rather, they were called from the impoverished, starving, and "heavy laden" countrypeople. They were tax collectors, sinners, women, children, fishers, housewives, those who had been healed from their infirmities or set free from bondage to their evil spirits. What they offered was not an alternative lifestyle but an alternative ethos: they were those without a future, but now they had

hope again; they were the "outcast" and marginal people in their society, but now they had community again; they were despised and downtrodden, but now they had dignity and self-confidence as God-Sophia's beloved children; they were, because of life's circumstances and social injustices, sinners with no hope to share in the holiness and presence of God, but now they were heirs of the *basileia,* experiencing the gracious goodness of God who had made them equal to the holy and righteous in Israel. As such they came together in the discipleship of equals and shared their meager bread with those who came to hear the gospel. (The stories about the miraculous feedings of the multitudes not only have eucharistic overtones but also speak of the worry and concern of Jesus' disciples that they had so little food to share.) They stand in the succession of Sophia-prophets, announcing *shalom* to Israel. As the disciples of Jesus-Sophia they continue what Jesus did, namely, making the reality of God's *basileia* and the all-inclusive goodness of the Sophia-God of Jesus experientially available.[81]

Whereas the Q traditions limit the prophetic ministry of Jesus and his movement to the people of Israel, the Galilean Jesus movement seems to have accepted gentiles at a very early date. The pre-Markan controversy dialogues Mark 2:1–3:6, as well as the pre-Markan miracle collection utilized in Mark 4:35–8:10, seem to address the question of inclusive table community with gentiles as an inner-Christian problem. The Galilean "missionaries" stress that many sinners were sitting down at table with Jesus and his disciples "for there were many who followed him" (Mark 2:15).[82] Sinners now meant not those Jews who in one way or the other had committed an offense against the Torah, but, as is often the case in Jewish discourse, it meant "pagans." Thus at an early stage some members of the Galilean Jesus movement justified their inclusive table community with pagans by reference to Jesus' own praxis and the fact that many non-Jews had become disciples of Jesus.

They do this, not so much as a defense against the Pharisees but rather against the criticism of other Christians, since the controversy collection evidences an inner-Christian debate. That such an inclusive table sharing of both Jews and gentiles was very controversial among Christians is obvious from Paul's statement (Gal 2:11–14) that Peter the Galilean had table community with gentile Christians in Antioch but ceased to do so when he was attacked. He and other Jewish Christians reversed themselves when they were under attack by some followers of James from Jerusalem. The conversion of the centurion Cornelius in Acts 10:1–11:18 reflects the same debate about ritual uncleanliness. After Peter had baptized the Roman's whole house he went up to Jerusalem and was attacked by the "circumcision party" (Acts 11:2f): "Why did you go to the uncircumcised [i.e., pagans] and eat with them?" Peter justifies his table sharing with gentile Christians by citing a heavenly vision in which he was directed to eat unclean food.

The pre-Markan story about the healing of the Gerasene demoniac (Mark 5:1–20) makes the same point but with a different theological-historical argument: it was Jesus himself who liberated the gentiles from their "unclean" spirits. Jesus did not ask him to stay "with him" but commanded him to proclaim to his friends the "great mercy" of the Lord (5:18–20). The *Sitz im Leben* of this strange exorcism story is, therefore, not the missionary preaching to gentiles but the inner-Christian debate over the mission to pagans and table sharing between them and Jewish Christians.

The same difficult problem is discussed theologically in the pre-Markan miracle story in Mark 7:24–30.[83] Surprisingly, the major theologian and spokesperson for such a table sharing with gentiles is a woman. As distinct from all other controversy dialogues, Jesus does not have the last word. Rather, the woman's argument prevails over that of Jesus. The parabolic saying of Jesus against the admission of gentiles to the community of Jesus provokes the intelligent retort of the woman. She takes up Jesus' parabolic image of the "table-children-housedogs" and uses it to argue against him. The woman "wins" the contest because Jesus, convinced by her argument (*dia touton ton logon*), liberates her daughter from the demon.

Except for the introduction in v. 24a and the addition in v. 27 (the children *first*), the story is a unified pre-Markan composition. If it was told together with the exorcism story of the unclean Gerasene demoniac, then these stories use the *example* of Jesus against those who use a *saying* of Jesus to justify a strict prohibition against the gentile mission. Thus the enigmatic saying in Matt 7:6 warns not to give food offered in sacrifice (and therefore holy) to dogs, and not to give pearls to swine. Since dogs and swine were considered unclean animals they could be used figuratively to characterize pagans. This saying ascribed to Jesus, then, argues that the gospel of the *basileia* which is compared to a pearl in Matt 13:45 (and the "holy" table sharing among Christians) should not be given to gentiles for fear they might misuse it.

If Mark 7:24a is Markan redactional introduction, then the original story is located in Galilee. The woman is characterized ethically and culturally as a gentile. Her daughter (her future?) is in bondage to evil and she expects liberation from Jesus. The Greek verb *chortasthēnai* ("become satisfied") connects the story with the two messianic pre-Markan feeding miracles, insofar as this verb is only found in Mark here and in 6:42; 8:4, 8).[84] The feeding miracles have strong eucharistic overtones which are toned down by Mark. The argument, then, that the children (Israel) should be fed and that their food should not be taken from them and given to the dogs (gentiles) is countered by the woman by referring to the messianic abundance of Christian table community. The gracious goodness of the God of Jesus is abundant enough to satisfy not only the Jews but also the gentiles. The power of the *basileia* liberates not only the "children" of Israel but also the woman-child who, as a female and as a gentile, is doubly polluted and subject to the "bondage" of ritual impurity.

If John 4:1–42 reworks a traditional mission legend about a woman's primary role in the beginnings of the Christian community in Samaria,[85] then there is evidence from two different strata of the gospel tradition that women were determinative for the extension of the Jesus movement to non-Israelites. Women were the first non-Jews to become members of the Jesus movement. Although the Syrophoenician respects the primacy of the "children of Israel," she nevertheless makes a theological argument against limiting the inclusive messianic table community of Jesus to Israel alone. That such a theological argument is placed in the mouth of a woman is a sign of the historical leadership women had in opening up Jesus' movement and community to "gentile 'sinners'" (Gal 2:15b).

This historical development was of utmost significance for the beginnings of Christianity. Women who had experienced the gracious goodness of Jesus' God were leaders in expanding the Jesus movement in Galilee and in developing a theological argument from the Jesus traditions for why pagans should have access to the power of Jesus' God and a share in the superabundance of the messianic table community. By challenging the Galilean Jesus movement to extend its table sharing and make the *basileia's* power and future experientially available also to gentiles, these women safeguarded the inclusive discipleship of equals called forth by Jesus. The Syrophoenician woman whose adroit argument opened up a future of freedom and wholeness for her daughter has also become the historically-still-visible advocate of such a future for gentiles. She has become the apostolic "foremother" of all gentile Christians.

3. Galilean women were not only decisive for the extension of the Jesus movement to gentiles but also for the very continuation of this movement after Jesus' arrest and execution. Jesus' Galilean women

disciples did not flee after his arrest but stayed in Jerusalem for his execution and burial. These Galilean women were also the first to articulate their experience of the powerful goodness of God who did not leave the crucified Jesus in the grave but raised him from the dead. The early Christian confession that "Jesus the Nazarene who was executed on the cross was raised" is, according to the pre-Markan resurrection story of Mark 16:1–6, 8a,[86] revealed in a vision first to the Galilean women disciples of Jesus.

In all likelihood, the Galilean disciples of Jesus fled after his arrest from Jerusalem and went back home to Galilee. Because of their visionary-ecstatic experiences, the women who remained in the capital came to the conviction that God had vindicated Jesus and his ministry. They, therefore, were empowered to continue the movement and work of Jesus, the risen Lord.[87] They probably sought to gather together the dispersed disciples and friends of Jesus who lived in and around Jerusalem—women disciples like Mary, Martha of Bethany, the woman who had anointed Jesus, the mother of John Mark who had a house in Jerusalem, or Mary, the mother of Jesus, as well as such male disciples as Lazarus, Nicodemus, or the "beloved" disciple. Some of these women probably also moved back, very soon, to Galilee, their native country. Such a reconstruction of the events after the death and resurrection of Jesus is historically plausible, since it might have been easier for the women of the Jesus movement to go "underground" than the men. By keeping alive the good news about the manifestation of God's life-giving power in Jesus of Nazareth, among the followers and friends of Jesus, the Galilean women continued the movement initiated by Jesus. Mary of Magdala was the most prominent of the Galilean disciples, because according to tradition she was the first one to receive a vision of the resurrected Lord.

Two different pre-Gospel traditions transmit names of Galilean women disciples. Although their names differ, Mary of Magdala seems to have been the leader among them, since she is usually mentioned first. The names vary in both the Palestinian (?) pre-Lukan and pre-Markan lists. However, Hengel has observed the tendency to group the women's names into groups of three, similar to the special groups of three among the twelve (Peter, James, John) and the leaders of the Jerusalem community (James the brother of the Lord, Cephas, and John). The membership in such a group of three, and the sequence of the names in it, indicates a preeminence in the latter community.[88] In Luke 8:3 the special Lukan source mentions Joanna, the wife of Herod's steward, who is characterized as a woman with higher social standing. How important she was for Luke is evident from his insertion of her name into the Markan list in Luke 24:10. Yet it is likely that Luke added her name to the orginal list because of his interest in wealthy women, as evident in Luke 8:1–3 and Acts.

Hengel concludes his article by noting that "the message of Jesus must have had a special impact on the women in Israel,"[89] but he does not explain why this was the case. We have seen that the Sophia-God of Jesus made possible the invitation of women to the discipleship of equals. However, one could object that the Q traditions not only image the gracious goodness of the God of Jesus as divine Sophia but also call this God "father." Do they thereby indirectly legitimize patriarchal structures and the "second class" status of women in such structures, or does their androcentric language have a critical impulse that radically denies any religious authority and power for the structures of patriarchy? To raise such a question is not to raise a modern question alien to the New Testament text, but to explore the Jesus traditions in terms of social-political structures. We have seen that, in the first century, patriarchy was well established as a social institution but also that it was undermined by religious practices and legal conventions that gave women more freedom and economic powers.

Liberation from Patriarchal Structures and the Discipleship of Equals

Previously I attempted to show that the early Christian movement was inclusive of women's leadership and can therefore be called "egalitarian." As a conflict movement within Palestine, Syria, Greece, Asia Minor, and Rome, it challenged and opposed the dominant patriarchal ethos through the praxis of equal discipleship. Luise Schottroff has objected, however, that since "liberation from patriarchal structures" was not of primary interest to the Palestinian Jesus movement it was never articulated as a "major theme." The emancipation or liberation "from patriarchal structure—if these still play a role for impoverished people in such dire social situations—stems from their hope for the kingdom of God."[90] Such an argument does not intend to be antifeminist but to do justice to the historical-social context of the women's passages in the Jesus traditions. As much as I share the concern for underlining the social *Sitz im Leben* of the Jesus traditions, I do not share the implied presupposition, namely, that patriarchal structures and poverty are two different issues and not two sides of the same coin. Therefore the common bases and different emphases of "social-historical" and "feminist-historical" interpretations need to be clarified further.

Only if one conceptualizes economic exploitation and patriarchal oppression as two different social-economic systems can one assume that liberation from patriarchal structures was probably not of much concern to destitute people. Yet such an assumption tends to overlook the reality that in the first century—as today—the majority of the poor and starving were women, especially those women who had no male agencies that might have enabled them to share in the wealth of the patriarchal system. In antiquity widows and orphans were the prime paradigms of the poor and exploited. Yet in Christian consciousness and theology "poor Lazarus" but not the "impoverished widow" has become the exemplification of poverty. Therefore, we have neglected to spell out theologically Jesus' hope for women who are poor and destitute.

Moreover, I do not think that the social category of "the poor" is sufficient to describe the inclusive character of the Jesus movement. Added to this category must be that of "the marginal," because the healing stories, as well as the descriptions of other persons in the Jesus traditions, indicate that Jesus and his movement were open to all, especially to the "outcast" of his society and religion. Although the majority of the tax collectors, prostitutes, and sinners might have been poor, some of them probably were not.

The assertion that liberation from patriarchal structures was not of primary concern to Jesus and his movement overlooks not only the androcentric tendencies that can be detected in the tradition and redaction of the Jesus materials,[91] but also the "intrusion" of Jesus and his movement into the dominant religious ethos of the people. The prescription of the Holiness Code, as well as the scribal regulations, controlled women's lives even more than men's lives, and more stringently determined their access to God's presence in Temple and Torah. Jesus and his movement offered an alternative interpretation of the Torah that opened up access to God for everyone who was a member of the elect people of Israel, and especially for those who, because of their societal situation, had little chance to experience God's power in Temple and Torah.

Underlining this renewal aspect of the Jesus movement does not imply anti-Judaism. Rather, overlooking it would mean subtle "downgrading" of first-century Judaism's most compelling religious avenues for salvation. The charismatic prophet Hanina ben Dosa, a near contemporary of Jesus, showed a similar Galilean attitude of independence toward "theology." Such a Galilean resistance to scribal proselytizing is summed up by a saying ascribed to Johannan ben Zakkai, who became one of the key figures in the reorganization of Judaism after 70: "Galilee, you hatest the Torah. Your end shall be destruction." If Neusner is correct in his delineation of the trajectory of the Holiness Code, then this code was the heart of patriarchal middle-class Jewish religion. The mere fact that the Palestinian and Galilean Jesus traditions not only speak of the liberation of women as well as of men from disease and illness but also "reflect" the objections against Jesus permitting himself to "be touched" by the sick and the sinners—this fact indicates how much the inclusive discipleship and praxis of the Jesus movement "intruded" upon the dominant ethos. It distinguishes the Jesus movement from other religious groups seeking to control access to the presence and power of God.

Finally, we must not oppose Jesus' "concern for the poor" to "emancipation from patriarchal structures." The Jesus traditions show both his stance on behalf of the poor as well as his concern for women, but they do not explicitly "articulate" in either case a strategy for "structural change." Jesus' proclamation does not address critically the structures of oppression. It implicitly subverts them by envisioning a different future and different human relationships on the grounds that *all* persons in Israel are created and elected by the gracious goodness of Jesus' Sophia-God. Jesus and his movement set free those who are dehumanized and in bondage to evil powers, thus implicitly subverting economic or patriarchal-androcentric structures, even though the people involved in this process might not have thought in terms of social structures.

The differences between a social-historical and a feminist-historical reading comes to the fore not so much in the interpretation of historical texts but in the perspective brought to such a reading. The following assertion of Schottroff can illustrate this: "A poor woman has become the mother of Israel's Messiah, in whose name the messengers proclaim the beginning of the kingdom of God. She *represents the hope of the poor*—men and women—not just solely the hope of women."[92] I completely agree with this interpretation, but I would qualify it with: she represents this hope *as a woman*. Only such a qualification would authenticate such a statement as feminist. I am not quibbling here merely with words, but am arguing against a whole direction of Christian theology, which has allowed women "to identify" with general (male) categories and groups, for example, the poor, the lonely, the brothers, the priests, but has not allowed them to identify themselves *as women* in solidarity with other women. The self-alienation of women promoted by Christian generic language will continue an exegetical and theological tradition that keeps poor women *as women* invisible.

Nevertheless, we find some texts in the pre-Gospel Jesus traditions that clearly address patriarchal structures, even if indirectly. These are: (1) the pre-Markan controversy stories in which Jesus challenges patriarchal marriage structures (Mark 10:2–9 and 12:18–27); (2) the texts on the a-familial ethos of the Jesus movement; and (3) the saying about domination-free relationships in the community of disciples.

1. The two pre-Markan controversy dialogues on patriarchal marriage are usually considered under the headings "divorce" and "the resurrection." However, these headings cause us to overlook the real issue in the debate. Mark 10:2–9 must be interpreted not only as separate from the saying on divorce in 10:10–12 but not even in light of it.[94] The question put before Jesus is totally androcentric (can a man dismiss his wife) and presupposes patriarchal marriage as a "given." The first exchange between Jesus and the Pharisees makes it clear that divorce is necessary because of the male's "hardness of heart," that is, because of men's patriarchal mind-set and reality. As long as patriarchy is operative, divorce is *commanded* out of necessity. One is not allowed to abolish it within the structures of patriarchy. However, Jesus insists, God did not create or intend patriarchy but created persons as male and female human beings. It is not woman who is given into the power of man in order to continue "his" house and family line, but it is man who shall sever connections with his own patriarchal family and "the two shall become one *sarx*." *Sarx* ("flesh") has a broad meaning: body, person, human being, everyone, human nature, human descent, that which is natural or earthly, human life in general, social relationships, earthly history. As opposed to spirit, flesh can also mean earthly, sinful human attitudes and behavior, but it never has solely sexual connotations. Therefore, the passage is best translated as "the two persons—man and woman—enter into a common human life and social relationship because they are created as equals." The text does not allude to the myth of an androgynous primal man but to the equal partnership of man and woman in human marriage intended and made possible by the creator God. What, therefore, God has joined together in equal partnership (yoked together; cf. the yoke of Sophia-Jesus as a symbol of discipleship), a human being should not separate.

The second text, Mark 12:18–27, critically questions patriarchal structures not with reference to creation but rather with reference to that eschatological future often seen in apocalyptic theology as a restitution of the original creation. The difficult legal-theological problem is raised by the Sadducees who object to the unwritten belief in the resurrection on the grounds that it is not found in the Pentateuch. They point out that belief in the resurrection cannot be harmonized with the Torah's commandment of "levirate marriage" (Deut 25:5–10). Such a belief would imply incest and abomination in heaven, since the resurrection would entail the simultaneity of persons who lived at historically different times. The woman who had been married to seven brothers serially, would, after the resurrection, be married to all of them. As the Sadducees of the story formulated it, the theological difficulty consists in the belief in an afterlife, since they cannot imagine that levirate marriage could be the theological issue at stake. The law of levirate marriage served the purpose of continuing the patriarchal family, by securing its wealth and the inheritance within it, a concern important to the Sadducees, many of whom were upper class and priests, rich landowners living in Jerusalem—thus profiting doubly from the fees due them as priests and those due them from the tenants who worked their land. For them the levirate law protecting and perpetuating the patriarchal structures of the "house" was of utmost importance. Although this law sometimes created more hardship for the brother of the deceased husband, while protecting the financial security of the widow, it nevertheless served the continuation of the family line and the maintenance of patriarchal structures.

Jesus' response states flatly that they are wrong. They do not know either the Scriptures or the power of God, because they do not recognize that "in the world" of the living God patriarchal marriage does not exist either for men or for women. They neither marry nor are given in marriage but are "like the angels in heaven." The last expression is often understood to mean that their "being as angels are" implies asexuality or freedom from sexual differentiation and sexual intercourse.[95] There is no doubt that this interpretation has claimed a long tradition but it has no basis in the text. The eschatological being of men and women "like the angels or heavenly messengers" must be understood with reference to the first part of the sentence. It is not that sexual differentiation and sexuality do not exist in the "world" of God, but that "patriarchal marriage is no more," because its function in maintaining and continuing patriarchal economic and religious structures is no longer necessary. This is what it means to live and be "like the angels" who live in "the world" of God.

The transitional sentence, "as for the dead being raised," (v. 26a) seems to be a secondary insertion by the later community since it is not interested in the debate but in the "proof" for the resurrection.

The reference to the revelation of God to Moses in the burning bush that follows does not address this question and interest. It must be artificially twisted in order to refer to the resurrection (e.g., the patriarchs of Israel are now alive—but that is not said!). However, this reference replies directly to the question of the continuation of the patriarchal family: in the burning bush God is revealed to Moses as the God of the promise and of the blessing given to the patriarchs and their posterity. The "house" of Israel is not guaranteed in and through patriarchal marriage structures, but through the promise and faithfulness of Israel's powerful, life-giving God. While the God of the patriarchal systems and its securities is the "God of the dead," the God of Israel is "the God of the living." In God's world women and men no longer relate to each other in terms of patriarchal dominance and dependence, but as persons who live in the presence of the living God. This controversy, which reflects the social world of Palestine and of the Jesus movement, ends therefore with the flat statement that the Sadducees have "erred much" in assuming that the structures of patriarchy are unquestionably a dimension of God's world as well. So, too, all subsequent Christians have erred in maintaining oppressive patriarchal structures.

2. Gerd Theissen has pointed to the a-familial ethos of the Jesus movement in Palestine. However, by choosing Luke 14:26 (Q) as the oldest text for this contention he turns the Jesus movement into a movement of itinerant charismatic *men* who have left not only house and children but also wives, while local communities of "sympathizers" did not live such a radical ethos. Although he never clearly spells out the assumption that the wandering charismatics were male, nevertheless he unreflectively suggests that this was the case: "Probably many families had the same feelings about their sons who had joined the Jesus movement as did the family of Jesus. . . . the tradition says nothing about the way in which the families who have been abandoned are to find a substitute for the earning power which they have lost."[96]

However, a more careful scrutiny of the synoptic texts, which speak about leaving one's house and family for the kingdom or Jesus' sake, clearly shows that it is not the Q traditions (but rather Lukan redaction) which count the wife among those family members who are to be left behind in following Jesus. The same saying occurs again in Luke 18:29b (a revision of Mark 10:29b). Here Luke shows the same redactional tendency to include the "wife" among those family members left behind, whereas Mark and Matthew mention only "house, brothers, sisters, mothers, fathers, children, lands." Thus Luke presents the only textual basis for assuming that the Jesus movement was a charismatic movement of wandering men, sons and husbands, who shirked family responsibilities in the discipleship of Jesus. By not including the wife among those left behind, the Q and pre-Markan traditions do not restrict entrance into the radical discipleship of Jesus to men.

The text preceding this discipleship saying in Q (Matt 10:34–36 and parallel Luke 12:51–53) also announces that Jesus brings to the patriarchal household not peace but rather the "sword," the symbol for bitter enmity between members of the same household. The message and claim of Jesus "destroys" natural family bonds, setting son against father and father against son, daughter against mother and mother against daughter, daughter-in-law against mother-in-law and mother-in-law against daughter-in-law (cf. Micah 7:6). This saying stresses that children are set over against their parents and parents against their children, thus emphasizing strongly that the problem occurs among female members of the household. Yet it does *not* make the same statement about wife and husband. The apocalyptic destruction and dissolution of the family announced for the cataclysmic last days before the end of the world in Micah 7:6 and Mark 13:12, characterize, according to the Q traditions, the present time of discipleship. Without question the discipleship of Jesus does not respect patriarchal family bonds, and the Jesus movement in Palestine severely intrudes into the peace of the patriarchal household. To claim that such a radical a-familial ethos is asked only of the male wandering charismatics but not of the local sympathizers is a serious misreading of the texts.

A similar critique of "natural" family claims and bonds is expressed in the double corrective macarism or beatitude in Luke 11:27f—a text which Luke derived either from Q or his special source (SL). A woman in the crowd cries out: "Happy [or blessed] the womb that bore you, and the breasts you sucked." But (corrective) he said, "Happy rather those who hear the word of God and keep it." Faithful discipleship, not biological motherhood, is the eschatological calling of women. That the saying includes Mary, the mother of Jesus, among his faithful disciples, can only be derived from the Lukan redactional context (cf. Luke 2:19, 51),[97] not from the older tradition. The parallelizing of the two macarisms and their connection with a Greek adversative particle[98] indicates that the original saying opposes religious claims made on grounds of motherhood but not on grounds of discipleship.

Such an interpretation is supported by the pre-Markan tradition which contrasts the patriarchal family with the community of equal discipleship. The pronouncement story in Mark 3:31–35 defines the circle of disciples around Jesus as his true family.[99] The saying of Jesus in v. 35, "Whoever does the will of God is my brother and sister and mother," which could have been circulated originally without the narrative context of vv. 31–34, is similar to Luke 11:28. Those who live the gracious goodness of God are Jesus' true family, which includes brothers, sisters, and mothers, but, significantly enough, no fathers. The exclusion of fathers from the "true family" of Jesus cannot be explained by biographical references or by reference to God as the true father of Jesus, since Mark 10:30 also omits fathers. However "mothers and sisters," that is, women, are clearly included among the followers of Jesus. This is underlined by the tension between the narrative context and the saying of Jesus. Whereas the narrative context stresses twice (Mark 3:31, 32) that "Jesus' mother and brothers were outside calling him," the saying of Jesus refers to brothers, mother, *and sisters*.

Moreover the narrative context makes it clear that those who "do the will of God" come together in discipleship to form a new "household." Jesus is "inside" the house, "at home" (cf. 3:19). He points to those who "sat around him" and declares them to be his true family (v. 34). The discipleship community abolishes the claims of the patriarchal family and constitutes a new familial community, one that does not include fathers in its circle.

The same understanding of the discipleship of equals is expressed in Mark 10:29–30, a pre-Markan Jesus saying introduced by Peter's question to which Mark has added "with persecutions." The traditional saying maintains that those who have left their patriarchal "households" and cut themselves off from their familial relationships in order to join Jesus and his movement will receive everything back a "hundredfold" *already, now,* in *this* time. The Jesus movement was the messianic community which brought together impoverished and marginal people, as well as "houseowners" and "farmers," and bound them together in a new kinship and family based on radical discipleship.

3. This new "family" of equal discipleship, however, has no room for "fathers." Whereas "fathers" are mentioned among those left behind, they are not included in the new kinship which the disciples acquire "already now in this time." Insofar as the new "family" of Jesus has no room for "fathers," it implicitly rejects their power and status and thus claims that in the messianic community all patriarchal structures are abolished. Rather than reproducing the patriarchal re-

lationships of the "household" in antiquity, the Jesus movement demands a radical break from it. The "house churches" in Galilee that might have transmitted these sayings are not divided into radical itinerant disciples and more bourgeois sympathizers, nor do they espouse love patriarchalism.

The child/slave who occupies the lowest place within patriarchal structures becomes the primary paradigm for true discipleship. Such true discipleship is not measured on the father/master position but on that of the child/slave. This can be seen in the paradoxical Jesus saying: "Whoever does not receive the *basileia* of God like a child (slave) shall not enter it" (Mark 10:15). This saying is not an invitation to childlike innocence and naiveté but a challenge to relinquish all claims of power and domination over others.

Just as this saying in its original setting reached beyond the circle of disciples to present a discipleship challenge to all of Jesus' hearers, so the saying about the first and greatest (among you) who is (or will be) your child or slave originally challenged all those in Palestine who were prominent in their society to be in "solidarity" with the slaves and powerless in Israel. This Jesus saying does not speak of eschatological reversal (the last will be first or the lowly will be exalted and vice versa), but about the "solidarity from below" required by the *basileia* of God. It clearly presupposes a society in which masters and slaves exist, and challenges those in positions of dominance in a feudal society to become "equal" with those who are powerless. Masters should relinquish domination over their slaves and tenants, and "serve" them in the same total fashion as a slave had to serve her/his master.

The importance of this saying for the Jesus movement is indicated by its inclusion in the synoptic tradition in a sevenfold combination, and in its transmission in very different forms and situations.[100] The ecclesial process of interpretation applied a saying originally addressed to the socially well-to-do in Israel to its own relationships within the discipleship of equals. Mark 10:42–45 and 9:33–37—adapted by Matt 20:26–27 and Luke 22:24–27 to their own situations and theological perspectives—contrasts the political structures of domination with those required among the disciples. Structures of domination should not be tolerated in the discipleship of equals, but those who "would be" great or first among the disciples must be slaves and servants of all. True leadership in the community must be rooted in solidarity with and in work for those who are "slaves and servants" in the community. But where Mark and Matthew acknowledge no "great" or "first" members of the community at all, Luke does. His only requirement is that their style of leadership orient itself according to the example of Jesus.

A second series of these sayings emphasizes that "the little child" should be the primary object of the community's care and service (Mark 9:35–37; Matt 18:1–4; Luke 9:48), because Jesus himself is present to the community in those children whom the community has accepted in baptism ("in my name"). This form of the tradition would seem to reflect a very concrete situation in which the community took care of its baptized children. However, such child care must already have caused problems, since the "great" and the "first" in the community seem not to have sought after it very much. According to Mark 9:35 (cf. Mark 10:13–16) the "twelve" male disciples constitute the circle of the "great" who are specifically addressed here. In this situation, where child care appears to have been a community problem, the saying insists that the discipleship of equals must be inclusive of children and serve their needs, if the community wants to have Jesus—and God—in their midst.

A third form of the sayings against "wanting to be" "great" and "first" in the community is found in Matt 23:8–11 (SM).[101] Matthew—or his tradition—has combined the saying about the "greatest who shall be the servant of all" (v. 11) on the one hand with the eschatological reversal saying about those who exalt themselves being humbled and vice versa (v. 12). On the other hand, he has combined it with an injunction against "patriarchal" roles and titles within the community of disciples (vv. 8–10). Although it is very difficult to situate these injunctions within the pre-Matthean tradition because Luke does not have such prohibitions, it is apparent, nevertheless, that the last prohibition, "Neither be called spiritual masters" (v. 10), restates v. 8 in explicitly Christian terms, insofar as the "absolute phrase 'the Christ' " is used. This saying, therefore, seems to be a secondary redaction of v. 8.[102]

In all likelihood the original form of the saying in v. 8 read "disciples" rather than "brothers," since the former is the usual antonym to teacher, while the latter, an antonym to "father," would better fit the second saying. Since it is a favored Matthean designation for the members of the Christian community, Matthew might have placed it here in order to be able to redact the second saying in terms of his own theology. The original prohibition, then, juxtaposes the terms "not to be called rabbi," "one teacher," "all disciples," in the form of an inclusion:

> But you are not to be called rabbi
> for you have one teacher
> and you are all disciples.

Either Matthew's tradition, his source, or Matthew's redaction combined this saying with a second prohibition (v. 9) which, in its present form, is not quite parallel to the first.

> Call no one father among you on earth
> for you have one heavenly father.

The parallelism of this saying contrasts earth and heaven, with the prohibition formulated in the active sense.[103] However, the phrase "heavenly father" indicates the redactional hand of Matthew, who also added "on earth." Thus the more original form of the saying may have read:

> Call no one father
> for you have one father
> (and you are all siblings).

This short injunction, "Call no one father, for you have one father," thus maintains the same relationships as the saying in Mark 10:29–30 did. The new kinship of the discipleship of equals does not admit of "fathers," thereby rejecting the patriarchal power and esteem invested in them.

In sum, regardless of what the original form of the sayings in Matt 23:8–9 may have looked like, the content of the sayings remains the same: the discipleship of equals rejects teachers because it is constituted and taught by one, and only one, teacher. Similarly, the kinship relationship in the discipleship of equals does not admit of "any father" because it is sustained by the gracious goodness of God whom the disciples and Jesus call "father" (Luke 11:2–4 [Q]; 12:30; cf. Mark 11:25). The "father" God is invoked here, however, not to justify patriarchal structures and relationships in the community of disciples but precisely to reject all such claims, powers, and structures. Since the social world evoked by these two sayings is that of Palestine and since they correspond to the theological emphasis found in the Q traditions, these sayings could have belonged to Matthew's source Q. The self-understanding and praxis of Jesus and his movement in Palestine are especially reflected in v. 9.

The address "father" used by Jesus and his disciples has caused many Christian feminists great scandal because the church has not obeyed the command of Jesus to "call no one father," for you have "one father," and because it has resulted in legitimizing ecclesial and societal patriarchy with the "father" name of God, thereby using the name of God in vain. But "the Lord will not hold him guiltless who takes his name in vain" (Exod 20:7). The saying of Jesus uses the "father" name of God not as a legitimization for existing patriarchal power structures in society or church but as a critical subversion of all structures of domination. The "father" God of Jesus makes possible "the sisterhood of men" (in the phrase of Mary Daly) by denying any father, and all patriarchy, its right to existence. Neither the "brothers" nor "the sisters" in the Christian community can claim the "authority of the father" because that would involve claiming authority and power reserved for God alone.[104]

However, we must also see that the original logion did not merely address the Christian community and its relationships. It also enjoined the disciples of Jesus from recognizing *any* father authority in their society, because there *is* only one father. The social-critical potential of this saying with respect to all patriarchal structures has yet to be brought to bear upon societal-political change. The monotheistic fatherhood of God, elaborated in the Jesus traditions as the gracious goodness usually associated with a mother, must engender liberation from all patriarchal structures and domination if it is to be rescued from the male projection of patriarchy into heaven. Thus liberation from patriarchal structures is not only explicitly articulated by Jesus but is in fact at the heart of the proclamation of the *basileia* of God.[105]

Conclusion

I have sought in this chapter to enter the "world" of Jesus and those who followed him. In doing so I have asked what it was like for a woman in Palestine to hear and be involved with Jesus and his movement. I have insisted on the importance of recognizing this "world" of Jesus as the Jewish "world" of Palestine and of seeing those who followed him as Jewish women. Even though Christianity and Judaism only subsequently became two distinct religions, I have not resorted to the term Judaeo-Christian tradition to describe the common history of Jewish and "Christian" women. Rather, for the most part, I have employed the term Israel in naming the people of Jesus and his Jewish followers who became our Christian foresisters. I am well aware of the problem raised by this characterization as well, but I have decided in favor of it on the grounds that it was positively used by the rabbis[106] and by early Christian writers to announce the gracious goodness of God in electing and caring for a historical oppressed people. I am well aware that this choice does not solve the problem, but it does open it up for a feminist discussion. Thus a feminist reconstruction of the world of first-century Jewish women, especially one undertaken by a Christian, while remaining very tentative and preliminary, nevertheless may serve to foster a feminist historical-theological exploration.

In reconstructing the world of Jesus and his movement, I have presupposed the methods and results of historical-critical exegesis, for example, the two-source theory for the synoptics, form-critical delineation of the most "original" stratum of the Jesus traditions, etc. However, any reader conversant with these scholarly results will recognize that my "reading" of these texts and traditions is often quite different. The difference is methodological. Where form criticism and tradition history stress the "word" component of a story or tradition, often favoring it as more original than the narrative, I have focused on the narrative text and the historical actors involved, because women are found in the story of Jesus and his movement. In stressing the narrative aspect I am not trying to eliminate the sayings and words of Jesus and his disciples. Rather, my purpose lies in modifying the view so widely held in form criticism that a miracle story or a controversy-dialogue setting is just an illustration or exemplification of the relevatory "word" or pronouncement of Jesus. If the revelatory word is a word in which God's praxis with respect to Israel is disclosed, the "word" is a story, and the story *may not be reduced* to an "ideological" statement. This insight has revolutionized parable interpretation in recent years and will do the same for the other Gospel narratives. The story, in turn, also should not be reduced to "text" as an ideologically fixed ontological structure, but rather be understood in the context of the social-historical world that it evokes. Only when we place the Jesus stories about women into the overall story of Jesus and his movement in Palestine are we able to recognize their subversive character. In the discipleship of equals the "role" of women is not peripheral or trivial, but at the center, and thus of utmost importance to the praxis of "solidarity from below."[107]

The story of the anointing of Jesus by a woman articulates this insight. In its final form it is told by a community that already envisions a world-wide mission: wherever the gospel—the good news of the *basileia*—is announced, in the whole wide world, the praxis of this woman will be remembered. Like the prophets anointing the kings of

Israel on the forehead, so the woman anoints Jesus. She publicly names him in a prophetic sign-action. She has spent much money to do so and is reprimanded sanctimoniously by the male disciples of Jesus. Those disciples who have projected their messianic dreams of greatness and dominance on Jesus use "the poor" as an argument against her. But Jesus defends her: "For you always have the poor with you, and whenever you decide to do so you can do good ['to them' is not found in all manuscripts], but me you do not always have." The community that tells this story knows that Jesus is no longer present in their midst. They do not "have" Jesus anymore with them. However, the poor (not just the impoverished Christians) are still very much present among them. Now is the time to decide to do good. Thus in remembering that a nameless woman prophet has anointed Jesus as the messianic inaugurator of the *basileia*, the community also remembers that the God of Jesus is on the side of the poor and that God's future, the *basileia*, belongs to the poor. The communal remembering of the woman's story always evokes the remembrance of the *basileia* promised to the impoverished and starving. Conversely, wherever the good news of the *basileia*—the gospel—is preached in the whole wide world, what the woman prophet has done will be remembered.

Luke no longer understands this powerful story as the story of a woman prophet, and therefore replaces it with the story of "the repentant sinner." At the same time, he no longer understands the "solidarity from below" that inspired Jesus and his first followers. The poor have become an object of almsgiving and charity, while poverty is seen as an ascetic challenge and "practice for special religious people." Although the eucharistic formula "in remembrance of me" (1 Cor 11:24, 25) is verbally similar to the gospel proclamation "in remembrance of her," the later church has not ritualized this story of the woman prophet, using it instead to assert as God's will that poverty cannot be eliminated. The "church of the poor" and the "church of women" must be recovered at the same time, if "solidarity from below" is to become a reality for the whole community of Jesus again. As a feminist vision, the *basileia* vision of Jesus calls all women without exception to wholeness and selfhood, as well as to solidarity with those women who are the impoverished, the maimed, and outcasts of our society and church. It knows of the deadly violence such a vision and commitment will encounter. It enables us not to despair or to relinquish the struggle in the face of such violence. It empowers us to walk upright, freed from the double oppression of societal and religious sexism and prejudice. The woman-identified man, Jesus, called forth a discipleship of equals that still needs to be discovered and realized by women and men today.

NOTES

1. Cf. Leander E. Keck, "Ethos and Ethics in the New Testament," in James Gaffney, ed., *Essays in Morality and Ethics* (New York: Paulist Press, 1980), pp. 29–49; Keck distinguishes four characteristic differences between Jesus and Paul: (1) Paul restricted his mission to the cities, Jesus to rural areas. (2) Paul and Jesus differed with respect to economic security. (3) Paul was the apostle of the gentile mission; Jesus restricted his mission to the "house of Israel." (4) Paul was creating a new community; Jesus sought to renew an old one.

2. See Martin Hengel, *Acts and the History of Earliest Christianity* (London: SCM Press, 1979), pp. 99–110.

3. Cf. David L. Dungan, *The Sayings of Jesus in the Churches of Paul* (Philadelphia: Fortress, 1971). The title of his book conveys this better than the author's conclusion, which argues for "Paul's intimate relation with the Synoptic traditions" (see pp. 139–50).

4. For extensive bibliographies of recent studies, see C. E. Carlston, "Form Criticism, NT," *Interpreter's Dictionary of the Bible*, Supp. Vol. (Nashville: Abingdon, 1976), pp. 345–48; and R. T. Fortna, "Redaction Criticism, NT," ibid., pp. 733–35. H. C. Kee, *Jesus in History: An Approach to the Gospels* (New York: Harcourt, Brace & World, 1970) is cited here as one of many such introductory studies on the remembrance of Jesus in the Gospels.

5. See David John Lull, *The Spirit in Galatia: Paul's Interpretation of Pneuma as Divine Power* (Chico, Calif.: Scholars Press, 1980), and the literature cited.

6. For the intersection between the inclusive ethos of Jesus and the Pauline doctrine of justification, see Nils Alstrup Dahl, "The Doctrine of Justification: Its Social Functions and Implications," in his *Studies in Paul: Theology for the Early Christian Mission* (Minneapolis: Augsburg, 1977), pp. 95–120.

7. See especially Judith Plaskow, "Christian Feminism and Anti-Judaism," *Cross Currents* 28 (1978) 306–9; now also Bernadette Brooten, "Jüdinnen zur Zeit Jesu: Ein Plädoyer für Differenzierung," in B. Brooten und N. Greinacher, eds., *Frauen in der Männerkirche* (Munich: Kaiser/Mainz: Grünewald, 1982), pp. 141–48.

8. Judith Plaskow, "Blaming Jews for Inventing Patriarchy," in *Lilith* 7 (1980) 11f.; and idem, "Feminists and Faith: A Discussion with Judith Plaskow and Annette Daum," ibid., pp. 14–17:14.

9. This is overlooked in Annette Daum's criticism of my writings in "Blaming Jews for the Death of the Goddess," *Lilith* 7 (1980) 12–13. Such careless criticism does not further feminist dialogue on the issue. Orthodox Jews, on the other hand, have chastised me for ascribing a Jewish prayer to the Greco-Roman patriarchal ethos of the time and thereby not respecting the genuine Jewish character of this prayer.

10. See especially Judith Plaskow's work.

11. See e.g. Leonard Swidler, *Women in Judaism: The Status of Women in Formative Judaism* (Metuchen, N.J.: Scarecrow Press, 1976), pp. 72–82, 97ff.

12. Bernard Prusak ("Woman: Seductive Siren and Source of Sin? Pseudepigraphical Myth and Christian Origins," in R. R. Ruether, ed., *Religion and Sexism: Images of Women in the Jewish and Christian Tradition* [New York: Simon & Schuster, 1974], pp. 89–116) has recognized the function of this mythology for "maintaining the cultural facts of male dominance and female subservience" (p. 97).

13. See e.g. Raphael Loewe, *The Position of Women in Judaism* (London: SPCK, 1966), p. 24. M. Meiselman (*Jewish Woman in Jewish Law* [New York: Ktav, 1978] pp. 45–57,

156–74) insists in response to issues raised by Jewish feminists that "a woman's primary concern must be the religious well-being of her family" (p. 169).

14. This is overlooked in all studies that take the Talmudic statements about women as descriptions of their actual role and status. Cf. e.g. Judith Hauptman, "Images of Women in the Talmud," in Ruether, *Religion and Sexism*, pp. 184–212.

15. Ulrike Türck, "Die Stellung der Frau in Elephantine als Ergebnis persisch-babylonischen Rechtseinflusses," *ZNW* 41 (1928) 166–69. But Reuven Yaron (*Introduction to the Law of the Aramaic Papyri* [Oxford: Oxford University Press, 1961] pp. 40–55) argues for Egyptian influence.

16. See E. Schürer, *A History of the Jewish People in the Times of Jesus* (New York: Schocken Books, 1971), pp. 91–93.

17. Cf. also the very influential friendship between Alexandra, mother of the queen Mariamme, and Cleopatra (ibid., pp. 131ff.); and that between Berenice, Agrippa I's mother, and Antonia, the sister-in-law of the emperor Tiberius (S. Safrai and M. Stern, eds., *The Jewish People in the First Century* [Philadelphia: Fortress, 1974], 1.288f.)

18. For the problem of using sources from Rabbinic Judaism for the reconstruction of pre-70 A.D. Judaism, see especially the work of Jacob Neusner. His summary statement appears in "The Formation of Rabbinic Judaism: Yavneh (Jamnia) from A.D. 70 to 100," in H. Temporini and W. Haase, eds., *Aufsteig und Niedergang der römischen Welt* (Berlin: de Gruyter, 1979), 2.3–42: esp. 3–16.

19. See especially the methodological reflections in R. A. Kraft, "In Search of 'Jewish Christianity' and Its 'Theology,' " *Recherches de Science Religieuse* 60 (1972) 81–92; idem, "The Multiform Jewish Heritage of Early Christianity," in J. Neusner, ed., *Christianity, Judaism and Other Greco-Roman Cults* (Leiden: Brill, 1975), 3.174–99; J. Neusner, *First-Century Judaism in Crisis* (Nashville: Abingdon, 1975), pp. 21–44:39.

20. See Elisabeth Schüssler Fiorenza, *Priester für Gott: Studien zum Herrschafts- und Priestermotiv in der Apokalypse* (NTAbh 7; Münster: Aschendorff, 1972), pp. 78–166.

21. Sheldon R. Isenberg, "Millenarism in Greco-Roman Palestine," *Religion* 4 (1974) 26–46.

22. Sheldon R. Isenberg, "Power through Temple and Torah in Greco-Roman Palestine," in Neusner, *Christianity, Judaism, and Other Cults*, 3.24–52:32.

23. Cf. Norman Perrin, *Jesus and the Language of the Kingdom: Symbol and Metaphor in New Testament Interpretation* (Philadelphia: Fortress, 1976), pp. 29–32.

24. Isenberg, "Temple and Torah," p. 25.

25. *Assumption of Moses* 10.1.7–8; R. H. Charles, *The Apocrypha and Pseudepigrapha of the Old Testament* (Oxford: Oxford University Press, 1913), pp. 421f.

26. On "kingdom" in Jewish prayers, cf. Norman Perrin, *Rediscovering the Teaching of Jesus* (London: SCM Press, 1967; New York: Harper & Row), pp. 57f.

27. This description of the different groups or "sects" in Judaism is based on Josephus, *Jewish Antiquities*, chaps. 17–20. See also S. Sandmel, *The First Christian Century in Judaism and Christianity: Certainties and Uncertainties* (Oxford: Oxford University Press, 1969).

28. For the references in Josephus and a general bibliography and description, cf. also David M. Rhoads, *Israel in Revolution 6–74 C.E.: A Political History Based on the Writings of Josephus* (Philadelphia: Fortress, 1976), pp. 32–46.

29. J. A. Fitzmyer (*The Gospel According to Luke (I–IX)* [New York: Doubleday, 1981], p. 671) argues that both texts are so different "that it is difficult to think that we are dealing with a 'Q' parallel."

30. For a historical-critical discussion of this passage, cf. especially W. Wink, *John the Baptist in the Gospel Tradition* (Cambridge: Cambridge University Press, 1968), pp. 8–13; J. Gnilka, "Das Martyrium Johannes des Täufers (Mk 6, 17–29)," in P. Hoffman et al., eds., *Orientierung an Jesus: Festschrift für Josef Schmid* (Freiburg: Herder, 1973), pp. 78–92. The *Sitz im Leben* of this story is the circle of disciples of John the Baptist (cf. 7:29).

31. Cf. the controversy on whether in 1QSa 1:11 the wife is accorded "general competence as a witness and jurist," in *JBL* 76 (1957) 108–22, 266–69.

32. E. Lohse, *Die Texte aus Qumran: Hebräisch und Deutsch* (Darmstadt: Wissenschaftliche Buchgesellschaft, 1964), p. 282, n. 3.

33. Horst R. Moehring, "Josephus on the Marriage Customs of the Essenes," in A. Wikgren, ed., *Early Christian Origins* (Chicago: Quadrangle Books, 1961), pp. 120–27.

34. F. H. Colson, ed. and trans., *Philo: On the Contemplative Life* (Loeb Classical Library; Cambridge Mass.: Harvard University Press, 1941), pp. 104–69.

35. Cf. especially the analysis of Prusak, "Woman: Seductive Siren," pp. 89–116; and Swidler, *Women in Judaism,* pp. 29–55.

36. Carsten Colpe ("Genossenschaft: Jüdisch," *RAC* 30 [1978] 117–41:134) maintains that the *havuroth* were not structured along patriarchal family lines, because husbands could become members without their wives, adult children without their parents, and slaves without their masters, and vice versa (*t. Demai* 2.15.7; 3.5.9).

37. Jacob Neusner, *Method and Meaning in Ancient Judaism* (Brown Judaic Studies 10; Missoula, Mont.: Scholars Press, 1979), p. 100.

38. Demetrius R. Dumm, "Tobith, Judith, Esther," *The Jerome Biblical Commentary* (Englewood Cliffs, N.J.: Prentice-Hall, 1968), pp. 620–32: esp. 624–28.

39. Patrick W. Skehan, "The Hand of Judith," *CBQ* 25 (1963) 94–110.

40. Ernst Haag, "Die besondere literarische Art des Buches Judith und seine theologische Bedeutung," *Trierer Theologische Zeitschrift* 71 (1962) 228–301.

41. George W. E. Nickelsburg, *Jewish Literature Between the Bible and the Mishnah* (Philadelphia: Fortress, 1981), p. 108.

42. In a similar fashion David Goodblatt ("The Beruriah Traditions," *Journal of Jewish Studies* 26 [1975] 68–85) has analyzed the Beruriah traditions in order to learn something about "the possible educational achievements of women in rabbinic society," rather than to treat them as "reliable biographical data about an historical person" (p. 82).

43. See also J. B. Segal, "The Jewish Attitude Towards Women," in *Journal of Jewish Studies* 30 (1979): "Nevertheless, there are, it may be suggested, indications, however imprecise, that the status of women in Jewish society may have been the subject of debate in the stormy centuries before and during the emergence of Christianity. Women had played a notable part in public life under the Hasmonean and Herodian regimes. . . . Women seem to have exercised control over property . . . [and] were emboldened to defy Jewish law by initiating divorce proceedings. Perhaps we may detect a measure of polarization in the attitudes of Jews toward women at this time" (p. 135).

44. See especially U. B. Müller, "Vision und Botschaft," *Zeitschrift für Theologie und Kirche* 74 (1977) 416–48; J. Becker, *Johannes der Täufer und Jesus von Nazareth* (Stuttgart: Katholisches Bibelwerk, 1972), pp. 71ff.

45. Perrin (*Rediscovering the Teaching of Jesus,* pp. 120f.) argues that this comparison between Jesus and John is authentic and comes from Jesus himself.

46. A. J. Hultgren, *Jesus and His Adversaries: The Form and Function of the Conflict Stories in the Synoptic Tradition* (Minneapolis: Augsburg, 1979), pp. 78–81.

47. N. Perrin, *The Kingdom of God in the Teaching of Jesus* (Philadelphia: Westminster, 1963), pp. 79–89, 185–201; W. G. Kümmel, *The Theology of the New Testament* (Nashville: Abingdon, 1973), pp. 32–39.

48. Cf. Paul Hoffman, " 'Eschatologie' und 'Friedenshandeln' in der Jesusüberlieferung," in G. Liedke, ed., *Eschatologie und Frieden* (Heidelberg: Evangelische Studiengemeinschaft, 1978), 2.179–223:190.

49. Earl Breech, "Kingdom of God and the Parables of Jesus," *Semeia* 12 (1978) 15–40.

50. Elizabeth Waller, "The Parable of the Leaven," *USQR* 35 (1979/80) 99–109.

51. R. Funk, *Language, Hermeneutic, and the Word of God* (New York: Harper & Row, 1966), pp. 162–98.

52. Müller, "Vision und Botschaft," pp. 442–47.

53. Cf. P. Hoffmann and V. Eid, *Jesus von Nazareth und seine christliche Moral* (Frei-

burg: Herder, 1975), pp. 29, 35; and Fitzmyer, *The Gospel According to Luke*, pp. 645f., for recent literature.

54. A. G. Wright ("The Widow's Mites: Praise or Lament?—A Matter of Context," *CBQ* 44 [1982] 256–65:262) argues that, in the Markan context, the story presents a critique of religion that encourages people to give their whole living to religious institutions: "She had been taught and encouraged by religious leaders to donate as she does, and Jesus condemns the value system that motivates her action, and he condemns the people who conditioned her to do it." See also J. D. M. Derrett, " 'Eating Up the Houses of Widows': Jesus' Comment on Lawyers?" *NovT* 14 (1972) 1–9.

55. H. Frankemölle ("Die Makarismen [Mt 5,1–12; Lk 6, 20–23]: Motive und Umfang der redaktionellen Komposition," *Biblische Zeitschrift* 15 [1971] 52–75) argues that the woes were part of Q, whereas Fitzmyer thinks that Luke has added them (*The Gospel According to Luke*, p. 627).

56. For a review of the discussion, cf. R. E. Brown, *The Birth of the Messiah* (New York: Doubleday, 1977), pp. 346–66; Luise Schottroff, "Das Magnifikat und die älteste Tradition über Jesus von Nazareth," *EvTh* 38 (1978) 298–313.

57. Cf. e.g. Kee, *Jesus in History*, pp. 86f.

58. Antoinette Clark Wire ("The Structure of the Gospel Miracle Stories and Their Tellers," *Semeia* 11 [1978] 83–113) argues that the structure of the miracle story is a juxtaposition of an oppressive context and the breaking open of it.

59. Perrin, *Rediscovering the Teaching of Jesus*, pp. 63–67.

60. For a discussion of the form and tradition history of these two miracle stories, cf. R. Pesch, *Das Markusevangelium* (Freiburg: Herder, 1976), 1.295–314, and the literature cited there.

61. See e.g. Rachel Conrad Wahlberg, *Jesus According to a Woman* (New York: Paulist Press, 1975), pp. 31–41.

62. See C. Dietzfelbinger, "Vom Sinn der Sabbatheilungen Jesu," *EvTh* 38 (1978) 281–97, for a review of the problem.

63. For a review, cf. Hultgren, *Jesus and His Adversaries*, pp. 111–15; and Pesch, *Das Markusevangelium*, 1.178–87.

64. Luise Schottroff and Wolfgang Stegemann, "Der Sabbat ist um des Menschen willen da," in W. Schottroff and W. Stegemann, eds., *Der Gott der kleinen Leute: Sozialgeschichtliche Bibelauslegungen*, vol. 2: *Neues Testament* (Munich: Kaiser, 1979), pp. 58–70.

65. For a review, see John R. Donahue, "Tax Collectors and Sinner," *CBQ* 33 (1971) 39–61; Martin Völkl, "Freund der Zöllner und Sünder," *ZNW* 69 (1978) 1–10.

66. L. Schottroff and W. Stegemann, *Jesus von Nazareth: Hoffnung der Armen* (Stuttgart: Kohlhammer, 1978), pp. 15–28.

67. H. Herter, "Die Soziologie der antiken Prostitution im Lichte des heidnischen und christlichen Schrifttums," *JAC* 3 (1960) 70–111.

68. Cf. Fitzmyer, *The Gospel According to Luke*, pp. 683–94, for discussion and bibliography.

69. H. Kessler, *Die theologische Bedeutung des Todes Jesu* (Düsseldorf: Patmos, 1970), pp. 227–329; S. K. Williams (*Jesus' Death as Saving Event: The Background and Origin of a Concept* [Missoula, Mont.: Scholars Press, 1975], p. 230) argues that the "concept originated among Christians who not only spoke Greek but were also thoroughly at home in the Greek-Hellenistic thought world." For a contrary opinion, cf. M. Hengel, *The Atonement: The Origins of the Doctrine in the New Testament* (Philadelphia: Fortress, 1981).

70. Carol Ochs, *Behind the Sex of God* (Boston: Beacon Press, 1977).

71. Müller, "Vision und Botschaft," p. 447.

72. See Perrin's review in his *Jesus and the Language of the Kingdom*, pp. 89–193; P. Perkins, *Hearing the Parables of Jesus* (New York: Paulist Press, 1981).

73. J. Lambrecht, *Once More Astonished: The Parables of Jesus* (New York: Crossroad, 1981), pp. 24–56.

74. L. Schottroff, "Die Güte Gottes und die Solidarität von Menschen: Das Gleichnis von den Arbeitern im Weinberg," in Schottroff and Stegemann, Der Gott der kleinen Leute, pp. 71–93.

75. "Redstockings, April 1969," in Feminist Revolution (New York: Random House, 1975), p. 205.

76. F. Christ, Jesus Sophia: Die Sophia Christologie bei den Synoptikern (Zurich: Zwingli Verlag, 1970); J. M. Robinson, "Jesus as Sophos and Sophia: Wisdom Tradition and the Gospels," in R. Wilken, ed., Aspects of Wisdom in Judaism and Early Christianity (Notre Dame: University of Notre Dame Press, 1975), pp. 1–16.

77. M. J. Suggs, Wisdom, Christology and Law in Matthew's Gospel (Cambridge, Mass.: Harvard University Press, 1970), pp. 31–62.

78. For a fuller development and discussion of the literature, cf. my article "Wisdom Mythology and the Christological Hymns of the New Testament," in Wilken, Aspects of Wisdom, pp. 17–42.

79. For a different "archetypal" interpretation, cf. J. Chamberlain Engelsman, The Feminine Dimension of the Divine (Philadelphia: Westminster, 1979), pp. 106–18.

80. S. Schulz, Die Spruchquelle der Evangelien (Zurich: Theologischer Verlag, 1972), pp. 336–45, for bibliography.

81. P. Hoffmann, Studien zur Theologie der Logienquelle (Münster: Aschendorff, 1972), pp. 287–311: esp. 296ff.

82. U. B. Müller, "Zur Rezeption gesetzeskritischer Jesusüberlieferung im frühen Christentum," NTS 27 (1981) 158–85; U. Luz, "Das Jesusbild der vormarkinischen Tradition," in G. Strecker, ed., Jesus Christus in Historie und Theologie (Tübingen: Mohr-Siebeck, 1975), pp. 347–74.

83. Cf. the discussion and literature in Alice Dermience, "Tradition et rédaction dans la péricope de la Syrophénicienne: Marc 7,24–30," Revue Théologique de Louvain 53 (1977) 15–29.

84. B. Flammer, "Die Syrophoenizerin," Theologische Quartalschrift 148 (1968) 463–78:468.

85. R. Bultmann, The Gospel of John (Philadelphia: Westminster, 1971), pp. 175f.

86. For a review and discussion, cf. H. Paulsen, "Mk xvi 1–8," NovT 22 (1980) 138–75; A. Lindemann, "Die Osterbotschaft des Markus: Zur theologischen Interpretation von Mark 16.1–8," NTS 26 (1980) 298–317.

87. This is completely neglected in the discussion of G. O'Collins, "Peter as Easter Witness," Heythrop Journal 22 (1981) 1–18.

88. M. Hengel, "Maria Magdalena und die Frauen als Zeugen," in P. Schmid, ed., Abraham unser Vater (Leiden: Brill, 1963), pp. 243–56:248.

89. Ibid., p. 256.

90. L. Schottroff, "Frauen in der Nachfolge Jesu in neutestamentlicher Zeit," in W. Schottroff and W. Stegemann, eds., Traditionen der Befreiung, vol. 2, Frauen in der Bibel (Munich: Kaiser, 1980), pp. 91–133:106.

91. Such tendencies are denied in her recent article: L. Schottroff, "Maria Magdalena und die Frauen am Grabe Jesu," EvTh 42 (1982) 3–25.

92. Schottroff, "Frauen in der Nachfolge Jesu," p. 112.

93. See B. Brooten, "Konnten Frauen im alten Judentum die Scheidung betreiben? Überlegungen zu Mk 10, 11–12 und 1 Kor 7,10–11," EvTh 42 (1982) 65–79.

94. For a review of the literature and a somewhat different interpretation, see Hultgren, Jesus and His Adversaries, pp. 119–23.

95. Cf. K. Niederwimmer, Askese und Mysterium (Göttingen: Vandenhoeck & Ruprecht, 1975), p. 53.

96. G. Theissen, Sociology of Early Palestinian Christianity (Philadelphia: Fortress, 1978), p. 12.

97. R. E. Brown et al., eds., Mary in the New Testament (Philadelphia: Fortress, 1978), p. 172.

98. M. E. Thrall, Greek Particles in the New Testament (Leiden: Brill, 1962), p. 35.

99. Cf. also R. Scroggs, "The Earliest Christian Communities as Sectarian Movement," in J. Neusner, *Christianity, Judaism, and Other Cults*, 2.14f.

100. See especially Hoffmann and Eid, *Jesus von Nazareth*, pp. 186–214, for an extensive discussion.

101. Cf. W. Trilling, "Amt und Amtsverständnis bei Matthäus," in K. Kertelge, ed., *Das kirchliche Amt im Neuen Testament* (Darmstadt: Wissenschaftliche Buchgesellschaft, 1977), pp. 524–42: esp. 525ff.

102. J. P. Meier, *Matthew* (Wilmington, Del.: Glazier, 1980), p. 265.

103. R. Bultmann (*History of the Synoptic Tradition* [Oxford: Blackwell, 1968], p. 144) thinks it is possible that vv. 8f. represent an authentic word of Jesus.

104. This is also recognized by F. Belo: "In ecclesial life the very image of the father should be eradicated. In fact, however, the ecclesiastical apparatus has multiplied 'fathers' and 'teachers' (the magisterium) and has given them the dominant function of producing the ideology" (*A Materialist Reading of the Gospel of Mark* [New York: Orbis Books, 1981], p. 324 n. 110).

105. But R. Hamerton-Kelly (*God the Father: Theology and Patriarchy in the Teaching of Jesus* [Philadelphia: Fortress, 1979], p. 102) suggests that Jesus "neutralizes" and "humanizes" the patriarchy by choosing the father symbol for God.

106. J. Neusner, *Method and Meaning in Ancient Judaism* (Chico, Calif.: Scholars Press, 1981), p. 104, n. 5.

107. Cf. Francis Schüssler Fiorenza, "Critical Social Theory and Christology: Toward an Understanding of Atonement and Redemption as Emancipatory Solidarity," *Proceedings of the Catholic Theological Society of America* 30 (1975) 63–110.

Chapter 5

The Early Christian
Missionary Movement
Equality in the Power of the Spirit

The beginnings of the early Christian missionary movement are shrouded in historical darkness. As was the case with the Jesus movement in Palestine, sources for the early Christian missionary movement in the Greco-Roman world are lacking for the crucial time between 30 and 50 C.E., since the Pauline letters were written in the 50s and 60s, while Acts belongs to the last decade of the first century. The historical picture that emerges when information from the Pauline letters and from Acts is pieced together is very sketchy and far from comprehensive.

> All too often we are only left with traces: names of people without specific details, isolated events, sporadic accounts or obscure legends—as from the Talmudic literature, except where suddenly larger fragments emerge, resting on individual lucky discoveries. We constantly come up against gaps and white patches on the map; our sources are uncertain and we have to content ourselves with more or less hypothetical reconstructions. All this is true of ancient history in general and even more of the history of early Christianity in particular, above all during its first 150 years.[1]

Since, in all probability, the author of Acts does not know the genuine Pauline letters, the Acts account must be supplemented and corrected by the information about early Christian developments found in the Pauline literature. Paul's letters, however, are occasional pastoral writings. They are not primarily interested in conveying information on the beginnings of early Christian mission. Their references to persons, places, or disputes are incidental, not comprehensive. Acts, in turn, intends to present not a history of the early Christian movement and the Christian communities, but a recounting of the "deeds" of the leading apostles Peter and Paul.[2] The author refers to other persons, events, or communities of the missionary movement only insofar as they shed light on or are connected with the dominant heroes of the book. Lacunae, contradictions, and loose ends in the narratives allow us to perceive the tension between Luke's traditional materials and his own redactional theological interests. Even Hengel, who pleads for the historical trustworthiness of Acts, must concede:

> He certainly knew a good deal more than he put down; when he is silent about something, there are usually special reasons for it. Only by this strict limitation of his material can he "put his heroes in the right perspective."[3]

When we ask which historical information about the involvement of women in the very beginnings of the Christian missionary movement has survived the "Lukan silence," the answer seems at first glance completely negative. No women are mentioned among the original apostles, the Jerusalem Hellenists, or in the Antiochene church. Moreover, the occasional Pauline references to women's names and leadership titles appear insignificant when read within the redactional framework of early Christian beginnings provided by Acts. Nowhere in his work does Luke picture women as missionaries and preachers. Rather he stresses that women, as wealthy proselytes or godfearers, support or oppose Paul's missionary work. The center stage of Acts is occupied by Paul, the great apostle and missionary to the gentiles. Women appear on this stage only as auxiliary supporters or influential opponents of Paul's mission.

However, when we read the occasional Pauline references to women in their own setting, we recognize that the Pauline and the post-Pauline literature know of women not merely as rich patronesses of the Christian missionary movement but as prominent leaders and missionaries who—in their own right—toiled for the gospel. These women were engaged in missionary and church leadership activity both before Paul and independently of Paul. Without question they were equal and sometimes even superior to Paul in their work for the gospel. As Jewish Christian missionaries, these women might have belonged to the Christian communities in Galilee, Jerusalem, or Antioch which stand at the very beginnings of the Christian missionary movement.[4] As I have shown, the Gospel traditions still reflect the fact that women were, on the one hand, instrumental in continuing the movement initiated by Jesus after his execution and resurrection and, on the other hand, involved in expanding this movement to gentiles in the adjacent regions. The tensions in Luke's account of the first Christian community in Jerusalem and the expulsion of the Hellenists indicate that women were also active in the Christian community of Jerusalem.

This chapter seeks to reconstruct the beginnings and the institutional, organizational forms of the early Christian missionary movement; to elaborate its overall theological perspective; and finally to situate its pre-Pauline baptismal self-expression (Gal 3:28) within the structural and theological framework of the movement.

"The Church in Her House"

It appears that very soon after the execution and resurrection of Jesus the community of so-called Hellenists gathered alongside the Aramaic-speaking community of Jerusalem. These Hellenists were probably Greco-Palestinians who, whether as families or as individuals, had resettled in Jerusalem. Archaelogical finds have shown that Greek-speaking synagogues existed in Jerusalem and that many of their members were women. Josephus tells us about Queen Helena of Adiabene who returned to Jerusalem to live out her life in the holy city. Most of these Greco-Palestinians were probably very observant Jews since they or their families had returned to Jerusalem. However, some of them might have been disappointed by the actual everyday life of Jerusalem and the Temple because it did not correspond to their expectations.[5]

Although the account of the Hellenists (Acts 6:1–8:3) is strongly overlaid by the redactional interests of Luke, it is still possible to reclaim some historical information from the Lukan redactional tendencies, as the following *aporias* in Luke's account[6] show.

Although Acts claims that the believers were "one heart and one soul" in the Jerusalem church, a conflict between the so-called Hebrews and Hellenists arises. In Luke's terms this conflict is resolved by a clear-cut division between the work of the apostles (the *diakonia* of the word) and that of the seven Hellenists (the *diakonia* of the tables). However, the subsequent narrative pictures the seven as powerful preachers and missionaries who were expelled from Jerusalem after the death of Stephen, while the church which gathered in Jerusalem around the apostles and James, the brother of the Lord, did not suffer expulsion. Moreover, Stephen was lynched because of his critique of the Temple, while James and the apostles are characterized by Luke as faithful observants of the Torah and the Temple rituals. Luke tries to gloss over these differences among the leadership in the Jerusalem church (or churches), but the facts were probably available not only to him but also to his readers, and he was compelled to incorporate some of the available historical information into his own account, although this information seems to have undermined his theological interest in picturing the mother community of Jerusalem as of one heart and one soul, sharing everything.

"Those who were scattered went about preaching the word" (8:4) to Samaria, Caesarea Damascus, and "as far as Phoenicia, Cyprus, and Antioch" (11:19). According to Luke, it was Peter who first admitted "gentiles" because he had received God's directive in a vision to do so. However, the remark of Acts, that some people from Cyprus and Cyrene preached "the Lord Jesus" (11:20f) to the "Greeks" in Antioch first and that "a large company was added to the Lord" (11:24) indicates that a larger group of missionaries stands at the beginning of the gentile mission. Among them was Barnabas,[7] a native of Cyprus who, like many Jews of the Diaspora, had moved to Jerusalem. According to Acts he was an emissary of the church in Jerusalem who approved the gentile mission—though this "approval" may have been emphasized mainly to support Luke's centralist image of early Christian beginnings. He appears to be the leader of the Antiochene church, who not only brought Paul to Antioch (11:25f) but also seems to have introduced him to Peter (Gal 1:18; cf. Acts 9:27). Barnabas, then, was the teacher of Paul, an apostle and missionary to the gentiles before and later with Paul (cf. 14:4, 14), and a prophet (13:1; cf. Acts 11:24).

Whether Barnabas belonged to the Hellenists or not, however, is unclear, since according to Acts, he was not expelled from Jerusalem. Again, this information might reflect Lukan redactional interest in making the Jerusalem church central to early Christian missionary beginnings. The description of Barnabas as a Levite born in Cyprus (4:36), as well as his initiative in the gentile mission and his leadership of the Antiochene church, speaks for his being one of the "Hellenists." On the other hand, he could also have represented a direction in the Jerusalem church distinct from either the Hellenists or James and the circumcision party. These theological circumstances would explain why it was so difficult for Paul, on the one hand, to distinguish his own theological emphasis from that of other Christian missionaries (Hellenists?) in Corinth and, on the other hand, to defend his "law"-free mission and apostleship to the gentiles in Galatia over and against the circumcision party of James. Paul's situation was further aggravated when both Peter and Barnabas retrenched on their earlier practice of table sharing with the gentile Christians (Gal 2:11–21). After this conflict with Peter and Barnabas, Paul seems to have lost all connection with and influence on the church in Antioch.

It is Barnabas, therefore, who seems to have forged the links not only between the two major communities of Jerusalem and Antioch but also between Antioch and the so-called Pauline missionary field. Thus Barnabas, and not his disciple Paul, was the most prominent and influential leader in the beginnings of the Christian missionary movement, with its center in Antioch, a cosmopolitan urban center of the Greco-Roman world and the third largest city in the Roman Empire after Rome and Alexandria. Yet we know very little about either the teaching of Barnabas or the beginnings of the Christian community in Antioch, Alexandria, or Rome, since the Pauline mission was centered in Greece and Asia Minor. We know from Paul's letter to the Romans that Paul had not founded the community there. If the Jewish-Christian pseudo-Clementine writings contain some historical reminiscences, then it was Barnabas who brought the gospel to Rome. He is characterized as belonging "to the circle of disciples" of Jesus,[8] an expression that, interestingly enough, emerges for the first time in Acts in connection with the Hellenists (cf. Acts 6:1, 2, 7).

Although Barnabas might not have visited Rome personally, it is more probable that members of the Antiochene church first evangelized in the capital. The peculiar role assigned to Antioch in the redactional plan of Acts, however, as well as the silence about Barnabas and the Antiochene church in other early Christian writings, indicates how difficult the reconstruction of the early Christian movement is, on the whole, if one of its most influential centers remains so elusive to historical inquiry. Such a reconstruction therefore must proceed like the restoration of an old painting which has been painted over again and again.

Although no women are mentioned among the seven Hellenists appointed to devote themselves to the *diakonia* at table, Luke mentions the daughters of Philip as well-known prophets in early Christianity.[9] The prominent prophet leader of Thyatira mentioned in Revelation 2 also appears to be associated with the followers of Nicolaus, who was one of the seven. Women are also involved in the original conflict which, according to Acts, led to the separation of the ministry into that of the apostles and that of the seven.

Acts' description of the incident and its resolution is clearly colored by the Lukan theological-historical interest in covering up a serious conflict that arose in the very beginnings of the Christian movement. This conflict resulted in the expulsion from Jerusalem of the Hellenists, who then initiated the Christian missionary movement to the gentiles. Although Luke seeks to subordinate the Hellenists to the apostles in Jerusalem and to reserve the ministry of the word to the latter, the Hellenists come to the fore as powerful missionary preachers and founders of communities.[10]

The division of the one *diakonia* into two, namely, the ministry at table and the ministry of the word, probably reflects a later practice of the Christian missionary movement, while the subordination of one to the other and the ascription of these ministries to certain groups clearly express Luke's own situation. This situation is remarkably similar to that in the Pastorals, which also distinguish between ministers who "labor in preaching and teaching" (1 Tim 5:17) and those who "serve" (1 Tim 3:8ff). Although the term *diakonos* does not occur in Acts, it is likely that the readers of Acts saw in Acts 6 the institution of the diaconate (cf. also Acts 19:22), since they were familiar with the office of the deacon. Luke's interest in subordinating one ministry to the other also comes to the fore in the story of Martha and Mary in Luke 10:38–42, where Martha is characterized as "serving at table", while Mary like a rabbinic disciple, listens to *the word* of Jesus.[11]

Exegetes usually explain the conflict in Acts 6 with reference to the plight of widows and orphans in the ancient world.[12] The Hebrews, so it is argued, had neglected the improverished widows of the Hellenists during the daily distribution of goods or food to the needy of the community. No doubt the plight of poor widows, especially those with small children, was very great, and the possibility of starving or of becoming a slave was very real.[13] Yet nothing is said in Acts 6 to indicate that the widows of the Hellenists were *poor*.

"Serving at table" (Acts 6:2; cf. Acts 16:34, also Luke 10:40; 12:37; 17:8) does not mean administration of funds but table service at a meal. According to 1 Cor 10:21 the "table of the Lord" was the eucharistic table. Table ministry, therefore, was most likely the eucharistic ministry, which included preparation of a meal, purchase and distribution of food, actual serving during the meal, and probably cleaning up afterwards. Such eucharistic table sharing, according to the Lukan summary statement in 2:46, took place "day by day": "And day by day, attending the temple together and breaking bread in their homes, they partook of food with glad and generous hearts." Moreover, the context of this statement in 2:45 as well as Acts 4:32–37, which speaks of the distribution of goods to the needy in the community, does not use the expression "serving at table," although, in the beginning chapters of Acts, the apostles are in charge of the community's economic welfare and financial administration.

It is possible, therefore, that the conflict between the Hellenists and the Hebrews involved the role and participation of women at the eucharistic meal. The expression that they were "overlooked" or "passed over" in the daily *diakonia* or ministry could indicate either that they were not assigned their turn in the table service or that they were not properly served. Whatever the problem was, it seems to have been of a nature similar to the problem of table sharing among Jewish and gentile Christians in Antioch. Since Greco-Roman women were used to participating in *symposia* and festive dinners, the "Hellenistic" women and men in Jerusalem or Antioch probably took for granted the participation of women in the "breaking of bread" in the house church, while the "Hebrews" might have had problems with such a practice.[14]

That the Hellenists—but not the group around James—gathered in the house of a woman in Jerusalem is clear from Acts 12:12–17. Peter tells those who were gathered in the house of Mary, that they should tell "James and the brethren" about his miraculous release from prison. Thus they were not present at the meeting. Moreover, Mary is identified as the mother of John Mark, who, according to Col 4:10, was the cousin of Barnabas. The Hellenistic nature of this house church might also be indicated by the Greek names Rhoda and Markos. Mary, thus, was a kinswoman of Barnabas and in charge of the (or a) house church of Hellenists in Jerusalem. The mere fact that her name is mentioned, since it would have been easy to characterize the house as that of John Mark, testifies to her importance in the Jerusalem community of Hellenists. Like Barnabas she would have been independently wealthy, since the house seems to have been large and to have had servants. Hengel has pointed out that, relatively speaking, women's names are mentioned quite often in Greek or bilingual tomb inscriptions found in Jerusalem.[15] Helena, the queen of Adiabene, was the paradigm of such well-placed women. Like Helena, many of these women probably were proselytes who had come to the holy city for religious reasons. Such women would have been attracted especially by the preaching of the Hellenists that accorded them full membership in the community. Mary might have been one of them. One can only speculate whether she was among the Greco-Palestinian "widows" who were passed over by the Hebrews in the daily eucharistic ministry, even though she had devoted herself "to the *diakonia* of the saints" (e.g., 1 Cor

16:15f which indicates what honor and respect would have been due her if she had been a man).

Acts probably reflects historical experience in stressing that women were involved in the Christian missionary movement at every stage of its expansion.[16] Tabitha of Jaffa represents the first stage of expansion, while Lydia is the first convert of Europe (Acts 16:14). God-fearing women of high standing at Antioch in Pisidia drove Paul and Barnabas out of their district (13:50ff), while many prominent Greek women, who were attracted to Judaism in Thessalonica (17:4), and the Greek women of Beroea, listened to the Christian preachers and some were converted. A woman convert, Damaris, is mentioned in Athens (17:34), and Prisca evangelized in Corinth (18:2ff). The son of Paul's sister informs the tribune of Jerusalem about a plot to ambush Paul (23:16). Drusilla, the wife of the governor Festus, and Bernice, the wife of King Agrippa, are present at Paul's defense and privately agree with each other that "this man has done nothing to deserve death or imprisonment" (26:31). Although these last remarks clearly evidence Lukan coloration, the whole narrative underlines the fact that many prominent and well-placed Greco-Roman women were attracted to the Christian movement. That more prominent women than men became Christians is especially reflected in the second- and third-century attacks against Christians, which speak of the problem of these women often being forced to marry pagans or to live with Christian slaves in a kind of "common-law marriage." Since this was prohibited in Roman civil law, it was acknowledged by the church only by Callistus, who was himself a slave before becoming bishop of Rome at the beginning of the third century.[17]

Acts is one-sided, however, in its presentation of the Christian missionary movement and of women's involvement in it. By stressing their status as prominent and wealthy, the author neglects their contribution as missionaries and leaders of churches in their own right. We are able to correct this one-sided picture to the degree that additional information derived from the Pauline literature allows us to question Acts' historical accuracy. Yet women's actual contribution to the early Christian missionary movement largely remains lost because of the scarcity and androcentric character of our sources. It must be rescued through historical imagination as well as in and through a reconstruction of this movement which fills out and contextualizes the fragmentary information still available to us. The historical texts and information on women's involvement in the beginnings of the Christian missionary movement, therefore, must not be taken as descriptive of the actual situation. Once again, they are the tip of an iceberg in which the most prominent women of the early Christian missionary movement surface, not as exceptions to the rule but as representatives of early Christian women who have survived androcentric redactions and historical silence. Their impact and importance must not be seen as exceptional, but must be understood within the structures of the early Christian missionary movement that allowed for the full participation and leadership of women.

This chapter, therefore, proceeds by reconstructing a model of that movement whose constitutive institutional elements were the missionary agents, on the one hand, and the house church and local associations on the other. The forms of religious propaganda and the reciprocal patronage system of Greco-Roman society, not the patriarchal structures of the Greco-Roman household, were constitutive organizational elements of this movement. Such a reconstruction of the Christian missionary movement in terms of organizational structures provides the social framework that makes women's leadership not only plausible but also intelligible. Traveling missionaries and house churches were central to the early Christian mission which depended on special mobility and patronage, and women were leaders in both areas.

Missionaries

The remarkable expansion of oriental mystery religions in the western Mediterranean has not lacked scholarly attention. Many preceded the Christian missionaries to Greece and Rome, thereby creating the climate in which a new Eastern cult such as Christianity could be propagated. The wandering preachers of that day manifest a whole range of missionary propagandists,[18] from philosophers, prophets, itinerant preachers, mendicants, and sorcerers to the traveling merchants, state officials, immigrants, slaves, and soldiers. Common to all were mobility and dedication to their philosophy or religion. Jewish proselytism of the first century must be seen in this context of Eastern cults. In Rome and throughout the Mediterranean, large numbers—many of whom were women—were attracted to the monotheism and high moral standards of Judaism. Among Godfearers and proselytes many women, often of high social status, are mentioned.[19]

Like Judaism the Christian gospel was spread by traveling missionaries, trade and business people, who depended on the hospitality and support provided by house churches.[20] Thus, the charismatic missionaries were not necessarily itinerant beggars. Barnabas seems to have been wealthy enough to support the community of Jerusalem by selling land. Paul was one of the distinguished circle of foreign Jews, who belonged to the privileged Hellenistic families in Tarsus and who had received Roman citizenship in turn for services rendered. E. A. Judge's conclusion, therefore, seems appropriate: "Christianity in its canonical form, then, is not so much the work of Galileans, as of a very cultivated section of internationalized Jewry; they were at any rate its principal sponsors."[21] The exceptional contribution of prominent women of wealth and social status to the Jewish as well as Christian missionary movements is more and more acknowledged in scholarship.[22]

The practice of missionary partners in the Jesus movement seems to have been followed by the Christian missionary movement as well.[23] This allowed for the equality of women and men in missionary work. It is likely that these missionary partners were at first couples. By the time of Paul, however, sexual ascesis and celibacy were being urged as preferred preconditions for missionary work. Whether or not some form of "spiritual marriage," in which two ascetics lived together as a couple, has its roots in this missionary practice of partnership is unclear, but possible. Pauline references to women missionaries, however, do not reflect on their sexual status and gender roles, or classify them as widows or virgins.

The Pauline letters mention women as Paul's coworkers, but these women were not the "helpers" of Paul or his "assistants." Only five of Paul's coworkers, all of whom are male (Erastus, Mark, Timothy, Titus, and Tychicus), "stand in explicit subordination to Paul serving him or being subject to his instructions."[24] The genuine Pauline letters apply missionary titles and such characterizations as co-worker (Prisca), brother/sister (Apphia), *diakonos* (Phoebe), and apostle (Junia) to women also. They usually equate co-workers and "those who toil." In 1 Cor 16:16ff Paul admonishes the Corinthians to be "subject to every co-worker and laborer" and to give recognition to such persons. 1 Thes 5:12 exhorts the Thessalonians to "respect those who labor among you, and are over you in the Lord, and admonish you." It is significant, therefore, that Paul uses the same Greek verb, *kopian*, "to labor" or "to toil,"[25] not only to characterize his own evangelizing and teaching but also that of women. In Rom 16:6, 12, he commends Mary, Tryphaena, Tryphosa, and Persis for having "labored hard" in the Lord.

Paul also affirms that women worked with him on an equal basis. Phil 4:2–3 explicitly states that Euodia and Syntyche have "contended" side by side with him. As in an athletic race these women have competed alongside Paul, Clement, and the rest of Paul's co-missionaries in the cause of the gospel.[26] Paul considers the authority of both women in the community at Philippi so great that he fears that their dissension could do serious damage to the Christian mission. The Philippians had entered with Paul into an equal partnership, a partnership endangered by the disagreement of these two outstanding women missionaries. J. P. Sampley has pointed out that, according to Roman legal traditions, consensual legal partnership "is operative as long as the partners are in *eodem sensu*, as long as they are 'of the same mind' about the centrality of the purpose around which the partnership was formed in the first place."[27] When, therefore, Paul admonishes the two women "to be of the same mind" he reminds them of their original shared partnership and commitment to the same gospel. At stake here, then, are not personal disagreements or quarrels but the shared ground and the purpose of their equal partnership in the "race" for the gospel.

Although Phoebe (Rom 16:1ff) is the only person in the Pauline literature to receive an official letter of recommendation and although she is given three substantive titles—sister, *diakonos*, and *prostatis*—her significance for the early Christian mission is far from acknowledged. Exegetes tend to denigrate these titles, or to interpret them differently, because they are given to a woman. Whenever Paul uses the title *diakonos* to refer to himself or another male leader, exegetes translate it "minister," "missionary," or "servant." In the case of Phoebe they usually translate it "deaconess." After characterizing Phoebe as an "obviously well-to-do and philanthropic lady," Lietzman goes on to say: "Even at that time there had long been women deacons in the Christian church whom, *when their sex made them especially suitable,* came forward and gave significant help in caring for the poor and sick, and at the baptism of women."[28] Similarly Michel notes: "It is possible that Phoebe 'served' women, the sick, or friends and perhaps gave also assistance at baptism of women."[29] Unconsciously these exegetes are projecting back into the first century the duties of deaconesses in later centuries. However, Phoebe's "office" in the church of Cenchreae is not limited by prescribed gender roles. She is not a deaconess of the women, but a minister of the whole church.[30]

The use of *diakonos* in Rom 16:1 is not identical to its use in Phil 1:1, where no named person receives this title, since saints, overseers, and ministers (*diakonoi*) are ascriptions of the whole community. The term is not used here in a formal, titular, and official way. Paul uses

the same title as a characterization of himself, Apollos, and his opponents in 2 Corinthians but appears to modify it with *synergos* ("co-
worker"). In 1 Cor 3:5, 9 he uses the expression to emphasize that it is
God who has called Apollos and himself and given them a common
ministry. In 2 Cor 6:1 he refers to the whole community "as working
together with God," while he commends himself as a *diakonos* who
suffered much in his missionary work. In 1 Thessalonians, Paul sends
Timothy "our brother" and "co-worker of God" in the gospel of
Christ (3:2). According to 1 Cor 16:15 the co-workers and laborers are
those who have "devoted themselves to the *diakonia* of the saints."
The *diakonos*, like the *synergos*, therefore, is a missionary entrusted
with preaching and tending churches.[31] Since the term is also used in
extrabiblical sources to refer to preaching and teaching, it seems clear
that the *diakonoi* of the Pauline mission served in the recognized and
"official" capacity of missionary preachers and teachers. It can be
concluded, therefore, that Phoebe is recommended as an official
teacher and missionary in the church of Cenchreae.[32]

This conclusion is justified by the affinity of her standing to that of
the so-called superapostles mentioned in 2 Corinthians. Friedrich has
pointed out that the word group *diakonos, diakonia, diakonein* is mostly
found in 2 Corinthians and that the rivals of Paul might have been
missionaries similar to the Hellenists of Acts 6–8.[33] They were charismatic missionaries and impressive preachers, visionary prophets and
true apostles, filled with Spirit and Sophia. Paul does not attack their
preaching and theology but is concerned to prove himself the true
pneumatic apostle of Christ. They seem to have attacked him for his
lack of support by the community, for his weak personal appearance,
and for his lack of letters of recommendation.

> The opponents in II Corinthians are not isolated teachers but, as
> their letters of recommendation (3:1) and their self-designation as
> "apostles," "ministers" and "workers" show, they are part of a
> larger group of missioners.[34]

The characterization of Phoebe is similar to that of these charismatic
preachers and effective missionaries.[35] However, she stands in a
friendly relationship to Paul and his missionary circle, since she receives from him a letter of recommendation and, like Timothy who is
called "brother," receives the title "our sister."

Unlike the *diakonoi* who worked as missionaries in Corinth, Phoebe
is not characterized as an "apostle." However, this can probably be
traced to Paul's desire to avoid a misunderstanding that she was an

apostle of the church at Cenchreae, since the "apostles of the churches" were commissioned only for a definite and limited function.[36] Another woman in Rom 16:7, however, does receive this title. Like Prisca and Aquila, Andronicus and Junia were missionary partners—Jewish Christians, perhaps from Tarsus.[37] Since they had become Christians before Paul, they seem to have worked together with Paul in Antioch and even shared imprisonment with him.[38] It can be conjectured that they belonged to the circle of apostles in Jerusalem who, together with James, received a vision of the resurrected Lord (see 1 Cor 15:7).[39] Paul even stresses that they were outstanding members of the circle of the apostles.

Since they were in Rome, they—like Paul and the community in Antioch—seem to have been engaged in the gentile mission. Like Barnabas and Paul (Acts 14:4, 14), they are itinerant missionaries engaged in the work of the gospel. In the discussion with his rivals in Corinth and Galatia, Paul stresses that he is a true apostle because he has received a resurrection appearance, has a call to missionary work, and has proven himself an outstanding missionary. For Paul, however, the mark of true apostleship does not consist in mighty speech and pneumatic exhibitions but in the conscious acceptance and endurance of the labors and sufferings connected with missionary work. (1 Cor 4:8–13; 2 Cor 11–12). Andronicus and Junia fulfill all these criteria of true apostleship. They were apostles even before Paul and had suffered prison in pursuit of their missionary activity.

However, in one signal aspect they are different from Paul, who worked mostly in tandem with male co-workers like Barnabas, Silvanus, or Timothy. As noted above, partnership or couple-mission, not individual missionary activity, seems to have been the rule in the Christian movement just as in the Jesus movement.[40] In 1 Cor 9:5 Paul maintains that he, like the other apostles, had the right to support and the right to be accompanied by a female co-missionary. The other apostles, the brothers of the Lord, and Cephas were accompanied on their missionary journeys by "sisters" as "wives" (lit., "as women"). Since the term *brother* can also characterize a member of a particular group of missionary co-workers (cf. Phil 4:21ff)[41], it can be surmised that "sisters" refers to the women as missionary co-workers. The difficult double accusative object ("sister," "woman") is best explained in this way.[42]

Thus the missionary couples Prisca and Aquila and Andronicus and Junia were not exceptions. Such pairs are probably also mentioned in Rom 16:15, as we have already seen. When Paul stresses celibacy as the best state for missionary work (1 Cor 7:24ff), he is expressing his own opinion, an opinion that does not square with the practice of the missionary movement. However, it must be noted that neither Prisca nor Junia are defined as "wives." Their traditional status and role as wives does not come to the fore, but rather their commitment to partnership in the work of the gospel. Moreover, we have no indication whatever that the work of these women missionaries laboring in tandem with their partners was restricted solely to women, as patristic exegetes suggest.[43]

The *Acts of Paul and Thecla* is a second-century writing devoted entirely to the story of a woman missionary.[44] In many regions this book was regarded as canonical in the first three centuries. It mentions a great number of women, besides the apostle Thecla. Thecla is converted by Paul. She takes a vow of continence and is persecuted for this by her fiance and her family. Condemned to death, she is saved by a miracle and goes with Paul to Antioch. A Syrian falls in love with Thecla, is rejected, and takes revenge. When Thecla is condemned to fight with wild beasts, she baptizes herself in a pit full of water, whereupon, since the beasts do not harm her, she is set free. Her protectress, Tryphena, together with a part of her household, is converted to Christianity. Thecla proclaims the word of God in the house of Tryphena, then follows Paul to Myra. After only a short while with him, she receives the commission "to teach the word of God" and goes to Iconium and from there to Seleucia, where she enlightens many with the gospel.

Since Paul does not stand in the foreground of the narrative, the author of the *Acts of Paul and Thecla* appears to have incorporated independent traditions about Thecla. The image of the woman missionary depicted here is striking. Thecla is commissioned by Paul to "go and teach the word of God." Women in Carthage at the beginning of the third century still appealed to the apostle Thecla for women's authority to teach and to baptize.

In other ways the picture of Thecla reflects usual feminine stereotypes. She falls in love with Paul, follows him, and is dependent on him. But her rejection of marriage brings her into conflict with the patriarchal values of her society. Motifs of the Hellenistic novel or romance are here taken over for missionary purposes. We find the motif of "love at first sight," the separation motif, the theme of the "devoted couple," and faithfulness despite great pressures. Of course, in the Christian work the apostle and the woman are not sexual partners but live in absolute continence. Obviously these legends and stories could present women as preachers and missionaries only in romantic disguise. Women renounce traditional family ties, not for the sake of mission but for a spiritual love relationship with the apostle. In the genre of romantic love, the woman is infatuated, follows the apostle, and remains faithful to him.

However, despite the romantic style of the Hellenistic novel, which is also found in *Joseph and Aseneth*, the image of Thecla retains reminiscences of the power and authority of women missionaries at the beginning of the Christian movement. As W. Ramsay has pointed out: "Thecla became the type of the female Christian teacher, preacher and baptizer, and her story was quoted as early as the second century as a justification of the right of women to teach and to baptize."[45] In time, however, "the objectionable features of the tale could be explained away," and those more in accordance with the prevailing women's image could be emphasized, until, finally, the objectionable features were totally eliminated, or—for those too well established in the tradition—reduced to a minimum. Thus we hear the short command that Thecla should preach the word of God, but none of her speeches is cited while several of her prayers are quoted. Similarly, we see her baptizing herself, but "in the extant MSS not a single trace remains of Thecla's administering the rite of baptism to others."[46]

Nevertheless, despite ecclesiastical redactions and romantic, erotic novelistic overlays, the *Acts of Paul and Thecla* still views women as followers of Paul and as celebrating an agape. Thecla's story as a follower of Paul takes shape on the model of the apostle's own, even in the extant manuscripts.

> Thecla is the disciple growing up to take the place of the Master. . . . In addition to many specific acts in her life which parallel or exceed Paul's exploits, Thecla is finally acclaimed as Paul's counterpart by Paul himself. Paul, on the contrary, assumes in the story an increasingly less important and less heroic role; in the end he exists only to be Thecla's inspiration and the apostolic validator of her mission.[47]

Thecla is not pictured as an isolated heroine, but is surrounded by a number of supportive women. The rejection by her own mother and the abandonment of her family are counterbalanced by the acquisition of "a new mother" in Queen Tryphaena and a new home in her "household." The "new family" promised in the Gospels to those who have left everything in the discipleship of Jesus, is here identified as the supportive community of women.[48] Not only the women of the city but also two fierce lionesses contribute to Thecla's deliverance and support her in her travails. When she is finally freed, "all the women cried out with a loud voice, and as with one voice gave praise to God, saying, 'One is God who has delivered Thecla' so that all the city was shaken by the sound" (3:38).

Although the *Acts of Paul and Thecla* might have had their original setting in a community of women,[49] the redactional tendencies and overlays suggest that their present form is the work of male ecclesiastical writers, who could tolerate women as ascetics persevering in contemplation and prayer but not as itinerant missionaries preaching the gospel. This is apparent, for example, from the way the author of the *Acts* treats Priscilla, the great woman missionary of early Christianity. He mentions that Paul at Ephesus stayed in the house "of Aquila and Priscilla." The second time their house is mentioned, it is referred to only as the "house of Aquila." Paul addresses only "the brethren and men"; Priscilla is here reduced to the lady of the house of Aquila and therefore soon forgotten. It is not very likely that a woman author would have developed so little interest in the great missionary of Paul's time.

The House Church

While Paul eloquently preaches about the building up of the community, he himself seems to have moved from missionary center to missionary center. By contrast, Prisca and Aquila founded and supported a "church in their house" wherever they moved. In their missionary endeavor the *diakonia* of the word and table was not yet divided. The house church was the beginning of the church in a certain city or district.[50] It provided space for the preaching of the word, for worship, as well as for social and eucharistic table sharing. The existence of house churches presupposes that some rather well-to-do citizens—who could provide space and economic resources for the community—joined the Christian movement.

It is not clear whether whole households converted to the new religion when the master or mistress of the house became a member of the church. Since the Greco-Roman household included not only the members of the immediate family, slaves, and unmarried female relatives, but also freed persons, laborers, tenants, business associates, and clients, this is not very likely. But a study of the house church not only sheds light on the social status of the leading members of the household but also explains why the members of such a community came from different groups and ranks of society associated with the household. As the household of faith (Gal 6:10) the community had to find new ways of living together, since the customary rules of behavior no longer applied.

The house church, by virtue of its location, provided equal opportunities for women, because traditionally the house was considered women's proper sphere, and women were not excluded from activities in it. This is recognized by Stephen B. Clark, even though he argues in the opposite direction:

> The men assume a more prominent place in the public life of the early Christian community than the women. This is understandable in terms of what we have observed about family life and the overall structure of the Christian community. The women had more responsibility within the household. This does not mean that women had no responsibility in the community, nor that men had no responsibility in the household. Men, however, had greater responsibility in community life outside of the household than did the women.[51]

Clark adopts the division between public and private sphere, community and household, which was as typical for Greco-Roman society as it is for our own. However, in doing so he overlooks the fact that the public sphere of the Christian community was *in* the house and not outside of the household. The community was "in her house." Therefore, it seems that the *domina* of the house, where the ecclesia gathered, had primary responsibility for the community *and* its gathering in the house church.

Moreover, wealthy women were notorious in the first century for opening their premises and houses to oriental cults and their ecstatic worship celebrations. The Christians were neither the first nor the only group to gather together in house communities for religious worship. A treatise on chastity attributed to members of a Pythagorean community in Italy in the second or third century B.C.E. warns women:

> They keep away from secret cults and Cibyline orgies in their homes. For public law prevents women from participating in these rites, particularly those rites which encourage drunkenness and ecstasy. The mistress of the house and head of the household should be chaste and untouched in all respects.[52]

An inscription from the first century B.C.E.—with rules for a house cult in Philadelphia, Phrygia—has been recovered, which stresses that both women and men, slaves and free, could participate in this cult whose guardian and mistress was Agdistis. In a satire Juvenal derides rich women who host oriental cults:

> And watch out for a woman who's a religious fanatic: in the summer she will fill the house with a coven of worshippers of strange oriental deities. Their minister will be a weird apparition, an enormous obscene eunuch, revered because he castrated himself with a jagged hunk of glass. He'll use his prophetic powers and solemnly intone the usual warning. . . . He claims that whatever dangers threaten will be absorbed by the cloak [that he wears as a gift] and promises protection for the coming year."[53]

The rites of the *Bona Dea*, the Good Goddess, were confined to women. But whereas Juvenal describes these rites as those of sex-crazy women burning with lust, Plutarch's picture of the cult is probably more accurate:

> It is not lawful for a man to attend the sacred ceremonies, nor even to be in the house when they are celebrated; but the women apart by themselves, are said to perform many rites during their sacred service which are orphic in character.[54]

These sacred rites took place in the house of the consul or praetor, who must leave "while his wife takes possession of the premises." Interesting, too, is the mystery cult of Dionysos, which Pompeia Agripinilla founded in Rome in the middle of the second century C.E., and in which she herself functioned as priestess. Similarly, synagogues in the Dispersion were often house cults. The founder of the synagogue of Stobi, for instance, reserved for himself and his descendants the right to live on the upper floor of the synagogue.[55] Women are honored in tomb inscriptions with the titles *mater synagogae, presbyteres,* and *archisynagogos,* but we do not quite know what the influence and power of these women was in the life and worship of the Jewish community.[56]

House churches were a decisive factor in the missionary movement insofar as they provided space, support, and actual leadership for the community. The house churches were the place where the early Christians celebrated the Lord's supper and preached the good news. Theologically, the community is called the "house of God," the "new temple" in which the Spirit dwells. Since women were among the wealthy and prominent converts (cf. Acts 17:4, 12), they played an important role in the founding, sustaining, and promoting of such house churches. The following texts which speak of women as leaders of house churches demonstrate this: Paul greets Aphia "our sister," who together with Philemon and Archippus was a leader of the house church in Colossae to which the letter to Philemon was written (Phlm 2).[57] Paul also mentions twice the missionary couple Prisca and

Aquila and "the church in their house" (1 Cor 16:19; Rom 16:5). In a similar fashion, the author of the letter to the Colossians refers to Nympha of Laodicea and the "church in her house" (Col 4:15). According to Acts the church of Philippi began with the conversion of the business woman Lydia from Thyatria who offered her house to the Christian mission (Acts 16:15). Lydia might have been a freed-woman, since she came from the East and sold purple goods which were luxury items. She was not necessarily, therefore, a wealthy, high-born woman.[58] Three women were thus initiators and leading figures in the church at Philippi, with whom Paul had entered into a "consensual partnership" (societas). Naturally, women also belonged to the household conversions and house churches, which are named after men (cf. Acts 10:1ff; 16:32ff; 18:8ff; 1 Cor 1:14; 1:16; 16:15ff [Stephanas]; Rom 16:23 [Gaius]).[59]

One of the most eminent missionaries and founders of house churches is Prisca or Priscilla who, together with her companion Aquila spread the gospel supported by their trade, and independent of any local church.[60] Like Barnabas and Apollos, Prisca was a missionary co-worker with Paul but she was independent of the apostle and did not stand under his authority. Paul is grateful to Prisca and Aquila because they have risked their lives for him. Not only he but the entire gentile church have reason to give thanks to these outstanding missionaries (Rom 16:4). Their house churches in Corinth, Ephesus, (2 Tim 4:19; Acts 18:18ff), and Rome (if Rom 16 is addressed to that community) were missionary centers. 1 Cor 16:19 has greetings from the couple. Even though she is mentioned here after her husband, it is remarkable that she is referred to by name at all, since normally the husband alone is named in such greetings. However, it is significant that whenever Paul sends greetings to the couple (Rom 16:3f), he addresses Prisca first, thus emphasizing that she is the more important of the two (cf. also 2 Tim 4:19).

Corresponding to the information of the Pauline letters, Acts also mentions Prisca and her husband (cf. Acts 18:2–4, 18, 26). Since Luke concentrates in the second part of the Acts on the achievements of Paul, he refers to the couple only in passing. Even these brief remarks, however, indicate the great influence of the couple. We can be assured, therefore, that Luke possesses much more information about them than he transmits to us. Like Paul, Priscilla and Aquila were tent makers by trade and supported their missionary activity through their own work. Like Paul they were Jewish Christians and financially independent of the churches they served. Like Paul they traveled to spread the gospel and suffered for their missionary activity. When Claudius banished the Jews from Rome the couple no longer could stay there and so moved on to Corinth, where they accepted Paul as co-worker in their trade and their house church. In Ephesus they took in Apollos, one of the most erudite and eloquent missionaries of the early Christian movement. Prisca, in particular, became the teacher of Apollos,[61] whose Sophia and Spirit theology might have been derived from her catechesis.

However, as noted earlier, Prisca and Aquila had adopted a different missionary method and practice from that of Paul. Insofar as they—like the "other apostles" (1 Cor 9)—traveled as a pair and gathered converts in house churches, they did not divide the apostolic *diakonia* into the eucharistic table sharing that establishes community and the word that aims at conversion of individuals. Insofar as Paul felt called "not to baptize but to preach the gospel," he did not concentrate on community building. Many of his subsequent problems, for example, with the community at Corinth, probably arose precisely because he had "baptized" so few, while such problems seem not to have emerged with the community in Philippi, with whom he had established *koinōnia*. Moreover, the example of the house churches of Prisca and Aquila suggests that the early house church is not constituted solely by the "family" of the *paterfamilias* or *materfamilias*, but also by converts who belonged to other families— since it is not likely that Prisca and Aquila were accompanied by children, former slaves, kinsfolk, or clients in their travels. Their house church, therefore, most likely was structured like a religious association rather than a patriarchal family.

If Prisca and Aquila already had presided at a church in Rome before being expelled in 49 C.E., they might have had contact or connections with some of the first Christians coming from the Hellenists of the Jerusalem or the Antiochene church. We have no reason to assume that the Roman community at first met solely in synagogues and then organized itself into house churches only after the persecution under Claudius.[62] The practice in Rome might have been similar to that in Jerusalem, in which the Christians did not, at first, sever their ties with the rather powerful Jewish community of Rome, thus remaining members of the synagogue in addition to a house community. The persecution, however, might have forced a separation of both communities for political reasons, and at the same time generated a greater influx of gentile Christians into the Roman church. The Roman church seems to have been organized in house churches well into the third century.[63] The participation of women in this church must have been remarkable. Among the twenty-five persons greeted by name in Romans 16, approximately one-third (eight) are women.[64] Two more women, the mother of Rufus and the "sister" of Nereus, are mentioned without proper names. In addition, women must also have been among those who belonged to the people of the house of Aristobulos and of Narkissos, as well as among the "brethren" or "saints" mentioned in 16:15. Interestingly enough, two pairs are mentioned here as well, Philologus and Julia, as well as Nereus and his sister. These seem to have been missionary couples like Prisca and Aquila, if *adelphē* is here, as elsewhere, an official title, since the woman is not mentioned as "wife" but in her significance for the community. As the movement spread, several house churches could come together as the *ekklēsia* of a city like Corinth. Many dissensions and disagreements which are usually interpreted theologically or ideologically might have their concrete roots in the diversity of house churches within a city or region. However, basic for their organizational structure was that as a religious cult or private association the local church conceded an equal share in the life of the association to all its members. Membership in such an association of equals, therefore, often stood in tension to the traditional partriarchal household structures, to which Christian members of pagan households still belonged.

While some of the religious clubs and associations admitted slaves, members of the lower classes, and women indiscriminately, others were reserved specifically to persons of high status, to certain ethnic groups, to lower-class people, or to women alone. On the whole, their social structures were socially less diversified and more homogeneous than those of the Christian groups. Many of the associations came together not primarily for religious but for social-economic purposes. Such clubs usually had not more than fifty and not less than three members. Unlike Judaism, they were local organizations and did not have international connections.

> The Builders and Carpenters, the Patchwork-Rug-Makers, the Porters, the Purple-dyers of the 18th Street met as did their counterparts of many other names to eat a meal, perhaps a bit better than usual, drink some pretty good wine, supplied by the member whose turn it was, celebrate the birthday of the founder or patron or the feast of Poseidon or Hermes, or Isis, or Silvanus, and to draw up rules to make sure that the members would all have a decent burial when their times came. The *ekklēsia* that gathered with the tentmakers Prisca, Aquila, and Paul in Corinth or Ephesus might well have seemed to the neighbors a club of the same sort."[65]

Those who joined the Christian house church joined it as an association of equals. It was especially attractive to those who had little stake in the rewards of religion based either on class stratification or on male dominance. Although we have little evidence for all-women associations, women joined clubs and became founders and patrons of socially mixed associations. They endowed the club with funds for specific, defined purposes and expected public honors and recognition in return for their benefactions. The officers of a club were usually elected for a specified term of one to five years and had much less influence than the patron of the club, to whom the members often stood in a client relationship.

The rich convert to Christianity, therefore, probably understood herself/himself as entering a club, and expected to exercise the influence of the patron on this club. Without question the house church, as a voluntary organization, was structured according to this patron-client relationship. Moreover, Christians like Phoebe also must have acted as guardians for the community or for individual Christians in dealings with the governments and the courts. With their network of connections, friendships, and influence, Christians from the upper strata eased the social life of other Christians in Greco-Roman society. However, we have no evidence that the Christian community bestowed particular honors and recognitions on its rich members.

The importance of Phoebe's position as minister in the church at Cenchreae is underlined by the title *prostatis,* usually translated "helper" or "patroness," although in the literature of the time the term has the connotation of leading officer, president, governor, or superintendent. Since Paul claims that Phoebe was a *prostatis* of many and also of Paul himself, scholars reject such a meaning here. However, in 1 Thess 5:12 the verb characterizes persons with authority in the community and in 1 Tim 3:4f and 5:17 it designates the functions of the bishop, deacon, or elder.[66]

In the context of Rom 16:2 such leadership must be understood in the more juridical, technical sense of *patrona,* although Ernst Käsemann has again recently argued against such an understanding. He maintains that the word cannot have the juridical sense of the masculine form, which connotes the leader and representative of an association. He declares categorically:

> There is no reference, then, to a "patroness". . . . Women could not take on legal functions, and according to Revelation only in heretical circles do prophetesses seem to have had official ecclesiastical powers of leadership. . . . The idea is that of the personal

care which Paul and others have received at the hand of the
deaconess.[67]

This assertion overlooks the fact, however, that the motif of reciprocity stressed by Paul speaks for a juridical understanding of the title.
Phoebe's patronage was not limited to the community in Cenchreae
but included many others, even Paul himself, who stood with Phoebe
in a patron-client relationship. Such patronage did not consist merely
in financial support and hospitality on behalf of clients but also in
bringing her influence to bear and in using her connections for them.
According to the "exchange law" of Greco-Roman patronage,[68] therefore, Paul asks that the community of Rome repay Phoebe for the
assistance and favors, which Paul owed her as her client.

Why would rich persons like Phoebe join the Christian movement?
The answer to this question might explain the relatively high participation of well-to-do women in the Christian missionary movement.
Although rich women, like rich men, received no honors in the Christian community in return for their patronage,[69] nevertheless they did
receive influence and standing they did not otherwise have in patriarchal society or in the official Roman patriarchal religion. Well-edu-
cated women in particular, with independent resources of wealth,
could develop leadership and have influence in this movement—
options denied them in society at large. Roman law—and apparently
Jewish-Hellenistic custom as well (see, again, Judith)—permitted
women to own and administer their own property and houses. Thus
a wealthy woman "might enjoy the prestige or at least the financial
resources usually reserved to a *paterfamilias*."[70] Such status discrepancy or status dissonance compelled women to break through the
traditional patriarchal patterns entrenched in law and custom. Not
only upper-class women but also women of lower standing had the
opportunity to follow their trade and to accumulate some wealth of
their own. Women were active in finance, trade, and commerce, and
could use their capital for patronage in order to gain recognition and
public honor in return for their benevolence. Archeological evidence
indicates that the women of Pompeii were actively involved in business as well as in civic and religious life during the last two centuries
of the city's existence. Eumachia, who lived during the first quarter of
the first century, donated a huge building as local club center for all
business people. She was a public priestess of Venus or Ceres, a
religious office surely facilitated by her wealth and business connections.[71]

Such status dissonance probably was also experienced by women who joined the Christian movement, founded house churches, and developed leadership. Their leadership in the missionary movement allowed those who were socially and politically marginal—because they were women—to gain new dignity and status. Their marginality was not—as Ross Kraemer has suggested—the result of childlessness or widowhood.[72] Greco-Roman women were chided by moralists for not wanting children and for getting rid of their husbands in easy divorces. Clearly, childlessness no longer bore such odium that it would relegate to marginal status women of wealth and high status. Yet Greco-Roman women had gained wealth, or at least moderate economic independence, without achieving comparable political influence and power. It is true, that by joining religious associations, clubs, or the Christian movement women did not achieve such political influence; they did gain religious influence and power, however. By joining the Christian movement and by building up the church in her house, a woman could derive religious authority and personal self-worth, both of which compensated well for the fact that the Christian community did not honor her as a rich person.

As mentioned earlier, Gerd Theissen has argued that the early Christian missionary movement outside Palestine was not in conflict with its society but was well integrated into it.[73] The radicalism of the Jesus movement was assimilated by the urban Hellenistic communities into a family-style love patriarchalism, which perpetuated the hierarchical relationships of the patriarchal family in a softened, milder form. He overlooks the fact, however, that the egalitarian community structures of private collegia or cultic associations provided the model for the early Christian movement in the Greco-Roman world, not the patriarchal family! This movement not only accorded women and slaves equal standing and the possibility of patronage, but—as a religious cult from the Orient—was suspect to the Greco-Roman authorities. Consisting of equal associations it stood in conflict with Greco-Roman society just as the Jesus movement did with respect to that of Palestinian.

In conclusion: The Pauline literature and Acts still allow us to recognize that women were among the most prominent missionaries and leaders in the early Christian movement. They were apostles and ministers like Paul, and some were his co-workers. They were teachers, preachers, and competitors in the race for the gospel. They founded house churches and, as prominent patrons, used their influence for other missionaries and Christians. If we compare their leadership with the ministry of the later deaconesses, it is striking that their authority and ministry were neither restricted to women and children, nor exercised only in specific feminine roles and functions.

True, we have only occasional remarks in Acts or the letters that allow us to glimpse the leadership and ministry of women in the Christian movement. Yet, the same is true for male leadership and ministry, as we have seen in the example of Barnabas. One could say that the more independent a woman missionary was from the Pauline mission the less chance she had to be remembered in history, since only the Pauline letters break the silence about the earliest beginnings of the Christian missionary movement. However, our sources still allow us to see that this movement was not structured after the Greco-Roman patriarchal household and did not espouse the love patriarchalism by which the later church adapted itself to the structures of its society.

Theological Self-Understanding of the Missionary Movement

Difficult as it is to trace the beginnings and organization of the Christian missionary movement, the reconstruction of Hellenist and Antiochene church theology is even more so. By carefully peeling away the Pauline and Lukan overlay, however, we tentatively can uncover its main features. This theology, first, is rooted in the experiences of the Spirit; second, christologically, it understands the ministry and life of Jesus in terms of Sophia; and therefore, third, it develops a prophetic-critical attitude to the Temple as the locus of the presence of God.

1. While the experience of God's gracious goodness in the ministry and life of Jesus is fundamental for the Jesus movement and its vision, the experience of the power of the Spirit is basic for that of the Christian missionary movement.[74] The God of this movement is the God who did not leave Jesus in the power of death but raised him "in power" so that he becomes "a life-giving Spirit" (1 Cor 15:45, *pneuma zōopoioun*). Christ is preached to Jews and Greeks as "the power of God" and "the sophia of God" (1 Cor 1:24). Therefore he is the Lord of glory, the Lord is the Spirit (Sophia) and the liberator (wherever the Spirit of the Lord is, there is freedom; cf. 2 Cor 3:17). The *basileia* of God does not consist in "mere talk" but in "power" (1 Cor 4:20).

Like Jesus (Luke 4:1), those who are "in Christ" are "filled with the Holy Spirit," possessed by God's Spirit. The expressions "full of the Holy Spirit" or "full of the Holy Spirit and of faith" or "full of the Spirit and of wisdom" all appear in Acts, either with respect to the

Hellenists (6:3, 5, 10; cf. also 6:8, "full of grace and power"), with respect to Barnabas (11:24), or with respect to all Christians (13:52). Those who "have called on the Lord" (Acts 2:21) or who have been "baptized into Christ," live by the Spirit (Gal 5:25)—they are pneumatics, Spirit-filled people (Gal 6:1). Women and men both have received the Spirit. Thus, in the second century, Justin—in his *Dialogue with Trypho*, chap. 88—still can assert that among the Christians all, women and men (*kai thēleias kai arsenas*), have received charisms from the Holy Spirit. This "equality" in the Spirit is summed up by the early Christian movement in the words of the prophet Joel (Acts 2:17f):

> I will pour out my Spirit upon all flesh
> and your sons and your daughters shall prophesy
> and your young shall see visions
> and your old shall dream dreams
> Yes, and on my male and female slaves (in those days)
> I will pour out my spirit and they shall prophesy.

The new community of believers living in the "force field" of the resurrected Lord is understood here in prophetic terms as the messianic community. What was promised in Isa 43:18 or 65:17f is now realized in the community of the baptized:

> Therefore if anyone is in Christ, they are a new creation.
> The old has passed away, behold the new has come. [2 Cor 5:17]

In Gal 6:15 the expression "new creation" characterizes the Christian community de facto as a "new religion." For those who have become a part of this new creation, Jewish concepts and rituals (circumcision or uncircumcision) "have lost their meaning. Faith in Christ has become the decisive basis for salvation."[75]

The expression "new creation" must already have been taken over by Paul because he uses it in an almost formulaic way and only twice in all his letters.[76] This expression probably belongs to the language of Jewish Christian missionary preaching. A similar understanding is also found in the Jewish missionary novel *Joseph and Aseneth*.[77] The prayer of Joseph praises God for the transforming power of conversion:

> Most High, Powerful
> Who makes all things to live
> Who calls out of darkness into light

and from error to truth
from death to life
You indeed are the Lord
who made alive and blessed this virgin
Renew her by your Spirit
Reform her by your hidden hand
Restore her to your life
and let her eat the bread of life
and drink the cup of Blessing
She whom I chose before her birth
and let her enter into your rest (*katapausis*)
which you prepared for your elect ones. [8:9]

In Aseneth's prayer her conversion experience is described as being cut off from her family; she has become an "orphan and alone" (12:11) and feels abandoned (13:1). She asks God to rescue her "from the hand of the enemy," "from those who harass her," and for deliverance from the devil, the father of the gods whom she has rejected (12:8f). As an initiate, Aseneth is given a new lustrous garment and a new name (14:4–15:5). She is granted permission to participate in the sacred meal shared with the angelic beings (15:14) and is promised that she will be the bride (15:5) in the sacred marriage (21:1ff). Aseneth thus becomes the prototype of all those proselytes of whatever race who turn to God in repentance.

At their baptism Christians are told: "You were buried with him in baptism in which you were also raised with him through faith in the working (energy) of God who raised him from the dead" (Col 2:12). Those who have entered the force field of the resurrected Lord, the liberating Wisdom (2 Cor 3:17), have been set free "to share in the glorious freedom of the children of God" (Rom 8:21). The life-giving power of the resurrected Lord has called forth a new creation, in the midst of this death-ridden world, the *sarx*. Therefore Paul can proclaim, "Behold now is the day of salvation" (2 Cor 6:2), and define the gospel "as God's power for salvation to everyone who has faith" (Rom 1:16).

When Paul proclaims that "the end of the ages has come" (1 Cor 10:11), he does not intend to nullify time. He does not speak of the "newness" in Christ Jesus as an atemporal or transtemporal event. God's sending of Christ-Sophia qualifies time and history in such a way that it inaugurates eschatological newness. "Fullness of time" is not the end of time but the beginning of a new epoch, while the end of time is still to be expected. The newness that has broken into this time and world with Jesus Christ does not abolish time and history but seeks to transform them. Therefore, Paul admonishes the Christians "to walk in the newness of life" (Rom 6:4) and not to adapt to the "old aeon" (Rom 12:2). Christians are the avant-garde of the new creation under the conditions of the old world and history. They have died with Christ to the power of sin, to the old humanity, the old ways of being human, but they have not yet shared in the resurrection of Christ in baptism (Rom 6:1–11). Therefore, Paul can speak of dying to the "old humanity" but, in distinction to the deutero-Paulines, he does not speak of "the new human being" that the Christians have become in baptism (Col 3:10; Eph 4:24). The baptized have entered the era of the new but still must daily realize their being "in Christ" anew.[78]

Since the baptized "were washed, sanctified, and justified" in the name of Jesus and in the Spirit of God (1 Cor 6:11), they were "set free from the law of sin and death" (Rom 8:2). They are "the first fruits of the Spirit," but they still wait eagerly for "the adoption as children," "for the redemption of our bodies." Although the baptized have died to the power of sin and death, the power of sin and death are not yet completely overcome. The newness of the era of the Spirit has entered history in Jesus Christ and the Christians, but has not yet completely transformed history. Therefore Paul insists: "Do not be conformed to this world but be transformed by the renewal of your mind, that you may prove what is the will of God, what is good and acceptable, and perfect" (Rom 12:2). "Newness" of God's new creation, according to Paul, should transform the "mind," but he does not stress that it should change the social-political relationship of Christians.

Christians have been crucified with Christ, they have been united in baptism with the suffering and death of Christ. Yet Paul does not understand the crucifixion in concrete political terms as the outcome of the conflict of Jesus' vision with that of the established powers of this world. This fact has far-reaching consequences for Pauline theology, which attempts to spell out the newness of Christian life in the context of history in order to prevent the evaporation of the Christian vision into a mere dream or fanciful ideology. However, whereas Jesus died on the cross because of his deviance from, and opposition to, the religious-social order of his time, the cross of Jesus becomes, in Paul's thought, so universalized that it applies to all human frailty and mortality.

The Pauline school uses the cross as a symbol to justify religiously the suffering of those oppressed by the present order of slavery or patriarchy (thus 1 Peter and Colossians). Cross and suffering are no longer understood as the necessary outcome of the tension between the newness of God's vision and new creation in Jesus Christ on the one hand and the old oppressive order of this world, which rules through suffering, sin, and death on the other. While Paul insists on the transforming power of the new for Christian personal life and practice, especially within the household of faith, he does not pay sufficient attention to the political concreteness of Jesus' crucifixion. Therefore, he does not insist that the power of the new must be brought to bear equally on Christian social-political relationships.

2. The theology of the Christian missionary movement identifies the resurrected Lord not only with the Spirit of God but also with the Sophia of God. (This was possible because in Hebrew and Aramaic both terms are grammatically feminine and can also be interchanged with the Shekinah, the presence of God.) The term Sophia in Acts is used only in relation to Stephen—and always in conjunction with Spirit—to characterize his ecstatic giftedness and proclamation. That the pre-Pauline Christian missionary movement understood the resurrected Christ in terms of Sophia-Spirit is evident in Paul's polemical argument in 1 Corinthians, and more emphatically in the so-called pre-Pauline christological hymns as well as in some traditional materials of the deutero-Pauline Colossians and Ephesians.

Whether or not Apollos, in particular, developed and preached this Sophia christology is debated. The debate will probably never be resolved, for in the words of F. F. Bruce:

> For one short spell Apollos flashes across the New Testament sky and then disappears into darkness as profound as that from which he emerged. But when we speak of darkness, we refer to our own ignorance, not to the historical facts. Apollos played probably a public part in early Christian life far longer than we realize but no further record of it has survived.[79]

We know from Paul's remark that Apollos fostered the church in Corinth after Paul's departure (1 Cor 3:6), and that some members of the community understood themselves as followers of Apollos. Paul stresses the friendly relationship prevailing between the two apostles, but he also must concede that (at least for the moment) Apollos chooses his own way in the missionary work (16:12).

Apollos was a cultured Jew from Alexandria, a theologian well versed in the Scriptures, who had been baptized with the baptism of John and had learned of the teaching of Jesus (Acts 18:24–19:1). We do not know whether he was converted in Alexandria, or who preached the gospel to him. It is possible he heard the story of Jesus from members of the Jesus movement who might have preached the baptism of repentance and the ministry and words of Jesus, as the communities in Galilee and those behind Q seem to have done. Be that as it may, Acts stresses that Priscilla, together with her husband (?) Aquila, instructed Apollos more accurately in the way of God.

Again what this more accurate instruction entailed is not certain, since "the way of God" is a stereotypical expression of Luke to characterize Christian preaching and life. In Acts 19:1–7, however, we encounter other disciples who, though baptized into John's baptism of repentance, had not heard of the Holy Spirit. In distinction to John's baptism of repentance, baptism in the name of the Lord Jesus mediates the Holy Spirit in ecstatic experiences. The more accurate teaching of Priscilla, then, would have entailed the gospel of the resurrected Christ, who is understood as cosmic Lord and life-giving Spirit-Sophia. If this assumption is correct, then Priscilla and Aquila not only provide the historical link of the Roman church to the Pauline missionary movement but also to the Christian movement in Alexandria—assuming Apollos was a missionary there. The content of this more accurate instruction might have been similar to the christological formula used in 1 Cor 1:24 which calls Christ "God's Power and Sophia" or to the characterization of Christ Jesus in 1 Cor 1:30, which also refers to baptism:[80]

> *You* however are in Christ Jesus, who has become for *us* Sophia from God; not only justice (righteousness) but also sanctification and liberation (redemption). [Note the change in pronoun.]

While the Jesus movement, like John, understood Jesus as the messenger and prophet of divine Sophia, the wisdom christology of the Christian missionary movement sees him as divine Sophia herself. Such a Sophia-christology is expressed especially in the pre-Pauline hymns Phil 2:6–11; 1 Tim 3:16; Col 1:15–20; Eph 2:14–16; Heb 1:3; 1 Pet 3:18, 22; John 1:1–14, delineated in form-critical studies. These hymns proclaim the universality of salvation in Jesus Christ in language derived from Jewish-Hellenistic wisdom theology and from contemporary mystery religions.[81] The ministry and significance of Christ the Lord is seen in terms of wisdom theology, for example, in 1 Tim 3:6 and Phil 2:6–11. The way of Jesus Christ was the same as that of Sophia:

Sophia found no place where she might dwell
Then a dwelling place was assigned her in the heavens
Wisdom went forth to make her dwelling among the children of humans

And found no dwelling place
Wisdom returned to her place
And took her seat among the angels. [*Enoch* 42:1–2]

Through his exaltation and enthronement Christ-Sophia has received his-her rulership over the whole cosmos, over heavenly and earthly powers. This is proclaimed in Phil 2:6–11 in language alluding to the Old Testament (Isa 45:23) and the contemporary Isis cult. Like Isis, Christ-Sophia is given a name "which is above all names" and worshiped by all the powers in the cosmos. Just as Isis's true acclamation is "Isis the Lord," so the true Christian acclamation is "Jesus Christ is the Lord."

This proclamation of the universal lordship of Christ-Sophia is addressed to people of the Hellenistic world who believed the world to be ruled by merciless powers, and above all by blind fate. It addresses the desires and longings of Hellenistic persons seeking liberation from the powers of this world and participation in the divine world. In this religious milieu of the mysteries, Christians proclaim Christ-Sophia as the ruler of the principalities and powers which have previously enslaved the world. In this milieu, where the hymns and aretalogies to Isis and other gods are sung, the Christian community sings hymns in praise of Jesus Christ the Sophia of God who appeared on earth and is now exalted as the Lord of the whole cosmos. These Christians believe they are already liberated from the bondage of death and freed from the cosmic evil spirits. They believe they already participate in the power and "energy" of Christ-Sophia, that they are the new creation because they have received the power of the Spirit in baptism.

This proclamation of Jesus Christ as the Sophia of God and the cosmic Lord functions in the Christian community as the foundational myth which engenders its own cult. The exaltation and enthronement of Christ to cosmic reconciliation and sovereignty are the central symbols of this myth. The understanding of Christ in terms of Sophia as the mediator in creation and as the power of the new creation underlines the cosmic significance of Christian faith, but also keeps alive the knowledge that this cosmic Lord is the same Jew, Jesus, who sought a "resting place" in Israel. This knowledge is expressed in the categories of humiliation, incarnation and death. The mythical features of these hymns are so strong, however, that there is a danger that this knowledge about the human life of Jesus Christ and the historical existence of Christians may be neglected.

This raises the fundamental theological question: how were Christians able to proclaim the historical person—Jesus of Nazareth—in terms of myth and with mythological language? This was made possible not only by the ecstatic experience of the Spirit and the resurrection but also by a Jewish-Hellenistic wisdom theology which had already provided the modes and language for a Sophia christology. The pre-Pauline christological hymns—already part of a trajectory of "reflective mythology" in Hellenistic Judaism and Jewish gnosticism—employ the language and motifs of various contemporary myths with a view to apologetic or missionary goals. This "theology expressed in mythological language" appears to have become dependent primarily on the myth of Isis-Osiris, and secondarily on myths of other oriental gods. The trajectory originated in the theology of post-exilic wisdom schools and moved through Hellenistic Judaism, gnosticism, and, in different ways, through early Christianity.

The conjunction of this wisdom trajectory with the pre-Pauline Sophia christology and the pre-Johannine Logos hymn seems to have been prepared for by Philonic theology, where the female figure of Sophia had already become identified with that of the masculine Logos.[82] Philo also had identified the Logos with historical figures such as Moses, Isaac or Israel. Philo, however, uses cosmological-mythological language, derived from the Isis-Osiris cycle to clarify psychological-mystical realities. The Logos as priest and king of the cosmos becomes the priest of the soul. The historical figures of Moses or Isaac are transformed into archetypes or symbols of virtues. The history of Israel is a psychological-mystical paradigm.

Similarly, the mythic material concerning Sophia found in gnostic texts evidences clear connections with Jewish wisdom literature and theology. The cosmic Sophia myth is psychologized and internalized here as well. Sophia and her fate exemplify the true gnostic, whose self can be set free from imprisonment in this world and restored to its divine nature through knowledge of its fall and redemption. It develops into metaphysical dualism constituted by masculine and feminine archetypes. This spiritualizing and psychologizing danger in gnostic dualism and Hellenistic wisdom speculation was already sensed by Paul who seeks to counter it by emphasizing the physical death of Christ and by stressing the historical reality of Christians. Yet this danger does not consist in taking over "female" language and "goddess" expressions, but in the dehistoricizing of Jesus Christ, our *Sophia* and *Kyrios*, as well as in the devaluating of Christian historical practice.

In counteracting the dehistoricizing tendencies of the Christ myth, Paul transfers it from its hymnic setting to that of moral exhortation.

In Phil 2:1–15 Christ becomes the example to be imitated by those who have to "work out" their "own salvation with fear and trembling." In this context Paul elaborates Christian equality. He points to Christ-Sophia who, according to the hymn, did not hold onto his "equality" with God, but "emptied himself" or "lowered himself," taking on the existence of a slave and becoming "obedient unto death." Paul explicitly qualifies the death of Christ as his violent execution on the cross. Yet, as noted, he does not reflect more deeply on the political significance of the death of Jesus, stressing instead, his obedience. Paul quotes the hymn in order to validate his admonitions: "Do nothing from selfishness or deceit, but in humility count others better than yourselves. Let each of you look not only to one's own interests but also to the interests of others (Phil 2:3f).

Equality for Paul, then, consists in looking out not only for our own interests but also for those of others. This understanding is borne out also by 2 Cor 8:13f, the second passage in which Paul speaks about equality. Paul appeals to the Corinthians to contribute their share to the collection for the community of Jerusalem. He does not mean to burden the Corinthians, "but that as a matter of equality" their "abundance at the present time should supply their want, so their abundance might supply" the Corinthians' want, "that there may be equality." Equality, then, consists in the reciprocal sharing of abundance with those Christians who are in need.

However, Paul does not elaborate what such a sharing of abundance would mean in social terms, although the key word *slave* in the hymn Phil 2:1–11 could have provided the occasion to do so. Paul's treatment of the death of Jesus also fails to spell out the political-social implications of this death. We can only speculate why Paul neglected to do this, and focused instead on the moral and ecclesial behavior of the individual Christians irrespective of their social status. Since he does not ground his theology of mutual love in the theology of the new creation and the social-political reality of the death of Christ and the existence of Christians, he necessarily privatizes Christian love and interiorizes it.[83] His attempt to ground the new creation and the story of Christ in history, therefore, does not fully develop its historical-critical impetus.

3. According to Acts 6:13f, Stephen is accused of having spoken against Temple and Torah, the central mediations of God's presence for all Jewish groups of the time. The identification of the Torah with Sophia and her localization in the Jerusalem Temple made the mediatory function of Temple and Torah authoritative, because both institutions thus became the preexistent, eternal, and final expression of

God's presence. The confession of Christ, the Lord, "who has been made our Sophia from God," thus challenges the theological claim of Temple and Torah. This seems to have been theologically articulated and recognized by the Hellenists and especially by Stephen.[84] In his defense he argues not only that—throughout Israel's history—the divine presence was never confined to one place but also that "the Most High does not dwell in houses made with hands" (7:48). The same Greek expression "made with hands" is also found in Mark 14:58 and Heb 9:11, 24. Its semantic and theological context is the missionary preaching of Hellenistic Judaism, which uses the term in its polemics against pagan idols.[85] The Jerusalem Temple is seen here and in Mark 14:58 as being on one level with idolatry, and therefore as belonging to the old aeon. Yet, while the speech of Stephen does not positively say what will replace the old Temple in mediating the presence of God, according to Mark its replacement will be the Christian community.

We find already in the pre-Pauline tradition the understanding that the Christian community is the temple of God. The texts 2 Cor 6:14–7:1; 1 Cor 3:16; Eph 2:22, and perhaps 1 Pet 2:4–10 transfer the notion of *naos* to the Christian community, while Paul adapts this tradition in 1 Cor 6:19 to refer to the body of the individual Christian.[86] Since Hellenistic and Jewish-Hellenistic literature considers not the human body but the soul or mind as the temple in which God or the Spirit dwells, and often understands the body as the prison of the soul, the transference of the notion of temple to the human body reflects typical Pauline theology and was, therefore, probably accomplished by Paul. In calling the body a temple, Paul warns against a "spiritualizing" of Christian self-understanding which considers the soul as the only essential divine part of the human person. In distinction to Paul, the pre-Pauline "temple tradition" understands the Christian community as "temple" of God in order to distinguish it from the unbelieving world. Its *Sitz im Leben* is not a "moral-anthropological discussion" but a missionary situation, interested in drawing the boundaries between the Christian community and the world.

1 Cor 3:16f uses the language complex "building, house, temple" in order to characterize the community. The form of the saying could indicate a baptismal tradition that is quoted here by Paul in order to counter Corinthian divisiveness. He warns the Corinthians that whoever destroys the unity of the community destroys the temple of God. This warning seems to be formulated by Paul for his own theological purposes and inserted into the traditional formula expressed in two parallelisms:

> You are God's temple
> and the Spirit of God dwells in you . . . .
> For the temple of God is holy (*hagios*),
> which you all are.

The traditional (baptismal) formula expresses the self-understanding of Christians that the community is the new temple and, therefore, that they all are sanctified. The missionary context of the temple motif transferred to the Christian community also appears in the passages of the Pauline school, Eph 2:18–22 and 1 Pet 2:4–10. Ephesians uses this motif in order to stress that Jews and gentiles are "made into one" people or race. Through Jesus Christ gentiles are no longer foreigners who are excluded from the inner sanctum of the temple, but have access in one Spirit to the Father. They have become full members of the temple community, the household of God, and are one with the holy angels.

1 Pet 2:4–10 transfers not only the images of temple but also those of priest and sacrifice to the Christian community, the household of God, in the interest of missionary theology. The Christians as the household of God are the new eschatological temple in which not just a special group but all members offer sacrifices worked by the Spirit. They have left their former cultural-religious milieu and form a new nation, new priesthood, and holy people. They are, therefore, characterized in Old Testament and political-cultic language as "a chosen race, a royal house, a priesthood, a holy nation, the true people of God," who proclaim the saving and mighty power of God. These latter passages have combined the tradition of the community as temple with that of the community as household, and their epistolary contexts strongly stress that life in the community must be lived in terms of the patriarchal household of antiquity.

This is not the case in the pre-Pauline[87] (but not necessarily anti-Pauline[88]) fragment 2 Cor 6:14–7:1, which most exegetes consider a segment of tradition inserted into the letter. It is debated, however, whether Paul himself could have used this tradition here, or whether it interrupts, and therefore does not fit into, the present Pauline context.[89]

> Do not get misyoked [or mismatched] with unbelievers.
> For what partnership have righteousness and lawlessness
> or what community has light with darkness?
> What harmony is there between Christ and Belial?
> Or what common lot a believer with an unbeliever?
> What agreement is there between God's temple and idols?
> For we are the temple of the living God; as God has said,

"I will dwell in them and walk among them;
and I will be their God
and they shall be my people.
Therefore come out of their midst
and separate,
says the Lord,
and touch nothing unclean.
Then I will receive you,
and I will be a father to you,
and you shall be to me sons and daughters,
says the Lord Almighty."
Since we have these promises, beloved,
let us cleanse ourselves from every defilement of flesh and spirit,
making holiness perfect in the fear of God.

Hans Dieter Betz has made a strong case that this paraenesis applies to the "theological position of the 'false brothers' at Jerusalem (see Gal 2:4f) and the 'men from James' (see Gal 2:11–14). . . . They would call 'misyoking' what Paul has done in bringing the Galatians into the church without subjecting them to the Torah covenant."[90] He points to Paul's understanding of freedom as opposed to the yoke of the Torah, "the yoke as of slavery" (Gal 5:1). However, while this litertary analysis has again proven that the vocabulary and theological perspective is non-Pauline, it must be questioned whether this generalized understanding of "misyoking" is appropriate.

The Greek word for *mismatch* is a metaphor deriving from Lev 19:19 where the LXX reads the same Greek word for *crossbreeding*. The same figure is also used in Deut 22:10 which forbids plowing with an ox and ass together. The whole complex of sayings prohibits the mingling of two different types of things, for example, seeds, animals, or woolen and linen stuff. It does not speak, however, of two different yokes. On the whole, the figure of the yoke seems to be different from what is in this context insofar as it usually refers to burdens imposed, especially by foreign oppressors (Isa 9:4; 10:27; 14:25; Jer 27:8, 11, 12; Gen 27:40; 1 Kgs 12:4). Therefore, the traditional translation and interpretation, which has generally taken the imperative "be not mismated," or "unevenly yoked together" as a warning against marriage between believers and unbelievers, appears more appropriate. This is not a general Jewish Christian prohibition against mixing socially and religiously with gentile Christians but a warning to avoid marriages with gentiles. The difficulty a woman would encounter in such a marriage is still, even in the second century, vividly described by Tertullian:

> For who would suffer his wife for the sake of visiting the breth-
> ren, to go around from street to street to other men's and indeed
> to all the poorer cottages? Who will willingly bear her being taken
> from his side by nocturnal convocations, if need be?. . . Who
> will, without some suspicion of his own, dismiss her to attend
> that Lord's Supper, which they defame?[91]

The warning in 2 Cor 6:14 is therefore similar to that in 1 Cor 7:39, but much more emphatic. It is based upon the theological self-under-standing of the community as temple and holy people of God, and it is argued with a string of scriptural texts.

The most striking adaptation of scriptural texts to the Christian situation is the alteration of 2 Sam 7:14 to show that God's promise of sonship given to David, the king of Israel, includes the male and female members of the church. The daughters as well as the sons are full members of the temple of the living God. Therefore, all Christians are called *hagioi*, "holy ones." Several exegetes have observed the "sexual egalitarianism" and even "feminism" that comes to the fore in this alteration. Robert Jewett underscores it but concludes: "It certainly speaks against either Qumran or Jewish Christian provenance, because these groups favored patriarchal views of women."[92] He further argues "this verse must be interpreted in light of the androgyny campaign in Corinth."[93] Yet both contentions are unproven. Certainly, the passage is not of Qumran provenance, although it has some affinities to Qumran theology. However, nothing speaks against its Jewish Christian provenance, since we have no evidence for such alleged patriarchal views of women in Jewish Christianity.

To the contrary, it seems this passage "fits" into the theology of the predominantly Jewish Christian missionary movement which conceives of itself as the new creation, filled with Sophia-spirit, embracing the sons and daughters, the male and female slaves who have received the Spirit and share in ecstatic experiences. This movement stresses that women and men are the children of God, the holy people, the temple community among whom the Spirit dwells. The boundaries here are not drawn between men and women, Jewish and gentile Christians, but between believers and unbelievers. Faith in Christ Jesus, and not religion, race, or sex, draws the line between the holy community and the domain of Belial, the temple of God and idol worship.

The *Epistle of Barnabas*, a Jewish Christian midrashic hortatory letter, probably written after the destruction of the Temple in 70 C.E.,[94] also combines the motifs of the holy people, the temple not made of hands, and the new creation in its theological outlook (16:3–5). The letter evidences a later stage of Jewish Christian theology, insofar as the Christian community is already understood as the new people of God in opposition to and as the replacement for the old covenant people. Nevertheless, parts of the epistle seem to reflect the same social and theological milieu as the Hellenistic-Jewish Christian movement. It is therefore difficult to decide whether these materials go back to Barnabas, or to one of his students and followers, or whether the letter simply uses Barnabas's name, without reflecting his theology at all. It appears likely, however, that the author stands in the same Antiochene theological tradition of which Barnabas was a part.[95]

Although the epistle stresses salvation as a future event and reward, it seeks to pass along to its readers special insight or gnosis, as a gift that God bestows on all of God's children enabling them to interpret the course of the history of salvation—past, present, and future (1:7; 5:3).

Such gnosis is available to all members of the community, whom the writer addresses as "sons and daughters," who have received "an implantation of the pneumatic gift" (1:1). The author understands himself as a teacher and calls the recipients, men and women, his children of love, joy, or peace and his "brethen." "He hopes that they too will become 'good lawgivers' and 'faithful advisers' (21:4) meditating on his teachings, which are the Lord's teachings (21:7f; see 1:4)."[96] He admonishes them not to seek solitary lives but to assemble together in order to search for the mutual good (see 4:10). They are admonished to love as the apple of their eye all those who proclaim the word to them. They themselves ought to pursue gnosis each day either by toiling and traveling to spread the word, to admonish, and to save a soul by the word, or by working with their hands and sharing all things with their neighbors since they cannot "claim that anything is exclusively" theirs (19:8–11). Except for the high estimation of those who teach and meditate on the "subtleties" of the word (10:11), there is no reference to any leadership in this community which celebrated Sunday as a "day of rejoicing" at Jesus' resurrection, and practiced baptism by immersion (11:8b, 11) for the forgiveness of sins (11:1b).

According to pseudo-Barnabas, Jesus appeared on earth in order to prepare "the new people" (5:7); he taught in Israel, worked great wonders and signs, and chose his own apostles to "preach his gospel." These apostles were "sinful beyond measure so that he might prove that he came not to call righteous but sinners" (5:9). The last emphasis indicates that pseudo-Barnabas sees the apostles as prototypes of every Christian who is called and baptized, while the few references to the ministry of Jesus picture him like one of the Hellenists or "the other apostles" mentioned in 2 Corinthians.

God's holy people, the members of the Christian community, are the true heirs of the Lord's covenant. As the new creation they are the new eschatological temple. The text is ambiguous as to whether the whole community, or only the individual, is the new temple. Yet in distinction to Paul it is not the body but, as in Jewish theology, "the heart" in which Christ dwells (6:11–14).

> When we receive the forgiveness of sins [in baptism] and place our hope in the Name, we become new, created again from the beginning. Wherefore God truly dwells in our 'dwelling place'— in us. In what way? The word of his faith, the invitation of his promise, the wisdom of his righteous ordinances, the commandments of his teachings; himself prophesying in us, himself dwelling in us. . . . This is the pneumatic Temple built for the Lord. [16:8b, 9ab, 10b]

Conclusion

The call of pseudo-Barnabas: "Let us be pneumatics, let us be the perfect Temple of God," sums up well the theological self-understanding of the pre-Pauline missionary movement. As the prophetic movement of the "sons and daughters of God," it gathers in house churches and spreads the gospel in missionary partnership. As the new temple, its members are "full" of Sophia and Spirit; they are the new creation and the new creatures of God. As a "new people" they gather together in house churches for the breaking of the bread and table sharing. Just like all other types of Greco-Roman associations— the professional collegia, the funeral associations, the mystery cults, or the Jewish-Pharisaic havuroth—the Christian house churches had the same unifying center: the communal banquet or meal which regularly gathered together all members of the group for table companionship. Eating and drinking together was the major integrative moment in the socially diversified Christian house community.[98] The diakonia at tables was crucial for early Christian community.

However, this diakonia was not yet separated from that of the word. The Christians gathered together for the breaking of the bread and the praise of God. They meditated on the promises of God in Scripture and sang new songs to Christ, the Lord. Like Isis, the Queen, who made "women and men equal," so Christ-Sophia has appeared in the midst of this old world of death and alienation in order to fashion a new people, "the sons and daughters of God."

In baptism Christians enter the force field of the Spirit, share in ecstatic experiences, and are "sent" to proclaim the gospel in the power of the Spirit, attested to by miraculous signs and persuasive eloquence. They have become "a new creation," the Spirit-filled people, those who have been purified, sanctified, and justified. They all are equal, because they all share in the Spirit, God's power; they are all called elect and holy because they are adopted by God, all without exception: Jews, pagans, women, men, slaves, free poor, rich, those with high status and those who are "nothing" in the eyes of the world. The household of God concretized in the house church constitutes the new family of God, where all without exception are "sisters and brothers." Gal 3:28 belongs to this theological setting and missionary environment. It is not a Pauline "peak formulation"[99] or a theological breakthrough achieved by Paul,[100] or an occasional, isolated statement of Paul that is outnumbered by the subordination passages.[101] Gal 3:28 is a key expression, not of Pauline theology but of the theological self-understanding of the Christian missionary movement which had far-reaching historical impact.

NOTES

1. M. Hengel, *Acts and the History of Earliest Christianity* (Philadelphia: Fortress, 1979), pp. 4f.

2. For a recent comprehensive discussion of the literature and interpretation of Acts, cf. the introduction in G. Schneider, *Die Apostelgeschichte*, part 1 (HThKNT 5; Freiburg: Herder, 1980).

3. Hengel, *Acts and the History*, p. 36.

4. H. Kasting (*Die Anfänge der urchristlichen Mission* [Munich: Kaiser, 1969], pp. 90ff.) suggests that the early Christian missionary movement originated in Galilee and spread from there to Jerusalem and to southern Syria (Damascus).

5. Cf. M. Hengel, "Zwischen Jesus und Paulus: Die 'Hellenisten,' die 'Sieben' und Stephanus," *Zeitschrift für Theologie und Kirche* 72 (1975) 150–206: esp. 181ff.

6. For discussions of the problem and the literature, see especially Hengel, ibid.; S. G. Wilson, *The Gentiles and the Gentile Mission in Luke-Acts* (SNTSM 23; Cambridge: Cambridge University Press, 1973), pp. 129–53; and Schneider, *Die Apostelgeschichte*, 1.405–80.

7. Cf. H. Evans, "Barnabas the Bridge-Builder," *Exp Tim* 89 (1977) 248–50; W. H. Ollrog, *Paulus und seine Mitarbeiter: Untersuchungen zur Theorie und Praxis der paulinischen Mission* (WMANT 50; Neukirchen-Vluyn: Neukirchener Verlag, 1979), pp. 14–17, 206–15.

8. *Recognitions* 1.7.7; cf. Edgar Hennecke, *New Testament Apocrypha*, ed. W. Schneemelcher, trans. R. McL. Wilson (Philadelphia: Westminster, 1965), 2.538.

9. Acts 21:8f.

10. R. Scroggs, "The Earliest Hellenistic Christianity," in J. Neusner, ed., *Religions in Antiquity* (Supplements to *Numen* 14; Leiden: Brill, 1970), pp. 176–206. For a critique of the division between Jewish-Palestinian and Jewish-Hellenistic Christianity, cf. I. H. Marshall, "Palestinian and Hellenistic Christianity: Some Critical Comments," *NTS* 19 (1973) 271–87.

11. Erling Laland ("Die Martha-Maria-Perikope in Lukas 10, 38–42," *Studia Theologia* 13 [1959] 70–85) has suggested that Martha expresses the opinion of some circles in the early church who sought to limit women's participation in the community to practical serving functions.

12. Cf. A. Strobel, "Armenpfleger 'um des Friedens willen' (Zum Verständnis von Act 6:1–6)," *ZNW* 63 (1972) 271–76, for a review of the literature.

13. Cf. G. Stählin, "Das Bild der Witwe: Ein Beitrag zur Bildersprache der Bibel und zum Phänomenon der Personifikation in der Antike," *JAC* 17 (1974) 5–20, for extensive bibliography.

14. H. W. Beyer ("*diakoneō*," *TDNT* 2.85) argues that a "radical difference of opinion" existed on "whether they should be admitted to the fellowship and therefore whether they really belonged to the community."

15. M. Hengel, "Zwischen Jesus und Paulus," p. 181.

16. Cf. among others C. Parvey, "The Theology and Leadership of Women in the New Testament," in R. R. Ruether, ed, *Religion and Sexism: Images of Women in the Jewish and Christian Traditions* (New York: Simon & Schuster, 1974), pp. 142–46.

17. H. Gülzow, "Kallist von Rom: Ein Beitrag zur Soziologie der römischen Gemeinde," *ZNW* 58 (1967) 102–21.

18. Cf. A. D. Nock, *Conversion: The Old and the New in Religion from Alexander the Great to Augustine of Hippo* (London: Oxford University Press, 1961); and the literature in E. Schüssler Fiorenza, ed., *Aspects of Religious Propaganda in Judaism and Early Christianity* (Notre Dame: University of Notre Dame Press, 1976).

19. Cf. M. Radin, *The Jews among the Greeks and Romans* (Philadelphia: Jewish Publication Society, 1915), pp. 149–62; K. G. Kuhn and H. Stegemann, "Proselyten," Supplement to Pauly-Wissowa 9 (1962) 1248–83; F. Siegert, "Gottesfürchtige und Sympathisanten," *Journal for the Study of Judaism* 4 (1973) 109–64.

20. Cf. D. W. Riddle, "Early Christian Hospitality: A Factor in the Gospel Transmission," *JBL* 57 (1938) 141–54; Helga Rusche, *Gastfreundschaft in der Verkündigung des Neuen Testaments und ihr Verhältnis zur Mission* (Münster: Missionswissenschaftliches Institut, 1958).

21. E. A. Judge, *The Social Patterns of Christian Groups in the First Century* (London: Tyndale Press, 1960), p. 57.

22. See especially H. Gülzow, "Soziale Gegebenheiten der altkirchlichen Mission," in H. Frohnes and U. W. Knorr, eds., *Kirchengeschichte als Missionsgeschichte* (Munich: Kaiser, 1974), 1.189–226: esp. 200–206; and already A. von Harnack, *The Mission and Expansion of Christianity in the First Three Centuries* (New York: Putnam, 1908), 2.64–84.

23. Cf. G. Schille, *Die urchristliche Kollegialmission* (Zürich: Zwingli Verlag, 1967), pp. 89ff., for mission by pairs; he does not mention couples, however.

24. E. E. Ellis, "Paul and his Co-Workers," *NTS* 17 (1970/71) 439.

25. A. von Harnack ("*'Kopos' [Kopian, Hoi Kopiountes]* im frühchristlichen Sprachgebrauch," *ZNW* 27 [1928] 1–10) argues against von Dobschütz that "those who labor" constituted an official circle of ministers, most of whom were probably presbyters.

26. Cf. W. D. Thomas, "The Place of Women in the Church at Philippi," *Exp Tim* 83 (1972) 117–20.

27. J. P. Sampley, *Pauline Partnership in Christ* (Philadelphia: Fortress, 1980), p. 62.

28. H. Lietzmann, *The History of the Early Church* (London: Lutherworth Press, 1963), 1.146. Emphasis added.

29. Otto Michel, *Der Brief an die Römer* (Göttingen: Vandenhoeck & Ruprecht, 1955), p. 377.

30. Against Klauck it must be stressed that the text does not refer to a house church; cf. his argument in *Hausgemeinde und Hauskirche im frühen Christentum* ([Stuttgart: Katholisches Bibelwerk, 1981], p. 31) that the ministry of Phoebe consisted in her function as hostess for the community at Cenchreae, to whom she opened her house.

31. Cf. A. Lemaire, "From Services to Ministries: Diakonia in the First Two Centuries," *Concilium* 14 (1972) 35–49; idem, "The Ministries in the New Testament: Recent Research," *Biblical Theology Bulletin* 3 (1973) 133–66.

32. But E. J. Goodspeed ("Phoebe's Letter of Introduction," *Harvard Theological Review* 44 [1951] 55–57) argues that Phoebe needed such a letter because as a decent woman she could not stay in disreputable inns. See also Klauck.

33. G. Friedrich, "Die Gegner des Paulus im 2. Korintherbrief," in O. Betz, M. Hengel, and P. Schmidt, eds., *Abraham unser Vater: Festschrift für Otto Michel* (Leiden: Brill, 1963), pp. 181–215. See also D. Georgi, *Die Gegner des Paulus im 2. Korintherbrief* (WMANT 11; Neukirchen-Vluyn: Neukirchener Verlag, 1964).

34. Ellis, "Paul and his Co-Workers," p. 291.

35. Cf., however, W. Michaelis, "Kenchreä (Zur Frage des Abfassungsortes des Rm)," *ZNW* 25 (1926) 140–44; he argues that Phoebe harbored a house church in Ephesus and that she occupied no official ministerial position.

36. This was overlooked in my article "The Apostleship of Women in Early Christianity," in L. and A. Swidler, eds., *Women Priests* (New York: Paulist Press, 1977), p. 137.

37. See E. Schüssler Fiorenza, "Die Rolle der Frau in der urchristlichen Bewegung," *Concilium* 7 (1976) 3–9; see also B. Brooten, "Junia . . . Outstanding among the Apostles (Romans 16:7)," in Swidler and Swidler, *Women Priests*, pp. 141–44.

38. Ollrog, *Paulus und Seine Mitarbeiter*, p. 51.

39. J. Roloff (*Apostolat-Verkündigung-Kirche* [Gütersloh: Mohn, 1965], pp. 60f.), however, assumes that both are men.

40. Cf. J. Jeremias, "Paarweise Sendung im Neuen Testament," in A. J. B. Higgins, ed., *New Testament Essays: Studies in Memory of T. W. Manson* (Manchester: Manchester University Press, pp. 136–43: esp. 136–39.

41. Ellis, "Paul and his Co-Workers," pp. 445–51.

42. Cf. B. Bauer, "Uxores Circumducere 1 Kor 9.5," *Biblische Zeitschrift* 3 (1959) 94–102.

43. Clement of Alexandria *Stromateis* 3.6.53.3f.: ". . . and took their wives with them not as women with whom they had marriage relations but as sisters that they might be their co-ministers (*syndiakonous*) in dealing with housewives. It was through them that the Lord's teaching penetrated also the women's quarters without any scandal being aroused."

44. For a basic bibliography, see my article "Word, Spirit, and Power: Women in Early Christian Communities," in R. Ruether and E. McLaughlin, eds., *Women of Spirit: Female Leadership in the Jewish and Christian Traditions* (New York: Simon & Schuster, 1979), pp. 29–70.

45. M. Ramsay, *The Church in the Roman Empire before A.D. 170* (New York: Putnam, 1893), p. 375.

46. Ibid., p. 376.

47. P. Wilson-Kastner, "Macrina: Virgin and Teacher," *Andrews University Seminary Studies* 17 (1979) 105–17:107.

48. This was pointed out in a seminar paper by Judith Sanderson, "Thecla and Her Sisters: Role Models in the Acts of Paul" (University of Notre Dame, fall 1980).

49. See especially S. L. Davies, *The Revolt of the Widows: The Social World of the Apocryphal Acts* (Carbondale: Southern Illinois University Press, 1980).

50. Cf. F. V. Filson, "The Significance of the Early House Churches," *JBL* 58 (1939) 105–12; Hans-Joseph Klauck, "Die Hausgemeinde als Lebensform im Urchristentum," *Münchener Theologische Zeitschrift* 32 (1981) 1–15; idem, *Hausgemeinde und Hauskirche;* R.

E. Brown, "New Testament Background for the Concept of Local Church," *Proceedings of the Catholic Theological Society of America* 36 (1981) 1–14.

51. S. B. Clark, *Man and Woman in Christ: An Examination of the Roles of Men and Women in Light of Scripture and the Social Sciences* (Ann Arbor: Servant Books, 1980), p. 135.

52. M. F. Lefkowitz and M. Fant, eds., *Women in Greece and Rome* (Toronto: Samuel-Stevens, 1977), p. 86.

53. Juvenal 6.511–41; cf. Juvenal, *The Sixteen Satires,* trans. P. Green (Baltimore: Penguin Books, 1967), pp. 146ff.

54. *Lives of the Caesars* 9.3f.

55. M. Hengel, "Die Synagogeninschrift von Stobi," *ZNW* 57 (1966) 145–83.

56. See especially B. Brooten, "Inscriptional Evidence for Women as Leaders in the Ancient Synagogue," *SBL Seminar Papers* 20 (1981) 1–17.

57. The traditional legal sentence "Tres faciunt collegium" might have been applied early on to the leadership group of a Christian community. Cf. B. Kötting, "Genossenschaft: Christlich," *RAC* 10 (1978) 148.

58. Cf. S. Pomeroy, *Goddesses, Whores, Wives, and Slaves* (New York: Schocken Books, 1957), p. 199.

59. Cf. the review chapter in A. J. Malherbe, *Social Aspects of Early Christianity* (Baton Rouge: Louisiana State University Press, 1977), pp. 60–91, on the house churches and their problems.

60. Cf. A. von Harnack, "Probabilia über die Addresse und den Verfasser des Hebräerbriefes," *ZNW* 1 (1900) 16–41: esp. 33ff; see also Klauck, *Hausgemeinde und Hauskirche,* pp. 21–26.

61. Although R. Schumacher ("Aquila und Priscilla," *Theologie und Glaube* 12 [1920] 86–99) points out that women played a significant role in the early Christian propaganda, he nevertheless maintains that Priscilla's teaching activity was not "official" (*amtlich*) but only private (p. 97).

62. For this hypothesis, see W. Wiefel, "Die jüdische Gemeinschaft im antiken Rom und die Anfänge des römischen Christentums," *Judaica* 26 (1970) 65–88: esp. 77ff.

63. See Joan M. Peterson, "House-Churches in Rome," *Vigiliae Christianae* 23 (1969) 264–72.

64. Whether or not Rom 16 is an integral part of the letter to the Romans is debated. See, however, the review article of K. P. Donfried, "A Short Note on Romans 16," *JBL* 89 (1970) 441–49, and H. Gamble, *The Textual History of the Letter to the Romans* (Studies and Documents 42; Grand Rapids: Baker, 1977), pp. 84–95; both argue that Rom 16 addresses Christians in Rome and not in Ephesus.

65. W. A. Meeks, "The Urban Environment of Pauline Christianity," *SBL Seminar Papers* 19 (1980) 113–22:119.

66. Cf. B. Reicke, "*prohistēmi,*" *TDNT* 6.703: The verb as well as the substantive "have the twofold sense of leadership and care."

67. Ernst Käsemann, *Commentary on Romans* (Grand Rapids: Eerdmans, 1980), p. 411.

68. See S. C. Mott, "The Power of Giving and Receiving: Reciprocity in Hellenistic Benevolence," in G. E. Hawthorne, ed., *Current Issues in Biblical and Patristic Interpretation* (Grand Rapids: Eerdmans, 1975), pp. 60–72.

69. Cf. L. W. Countryman, "Patrons and Officers in Club and Church," *SBL Seminar Papers* 11 (1977) 135–41; idem, "Welfare in the Churches of Asia Minor under the Early Roman Empire," *SBL Seminar Papers* 16 (1979) 131–46.

70. See J. E. Stambaugh, "Social Relations in the City of the Early Principate: State of Research," *SBL Seminar Papers* 19 (1980) 75–99:76.

71. E. Lyding Will, "Women's Roles in Antiquity: New Archeological Views," *Science Digest,* March 1980, 35–39; R. MacMullen, "Women in Public in the Roman Empire," *Historia* 29 (1980) 208–18.

72. Ross S. Kraemer, "Ecstasy and Possession: The Attraction of Women to the Cult of Dionysos," *Harvard Theological Review* 72 (1979) 55–80: esp. 73f.

73. Cf. chap. 3 of this book.

74. See E. Schweizer, *"pneuma, pneumatikos,"* *TDNT* 6.415–37 (Paul); V. P. Furnish, *Theology and Ethics in Paul* (Nashville: Abingdon, 1968), pp. 115–81.

75. H. D. Betz, *Galatians* (Hermeneia; Philadelphia: Fortress, 1979), p. 263.

76. See G. Schneider, "Die Idee der Neuschöpfung beim Apostel Paulus und ihr religionsgeschichtlicher Hintergrund," *Trierer Theologische Zeitschrift* 68 (1959) 257–70.

77. See C. Burchard, *Untersuchungen zu Joseph und Asenath* (WUNT 8; Göttingen: Vandenhoeck & Ruprecht, 1965); R. I. Pervo, "Joseph and Asenath and the Greek Novel," *SBL Seminar Papers* 10 (1976) 171–81; H. C. Kee, "The Socio-Religious Setting and Aims of 'Joseph and Asenath,' " ibid., pp. 183–92.

78. For this section, cf. especially E. Stegemann, "Alt und Neu bei Paulus und in den Deuteropaulinen (Kol-Eph)," *EvTh* 37 (1977) 508–36 (literature).

79. F. F. Bruce, *Peter, Stephen, James and John: Studies in Early Non-Pauline Christianity* (Grand Rapids: Eerdmans, 1979), p. 84.

80. See B. A. Pearson, "Hellenistic-Jewish Wisdom Speculation and Paul," in R. L. Wilken, ed., *Aspects of Wisdom in Judaism and Early Christianity* (Notre Dame: University of Notre Dame Press, 1975), pp. 43–66.

81. For the following section and bibliographical references, see my article "Wisdom Mythology and the Christological Hymns of the New Testament," in Wilken, *Aspects of Wisdom*, pp. 17–42.

82. See B. L. Mack, *Logos und Sophia: Untersuchungen zur Weisheitstheologie im hellenistischen Judentum* (SUNT 10; Göttingen: Vandenhoeck & Ruprecht, 1973), pp. 118–78.

83. But this should not be misunderstood in terms of "the introspective conscience of the West"; see especially K. Stendahl, *Paul Among Jews and Gentiles* (Philadelphia: Fortress, 1976), pp. 78–96, 130ff.

84. See e.g. O. Cullmann, *The Johannine Circle* (Philadelphia: Westminster, 1976), pp. 41ff.; and Hengel, *Acts and the History*, pp. 71–80. Schneider (*Die Apostelgeschichte*, 1.452ff.) argues for Lukan redaction.

85. So M. Simon, *St. Stephen and the Hellenists in the Primitive Church* (London: Longmans, Green, & Co., 1958), pp. 87ff; C. H. Scobie ("The Use of Source Material in the Speeches of Acts III and VII," *NTS* 25 [1979] 399–421) argues for a Samaritan origin.

86. For this whole section, see my article "Cultic Language in Qumran and in the New Testament," *CBQ* 38 (1976) 159–77, and the cited literature.

87. Cf. J. A. Fitzmyer, "Qumran and the Interpolated Paragraph on 2 Cor 6:14–7:1," *CBQ* 23 (1961) 271–80; J. Gnilka, "2 Cor 6:14–7:1 in the Light of the Qumran Texts and the Testaments of the Twelve Patriarchs," in J. Murphy-O'Connor, ed., *Paul and Qumran* (London: G. Chapman, 1968), pp. 48–68.

88. H. D. Betz, "2 Cor 6:14–7:1: An Anti-Pauline Fragment?" *JBL* 92 (1973) 88–108.

89. For a review of the question, cf. M. E. Thrall, "The Problem of II Cor vi.14–vii.1 in Some Recent Discussion," *NTS* 24 (1977) 132–49.

90. Betz, *Galatians*, p. 329, n. 2.

91. Tertullian *To His Wife* 2.4 (ANF 4:39–49).

92. R. Jewett, "The Sexual Liberation of the Apostle Paul," *JAAR* Supplements · 47/1 (1979) 55–87:68.

93. Ibid., p. 69.

94. The epistle proves of very little help for dating. K. Wengst (*Tradition und Theologie des Barnabasbriefes* [Berlin: de Gruyter, 1971]) dates it between 130 and 132 and situates it in western Asia Minor (pp. 113ff.), but his arguments are not conclusive.

95. Wengst's assumption of a "school-tradition" seems to be the most comprehensive hypothesis.

96. R. A. Kraft, *The Apostolic Fathers*, vol. 3, *The Didache and Barnabas* (New York: Thomas Nelson, 1965), p. 21.

97. Wengst (*Tradition und Theologie*, pp. 52f.) suggests that 16:1.7b–10 is taken over from the tradition. L, the ancient Latin version, concludes with 17:2 and thus lacks the Two Ways material; see Kraft, *Apostolic Fathers*, 3.133.

98. See my "Tablesharing and the Celebration of the Eucharist," in M. Collins and D. Power, eds., *Can We Always Celebrate the Eucharist?"* (Concilium 152; New York: Seabury, 1982), pp. 3–12.

99. See e.g. P. Stuhlmacher, *Der Brief an Philemon* (EKKNT; Zurich: Benziger Verlag, 1975), p. 67.

100. K. Stendahl, *The Bible and the Role of Women* (Philadelphia: Fortress, 1966), p. 32.

101. Clark, *Man and Woman in Christ*, pp. 138ff.

Chapter 6

Neither Male Nor Female ·
Galatians 3:28—Alternative Vision and Pauline Modification

Although many have seen Gal 3:28 either as the *locus classicus* of Paul's teaching on women or as the focal point and organizing center of his theology, others have denied such a claim on the basis of the so-called household-code tradition of the New Testament and the early Fathers, which stresses the subordination of women to men. J. E. Crouch, in turn, has maintained that both texts, Gal 3:28 and the household code of Colossians (which is the first one in the New Testament), are related to each other. He argues that the household code was developed in Christian preaching in order to counteract excessively enthusiastic claims that appealed to Gal 3:28.[1]

Wayne Meeks has highlighted the ritual setting of the "reunification formula" in Gal 3:28 and argued that it evokes the myth of androgyny that was widespread in Hellenism, Judaism, and especially gnosticism. However, for this myth he refers especially to the "'new man' symbolized by the clothing who is 'renewed after the image of his creator'" of Col 3:10 (cf. Eph 4:24) and to gnostic texts. In doing so he understands "neither male and female" in Gal 3:28 in terms of the "eschatological restoration of man's original divine, androgynous image."[2] In 1 Cor 11:2–16 and 14:33b–36 "Paul seems primarily concerned to reassert the distinction between male and female."[3] Paul insists on "the *symbolic* distinctions belonging to the humanity of the old Adam" but concedes the abandonment of "functional distinctions," so long "as the result leads to the 'building up' of the community."[4] In doing so Meeks follows Robin Scroggs who argues "that Paul wanted to eliminate the inequality between the sexes, while the gnostics wanted to eliminate the distinction between the sexes."[5]

In a similar vein, Robert Jewett concludes his article "The Sexual Liberation of the Apostle Paul": "The authentic Pauline letters therefore move on a progression that leads to a full acknowledgment of equality, while maintaining an insistence on the divinely given quality of sexual difference."[6] Jewett explicitly approves Crouch's judgment that the household-code's concern "was with the excesses of women and slaves," which threatened the "stability of the Pauline churches." However, in Colossians "the balance between equality and sexual differentiation is lost" in the argument against androgyny. Paul then "was struggling to maintain two seemingly contradictory points: differentiation of sexual identity on the one hand and equality of honor and role on the other hand."[7]

Widespread in exegetical commentaries and articles on women in the Bible is the distinction between the "order of creation," to which the household codes belong, and the "order of redemption"— though neither expression is found in the New Testament. While some traditionalists maintain that women have a different role from men in the order of creation and redemption and are assigned a position of subordination by God in creation, others maintain that "before God" all are equal. With respect to redemption and the gifts of the Spirit all have equal standing before God. The sociological implications of this equal standing cannot be applied either to society or church ministry, however, but are postponed until the age to come.

Against such an interpretation of Gal 3:28, which restricts equality and oneness to the soul or to one's standing before God, Krister Stendahl has forcefully argued:

> The statement is limited to what happens in Christ through baptism. But in Christ the dichotomy *is* overcome through baptism, a new unity is created, and that is not only a matter discerned by the eyes of faith but one that manifests itself in the social dimensions of the church.[8]

However, he also maintains that in 1 Corinthians Paul argues against a kind "of spiritual snobbishness" and directs his Christian eschatology "against those who think that they have already transcended the world of death and limitations."

When Paul fought those who defended the old—his bold vision of the new expressed itself most strongly as in Gal 3:28. When he discerned the overstatement of the new he spoke up for the old, as in Corinthians.[9]

Paul, then, wanted to maintain the tension between the new and the old, the age to come and this age. On the one hand, the old hierarchy associated with men and women, slaves and free has been overcome; on the other, wholesale emancipation from societal constraints is illusionary enthusiasm that hinders the advancement of the gospel and threatens the unity of the church.

All these different interpretations seem to be based on certain presuppositions and modern categories of interpretation. While the older exegesis insisted on the subordination and difference between women and men, slaves and free—and I would add, also, Greeks (Americans, Germans, etc.) and Jews—as valid in society and church, more recent exegesis proceeds from the "equal but different assumption." Interestingly enough, it does not insist on a "symbolic" difference of race or class, but only on sexual difference, which still must be lived out by women in "subordination." Stephen Clark, for example, spends a good deal of time showing that the first two pairs in Gal 3:28 are quite distinct from the last pair, in order to prove that one may not also advocate the subordination of slaves and of Jews, if one argues for that of women.[10] In pointing out the presuppositions of contemporary exegetes for interpreting Gal 3:28, I do not want to advocate a value-free exegesis but only to clarify the values at stake.

The contemporary discussion linking Gal 3:28 and the household-code tradition seems to point to a historical-political dynamic that does not come to the fore when it is forced into the oppositions of "order of creation" and "order of redemption" on the one hand, and of "enthusiastic excess, or gnostic heresy" and "Pauline theology and New Testament orthodoxy" on the other. Hans Dieter Betz has acknowledged that commentaries on Galatians "have consistently denied that Paul's statements have political implications."[11] Such commentaries are prepared to state the opposite of what Paul actually says in order to preserve a "purely religious" interpretation. In doing so, they can strongly emphasize the reality of equality before God sacramentally and at the same time "deny that any conclusions can be drawn from this in regard to the ecclesiastical offices(!) and the political order"—all of which, I would add, rest on the assumed natural differences between the sexes institutionalized in patriarchal marriage.

Analysis and Interpretation of Galatians 3:28

Form critical analyses converge in the delineation of Gal 3:26–28 and its classification as a baptismal confession quoted by Paul.[12] The following observations speak for such a traditional formula. The same formula occurs in various New Testament and early Christian texts, but with a consistency of motifs and their variations. Moreover, Paul shifts from "we" in v. 25 to "you" in v. 26 and returns to the "we" again in 4:3. In addition, the immediate context in Galatians speaks neither about baptism nor about social relationships. Theologically the baptismal formula differs from its immediate context. Paul's concern in Galatians is the religious relationship between Jews and gentiles, not the cultural-political distinctions between Jews and Greeks as two different types of people and cultures. Therefore, he does not use the expression in Gal 5:6 and 6:15 (cf. 1 Cor 7:19), and instead refers to circumcision/uncircumcision. Further, the immediate context speaks about bondage and slavery, the slave woman and the free woman (Galatians 4). However, "slavery" and "freedom" are used to characterize the religious but not the social situation of the Galatian Christians, while the pair "male" and "female" plays no role at all in the argument of Paul in Galatians.

Finally, within the baptismal unit one can distinguish several Pauline additions. The syntactic transitions "therefore" and "through faith in Christ Jesus," as well as v. 29, are clearly Pauline insertions. Since Paul uses the concept of sonship in the immediate context, he also might have changed children into sons, because the traditional formula "that we are children of God" (Rom 8:16c) indicates that the Christian missionary movement conceived the gift of the Spirit as the attestation that Christians were indeed children of God "and if children, then heirs" (Rom 8:17). The baptismal announcement quoted by Paul, then, might have consisted of the following:

  i. 3:26a For you are all children of God
 ii. 3:27a For as many as were baptized into Christ
      b have put on Christ
iii. 3:28a There is neither Jew nor Greek
      b There is neither slave nor free
      c There is no male and female
 iv. 3:28d For you are all one

Though scholars differ on the delineation of the different lines, they agree that the core of the traditional formula is Gal 3:28abc. Because of the opposition pair Jew/Greek they assume it was formulated in a Jewish-Hellenistic community. Therefore, nothing prevents us from attributing it to the pre-Pauline missionary movement and seeing it as an integral part of this movement's theology of the Spirit. The function of this pronouncement is best captured in the description of Meeks:

> . . . a resident of one of the cities of the province Asia who ventured to become a member of one of the tiny Christian cells in their early years would have heard the utopian declaration of mankind's [sic] reunification as a solemn ritual pronouncement. Reinforced by dramatic gestures (disrobing, immersion, robing), such a declaration would carry—within the community for which its language was meaningful—the power to assist in shaping the symbolic universe by which that group distinguished itself from the ordinary "world" of the larger society. As a "performative utterance" it makes a factual claim "about an "objective" change in reality that fundamentally modifies social roles. New attitudes and altered behavior would follow—but only if the group succeeds in clothing the novel declaration with an "aura of factuality."[13]

We have seen that such new behavior was engendered by this baptismal declaration, at least with respect to women who exercised leadership roles in the house churches and mission of the early Christian movement. A letter of Pliny to the Emperor Trajan confirms that at the beginning of the second century women "servants" (slaves?) were ministers in the church of Bithynia.[14] Around the same time, Ignatius writes to the bishop Polycarp of Smyrna, telling him not to set free either male or female slaves at the expense of the church (4:3). This exhortation presupposes that slaves who joined the Christian community expected their freedom to be bought by the church.

Such expectations were supported by the Christians' belief that they were truly set free by Christ. Such formulas occur again and again in the Pauline letters: "You were bought with a price, do not become human slaves" (1 Cor 6:20; 7:23). Or "For freedom Christ has set us free . . . do not submit again to a yoke of slavery" (Gal 5:1). The goal of Christian calling is freedom: "You were called to freedom" (Gal 5:13), because "where the Spirit of the Lord is there is freedom" (2 Cor 3:17). To argue that Christian slaves who understood their call to freedom had only "a superficial understanding of the gospel"[15] is to minimize the impact of this language in a world where slavery was a commonly accepted institution. Liberation from the slavery of sin, law, and death, from the conditions of the "present evil age" (Gal 1:4) has "freedom" as its purpose and destiny. "As a result, *eleutheria* (freedom) is the central theological concept which sums up the Christian's situation before God as well as in this world."[16] Therefore, a slave woman who became a Christian in the first century heard this baptismal pronunciation as a ritual, "performative utterance," which not only had the power to shape the "symbolic universe" of the Christian community but also determined the social interrelationships and structures of the church.

That such an expectation of free status on the grounds of baptism was not merely excessive enthusiasm is apparent if we look at the first opposites of the baptismal formula—Jew/Greek. One could show that Paul's whole work centered around the abolition of the religious distinctions between Jew and Greek. "For there is no distinction between Jew and Greek. The same Lord is Lord of all and bestows his riches upon all who call upon him" (Rom 10:12). Equality among all those who call upon the Lord is based on the fact that they have all one and the same master who shares his wealth with all of them (cf. also Rom 3:22). That such "religious equality" had social-ecclesial consequences for the interrelationship between Jewish and gentile Christians is apparent from the Antioch incident, which seems to have been well known in the early church.[17] Peter and Barnabas had entered into table sharing with the gentile Christians in Antioch but, after pressure from Jerusalem, discontinued it. They again adhered to the Pharisaic Christian purity rules against eating together with the "unclean." Paul publicly confronts Cephas and the Jewish Christian group around him because "they did not act in consistency with the truth of the gospel" (Gal 2:14). The whole letter to the Galatians is written to make the same point. It is not circumcision or uncircumcision that counts, but the new creation.

This struggle of Paul for equality between gentile and Jewish Christians had important ramifications for Jewish and gentile Christian women alike. If it was no longer circumcision but baptism which was the primary rite of initiation, then women became full members of the people of God with the same rights and duties. This generated a fundamental change, not only in their standing before God but also in their ecclesial-social status and function, because in Judaism religious differences according to the law were also expressed in communal behavior and social practice. While one was *born* into Judaism—even the full proselyte could not achieve the status of the male Israelite— the Christian movement was based not on racial and national inheritance and kinship lines, but on a new kinship in Jesus Christ.[18] In baptism Christians entered into a kinship relationship with people coming from very different racial, cultural, and national backgrounds. These differences were not to determine the social structures of the community, nor were those of family and clan. Therefore both Jewish and gentile women's status and role were drastically changed, since family and kinship did not determine the social structures of the Christian movement.

This seems to be stated explicitly in the final pair of the baptismal pronunciation: "There is no male and female." This last pair differs in formulation from the preceding two, insofar as it does not speak of opposites but of man *and* woman. Exegetes have speculated a good deal over the fact that "male and female" are used here, but not "man and woman."[19] It is often argued that not only "the *social* differences (roles) between men and women are involved but the *biological* distinctions" as well.[20] Therefore, as we have seen, it is conjectured that the formulation is gnostic and advocates androgyny. Paul does not repeat the formulation in 1 Cor 12:13—according to this argument—because he had special problems in Corinth due to the gnostic or enthusiastic consequences women drew from Gal 3:28. However, such a conjecture is based on the unproven assumption that the behavior of Corinthian women was determined by gnostic beliefs and not by early Christian prophetic experiences.

The argument, moreover, overlooks the fact that designations of the sexes in the neuter can simply be used in place of "woman and man." Such designations do not imply a denial of biological sex differences.[21] The reference here probably alludes to Gen 1:27, where humanity created in the image of God is qualified as "male and female" in order to introduce the theme of procreation and fertility. Jewish exegesis understood "male and female," therefore, primarily in terms of marriage and family. In early Christian theology the expression also evokes the image of the first couple, and not that of an androgynous being, as can be seen from Mark 10:6. "No longer male and female" is best understood, therefore, in terms of marriage and gender relationships. As such, Gal 3:28c does not assert that there are no longer men and women in Christ, but that patriarchal marriage—and sexual relationships between male and female—is no longer constitutive of the new community in Christ.[22] Irrespective of their procreative capacities and of the social roles connected with them, persons will be full members of the Christian movement in and through baptism. This interpretation is also supported by the noncanonical tradition.

The apocryphal literature transmits a saying of Jesus that appears to reflect a Christian self-understanding similar to that in Gal 3:28c. In passing, Jesus sees mothers nursing their children and says to the disciples: "These infants being suckled are like those who enter the kingdom." The disciples want to make sure that they understand him correctly and ask: "Shall we then, as children, enter the kingdom?" and Jesus answers:

> When you make the two one, and when you make the inside like the outside, and the outside like the inside, and the above like the below, and when you make the male and the female one and the same so that the male not be male nor the female. . . . [*Gosp. Thom.* log. 22]

Similarly, the *Second Epistle of Clement*, an anonymous sermon dated early in the second century and ascribed to Clement of Rome, addresses gentile converts (probably from Egypt) who "are in danger of falling prey to gnostic teachings."[23] The preacher quotes this saying in the context of eschatological preaching:

> For when someone asked the Lord when his Kingdom was going to come, he said, "When the two shall be one and the outside like the inside, and the male with the female neither male nor female."

He then goes on to explain that the inside and outside are soul and body respectively.

> Furthermore "male with the female neither male nor female" means this: that when a brother sees a sister he should not think of her sex any more than she should think of his. [12.1–6]

This interpretation still clearly reflects the same community situation as Gal 3:28. It does not yet understand this Jesus saying in anthropological, androgynous terms, as gnostic writings do. Although the ecclesial context is not clear in the saying of the *Gospel of Thomas*, the saying does not yet speak of bisexuality or androgyny, but more likely of presexuality, as the image of the nursing babies suggests. What this sayings tradition asserts, then, is that sexual dimorphism, and gender roles based on it, must be relinquished to enter the kingdom. Or, in terms of the anonymous preacher, a Christian ought not to look at other Christians as sex objects, as males or females, but as members of the same "family of God," as brothers and sisters. The saying tradition ascribed to Jesus, then, expresses in different words the same understanding of being Christian as the baptismal formula of Gal 3:28. Women and men in the Christian community are not defined by their sexual procreative capacities or by their religious, cultural or social gender roles, but by their discipleship and empowering with the Spirit.

In antiquity not only were sexual or gender roles considered to be grounded in biological nature but also cultural, racial, and social differences. Religious, social, racial, and sexual properties were not differentiated in antiquity as much as they are today. Although most would concede today that racial or class differences are not natural or biological, but cultural and social, sexual differences and gender roles are still proclaimed as given by nature. However, feminist studies have amply documented that most perceived sex differences or gender roles are cultural-social properties. We are socialized into sex and gender roles as soon as we are born. Every culture gives different symbolic significance and derives different social roles from the human biological capacities of sexual intercourse, childbearing, and lactation.[24] Sexual dimorphism and strictly defined gender roles are products of a patriarchal culture, which maintain and legitimize structures of control and domination—the exploitation of women by men.[25] Gal 3:28 not only advocates the abolition of religious-cultural divisions and of the domination and exploitation wrought by institutional slavery but also of domination based on sexual divisions. It repeats with different categories and words that within the Christian community no structures of dominance can be tolerated. Gal 3:28 is therefore best understood as a communal Christian self-definition rather than a statement about the baptized individual. It proclaims that in the Christian community all distinctions of religion, race, class, nationality, and gender are insignificant. All the baptized are equal, they are one in Christ. Thus, taken at face value, the baptismal declaration of Gal 3:28 does not express "excessive enthusiasm" or a "gnosticizing" devaluation of procreative capacities.

Except for Mithraism, oriental cults initiated women as well as men without distinction of family, class, or social status. At Eleusis initiation was open to women as well as to slaves, and even to *hetairai* and to foreigners if they spoke Greek. An inscription from the first century B.C.E. reproducing the rules for a house cult in Philadelphia (Lydia) explicitly mentions men and women and slaves and free:

> The commandments given to Dionysos by Zeus, granting access in sleep to his own house both to free men and women and to household slaves. . . . Those who enter this house both men and women, both bond and free are to take oath before the Gods. . . . These commandments were placed [here] by Agdistis, the most holy Guardian and Mistress of this house, that she might

show her good will [or intention] to men and women, bond and
free, so that they might follow the [rules] written here and take
parts in the sacrifices.[26]

The figurative language of "putting on Christ" like a robe has parallels in the mystery religions, where "putting on or putting off" the
redeemer figure is also connected with the initiation rite[27]. The same
language of Gal 3:26f is found in Col 3:10 and Eph 4:24, and in gnosticism, where it is connected with putting off the "old man" and putting on the "new man." However such an anthropological-cosmic
interpretation is not explicit in Gal 3:28. Being baptized into Christ
means entering the sphere of the resurrected Lord, the life-giving
Spirit whose reality and power are manifested in the Christian community. It is not anthropological oneness but ecclesiological oneness
or unity in Christ Jesus which is the goal of Christian baptism. Unlike
initiation into mystery cults—which usually had no social consequences—Christian baptism accomplishes both individual salvation
and initiation into a community, into a religious association.

Although the traditional philosophical schools (which were often
cultic associations as well) espoused equality of women and men in
theory or as an ideal, only the Epicurean Garden admitted women on
an equal basis.[28] We even know of one woman president (Deontion).
They based their community on friendship (*philia*) and communal
living (*koinōnia*)—the same term often describes the marriage relationship. Since they were pessimistic about the societal public order, they
recommended the "private life," in which individual independence
(*autarkeia*) could be enhanced by mutual support. Although they rejected erotic love and marriage in favor of friendship between women
and men, they numbered couples among their members. Thus they
created a community and theory, in which men and women able to
withdraw from society were equal. This philosophical ideal later had
great impact in the third and fourth centuries on Christian communities founded by women. In that context, however, it was connected
with sexual asceticism.[29]

We do not know the social effects initiation into Judaism had upon
women, but we have some indication that it could spell "freedom"
for slaves. The manumission or setting free of the slave was an act of
the slave owner performed with the assent of the synagogue. The
slave gained complete freedom except for the requirement to attend
the synagogue. Connected with the act of manumission was a second
washing that corresponded so closely to proselyte baptism that both
could be seen as one and the same. Against the background of orien-

tal cultic and Jewish religious manumission practices it is obvious that slaves would expect freedom from their initiation into the Christian community.[30] Paul seems to assume this when he sends the baptized Onesimus back to Philemon "no longer as a slave" but as a beloved brother "both in the flesh and in the Lord," that is, socially as well as ecclesially, as a human being as well as a Christian (Phil 16). Paul has neither the legal ability to set Onesimus free himself nor the authority to *command* Philemon to do so. But by sending Onesimus back as a new member of the church in Philemon's house, he expects Philemon to acknowledge the new *status* of the former slave as a "brother."

In his description of the "contemplative" or "philosophical" life of the Therapeutae and Therapeutrides, Philo stresses that this ascetic community has "no slaves to wait upon them them as they consider that the ownership of servants is entirely against nature. For nature has borne all to be free, but the wrongful and covetous acts of some who pursued that source of inequality, have imposed their yoke and invested the stronger with power over the weaker."[31] Instead of slaves, young freeborn men serve at table, where the men recline on the right side and the women on the left.

> They give their services gladly and proudly like sons to their real fathers and mothers judging them to be the parents of them all in common, in a closer affinity than that of blood, since to the right minded there is no closer tie than noble living.[32]

In this ascetic community of the wise, women seem to participate equally with men "with the same ardour and the same sense of calling," although for ascetic resons and for the sake of the "modesty of the women" their sanctuary is divided by a three or four cubit wall.[33] These women "have kept their chastity, not under compulsion, like some of the Greek priestesses, but of their own free will in their ardent yearning for Wisdom" whom they are eager "to have for their life mate." Most of these women are "aged virgins" who have dedicated their lives to Scripture study, prayer, the composing of hymns, in short to "the verities of wisdom." It is not noted whether they also participated actively in the weekly scriptural discussion, whether their "senior" was also allowed to expound on the Scriptures in the assembly, or take her turn in singing a hymn she had composed. However, it is explicitly stated that for the "sacred vigil" they would divide in two choirs, for each of which a leader would be chosen "who is the most honored among them and the most musical."[34] After they have sung their own songs the choirs merge.

> This wonderful sight and experience, an act transcending word
> and thought and hope, so filled with ecstasy both men and
> women that forming a single choir they sang hymns of thanks-
> giving to God their Saviour, the men led by Moses, and the
> women by the prophetess Miriam.[35]

Although the early Christian house churches were not ascetic monastic communities which withdrew to an isolated spot but lived in the
urban centers of the Greco-Roman world, they did share the ecstatic
experiences of Spirit-Wisdom, and considered themselves the
new family of God. Their worship gatherings were similar to those of
the Therapeutae insofar as they expounded the Scriptures, sang new
hymns and psalms, experienced prophecy and ecstasy in their midst,
and concluded with a communal meal shared by all members of the
community. Finally Philo's description of the Therapeutae and the
Therapeutrides provides us with one instance where Jewish women
participated fully in the study of the Torah and in the communal
worship of the community. However, the ascetic character of this
Jewish community seems to have generated an institutionalized division between the male and female members of the community which
is not evident in the traditions of the early Christian movement,
though it emerges in Christian literature toward the end of the first
century.

Moreover, insofar as the Christian community did not withdraw
from society, as the Epicurean Garden or the Jewish Therapeutae did,
it provided an experience of an alternative community in the midst of
the Greco-Roman city for those who came in contact with it. As an
alternative association which accorded women- and slave-initiates
equal status and roles, the Christian missionary movement was a
conflict movement which stood in tension with the institutions of slavery and the patriarchal family. Such conflict could arise not only
within the community but even more within the larger society, since
Christians admitted to their membership women as well as slaves
who continued to live in pagan marriages and households. This tension between the alternative Christian community and the larger society had to cause conflicts that demanded resolution, often in different
ways. The Pauline exhortations and the household-code tradition
within the New Testament testify to these tensions.

Yet unconsciously these injunctions of men, which demand the
subordination of slaves, women, and children, may also express the
interests of the "owner and patron class,"[36] as Judge has suggested—
as well as reflect the interests of husbands and masters, the heads of

families, who felt that their prerogatives were being undermined. Of course, it is difficult for us to decide whether or not such motivations played a role in the modifications of the Christian baptismal self-understanding, that is, which admonitions to subordination were due to a genuine concern for the Christian group's embattled situation and which arose from a defense of patriarchal dominance couched in theological terms. The theological counterarguments by slaves or women have not survived in history.

To assume such resentment is historically plausible, to the extent that the baptismal declaration of Gal 3:28 runs counter to the general acceptance of male religious privileges among Greeks, Romans, Persians, and also Jews in the first century C.E.[37] It was a rhetorical commonplace that Hellenistic man was grateful to the gods because he was fortunate enough to be born a human being and not a beast, a Greek and not a barbarian, a free man and not a slave, a man and not woman. This cultural pattern seems to have been adopted by Judaism in the first or second centuries C.E. and found its way into the synagogue liturgy.[38] Three times a Jewish man thanked God that he did not create him a gentile, a slave, or a woman. This is not a misogynist prayer but an expression of gratitude for religious male privilege, as the comment of Rabbi Jehuda (second century C.E.) elucidates.

> Rabbi Jehuda said, One must speak three prayers every day:
>   Blessed be God that he has not made me a Gentile.
>   Blessed be God that he has not made me a woman.
>   Blessed be God that he has not made me a boor.
> Blessed be God that he has not made me a Gentile:
> "because all Gentiles are nothing before him" (Jer 40:17).
> Blessed be God that he has not made me a woman: because
> woman is not obligated to fulfill the commandments.
> Blessed be God that he has not made me a boor: because
> a boor is not ashamed to sin.[39]

Although it is difficult to say whether this prayer was already known to Jewish converts to Christianity in the fortieth year of the first century, its consciousness of religious male privilege was widespread not only among Jews but among Greeks and Romans as well. Conversion and baptism into Christ for men, therefore, implied a much more radical break with their former social and religious self-understandings—especially for those who were also wealthy slave owners—than it did for women and slaves.

While the baptismal declaration in Gal 3:28 offered a new religious vision to women and slaves, it denied all male religious prerogatives in the Christian community based on gender roles. Just as born Jews had to abandon the privileged notion that they alone were the chosen people of God, so masters had to relinquish their power over slaves, and husbands that over wives and children. Since these social-political privileges were, at the same time, religious privileges, conversion to the Christian movement for men also meant relinquishing their religious prerogatives. It is often argued that it was impossible for the tiny Christian group to abolish the institution of slavery and other social hierarchies. That might have been the case or it might not. However, what is often overlooked is that relinquishment of religious male prerogatives within the Christian community was possible and that such a relinquishment included the abolition of social privileges as well. The legal-societal and cultural-religious male privileges were no longer valid for Christians. Insofar as this egalitarian Christian self-understanding did away with all male privileges of religion, class, and caste, it allowed not only gentiles and slaves but also women to exercise leadership functions within the missionary movement.

The pre-Pauline baptismal formula however does not yet reflect the same notion of anthropological unification and androcentric perspective that has determined the understanding of equality found in later gnostic and patristic writings.[40] According to various gnostic and patristic texts, becoming a disciple means for a woman becoming "male," "like man," and relinquishing her sexual powers of procreation, because the male principle stands for the heavenly, angelic, divine realm, whereas the female principle represents either human weakness or evil.[41] While patristic and gnostic writers could express the equality of Christian women with men only as "manliness' or as abandonment of her own sexual nature, Gal 3:28 does not extol maleness but the oneness of the body of Christ, the church, where all social, cultural, religious, national, and biological gender divisions and differences are overcome and all structures of domination are rejected. Not the love patriarchalism of the post-Pauline school, but this egalitarian ethos of "oneness in Christ" preached by the pre-Pauline and Pauline Christian missionary movement provided the occasion for Paul's injunction concerning the behavior of women prophets in the Christian community.

Pauline Modifications of Galatians 3:28

Paul explicitly refers to Gal 3:28 in 1 Cor 12:13[42] and 1 Cor 7:17–24.[43] Nevertheless, it is difficult to ascertain with certainty Paul's position with respect to women and slaves in the community. Although he quotes Gal 3:28 in 1 Cor 12:13 explicitly in connection with baptism and the reception of the Spirit, he does not mention the third pair—"male and female"—of the baptismal formula. Moreover, the meaning of his advice to slaves in 7:21 is much debated, and the argument in 11:2–16 with respect to the behavior of women prophets in the worship assembly is very convoluted and far from being intelligible even today. Finally, it is not clear what the Corinthians' theology and practice was in the matters raised. If the suggestion is correct, that the third pair—"male and female"—of the baptismal formula refers to marriage and declares it no longer constitutive for the community of Christians, then the extensive discussion of questions like: should married Christians continue or abstain from sexual intercourse? should unmarried people get married? what is to be done if one's marriage partner is an unbeliever, either Jew or pagan? what about women who are virgins or widows? can be seen as direct practical elaborations of Gal 3:28c, even though the third pair of the formula is never explicitly mentioned.

Moreover, we must recognize that the Corinthian community probably consisted of a large number of active Christian women, who had a voice in the community's theology and practice. Although only very scanty information on women's leadership in early Christianity has survived, the communities of Corinth and vicinity had, as we have noted, at least three outstanding women leaders in their midst: Chloe, Prisca, and Phoebe. All three of these women leaders had good working relationships with Paul, although we do not know how much they influenced his theology or whether they agreed with him theologically. Paul at least expresses his respect and praise for them as his co-workers.

We also know from Paul that women were prophets and charismatics in the community, but we do not know the names of any women prophets or women leaders in Corinth. In any case, despite Paul's consistent use of the address "brothers," it seems safe to assume that among the Christians in Corinth there were women who were both well educated and prosperous, and poor and slave. The attention paid to the relationship between women and men and their sexual intercourse, as well as to women's role in the worship assembly, indicates that women were very active in the community. Moreover, as we have seen, like the Therapeutae and Therapeutrides the Corinthian Christians understood their faith in terms of Sophia theology. "The Spirit" was believed to be "the 'Wisdom of God,'" and the Spirit-Wisdom bestows the gift of wisdom upon those who cultivate her gifts, and who live according to her calling."[44] The Corinthians and Paul understand the significance of Jesus Christ in terms of wisdom theology, as the pre-Pauline christological hymns indicate. Since in this theology Sophia was conceived as a semihypostatic divine female figure, women probably were especially attracted to become devotees. In the worship service of the community the divine Sophia-Spirit was present. All received her spiritual gifts and powers. Women as well as men were pneumatics and could, therefore, pray, and prophesy, publicly before the whole congregation under the influence of divine Sophia. They were the new creation in Christ and could call on the name of God in the power of the Spirit as "children of God."

Paul shares this theology and Christian self-understanding. In no way does he reject it; rather he seeks to elaborate it in terms of the concrete situation in Corinth. In doing so he interprets and adapts the baptismal declaration of oneness and equality in Christ. Paul addresses the problem of marriage, slavery, divorce, and celibacy in 1 Corinthians 7,[45] discusses "custom" and "propriety" with respect to the worship assembly in chapters 11 and 14, and develops in his discussion with the other Christian "parties" in Corinth his understanding of the missionary as "a father" of those whom he has baptized (4:14–17). Finally, in 2 Corinthians (11:2–3) he introduces the image of Eve as the counterimage to that of the church as bride and Christ as the husband. All these qualifications of Gal 3:28, made in a concrete pastoral situation, were developed further in a patriarchal direction by the Pauline "school."

Marriage and Celibacy (1 Corinthians 7)

The introduction to 1 Corinthians 7 clearly states that Paul is responding here to matters about which the Christians had written him. Although all the problems raised seem to refer in one way or another to marriage and the relationship between the sexes, Paul also mentions in 7:17–24 the question of circumcision/uncircumcision and slave/free. Since he also speaks in this section about the Christian calling by God, he clearly had the baptismal formula in mind when elaborating the general theological foundation for his advice in chapter 7. His reference to circumcision/uncircumcision in particular indicates that he has the three pairs Jew/gentile, slave/free, male/female in mind, since this reference to circumcision does not quite fit the tenor of the whole chapter, that is, it is not the social situation in which one finds oneself as a Christian that determines one's Christian standing, but rather living according to the will of God.[46] Exegetes misread

Paul's advice to Jewish or gentile Christians, when they argue that Paul here means to say that they should remain in the social state and religious role they had when they heard the call to conversion. Paul clearly does not advise the former Jew or the former gentile to remain in their Jewish or pagan state. Rather he insists that the religious/biological sign of initiation to Jewish religion is no longer of any relevance to Christians.

Similarly, the advice to slaves cannot mean that slaves should remain in the state in which they were called. The advice in 7:21 is difficult to understand, since it is not clear whether they should "use" freedom or slavery to their advantage, if they have the possibility of being set free.[47] Although most exegetes and translators assume that slaves were to remain in the state of slavery when they became Christians, in my opinion the context speaks against such an interpretation. The injunction of v. 23—"You were bought with a price, do not become slaves of people"—prohibits such an interpretation. The advice Paul gives to Christian slaves, then, seems best understood as: "If you still must live in the bondage of slavery, with no possibility of being freed, even though you were called to freedom, do not worry about it. However, if you have the opportunity to be set free, by all means use this opportunity and live in accordance with your calling to freedom. Those of you who were slaves when called to become a Christian are now freedwomen and freedmen of the Lord, just as those of you who were freeborn have now a master in Jesus Christ." Paul argues here, then, that both slaves and freeborn are equal in the Christian community, because they have one Lord. Therefore, it is possible to be a Christian even as a slave, if no possibility of becoming free exists. Of course it is more in line with one's calling to freedom to live as a free person. Much would be gained by a change in social status, if such a change is possible. Regardless of one's social status, however, the decisive thing is to continue in the calling to freedom which one has heard and entered into in baptism.[48] Thus it seems clear that Paul had the baptismal declaration of Gal 3:28 in mind when addressing the problem of the relationship between the sexes in chapter 7, even though the reference to the first two pairs of the formula is made only in passing.[49]

Paul's theological advice with respect to the relationship between the sexes is basically similar to the advice given to slaves. It is quite possible to live a Christian life as a married person, if that was the state in which one lived when becoming a Christian. However, Paul explicitly bases his argument not on the social order, but on a word of the Lord that prohibits divorce. The eschatological ideal of Jesus' declaration on marriage is here turned into an injunction of Jesus against divorce. However, despite this explicit instruction of the Lord, wives—who are mentioned first and with more elaboration in 7:10f—still have the possibility of freeing themselves from the bondage of patriarchal marriage, in order to live a marriage-free life. If they have done so, however, they must remain in this marriage-free state. They are allowed to return to their husbands, but they may not marry someone else.

A somewhat different problem is raised with respect to mixed marriages between Christians and "unbelievers" who might be either gentiles or Jews. In the preceding chapter (6:12–20) Paul had raised the rhetorical question: "Do you not know that your bodies are members of Christ? Shall I therefore take the members of Christ and make them members of a prostitute?" Likewise, Christians who had remained married with unbelieving spouses could have asked: Can I as a "member of Christ" have sexual intercourse with someone who does not belong to the body of Christ? Do I then become conformed to her/his pagan existence and lose my standing in Christ? In addition, Jewish and early Christian missionary theology held that converts became a new creation in baptism. They were like newborn children and became members of the new family of God. According to Jewish theology and practice, initiation into Judaism dissolved previous kinship and marriage bonds.[50] Therefore, proselytes or Jews who had become Christians rightly might have raised the questions: Does Christian baptism also dissolve all former marriage bonds? If so, does my marriage still exist after I have become a Christian and my spouse has not done so?

In response to this problem, Paul insists that because of the missionary situation (God has called us to peace!), the decision to continue or not to continue the marriage relationship is up to the unbelieving partner but not up to the Christian. If the unbelieving spouse wants to separate, then the Christian should respect this decision, because she/he has no guarantee that she/he will be able "to save" the unbelieving partner. If, however, the unbeliever wants to stay married, the Christian should also respect this decision. The Christian partner has reconstituted the marriage bond "by intercourse." Therefore the children of the marriage are holy and legitimate. David Daube has pointed out that "to sanctify" or "to consecrate" means, in Jewish language, to "take someone in marriage." However, "in Judaism it is invariably the woman who is consecrated as spouse by the man. . . . His [Paul's] extension of consecration is totally untraditional."[51] Paul thus ascribes here to Christian wives the same consecrating power bestowed traditionally on husbands.

However, Paul's insistence that the pagan partner had the final decision about the continuance of the marriage must have been more difficult for Christian women than for men. Moreover, the early church seems not to have adhered to it. The apocryphal Acts are full of stories about women who became converts to Christianity and left their husbands.[52] Moreover, more upper-class women than men seem to have converted to Christianity, since this is one of the constant points of attack by pagan writers against Christians. The apologist Justin, writing one hundred years after Paul, still knows of the problem. He tells of a Roman matron converted to Christianity who, against the advice of her Christian counselors, divorced her husband because she could no longer share his licentious ways of living. Subsequently, she was accused in court by her husband as a Christian. When she asked the emperor to postpone her trial until she had ordered her estate and economic affairs, her husband also denounced her teacher Ptolemy as a Christian. This case indicates how difficult it must have been for Christian women to participate in the pagan lifestyle and social obligations of their households.[53] On the other hand, poor women who became Christians risked being divorced by their husbands and, as a result, losing their economic sustenance. Paul tells them not to prohibit such a decision by the unbelieving husband. By leaving the decision to the unbelieving spouse, for missionary reasons, Paul sacrifices the right of the Christian to determine his or her marital status. This is even more astonishing since Paul on the whole prefers the marriage-free Christian life over the married state.

Despite his preference for celibacy, however, Paul maintains that both marriage and freedom from marriage are callings and charisms from God. It is clear he would prefer that everyone live unmarried like himself, but he is careful to stress this advice as his own opinion. However, marriage is a necessity if one cannot live the asexual life demanded by freedom from the marriage bond. It is advantageous or "good" (not in a moral sense) "not to touch a woman" (formulated from his own male perspective), that is, not to have sexual intercourse, if one has the "charism" to do so. But those who are tempted should have intercourse with their own wives or husbands. Both partners have the mutual obligation and the mutual right to such intercourse, except for some celibate periods set aside for worship. As in other oriental cults, Paul advises temporary ritual chastity. Yet it is noteworthy that Paul does not relate the right to sexual intercourse to the purpose of procreation alone. Only later will abstinence for the sake of birth control play a role in Christian apologetic writings.

Exegetes have pointed out how Paul carefully repeats every injunction in 7:1–5 in order to make sure that husband and wife have equal conjugal obligations and equal sexual rights.[54] Thus we can see that Paul has taken great care to give a double command covering each case of active sexual interaction between husband and wife. However, it would be reaching too far to conclude from this that women and men shared an equality of role and a mutuality of relationship[55] or equality of responsibility, freedom, and accountability in marriage.[56] Paul stresses this interdependence only for *sexual* conjugal relationships and not for all marriage relationships. Moreover, even though Paul feels compelled to acknowledge marriage, his own personal ideal was the asexual life and the marriage-free state.[57]

This comes to the fore throughout the whole chapter, especially in his advice to the "unmarried," that is, those who are widowed or divorced as well as those who are engaged to be married (this is probably the best explanation for the thorny problem of 7:32–35). If sexual desire requires it, they should get married. However, if at all possible, it is better not to marry and to remain in the marriage-free state. If the unmarried and widows cannot exercise self-control they should get married in the Lord; but in Paul's opinion they would be happier if they were to remain in the state they are. For this opinion he appeals to his own prophetic-charismatic inspiration.

It is not only remarkable that Paul insists on equality and mutuality in sexual relationships between husbands and wives, but even more that he advises Christians, especially women, to remain free from the marriage bond. This is often overlooked because Paul's option for celibacy has become "the higher calling" in Christian tradition. However, in the first century, permanent abstinence from sexual relations and remaining unmarried were quite exceptional. The discoveries of Qumran and Philo's description of the community of the Therapeutae give evidence of such an ascetic lifestyle within Judaism, but it was lived in isolation from the mainstream urban culture. Temporary chastity was known in most oriental cults; castration was practiced in the worship of the Great Mother, and in Rome the Vestal Virgins remained chaste for the thirty years of their service; but virginity was a privilege and not a right according to Roman law.

> The lives of the Vestals were severely regulated but in some respects they were the most emancipated women in Rome. As

noted in our discussions of unmarried goddesses, the most liberated females are those who are not bound to males in a permanent relationship. . . . . Further evidence of the freedom from the
restrictions of ordinary women is to be found in the privileges
enjoyed by the Vestals. . . . These privileges had such implications of status that the "rights of Vestals" were often conferred
upon female members of the imperial family, who were frequently portrayed as Vestals on coins.[58]

The privileges of virginity were not open to "ordinary women" in the
Roman empire. In order to strengthen the traditional Roman family,
Augustus had introduced severe marriage legislation and openly
used religion to promote his marriage ideals.[59] In order to increase the
birthrate, he granted freeborn women with three children and
freedwomen who had given birth to four children emancipation from
patriarchal tutelage. However, since he gave this privilege to his wife,
the Vestal Virgins, and soldiers who could not marry during their
time of service, other women who had not fulfilled the prescribed
number of births also acquired this privilege. The rate of birth and the
number of children were of great political concern, however, to the
patriarchal establishment of the empire. The emperor levied sanc-
tions and taxes upon those who were still bachelors. Moreover, wid-
owers and divorcees of both sexes were expected to remarry after a
period of one month. Widows at first were expected to remarry after a
one year period, but, following protests, this period was extended to
three years. Only those who were over fifty years of age were allowed
to remain unmarried. Although these laws were probably not strictly
kept throughout the empire, they evidence the general cultural
ethos and the legal situation with respect to a marriage-free state. At
the end of the first century, the Emperor Domitian reinforced the
Augustan marriage legislation particularly in order to strengthen the
leading families of the empire.

It is therefore important to note that Paul's advice to remain free
from the marriage bond was a frontal assault on the intentions of
existing law and the general cultural ethos, especially since it was
given to people who lived in the urban centers of the Roman empire.
It stood over and against the dominant cultural values of Greco-Roman society. Moreover, his advice to women to remain nonmarried
was a severe infringement of the right of the *paterfamilias* since, according to Roman law, a woman remained under the tutorship of her
father and family, even after she married. Paul's advice to widows
who were not necessarily "old"—since girls usually married between
twelve and fifteen years of age—thus offered a possibility for "ordi-

nary" women to become independent. At the same time, it produced conflicts for the Christian community in its interaction with society.

Paul's theological argument, however, that those who marry are "divided" and not equally dedicated to the affairs of the Lord as the nonmarried, implicitly limited married women to the confines of the patriarchal family. It disqualified married people theologically as less engaged missionaries and less dedicated Christians. It posited a rift between the married woman, concerned about her husband and family, and the unmarried virgin who was pure and sacred and therefore would receive the pneumatic privileges of virginity. One can only wonder how Paul could have made such a theological point when he had Prisca as his friend and knew other missionary couples who were living examples that his theology was wrong.

Women in the Worship of the Community (1 Corinthians 11–14)

In his section of 1 Corinthians on the pneumatic worship of the community (chaps. 11–14) Paul probably refers to women twice, if 14:34–36 is not a later interpolation.

The injunctions concerning women's behavior, however, are not peripheral to Paul's argument but of great concern to him, as their place in the structure of the letter indicates. The whole of chapters 11–14 speaks of the pneumatic worship service of the community and is composed in the form of a thematic inclusion, insofar as the section begins and ends with the problem of women's correct behavior in the worship assembly.[60] The immediate context of Paul's injunctions concerning women's behavior in the worship service of the community gives evidence that women as well as men share in the pneumatic gifts of Sophia Spirit, and pray and prophesy publicly under the influence of the divine Spirit. Paul explicitly affirms that in doing so the Corinthians have followed his teachings and example (11:2), and he does not disqualify this "spiritual" self-understanding and practice of the Corinthian pneumatics. The contrast between 1 Cor 11:2 and 11:17 emphasizes that Paul is not referring here to any particular abuse but is introducing regulations and customs which were observed in other Christian communities (11:16; 14:33).

The concluding verses 14:37–40 indicate how serious the issues are for Paul and how much he expects resistance to his viewpoint. Paul appeals to the prophets and pneumatics to accept his arguments as a revelatory word of the Lord himself (v. 37).[61] He assures the Corinthians that he does not want to hinder prophetic and ecstatic speaking but is concerned that everything "should happen decently and in the right order" (v. 40). Thus it seems to be Paul, and not the Corinthians, who is attempting to qualify or to change the pneumatic behavior of the community. His major line of argument involves decency and right order, values which are not specifically Christian.[62] At the same time, Paul is in a difficult position since he had originally spoken to them about the new life in the Spirit and the Christian freedom evolving from it.[63] In order to understand Paul's situation we must analyze the injunctions of 1 Cor 11:2–16 and 14:33–36 more fully.

1 Cor 11:2–16: We no longer are able to decide with certainty which behavior Paul criticizes and which custom he means to introduce in 1 Cor 11:2–16.[64] Traditionally, exegetes have conjectured that Paul was insisting that the pneumatic women leaders wear the veil according to Jewish custom.[65] Yet v. 15 maintains that women have their hair instead of a head-covering, and thus militates against such an interpretation. It is therefore more likely that Paul is speaking here about the manner in which women and men should wear their hair praying and prophesying.[66] It seems that during their ecstatic-pneumatic worship celebrations some of the Corinthian women prophets and liturgists unbound their hair, letting it flow freely rather than keeping it in its fashionable coiffure, which often was quite elaborate and enhanced with jewelry, ribbons, and veils.[67] Such a sight of disheveled hair would be quite common in the ecstatic worship of oriental divinities. In 14:23 Paul points out that the Corinthians' pneumatic worship impresses the outsider as ritual madness. Such ecstatic frenzy in oriental cults was a highly desirable spiritual phenomenon and a mark of true prophecy. Disheveled hair and head thrown back were typical for the maenads in the cult of Dionysos, in that of Cybele, the Pythia at Delphia, the Sibyl, and unbound hair was necessary for a women to produce an effective magical incantation.[68] In resistance to the decree of her husband, the king, Vergil's Amata calls upon the other women to discard their hair-ribbons and nets.

Flowing and unbound hair was also found in the Isis cult, which had a major center in Corinth. For instance, a woman friend of the poet Tibullus is said to have had to let her hair down twice daily in the worship of Isis to "say lauds."[69] Archeological evidence also shows that female devotees of Isis usually wore long hair "with a band around the forehead and curls falling on the shoulder," while the male initiates had their hair shaven.[70] Hence Paul's sarcastic statement in vv. 5f that women who loosen their hair might as well have it cut short or shaven. It is as disgraceful for a women to loosen her hair as it is to shave it.

The Corinthian pneumatics presumably took over such a fashion because they understood their equality in the community and their devotion to Sophia-Spirit by analogy to the worship of Isis, since Isis was also said to have made the power of women equal to men[71]; and her associations—like the Christian communities—admitted women and slaves to equal membership and active participation.[72] For the Christian women at Corinth, such loose and unbound hair was a sign of their ecstatic endowment with Spirit-Sophia and a mark of true prophetic behavior. Paul, on the other hand, is bent on curbing the pneumatic frenzy of the Corinthians' worship. For Paul, building up of the community and intelligible missionary proclamation, not orgiastic behavior, are the true signs of the Spirit. In this context it is understandable why Paul insists that women should keep their hair bound up.

In addition, loose hair probably had even a more sinister meaning in a Jewish Christian context. According to Jewish sources loose hair continued to be a sign of uncleanness, even to Paul's day.[73] Num 5:18 (LXX) prescribes that the woman accused of adultery be marked publicly by loosening her hair. Similarly, in Lev 13:45 (LXX), one of the signs for the uncleanness of a leper is loose hair. Jewish women very artfully braided their hair and pinned it up so that it formed a kind of tiara on their head (cf. Jdt 10:3; 16:8), an effect heightened by adorning it with gold, jewelry, ribbons, or gauze.[74] In view of this hairstyle, the exegetically difficult statement in v. 10 becomes more understandable. As Paul argues, since the angels are present in the pneumatic worship service of a community that speaks the "tongues of angels,"[75] women should not worship as cultically unclean persons by letting their hair down but should pin it up as a sign both of their spiritual power and of control over their heads. The Greek word *exousia* in v. 11 can only be read in the active sense as power over their head,[76] whereby "head" has a double meaning: the actual head as well as man—who is the "head" of women according to 11:3ff.[77] Women have such power through the angels, who according to Jewish and Christian apocalyptic theology mediate the "words of prophecy."[78]

In a very convoluted argument, which can no longer be unraveled completely, Paul adduces several points for "this custom" or hair fashion. The key to these points, in my opinion, however, is the opening statement praising the Corinthian pneumatics for having kept the traditions Paul has transmitted to them. These traditions are those of liberation, freedom, equality, and Spirit-empowerment in Christ or in the Lord. Paul's arguments in 1 Cor 11:2–16 seek to introduce the community to a deeper understanding. Since Paul praises the Corinthians for having kept the traditions, we do not know whether or not they were already practicing a new orgiastic liturgical style of loose and uncovered hair, or whether Paul was warning them not to introduce such a custom. His "theological" arguments are: first, there is a descending hierarchy, God-Christ-Man-Woman, in which each preceding member, as "head" or "source," stands above the other "in the sense that he establishes the other's being." Therefore, Paul can declare that man is created to be the image and manifestation of God, while woman is the glory of man, and hair is the glory of woman. It is important to note, that woman is not said to be the image of man. Thus the statement does not deny woman the "image of God" status, but explains why man is the glory of God. The argument focuses on "glory" and climaxes with "hair as the glory of woman" (v. 15). In order to make his point Paul resorts to the Stoic argument "from nature"[79] which was widely used to insist on the difference between men and women. Paul concludes that mixture of scriptural and philosophic-midrashic argument with an authoritarian appeal, probably because he himself senses that his reasoning is not very convincing. He insists that he and the churches have no such practice of loose and uncovered hair. This is the point he wants to make.

Second, perhaps sensing that his midrashic proof could be misunderstood, Paul insists that he does not want to deny the equality of women and men "in the Lord." 1 Cor 11:11 is usually translated, "In the Lord woman is not independent of man nor man of woman." The Greek term *choris* is thus interpreted in the sense of v. 12, which states that even in creation women and men are interdependent, because woman was (in the beginning) made from man, but now man is born of woman and in any case "all things are from God." Clearly, v. 12 states that Paul's midrashic scriptural argument does not want to deny the creational interdependence and mutuality of men and women. If *choris* is translated as "without" or "independent," then v. 11 would maintain the same for their relationship in the Lord.

However, Josef Kürzinger has reviewed the evidence for such a translation and found that it has little basis. Usually the term means not "without," but "different from," "unlike," "otherwise," "heterogeneous," or "of another kind."[80] The best translation of v. 11, then, would be, "In the Lord woman is not different from man nor man from woman." In other words, as Christians women and men are equal. Bound-up hair must be understood as a liturgical symbol of woman's prophetic power, because in the Christian community women and men are not different from each other. Differences which might exist on the basis of nature and creation are no longer present in the worship assembly of the Christians.

To sum up, Paul does not argue in 11:2–16 for the "creational" or "symbolic" *difference* between women and men despite their equality in Christ, but for the custom of bound-up hair, as the symbol of women's prophetic-charismatic power. Like his other arguments in 1 Cor 11:2–14:40 his instruction aims at playing down the impression of madness and frenzy so typical of orgiastic cultic worship. Decency and right order in the community require women prophets and charismatics actively engaged in the worship of the community to look "proper." Paul therefore makes a more or less convincing theological argument for the "proper" hairstyle as the cultic symbol for women's spiritual power and equality in the Lord. The goal of his argument, then, is not the reenforcement of gender differences but the order and missionary character of the worship community.

1 Cor 14:33b–36: It is debated whether these verses are an authentic Pauline injunction or whether they were added by a later editor of the Pauline school.[81] Since these verses cannot be excluded on textual-critical grounds but are usually declared inauthentic on theological grounds, it is exegetically more sound to accept them as original Pauline statements and then explain them within their present context. As in chapter 11 so in chapters 12–14 Paul seeks to persuade the Corinthians that decency and order should be more highly esteemed than the spiritual status and exercise of individual pneumatic inspiration. While the Corinthians seem to have valued glossolalia above all, Paul favors the gift of prophecy and interprets it in terms of reason, order, and mission (14:4, 5, 19).[82] The Corinthian pneumatics should not be concerned with the exhibition of their spiritual gifts but with the building up of the community and with the impression they make on interested outsiders (14:16, 17, 23ff).

14:26–36 is best understood as a church order with rules for glossolalists (vv. 27ff), prophets (vv. 29–33), and wives (vv. 34–36).[83] These three rules are formulated in a structurally similar fashion. General sentences of regulation (vv. 27, 29, 34) are complemented by sentences that concretize them (vv. 28, 30, 35). The second and third rules are expanded with reasons for the regulation (vv. 31–32, 34a, 35b). However, the rule for wives is different insofar as it ends with a double rhetorical question (v. 36), thus appearing to underline the importance of the last regulation.

1 Cor 14:33–36 is often understood to speak about women in general and therefore to contradict 11:2–16 which presupposes that

women are pneumatics, and as such pray and prophesy within the worship of the community. However, the difficulty is resolved if we recognize that the injunction does not pertain to all women but solely to wives of Christians, since chapter 7 makes it clear that not all women in the community were married or had Christian spouses. They therefore could not ask their husbands at home. 1 Cor 7:32–35 confirms the interpretation that the prohibition in 14:33–36 applies only to wives. Although in 1 Corinthians 7 Paul acknowledges the equality and reciprocity of husband and wife, his ascetic preference for the unmarried state is plain.[84] In 7:32–35 he interprets the apocalyptic "as if not" tradition of 7:29–31 in a christological missionary perspective. The married person, Paul argues, is divided and concerned with the issues of marriage and family, while the unmarried person is completely dedicated to the affairs of the Lord. It is apparent that Paul is here "taking over bourgeois moral concepts which denote not absolute but conventional values."[85] Paul's argument is surprising, as noted earlier, since we know of leading missionary couples who spent their lives in the service of the Lord.

The single-minded dedication of the unmarried woman and virgin, but not the unmarried man, however, is further qualified with the subordinate clause "that she may be holy in body and spirit" (7:34). Paul here ascribes a special holiness to the unmarried woman and virgin, apparently because she is not touched by a man (cf. 7:1).[86] We therefore can surmise that Paul is able to accept the pneumatic participation of such "holy" women in the worship service of the community, but argues in 14:34f against such an active participation of wives. As in 1 Cor 7:35 so also here Paul concludes his injunction by invoking propriety (14:35b).

Paul probably derives his theological argument from Jewish-Hellenistic missionary tradition, which, as Josephus documents, had adopted the Greco-Roman exhortations for the subordination of wives as part of the "law."[87] The traditional Roman sentiment against matrons speaking in public and gathering for public demonstration is expressed in the speech of the consul Cato against the Roman women who sought abolition of the Oppian law. Although this incident happened at the end of the third century B.C.E., the speech was composed by Livy in the first century.

> If each man of us fellow citizens, had established that the right and authority of the husband should be held over the mother of his own family, we should have less difficulty with women in general; now at home our freedom is conquered by female fury,

here in the Forum it is bruised and trampled upon. . . . What kind of behavior is this? Running around in public, blocking streets, and speaking to other women's husbands! Could you not have asked your husband the same thing at home? . . . Give the reigns to their unbridled nature and this unmastered creature, and hope that they will put limits on their own freedom? Unless you do something yourselves, this is the least among the things imposed upon them either by custom or by law which they endure with hurt feelings. They want freedom, nay licence (if we are to speak the truth) in all things. . . . As soon as they begin to be your equals, they will have become your superiors.[88]

The community rule of 1 Cor 14:34–36 presupposes that, within the Christian worship assembly, wives had dared to question other women's husbands or point out some mistakes of their own during the congregational interpreting of the Scriptures and of prophecy. Such behavior was against all traditional custom and law. However, the text does not say that wives should subordinate themselves either to the community leadership or to their husbands. It asks simply that they keep quiet and remain subdued in the assembly of the community.

Paul's major concern, however, is not the behavior of women but the protection of the Christian community. He wanted to prevent the Christian community from being mistaken for one of the orgiastic, secret, oriental cults that undermined public order and decency. For, as we have seen, already in the second or third century B.C.E., a neo-Pythagorean treatise from Italy, in discussing the behavior of women, had stated: "Public law prevents women from participating in these rites [secret cults and Cybeline orgies], particularly those rites which encourage drunkenness and ecstasy."[89]

The concluding rhetorical questions in v. 36 indicate the counter-argument which Paul expects. It is often suggested that these questions refer to the whole community because the wives could not have argued that the word of God originated with them or that they were the only ones whom it has reached. However, when we consider that such leading early Christian missionaries as Prisca, Junia, and perhaps Apphia were married, and that in general the other leading women mentioned in the Pauline letters are not characterized as virgins, widows, or unmarried, such a counter-argument becomes plausible. Since we have seen that wives were called to missionary preaching and were founders of house churches, Paul's claim that these women should be silent and ask their husbands at home sounds preposterous. Paul realizes that this regulation goes against the accepted practice of the missionary churches in the Hellenistic urban centers. He therefore claims for this and the preceeding regulations the authority of the Lord (v. 37). In the final analysis, however, it is not theology but concern for decency and order which determines Paul's regulation concerning the behavior of pneumatic women and men in the worship service of the community (v. 40).

In Conclusion: In the preceding analysis I have attempted to argue that the Pauline injunctions for women in 1 Corinthians should be understood in the context of Paul's argument against orgiastic behavior in the worship of the community. On the one hand, 11:2–16 does not deny women's prophecy and prayer in the worship assembly but insists that in the Christian community women and men are equal. They are not to exhibit in their behavior the symbols of behavior of orgiastic worship. The community rule of 14:33–36, on the other hand, has a specific situation in mind, namely, the speaking and questioning of wives in the public worship assembly. Here, as in 7:34 and 9:5, Paul appears to limit the active participation of wives in the "affairs of the Lord." His concluding rhetorical questions indicate that he does not expect his regulation to be accepted without protest by the Corinthian community which knows of wives as leading Christian apostles and missionaries. Yet Paul is more concerned that order and propriety be preserved so that an outsider cannot accuse the Christians of religious madness. In both passages, then, Paul places a limit and qualification on the pneumatic participation of women in the worship service of the community. We do not know whether the Corinthian women and men accepted his limitations and qualifications. However, the love patriarchalism of the deutero-Pauline household codes and the injunctions of the Pastorals are further developments of Paul's argument, developments that will lead in the future to the gradual exclusion of all women from ecclesial office and to the gradual patriarchalization of the whole church.

Patriarchal Images and Metaphors

While the two previously discussed modifications of Gal 3:28 by Paul are much debated in scholarship on Paul and women, little attention has been paid to the patriarchal imagery and language introduced by Paul. Of particular significance here are his missionary self-understanding of the "father of the community" and the bride image for the Christian community.

Paul not only uses the metaphor of "father" but also that of "mother" and "nurse" to describe his relationship to the communities he founded and to the individuals he converted to the gospel. By the transmission of the gospel he has begotten them, given them new life, nourished them like babes, and formed them as children of God.[90] The slave Onesimus has become his child and Paul, in turn, is his father (Phlm 10). Timothy has served with Paul in the gospel as a son with his father (Phil 2:22). He is Paul's "beloved and faithful child in the Lord" (1 Cor 4:17). Paul exhorts the Corinthians to imitate him, because he became their "father in Christ Jesus through the gospel" (4:15). They have many guides, but not many fathers. Paul threatens to come to Corinth and find the arrogant ones, asking: "What do you wish? Shall I come to you with a rod, or with love in a spirit of gentleness?" (4:21)

Although Paul stresses his parental affection toward his "children," whom he has converted, he nevertheless opens the door for the reintroduction of patriarchal authority within the Christian community. By this "spiritual" fatherhood[91] he allows for an understanding of the Christian community as the "new family of God" that has "fathers" here on earth, not just one and only one "father" in heaven. Although Paul can still "mix" the metaphors of father, mother, and wet nurse, he nevertheless understands himself and his authority in terms of "fatherhood," since he himself was a man. By claiming "to have given" life to his children he plays down the natural birthing power of mothers, and associates "fatherhood" with baptism and rebirth. Thus Paul makes it possible for later generations to transfer the hierarchy of the patriarchal family to the new family of God. This is true, even though he himself certainly does not understand his authority[92] and ministry as patriarchal, but as the nurturing, life-enhancing service of a nurse or a mother.

In his debate with the superapostles Paul introduces himself in 2 Cor 11:2–3[93] as a parent who has betrothed his daughter, the church of Corinth, as a pure virgin to Christ. While the figure of Christ as the bridegroom is known from the synoptic traditions, it is here that we encounter for the first time the bride metaphor for the church. With this image Paul hearkens back to the Old Testament prophets who repeatedly saw Israel as the spouse of Yahweh. Hos 2:19–20 presents this relationship as an engagement, but no matchmaker is mentioned.[94] In Revelation the image of the bride does not refer to the historical Christian community but to the eschatological community of the new Jerusalem. In 2 Cor 11:2, the whole community, both women and men, are likened to the virgin bride, who expects Christ as the eschatological bridegroom.[95]

The counter-image to the virgin-bride/bridegroom-Christ image is that of Eve and the serpent. Paul fears that the community might be more like Eve—who was deceived by the cunning of the serpent—if it follows the "superlative apostles" (11:5) who led the Corinthians' thoughts away from their pure and sincere devotion to Christ. Paul is "jealous" that these false teachers might be able to seduce them from their commitment to Christ just as Eve was seduced. Whenever Paul mentions the power of sin elsewhere he mentions Adam, the representative of the "old humanity," whose counter-image is Jesus Christ, the representative of the "new humanity."[96] He refers to Eve in order to stress the gullibility of the Corinthian community, pictured here as a virgin-bride.

The difference between Paul's use of the Eve image and that of later theology becomes apparent when we compare 2 Cor 11:3 with 1 Tm 2:13ff, the only other passage in the New Testament to mention Eve. In 1 Tm 2:13ff Adam and Eve are juxtaposed, but it is stressed that Adam was created first, while Eve was created after him.[97] Adam was not deceived, but Eve was deceived and became a transgressor. This passage thus explicitly restricts the image of Adam to men and Eve to women in order to stress the priority and fidelity of men over and against women. Paul, by contrast, refers the image of Eve to both women and men, that is, to the whole community. His interest is not in associating women with Eve and ascribing secondary status to them in the community. Nevertheless, by employing the metaphor of the virgin-bride-church who, like Eve, is in danger of being seduced by the superapostles, he opens the door for those later speculations that transfer the marriage relationship—between Israel and Yahweh, between the church and Christ, and between Eve and the serpent—to women.

Conclusion

Paul's interpretation and adaptation of the baptismal declaration Gal 3:28 in his letters to the community of Corinth unequivocally affirm the equality and charismatic giftedness of women and men in the Christian community. Women as well as men are prophets and leaders of worship in the community. Women as well as men have the call to a marriage-free life. Women as well as men have mutual rights and obligations within the sexual relationships of marriage.

However, in introducing a distinction, between those who are married and those who are not, with respect to missionary work, Paul relegates the former to the cares of this world and ascribes to the latter a special pure and holy state. Therefore, he restricts more severely the active participation of Christian wives in the worship of the community. His use of the virgin-bride metaphor for the church, as well as his figurative characterization of his apostleship as fatherhood, opens the door for a reintroduction of patriarchal values and sexual dualities.

Although he introduces an element of severe tension between the Christian community and the wider society with his emphasis on the marriage-free state of Christians, in his injunctions concerning the worship assembly of the Corinthians he is concerned to reduce this tension as much as possible.[98] Since he wants to prevent "outsiders" from mistaking the Christian assembly as the celebrations of an orgiastic cult, he insists on the "proper" hairstyle for women active in the worship assembly. He then justifies this custom theologically by interpreting it as a symbol of their spiritual power in Christ. Moreover, he silences wives' public speaking, according to traditional Roman sentiment, as being against "law and custom." Similarly, in the case of mixed marriages, he restricts the freedom of Christian partners to separate from their unbelieving spouses by making the separation dependent on the decision of the nonbeliever. Paul's interests in doing so, however, are missionary and not directed against the spiritual freedom and charismatic involvement of women in the community.

Thus Paul's impact on women's leadership in the Christian missionary movement is double-edged.[99] On the one hand he affirms Christian equality and freedom. He opens up a new independent lifestyle for women by encouraging them to remain free of the bondage of marriage. On the other hand, he subordinates women's behavior in marriage and in the worship assembly to the interests of Christian mission, and restricts their rights not only as "pneumatics" but also as "women," for we do not find such explicit restrictions on the behavior of men *qua* men in the worship asembly. The post-Pauline and pseudo-Pauline tradition will draw out these restrictions in order to change the equality in Christ between women and men, slaves and free, into a relationship of subordination in the household which, on the one hand, eliminates women from the leadership of worship and community and, on the other, restricts their ministry to women.

NOTES

1. J. E. Crouch, *The Origin and Intention of the Colossian Haustafel* (FRLANT 109; Göttingen: Vandenhoeck & Ruprecht, 1972), p. 144.
2. W. A. Meeks, "The Image of the Androgyne: Some Uses of a Symbol in Earliest Christianity," *History of Religions* 13 (1974) 165–208:197.
3. Ibid., p. 200.
4. Ibid., p. 202.

5. Ibid., p. 203, n. 153.

6. R. Jewett, "The Sexual Liberation of the Apostle Paul," *JAAR* Supplements 47/1 (1979) 55–87:74f.

7. Ibid., p. 67.

8. K. Stendahl, *The Bible and the Role of Women* (Philadelphia: Fortress, 1966), p. 33.

9. Ibid., p. 37.

10. S. B. Clark, *Man and Woman in Christ: An Examination of the Roles of Men and Women in Light of Scripture and the Social Sciences* (Ann Arbor: Servant Books, 1980), pp. 155ff.

11. H. D. Betz, *Galatians* (Hermeneia; Philadelphia: Fortress Press, 1979), p. 189, n. 68.

12. Meeks, "Image of the Androgyne"; see also H. D. Betz, "Spirit, Freedom, Law: Paul's Message to the Galatian Churches," *Svensk Exegetisk Årsbok* 39 (1974) 145–60, and his *Galatians*, pp. 181–201; J. Becker, *Auferstehung der Toten im Urchristentum* (SBS 82; Stuttgart: Katholisches Bibelwerk, 1976), pp. 56f.; H. Paulsen, "Einheit und Freiheit der Söhne Gottes—Gal 3:26–29," *ZNW* 71 (1980) 74–95, for literature.

13. Meeks, "Image of the Androgyne," p. 182.

14. Pliny *Epistles* 10.96. According to A. N. Sherwin-White, "Pliny treats the *diakonoi* as these 'servants' evidently were, as slaves, whose evidence was commonly taken under torture. The torture of freeborn witnesses in ordinary criminal procedures was an innovation of the Late Empire. . . . Pliny stresses that many of 'every age, every class, and of both sexes are being accused . . .' " (*The Letters of Pliny: A Historical and Social Commentary* [Oxford: Clarendon Press, 1966], p. 708).

15. Cf. Crouch, *Colossian Haustafel*, p. 127.

16. Betz, *Galatians*, p. 255.

17. For literature and discussion, cf. Betz, *Galatians*, pp. 103f.

18. This is stressed by R. Loewe: "The sociological basis on which Christianity rests is not the tie of kinship as in the case of Judaism, but that of fellowship—fellowship in Christ" (*The Position of Women in Judaism* [London: SPCK, 1966], p. 52).

19. See especially H. Thyen, " '. . . nicht mehr männlich und weiblich . . .' Eine Studie zu Galater 3.28," in F. Crüsemann and H. Thyen, eds., *Als Mann und Frau geschaffen* (Gelnhausen: Burkardthaus-Verlag, 1978), pp. 109f.

20. Betz, *Galatians*, p. 195.

21. For documentation, see M. de Merode, "Une théologie primitive de la femme?" *Revue Théologique de Louvain* 9 (1978) 176–89: esp. 184ff.

22. For a similar exegetical argument but a different systematic conclusion, see also B. Witherington, "Rite and Rights for Women—Galatians 3.28," *NTS* 27 (1981) 593–604. According to Witherington, the "Judaizers may have been insisting on the necessity of marriage and propagation, perhaps as a way of including women into the community and giving them an important role. . . ." But he insists that the mere fact that Paul speaks here of such sexual, racial, religious, and class distinctions means Paul recognizes quite well that they exist. He wishes not to obliterate them but to orient them properly. . . . Thus he rejects their *abuse* and not their proper *use*" (pp. 601f.). However, such a conclusion cannot be derived from the text.

23. C. C. Richardson, *Early Christian Fathers* (New York: Macmillan, 1970), p. 200.

24. See espcially M. Zimbalist Rosaldo, "The Use and Abuse of Anthropology: Reflections on Feminism and Cross-Cultural Understandings," *Signs* 5 (1980) 389–417; and chap. 1 of this book.

25. For the delineation of sex and gender, see A. Oackley, *Sex, Gender and Society* (New York: Harper & Row, 1972), pp. 158ff.

26. F. C. Grant, *Hellenistic Religions* (Indianapolis: Bobbs-Merrill, 1953), p. 28f.

27. Betz, *Galatians*, p. 188, n. 60.

28. See Meeks, "Image of the Androgyne," pp. 172ff.

29. A. Yarbrough, "Christianization in the Fourth Century: The Example of Roman Women," *Church History* 45 (1976) 149–65; E. A. Clark, *Jerome, Chrysostom and Friends*

(Studies in Women and Religion 2; New York: Edwin Mellen Press, 1979), pp. 35–106; idem, "Ascetic Renunciation and Feminine Advancement: A Paradox of Late Ancient Christianity," *Anglican Theological Review* 63 (1981) 240–57.

30. See Crouch, *Colossian Haustafel*, pp. 126–29.

31. *De vita contemplativa* 70; the translation used here and in the following references is from F. H. Colson, ed. and trans., *Philo: On the Contemplative Life* (Loeb Classicial Library; Cambridge, Mass.: Harvard University Press, 1941).

32. Ibid., 72.

33. Ibid., 32f.

34. Ibid., 83.

35. Ibid., 87.

36. E. A. Judge, *The Social Pattern of the Christian Groups in the First Century* (London: Tyndale Press, 1960), p. 60.

37. For references, cf. Meeks, "Image of the Androgyne," p. 167, nn. 7–8.

38. See H. Fischel, "Story and History: Observations on Greco-Roman Rhetoric and Pharisaism," in D. Sinor, ed., *American Oriental Society Middle West Branch Semi-Centennial Volume* (Bloomington: Indiana University Press, 1969), pp. 74ff.

39. *T. Berakot* 7:18 (ed. S. Liebermann, p. 38). This prayer expresses a patriarchal cultural-religious attitude of male superiority, and should not be used to single out Jewish patriarchal attitudes for criticism.

40. See especially W. Schmithals, *Die Gnosis in Korinth* (FRLANT 66; Göttingen: Vandenhoeck & Ruprecht, 1956), p. 227, n. 1.

41. See my article "Word, Spirit, and Power: Women in Early Christianity," in R. Ruether and E. McLaughlin, eds., *Women of Spirit: Female Leadership and the Jewish Christian Traditions* (New York: Simon & Schuster, 1979), pp. 44–57.

42. M. Bouttier, "Complexio Oppositorum: Sur les formules de I Cor xii.13; Gal iii.26–28; Col iii.10.11," *NTS* 23 (1976) 1–19.

43. This was recognized by S. S. Bartchy, *First-Century Slavery and 1 Corinthians 7:21* (SBL Diss. 11; Missoula, Mont.: Scholars Press, 1973), pp. 162–65; and D. Lührmann, "Wo man nicht mehr Sklave oder Freier ist: Überlegungen zur Struktur frühchristlicher Gemeinden," *Wort und Dienst* 13 (1975) 53–83.

44. B. A. Pearson, *The Pneumatikos-Psychikos Terminology in 1 Corinthians* (SBL Diss. 12; Missoula, Mont.: Scholars Press, 1973), p. 37.

45. It is questionable whether 1 Thess 4:4 speaks about a marriage relationship ("to acquire a wife") or means "to gain mastery over one's body" (*skeuos* is used to refer to the human body in Jewish and Greek writings); both readings are possible. See e.g. W. Klassen, "Foundations for Pauline Sexual Ethics as Seen in I Thess. 4:1–8," *SBL Seminar Papers* 14 (1978), pp. 159–81:166.

46. For a different interpretative emphasis, see H. Conzelmann, *1 Corinthians* (Hermeneia; Philadelphia: Fortress, 1975), p. 126: "And grace embraces the world and holds me fast in my worldliness. No change of status brought about by myself can further my salvation."

47. See Bartchy, *First-Century Slavery*, pp. 6–7, for a synopsis of the interpretations of 1 Cor 7:21.

48. For a similar interpretation, see also P. Trummer, "Die Chance der Freiheit: Zur Interpretation des *mallon chrēsai* in 1 Kor 7,21," *Biblica* 56 (1975) 344–68.

49. See e.g. D. Cartlidge, "I Cor 7 as a Foundation for a Christian Sex-Ethic," *Journal of Religion* 55 (1975) 220–34; W. Schrage, "Zur Frontstellung der paulinischen Ehebewertung in 1 Kor 7.1–7," *ZNW* 67 (1976) 214–34; and the commentaries for bibliographical reviews.

50. See G. Schneider, "Die Idee der Neuschöpfung beim Apostel Paulus und ihr religionsgeschichtlicher Hintergrund," *Trierer Theologische Zeitschrift* 68 (1959) 260f. For *Joseph and Asenath*, see the summary review by E. W. Smith, *"Joseph and Asenath" and Early Christian Literature* (Ann Arbor: University Microfilms, 1975), pp. 1–44.

51. D. Daube, "Pauline Contributions to a Pluralistic Culture: Re-Creation and Be-

yond," in D. G. Miller and D. Y. Hadidian, eds., *Jesus and Man's Hope* (Pittsburgh: Pittsburgh Theological Seminary, 1970), 2.223–45:240.

52. See R. Kraemer, *Ecstatics and Ascetics: Studies in the Functions of Religious Activities for Women* . . . (Ann Arbor: University Microfilm, 1976), pp. 134–67.

53. Justin *Apologia* 2.2. See H. Gülzow, "Soziale Gegebenheiten der altkirchlichen Mission," in *Kirchengeschichte als Missionsgeschichte*, vol. 1, *Alte Kirche* (Munich: Kaiser, 1974), p. 203.

54. See especially R. Scroggs, "Paul and the Eschatological Woman," *JAAR* 40 (1972) 283–303.

55. Meeks, "Image of the Androgyne," p. 200.

56. Scroggs, "Paul and the Eschatological Woman," p. 294.

57. Cartlidge, "I Cor 7 as a Foundation," p. 232.

58. S. B. Pomeroy, *Goddesses, Whores, Wives, and Slaves* (New York: Schocken Books, 1975), pp. 213f.

59. See L. Naphtali, *Roman Civilization* (New York: Columbia University Press, 1955), pp. 52ff.; P. E. Corbett, *The Roman Law of Marriage* (Oxford: Oxford University Press, 1930), pp. 106–46:120f.

60. H. Wendland, *Die Briefe an die Korinther* (NTD 7; Göttingen: Vandenhoeck & Ruprecht, 1965), p. 80. E. Kähler (*Die Frau in den Paulinischen Briefen* [Zurich: Gotthelf Verlag, 1960], pp. 43f.) maintains that 10:32–11:2 are the introduction and headline to the following.

61. Conzelmann (*1 Corinthians*, p. 246) argues that "this idea is better suited to an interpolation than to Paul, and is suggested by it."

62. For the concept of "good order," see G. Dautzenberg, *Urchristliche Prophetie: Ihre Erforschung, ihre Voraussetzungen im Judentum, und ihre Struktur im 1. Korintherbrief* (BWANT 104; Stuttgart: Kohlhammer, 1975), p. 278–84.

63. Cf. J. C. Hurd, *The Origin of 1 Corinthians* (New York: Seabury, 1965); p. 287; J. W. Drane, "Tradition, Law, and Ethics in Pauline Theology," *NovT* 16 (1974) 167–87.

64. The non-Pauline character of 1 Cor 11:2–16 is argued in W. O. Walker, "1 Corinthians 11:2–16 and Paul's View Regarding Women," *JBL* 94 (1975) 94–110; and in Lamar Cope, "1 Cor 11:2–16: One Step Further," *JBL* 97 (1978) 435–36. For a discussion and rejection of their arguments, see J. Murphy-O'Connor, "The Non-Pauline Character of 1 Corinthians 11:2–16?" *JBL* 95 (1976) 615–21; idem, "Sex and Logic in 1 Corinthians 11:2–16," *CBQ* 42 (1980) 482–500; J. P. Meier, "On the Veiling of Hermeneutics (1 Cor 11:2–16)," *CBQ* 40 (1978) 212–26.

65. See e.g. S. Lösch, "Christliche Frauen in Korinth," *Theologische Quartalschrift* 127 (1947) 216–61; A. Jaubert, "Le voile des femmes (1 Cor xi.2–16)," *NTS* 18 (1972) 419–30; A. Feuillet, "La dignité et le rôle de la femme d'après quelques textes pauliniens," *NTS* 21 (1975) 157–91; and the articles by Meeks, Scroggs, and Jewett.

66. See especially J. B. Hurley, "Did Paul Require Veils or the Silence of Women?" *Westminster Theological Journal* 35 (1972/73) 190–220; W. J. Martin, "1 Cor 11:2–16," in W. W. Gasque and R. P. Martin, eds., *Apostolic History and the Gospel* (Grand Rapids: Eerdmans, 1970), pp. 231–34; A. Isaakson, *Marriage and Ministry in the New Testament* (ASNU 24; Lund: Gleerup, 1965), pp. 165–86; Murphy-O'Connor, "Sex and Logic," pp. 488ff.

67. See e.g. J. P. V. D. Balsdon, "Women in Imperial Rome," *History Today* 10 (1960) 24–31.

68. R. and K. Kroeger, "An Inquiry into Evidence of Maenadism in the Corinthian Congregation," *SBL Seminar Papers* 14 (1978), 2.331–46.

69. Tibullus 1.3.29–32; for other cults, see Lösch, "Christliche Frauen," pp. 240ff.

70. S. Kelly Heyob, *The Cult of Isis Among Women in the Greco-Roman World* (Leiden: Brill, 1975), p. 60.

71. Ibid., p. 52.

72. Ibid., pp. 105f. See also R. E. Witt, "Isis-Hellas," *Proceedings of the Cambridge Philological Society* 12 (1966) 62; idem, *Isis in the Greco-Roman World* (Ithaca, N.Y.: Cornell

University Press, 1971); J. Z. Smith, "Native Cults in the Hellenistic Period," *History of Religions* 11 (1971/72) 236–49.

73. W. C. van Unnik, "Les cheveux défaits des femmes baptisées," *Vigiliae Christianae* 1 (1947) 77–100; however, Murphy-O'Connor ("Sex and Logic," pp. 485ff.) suggests that the real issues here are "long-haired men" and "the way hair is dressed."

74. H. L. Strack and P. Billerbeck, *Kommentar zum Neuen Testament aus Talmud und Midrasch* (Munich: C. H. Beck, 1926), 3.428f.

75. Cf. especially J. A. Fitzmyer, "A Feature of Qumran Angelology and the Angels of 1 Cor 11:10," *NTS* 4 (1957/58) 48–58.

76. See M. D. Hooker, "Authority on Her Head: An Examination of I Cor xi.10," *NTS* 10 (1964/65) 410–16; A. Feuillet, "Le sign de puissance sur la tête de la femme (I Cor xi.10)," *Nouvelle Revue Théologique* 55 (1973) 945–54.

77. See H. Schlier, "*kephalē*," *TDNT* 3.679; S. Bedale, "The Meaning of *kephalē* in the Pauline Epistles," *Journal of Theological Studies* 5 (1954) 213f.; Scroggs, "Paul and the Eschatological Woman," pp. 298f.

78. In the NT see especially the Book of Revelation; cf. my *Invitation to the Book of Revelation* (Garden City, N.Y.: Doubleday, Image Books, 1981); and my "Apokalypsis and Propheteia: The Book of Revelation in the Context of Early Christian Prophecy," in J. Lambrecht, ed., *L'Apocalypse johannique et l'Apocalyptique dans le Nouveau Testament* (BETL 53; Gembloux: Duculot, 1980; Leuven: University Press, 1980), pp. 105–28.

79. See Conzelmann, *1 Corinthians*, p. 190, nn. 96–97.

80. J. Kürzinger, "Frau und Mann nach 1 Kor 11.11f," *Biblische Zeitschrift* 22 (1978), 270–75; Murphy-O'Connor ("Sex and Logic," pp. 497f.) also accepts Kürzinger's correction but again ends up with an "equal but different" interpretation: ". . . the recreated woman has an authority equal to that of the man (vv. 10–12). The two are related (*dia touto*, v.10) inasmuch as the woman has this power precisely as a woman. New status is accorded to woman, not to an ambiguous being whose 'unfeminine' hairdo was an affront to generally accepted conventions" (p. 498).

81. Many scholars have accepted 1 Cor 14:33b–36 as a post-Pauline interpolation; see especially G. Fitzer, "*Das Weib schweige in der Gemeinde*" (TEH 110; Munich: Kaiser, 1963); Conzelmann, *1 Corinthians*, p. 246; and the review of the arguments by Feuillet, "La dignité et le rôle," pp. 162–70.

82. See E. E. Ellis, " 'Spiritual' Gifts in the Pauline Community," *NTS* 20 (1974) 128–44; U. B. Müller, *Prophetie und Predigt im Neuen Testament* (StNT 10; Gütersloh: Mohn, 1975), pp. 11–45.

83. Dautzenberg, *Urchristliche Prophetie*, pp. 253–88.

84. See K. Niederwimmer, *Askese und Mysterium* (FRLANT 113; Göttingen: Vandenhoeck & Ruprecht, 1975), pp. 80–123.

85. Conzelmann, *1 Corinthians*, p. 134.

86. Niederwimmer, *Askese und Mysterium*, p. 115.

87. S. Aelan, "A Rabbinic Formula in I Cor. 14.34," *Studia Evangelica* 87 (1964) 513–25: esp. 517ff; and especially Crouch, *Colossian Haustafel*, pp. 138ff.

88. M. F. Lefkowitz and M. Fant, eds., *Women in Greece and Rome* (Toronto: Samuel-Stevens, 1977), p. 135. For the androcentric tendency of Livy's historiography, see S. E. Smethurst, "Women in Livy's History," *Greece and Rome* 19 (1950) 80–87; N. P. Miller, "Dramatic Speech in the Roman Historians," *Greece and Rome*, n.s. 22 (1975) 45–75.

89. Lefkowitz and Fant, *Women in Greece and Rome*, p. 86.

90. For "spiritual motherhood," see Gal 4:19 and Betz, *Galatians*, pp. 233ff; for "spiritual parenthood," see 2 Cor 2:14; and for the comparison with a "wet-nurse," see 1 Thess 2:11 and especially A. Malherbe, " 'Gentle as a Nurse': The Cynic Background to I Thess ii," *NovT* 12 (1970) 203–17.

91. See Strack and Billerbeck, *Kommentar*, 3.340f.; G. Schrenk, "patēr," *TDNT* 5.958f.; P. Gutierrez, *La paternité spirituelle selon Saint Paul* (Paris: Gabalda, 1968); P. A. H. De Boer, *Fatherhood and Motherhood in Israelite and Judaean Piety* (Leiden: Brill, 1974).

92. For an analysis of the sociology of "apostolic authority" in Paul, see J. H. Schütz,

Paul and the Anatomy of Apostolic Authority (Cambridge: Cambridge University Press, 1975), p. 278. He stresses that Paul's authority was based on the appeal to "what it shares with common Christian charisma and not by reference to what it distinguishes from all the others."

93. See e.g. P. C. Hanson, *II Corinthians* (London: SCM Press, 1954), pp. 79f; Jean Hering, *The Second Epistle of St. Paul to the Corinthians* (London: Epworth Press, 1967), pp. 783ff.

94. See my "Interpreting Patriarchal Traditions," in L. Russell, ed., *The Liberating Word: A Guide to Nonsexist Interpretation of the Bible* (Philadelphia: Westminster, 1976), pp. 46f.; H. Balz-Cochois, "Gomer oder die Macht der Astarte: Versuch einer feministischen Interpretation von Hos 1–4," *EvTh* 42 (1982) 37–65.

95. Cf. D. C. Smith, "Paul and the Non-Eschatological Woman," *Ohio Journal of Religious Studies* 4 (1976) 11–18:16.

96. See R. Scroggs, *The Last Adam* (Philadelphia: Fortress, 1966); and especially E. Käsemann, "On Paul's Anthropology," in his *Perspectives on Paul* (Philadelphia: Fortress, 1971), pp. 1–31; see also R. Scroggs, *Paul for a New Day* (Philadelphia: Fortress, 1977).

97. C. K. Barrett (*The Pastoral Epistles* [Oxford: Clarendon Press, 1963], p. 56) sums it up: "Adam, first in creation. Eve, first in sin." For the Jewish interpretation of Gen 3:13, cf. Hanson, *II Corinthians*, pp. 65–77.

98. For this fundamental ambiguity in Paul, see W. A. Meeks, "'Since Then You Would Need to Go Out of the World': Group Boundaries in Pauline Christianity," in T. J. Ryan, ed., *Critical History and Biblical Perspective* (Villanova, Pa.: College Theology Society, 1979), pp. 4–29.

99. If this practical tension in Paul's writings is overlooked, then Paul is alternately condemned as a "chauvinist" or hailed as a "liberationist."

Part III

TRACING THE STRUGGLES
Patriarchy and Ministry

In the last decades of the first century Christian texts emerge that seek to order relationships in terms of the Greco-Roman household. (The authors of Colossians, Ephesians, and the Pastorals claim the authority of Paul.[1] Although 1 Peter is written in the name of Peter, the letter contains many traces of Pauline traditions.[2]) The writers of the post-Pauline literature advocated the adoption of the Greco-Roman patriarchal order of the house with its injunctions to subordination and submission of the socially weaker party.[3] At first they might have done so with a view to lessening the political tensions between the Christian group and the pagan patriarchal household. However, at the same time, Christian writers apply this pattern of patriarchal submission also to their own communal self-understanding and life in the church as the household of God. Interestingly, most of the early Christian writings that promulgate such as model of the patriarchal household are written to churches in Asia Minor.

The situation of the churches in Asia Minor[4] seems to have been still very fluid and diversified. Neither a stabilized form of monepiscopal office nor a unified structure of organization yet existed. The prevalent organizational form was probably the house church, although itinerant charismatics and "schoollike" gatherings also continued the Pauline mission.[5] Theologically several strands of early Christian tradition seem to have coalesced in the communities of Asia Minor. Prophetic authority, apocalyptic expectation, pressure of adapting to the dominant society, ascetic withdrawal from marriage and family, Judaizing tendencies, avowal of docetism, strife and rivalries among different leaders and groups, persecution by Rome, and harassment by neighbors—all these elements provided the exciting mix of life for women in the Asian churches at the end of the first century.

John, the author of Revelation, and Ignatius of Antioch wrote letters to the most important churches of the region. Luke-Acts and the Fourth Gospel in its final form might have been written for such communities. The *Acts of Paul and Thecla* were written by one of the Asian elders. The correspondence between Pliny and Trajan, the fourth book of the *Sibylline Oracles*, the book of Revelation, and 1 Peter testify to the precarious political situation of these communities, partially engendered by their resistance to the imperial cult and policies. Important Asiatic Christians still known to us in the second century are: "Jezebel," the head of a prophetic school in Thyatira, Polycarp of Smyrna, Papias of Hierapolis, Alce of Smyrna, Polycrates of Ephesus, Marcion and Markus together with their women followers, as well as the Montanist prophets Maximilla, Priscilla, and Montanus.

The excellent roads of Western Asia Minor allowed for extensive travel and diversified communication.[6] The churches of Asia Minor might have been small, but they were not isolated. They had strong links with other Christian centers, especially with Antioch and Rome. Merchants, such as Lydia of Thyatira, trade people like Prisca and Aquila, prisoners like Ignatius of Antioch kept a lively exchange going between various missionary areas of the Christian movement. Itinerant prophets, traveling missionaries, and ecclesial emissaries brought new ideas and theological perspectives or customs to the Christians in Asia. While in retrospect scholars might be able to sort out different Christian traditions and to distinguish between Pauline, Johannine, or Lukan strands of theology, ordinary members of the Asian churches were probably not able to do so. Thus a coalescing and amalgamation of various traditions and influences must be taken into account when discussing the situation of the Christian missionary movement in Asia Minor around the turn of the first century. The variety of literary theological expressions available from this area, however, must have been rooted in a very diffused actual historical situation. However, if the major organizational form of the Christian community was the house church, then such a plurality of theological perspectives and self-understandings is easily understandable.

Women belonged to the leadership of such house churches in Asia Minor. We have seen that Paul greets Apphia as a leading member of Philemon's house church.[7] He does not call her Philemon's sister and thereby imply that she is Philemon's wife as many contemporary exegetes do. Like Philemon and Archippus, she is also described as a co-missionary of Paul. The author of Colossians sends special greetings to Nympha and the church in her house, while the writer of 2 Timothy recalls the missionary endeavors of Prisca and Aquila at Ephesus by sending special greetings to them (4:19). He also sends greetings from a woman by the name of Claudia, about whom we know nothing more than her name. Like Eubullus, Linus, and Pudens she must have been well known to the recipients of the letter (4:21). The same letter stresses that Timothy derives his own faith from that of his grandmother Lois and his mother Eunice. Since Timothy's father is not mentioned we can assume that only the female line of the family was Christian. Women are here understood as the faithful transmitters and guarantors of Christian faith (1:5). This enumeration of women as the transmitters of faith—Lois, Eunice, Timothy—parallels Paul's own lineage of faithful service—"my fathers" (1:3), Paul himself, and Timothy, who is called Paul's "beloved child" (1:2).[8]

At the beginning of the second century, Ignatius of Antioch greets women only in two letters. However, in these letters the women are given prominence almost to the near exclusion of men. Moreover, the salutations of Ignatius's other letters mention only Polycarp and the church in Smyrna (*Ephesians, Trallians, Magnesians*), some persons who are with him in Troas (*Philadelphians*), and Crocus, a representative of the Ephesian community who might have carried the *Letter to the Romans*. The personal greetings in the letters to Smyrna and Polycarp are explained when we consider that Ignatius only stayed long enough in Smyrna and Philadelphia to become acquainted with the actual situation and leading persons of the community. While his relationship to the Christians in Philadelphia was somewhat strained, he had prolonged and positive contacts with those in Smyrna.[9]

In the *Letter to the Smyrnaeans* (13:1) he sends greeting not only to the households of "brothers with their wives and children" but also to the "virgins called widows" who seem to be viewed as a distinct social group. He greets by name two men, "the inimitable Daphnus and Eutecnus," and two women. They are Tavia and her household, whom he wants to be "grounded in faith and love both in the flesh and in the Spirit," and Alce, "who means a great deal" to Ignatius. In the *Letter to Polycarp* he again greets Alce (8:3) and the wife (or widow or divorcee) of Epitropus with her children and her whole house. Epitropus however might not be a proper name but a title meaning "procurator." Since it is not the *paterfamilias* but a woman who is mentioned, she is either the widow or wife of Epitropus (or of the procurator) who himself is not a Christian. We are no longer able to decide the matter.

Alce is also mentioned in the *Martyrdom of Polycarp* (17:2), written about fifty years later. Her brother, Nicetas, is a pagan and an opponent of the Christians. To identify him as "brother of Alce" makes sense only if Alce is well known to the Christians in Smyrna and Philomelium to which the report is addressed. Both of these passages from Ignatius, in short, throw light upon the fact that Alce was a Christian of particular influence and energy in Smyrna who, as late as 150, was well known throughout the churches of Asia.[10] We do not know what role Alce had in Smyrna and in the Asian churches and why she meant a great deal to Ignatius. However, her name is only one among the many women who—as Grant has pointed out—"in the church as in society in general, were highly influential in the second century."[11] Grant also suggests that the misogynism of Tertullian or Hippolytus might reflect their personal resentment.

It seems that the nameless woman to whom the second Johannine letter is written must be understood as the head of her house church. Although most scholars understand "the elect lady" and her "elect sister" as symbolic names for churches in Asia Minor,[12] there is no compelling reason to do so. These expressions are best understood as honorifics for the women leaders of house churches,[13] since *kyria* or *domina* is a familiar title for the *materfamilias* and "sister" is used as a missionary title by Paul. The expression "children" can connote biological children, but in the context of the Christian mission it designates more frequently "spiritual children" who are converts. "Children" is also used to characterize the disciples or members of a philosophical school.[14]

Since 3 John is also addressed to the head of a house church, nothing prevents us from assuming the same for 2 John. Malherbe has observed that Diotrephes who is addressed in 3 John had a position of power and eminence. "The picture that we get is of one man exercizing his power, not of someone lobbying in order to impose his will. . . . He may not have had ecclesiastical authority, but he did have the power to exclude from the assembly in his house those who opposed him."[15] Similarly, the "elect lady" is admonished not to admit anyone to her house who does not teach the same doctrine that the elder teaches. The presbyter who writes the letter had no power to command but "begs" or "entreats" the head of this house church. He reminds her of the commandments and warns her against docetic preachers, yet he cannot prevent her from giving hospitality to such preachers. Here we have a glimpse of the great influence and personal power exercised by those wealthy Christians who provided for the local church a meeting place, funds, and social-political standing. The presbyter can make appeals and plead that hospitality is granted to his own emissaries, he can warn and announce his personal intervention, but neither Diotrephes nor "the elect lady" are subject to his authority.

Such influential position and leadership of women in the Asian churches is quite in keeping with the general religious position and social influence women had in Asia Minor. Even under Roman rule women were of remarkable prominence in the political, social, and religious life of the country. The large number of inscriptions and ancient monuments mentioning women are unusual.[16] Even in the most Hellenized and Romanized cities women functioned as magistrates and officials, as priestesses and cultic staff. Under the empire the chief priest of the Ephesian Artemis, whose temple was one of the seven wonders of the world, was no longer a eunuch but a high priestess. The priestly organization of the Artemisium included a large number of officers, both male and female. The cult and festivals of the Ephesian Artemis[17] attracted pilgrims from all over the world, especially from the neighboring regions of Asia Minor. Women and men equally participated in the rites of the Great Goddess. That the early Christians were conscious of their competition with this cult comes to the fore in Acts 19:23–41.[18] This apologetic account blames the Jewish competition for the unrest and has the city sacristan of the great Artemis assert that Paul and his companions are "neither sacrilegious nor blasphemers of our goddess" (19:37). At the same time, the story emphasizes that the Pauline mission not only threatened the business people who made and sold the image of the goddess as souvenirs but also endangered the temple of the Great Goddess, "whom all Asia and the world worships" (19:27).

Jewish communities were numerous and influential in Western Asia Minor.[19] The rights afforded to the Jewish *politeuma* of Sardis, for example, illustrate the interpenetration of civil and religious affairs; this community is permitted to worship and practice its ancestral laws, to have a defined place for cultic activities, to adjudicate internal matters in its own courts, to pay to Jerusalem the half-shekel tax, and to represent its members to the imperial government. For many generations the Jews of Sardis were integrated into the community and played an important and powerful role in civic life. Kraabel, who has studied the Jewish communities in western Asia Minor, has pointed out that women were prominent members of Jewish communities in

Asia Minor.[20] A tomb inscription from Smyrna, dating from the second or third century, reads:

> Rufina, a Jewess, president of the synagogue (*archisynagōgos*), built this tomb for her freed slaves and the slaves raised in her house. No one else has the right to bury anyone [here]. If someone should dare to do so, they will pay 1500 denars to the sacred treasury and 1000 denars to the Jewish people. A copy of this inscription has been placed in the archives.[21]

This inscription gives us a clue to the influential positions women had in Jewish communities. At least some women had so much property at their disposal that they could build synagogues out of their own funds, own slaves and set them free, as well as be leading officers in the synagogue. As president of the synagogue Rufina would have had to care for the proper execution of the synagogue services, to collect money, as well as to preach and to teach.

Asian women who converted either from Judaism or from their native religion to Christianity would have expected to have the same influence in the Christian community. Wealthy women especially must have taken for granted their influence in the church, since their culture and religion had socialized them to assume important positions in civic life and religious institutions. However, we know from Pliny that ministerial leadership in the Christian community was not restricted to wealthy and free matrons but that slave women were also "ministers" among the Christians. The Pastoral and Ignatian letters indicate that such slave women and men expected to be bought free by the Christian community "on the grounds that they are 'brethren' "—full members of the new Christian family. While the names of prominent Christian women give us a clue to women's leadership in the Christian movement, the mention of slave women as "ministers" indicates that the discipleship of equals was in the process of being transformed into a community of patriarchal submission. The dynamics of the repression of women's leadership and the continuing oppression of enslaved and poor people, especially of women, in the name of Christianity are historically intertwined and have the same roots in the patriarchal structures of dominance and submission.

Notes to this section follow chapter 7 on page 279.

Christian Mission and the Patriarchal Order of the Household

A s we have seen, the early Christian vision of the discipleship of equals practiced in the house church attracted especially slaves and women to Christianity but also caused tensions and conflicts with the dominant cultural ethos of the patriarchal household. True, women as well as men, slaves as well as free, Asians as well as Greeks and Romans, participated fully in the cult of the Great Goddess; and in such a religious context the baptismal confession of Gal 3:28 was not utopian. However, in contrast to the public cult of the goddess, in the Christian context, the public religious sphere of the church and the private sphere of the patriarchal house were not clearly separated. Insofar as Christians understood themselves as the new family[22] and expressed this self-understanding institutionally in the house church, the public-religious and private patriarchal spheres were no longer distinguished. In fact, it was the religious ethos—of equality—that was transferred to and came in conflict with the patriarchal ethos of the household. The Christian missionary movement thus provided an alternative vision and praxis to that of the dominant society and religion.

Colossians and the Household Code

Colossians, written by a disciple of Paul,[23] quotes Gal 3:28 but changes it considerably. Moreover, he balances it out with a household code of patriarchal submission. The relationship of Jews and gentiles was no longer a great problem and concern for the author. The separation between the Jewish and Christian communities probably had already taken place at the time of his writing. In quoting the baptismal formula[24] Colossians mentions Greeks first and elaborates the second member of the pair circumcision and uncircumcision with "barbarian and Scythian," in order to stress that national and cultural differences and inequalities are overcome in the new humanity of Christ. Since Scythians were the proverbial boors of antiquity, it is obvious that the author of Colossians is especially interested in the opposite pair Greek and barbarian. While the third pair of Gal 3:28— male and female is not mentioned at all, Col 3:11 also dissolves the slave-free polarization that defines the social-political stratifications of institutional slavery. Col 3:11 no longer juxtaposes slave-free as opposite alternatives but adds them to the enumeration and elaboration of those who are uncircumcised: barbarian, Scythian, slave, freeborn.

Although the letter to the Colossians still refers to the baptismal liturgy and theology of the Asian churches,[25] it celebrates not so much the restoration of human equality in the new community but rather "a cosmic event, in which the opposing elements of the universe were reconciled to each other." The so-called enthusiastic theology ascribed to Paul's opponents in Corinth is fully expressed here. Baptism means resurrection and enthronement with Christ in heaven, "stripping away the body of flesh" (2:11), and life in heaven rather than on earth (2:1–4; cf. 2:12, 20). The baptized are delivered from "the dominion of darkness" and transferred into "the kingdom of his beloved son" (1:13). They are "dead to the cosmos," have received a secret mystery (1:26f; 2:2–3), and have the assurance of an inheritance among the "holy ones" in the realm of light. The writer of Colossians agrees with his audience on this theology of exaltation but disagrees with some of the Colossians on how this baptismal "symbolic universe" and drama should be remembered and made effective. While some in the community of Colossae believed that the "removal of the fleshly body" and the "new humanity" in baptism must be realized in ascetic practices and elaborate ritual observances, the author insists on the finality of Christ's reconciliation and unification. The new "angelic religion" and the life in heaven are not to be realized by ascetic and ritual practice but in ethical behavior and communal life.[26] Since they have been raised with Christ, they are to "seek the things that are above," and to set their "minds on the things that are above." They do so "by putting away" anger, wrath, malice, slander, and foul talk and by "putting on" compassion, kindness, lowliness, meekness, and patience, forebearing one another and forgiving each other. Above all, they should "put on love, which binds everything together in perfect harmony" (3:5–17). They should behave wisely to outsiders and be able to answer everyone (4:5f).

This is the context of the household code (3:18–4:1), the first and most precise form of the domestic code in the New Testament. The basic form of this code consists of three pairs of reciprocal exhortations addressing the relationship between wife and husband, children and father, and slaves and masters. In each case, the socially subordinate first member of the pair is exhorted to obedience to the superordinate second. The formal structure of such a household code, then, consists of address (wives), exhortation (submit to your husbands), and motivation (as is fitting in the Lord). The only Christian element in the Colossian code is the addition "in the Lord."[27] However, the author of Colossians quotes the code here, not because he is concerned about the behavior of wives, but that of slaves.

The expansion of the code's third pair, slave-master, indicates that the obedience and acceptance of servitude by Christian slaves are of utmost concern.[28] Colossians asks slaves to fulfill their task with single-mindedness of heart and dedication "as serving the Lord and not men" (3:23). He not only promises eschatological reward for such behavior but also threatens eschatological judgment and punishment for misbehavior (3:24f). The injunction to masters, in turn, is very short and has no Christian component except the reminder that they, too, have a master in heaven. Slave behavior is likened here to the Christian service of the Lord, while the "masters" are likened to the "Master" in heaven. It is obvious that the good behavior of slaves, according to the author, is the concrete realization of Gal 3:28, insofar as both slaves and freeborn have one Lord in heaven, Christ, and belong to the new humanity, now "hid with Christ in God" (3:3). There is no question that E. A. Judge is right when he asserts that what we hear in these injunctions is "the voice of the propertied class."[29] We have no way of determining whether "those who are your earthly masters" are only pagan or also Christian masters. The injunction to the masters presupposes that they still have slaves who might or might not have been Christian.

In taking over the Greco-Roman ethic of the patriarchal household code, Colossians not only "spiritualizes" and moralizes the baptismal community understanding expressed in Gal 3:28 but also makes this Greco-Roman household ethic a part of "Christian" social ethic. However, it is important to keep in mind that such a reinterpretation of the Christian baptismal vision is late—it did not happen before the last third of the first century. Moreover, it is found only in one segment of early Christianity, the post-Pauline tradition, and had no impact on the Jesus traditions. The insistence on equality and mutuality within the Christian community that seems to have been expressed by slaves as well as by women is not due to later "enthusiastic excesses"[30] or to illegitimate agitation for emancipation. The opposite is true. Colossians shows how a so-called "enthusiastic" realized eschatological perspective can produce an insistence on patriarchal behavior as well as an acceptance of the established political-social status quo of inequality and exploitation in the name of Jesus Christ.

In discussing the *Sitz im Leben* of the household code form, exegetes have arrived at different interpretations. While a few scholars think that the demands for the obedience and submission of wives, children, and slaves are genuinely Christian, the majority sees the domestic code as a later Christian adaptation of a Greco-Roman or Jewish-Hellenistic philosophical-theological code. While Dibelius (cf. also Weidinger and Lohse) holds that the household code in Colossians is a slightly Christianized version of a Stoic ethical code, Lohmeyer (and recently Crouch) has stressed the Jewish-Hellenistic origin of the code in an apologetic missionary context. Not Stoicism but oriental Jewish religion provides the background for the code. In adopting the code, Christians followed the example of Hellenistic Judaism and utilized the form of the code developed in Jewish-Hellenistic missionary apologetics.[31]

Most recently scholars have pointed to the treatises on economics and politics that reflect a form already codified by Aristotle and at home in the philosophical schools and morals of the first century C.E. Thraede stresses that the moralists of the early empire sought to formulate an ethics that would find a balance between the absolute traditional demands of subordination and obedience to the *paterfamilias* and the ideals of equality formulated in the Hellenistic age. What comes to the fore in the household code form of the New Testament is the option for "an ethically softened or humanized notion of domination and rule."[32] But while Lührmann stresses the *Sitz im Leben* of the form and of the *topos* in economics[33] with indirect implications for politics, Balch highlights the political context of the teachings about the right order of the house and economics.[34] Both are intertwined because in antiquity the household was economically independent, self-sufficient, hierarchically ordered, and as such the basis of the state. Therefore, the three *topoi*, "concerning the state," "concerning household management," and "concerning marriage," were closely interrelated.[35]

Aristotle, who has decisively influenced Western political philosophy as well as American legal concepts[36] argues against Plato that one must begin the discussion of politics with thoughts about marriage, defined by him as a union of "natural ruler and natural subject."[37] When slaves are added to the family, it can be called a "house." Several households constitute a village and several villages a city-state, or *politeia:*

> The investigation of everything should begin with its smallest parts, and the smallest and primary parts of the household are master and slave, husband and wife, father and children. We ought therefore to examine the proper constitution and character of each of the three relationships, I mean that of mastership, that of marriage and thirdly the progenitive relationship. [*Politics* I.1253b]

It is part of the household science to rule over wife and children as freeborn. However, this is not done with the same form of government. Whereas the father rules over his children as a monarch rules, the husband exercises republican government over the wife:

> for the male is by nature better fitted to command than the female . . . and the older and fully developed person than the younger and immature. It is true that in most cases of republican government the ruler and ruled interchange in turn . . . but the male stands in this relationship to the female continuously. The rule of the father over the children on the other hand is that of a king. [*Politics* I.1259b]

Against those who argue that slavery is contrary to nature, Aristotle points to the rule of the soul over the body.

> It is manifest that it is natural and expedient for the body to be governed by the soul and for the emotional part to be governed by the intellect, the part possessing reason, whereas for the two parties to be on equal [*ison*] footing or in the contrary positions is harmful in all cases. . . . Also as between the sexes, the male is by nature superior and the female inferior, the male ruler and the female subject. And the same must also necessarily apply in the case of humankind generally; therefore all human beings that differ as widely as the soul does from the body . . . these are by nature slaves for whom to be governed by this kind of authority is advantageous. [*Politics* I.1254b]

These "natural" differences justify the relationships of domination in household and state.

> Hence there are by nature various classes of rulers and ruled. For
> the free rules the slave, the male the female, the man the child in
> a different way. And all possess the various parts of the soul but
> possess them in different ways; for the slave has not got the
> deliberative part at all, and the female has it but without full
> authority, while the child has it but in an undeveloped form.
> [*Politics* I.1260a]

Interestingly enough, Aristotle acknowledges one exception when
women can rule with "authority." Usually the relationship between
husband and wife is that of "aristocracy" but when the husband
controls everything it becomes an "oligarchy," "for he governs in
violation of fitness and not in virtue of superiority." "And sometimes
when the wife is an heiress, it is she who rules. In these cases, then,
authority goes not by virtue but by wealth and power, as in an oligarchy" (*Nicomachean Ethics* VIII.1160b).

Since, however, every household is part of the state, the state is
jeopardized if the different forms of household rule are not exercised
faithfully.

> The freedom in regard to women is detrimental both in regard to
> the purpose of the *politeia* and in regard to the happiness of the
> state. For just as man and wife are part of a household, it is clear
> that the state also is divided nearly in half into its male and
> female population, so that in all *politeia* in which the position of
> women is badly regulated one half of the state must be deemed
> neglected in framing the law. [*Politcs* II.1269b]

Such was the case in Sparta, where women controlled their own
wealth. Although the Spartans did attempt to bring their women
under the law, they gave up when the women resisted. Therefore,
they loved and respected wealth and were under the sway of their
women. The women controlled not only many things but also ruled
their own rulers! These remarks make it clear that Aristotle knows of
a historical state that was differently constituted.

Although the negative influence of Aristotle on Christian anthropology is widely acknowledged today,[38] it is not sufficiently recognized that such an anthropology was rooted in Aristotle's understanding of political rule and domination. Just as he defined the
"nature" of slaves with respect to their status as property and to their
economic function, so Aristotle defined the "nature" of woman as
that of someone who does not have "full authority" to rule, although
he is well aware that such rule was an actual historical possibility and
reality. The definition of "woman's nature" and "woman's proper

sphere" is thus rooted in a certain relation of domination and subordination between man and woman having a concrete political background and purpose. Western misogynism has its root in the rules for
the household as the model of the state. A feminist theology therefore
must not only analyze the anthropological dualism generated by
Western culture and theology, but also uncover its political roots in
the patriarchal household of antiquity.

Balch cites considerable evidence that Aristotle's political philosophy was revitalized in neo-Pythagorean and Stoic philosophy.[39] It
was also accepted in Hellenistic Judaism, as the writings of Philo and
Josephus demonstrate. For instance, Philo stresses the interrelationship between household and state management.

> For the future statesman needed first to be trained and practiced
> in house management, for a house is a city compressed into small
> dimensions, and a household management may be called a kind
> of state management [politeia]. . . . This shows clearly that the
> household manager is identical with the statesman. [Joseph 38–
> 39]

And he asserts in *Special Laws*:

> Organized committees are of two sorts, the greater which we call
> cities and the smaller which we call households. Both of these
> have their governors [prostasian], the government of the greater
> is assigned to men, under the name of statesmanship [politeia],
> that of the lesser known as household management to women. A
> woman then should not be a busybody, meddling with matters
> outside her household concerns, but should seek a life of seclu-
> sion. [III.170f]

Philo insists that Jews are not impious, they respect father and
mother, and wives must be in servitude to their husbands. Crouch[40]
has argued that the closest parallel to the New Testament domestic
code is *Hypothetica* VIII.7.14:

> Any of them whom you attack with inquiries about their ances-
> tral institutions can answer you rapidly and easily. The husband
> seems competent to transmit knowledge of the laws to his wife,
> the father to his children, the master to his slaves.

In discussing the *politeia* of Moses and comparing it to that of Romulus, Josephus stresses that Jewish laws do not teach impiety but
piety, not the hatred of others but the communal life. They oppose
injustice and teach justice, they deter from war and encourage people

to work. Therefore, there can be nowhere a greater justice, piety, and harmony than among the Jews. In their marriage laws and the birth and upbringing of children Jews fulfilled the laws of Romulus's *politeia*, which the Romans had imposed on the whole empire. Jewish women were good Roman citizens:

> The woman, says the Law, is in all things inferior to the man. Let her accordingly be submissive, not for her humiliation, but that she may be directed, for the authority has been given by God to the man. [*Against Apion* II.201]

Since the Jews were criticized on the ground that Moses, the founder of the Jewish state, had incited a revolt and introduced different marriage and burial laws, Josephus[41] stresses that Jewish wives, unlike Spartan women, are entirely submissive to their husbands. The context of this statement, as for that of Philo, is clearly apologetic. Dionysos of Halicarnassus had in a similar fashion elaborated the position of women in the *politeia* of Romulus:

> The law led the women to behave themselves with modesty and great decorum. The law was to this effect that a woman joined to her husband by a holy marriage should share in all his possessions and sacred rites. . . . This law obliged both the married women, as having no other refuge, to conform themselves entirely to the temper of their husbands, and the husbands to rule their wives as necessary and inseparable possessions. Accordingly if a wife was virtuous and in all things obedient to her husband she was the mistress of the house in the same degree as the husband was master of it, and after the death of her husband, she was heir to his property. [*Roman Antiquities* II.25.2]

However, Thraede is correct when he points out that we must not overlook the fact that alongside this Aristotelian ethics of submission and rule, a marriage ethos developed which stressed the harmony between the couples.[42] Plutarch describes the ideal marriage as a copartnership:

> It is a lovely thing for a wife to sympathize with her husband's concerns and the husband with the wife's so that, as ropes, by being intertwined, get strength from each other, thus . . . the co-partnership may be preserved through the joint action of both. [*Conjugal Precepts* 140e]

Although the wife is clearly the subordinate of the husband, the husband should train her in philosophy and she should respect him as "guide, philosopher and teacher in all that is most lovely and divine." She should not be aggrieved "if like the flute-player, she makes a more impressive sound through a tongue not her own."[43] Therefore, she should always behave with modesty and moderation, appear in public only with her husband, be carefully guarded in her speech, and avoid excessive adornment and luxury. So the neo-Pythagorean Callicratidas advises men to marry virgins in the flower of their youth (usually between 12 and 15 years) because

> such virgins are easily fashioned, and are docile and are also naturally well disposed to be instructed by, and to fear and love their husbands.

If the husband, however, wants to be admired and loved, he should

> exercise his power so that it might be mingled with pleasure and veneration; pleasure indeed being produced by his fondness, but veneration from doing nothing of a vile or abject nature.[44]

The marriage will be happy if both husband and wife are in accord with each other in prosperous and adverse times. The husband's role is that of a master, teacher, and regulator, the wife's behavior that of prudence, modesty, and respect. Perictione stresses that the wife must venerate the gods by obeying the laws and sacred institutions of her country. She should honor and respect her parents, and live with her husband "legally and socially," especially concerned with performing her duties toward him in "domestic harmony" and being the guardian of his bed,

> then she will not only benefit her husband, but also her children, her kindred, her servants, and the whole of her house; in which possessions, friends, citizens, and strangers are contained.[45]

Plutarch also emphasizes that the wife should not only share her husband's friends but also his gods. She must therefore "shut the front door tight upon all queer rituals and outlandish superstitions. For with no god do stealthy and secret rites performed by a woman find any favor" (140d). Thus it is apparent that in antiquity rules of the household are part of economics and politics, as are religious rites and ancestral customs. The well-being of the state and the religious observance of the laws and customs of the patriarchal family are intertwined. Slaves and wives who do not worship the gods of the *paterfamilias* violate not only their household duties but also the laws of the state.

1 Peter and the Household Code

The household code in 1 Pet 2:11–3:12[46] no longer consists of three pairs of reciprocal injunctions, for it only mentions slaves, wives as well as husbands, but not children and parents. Moreover, it stresses primarily the duties of the subordinate members of the household. Its context, however, is the Greco-Roman discussion on the *politeia* with its three sections: the discussion of the duties concerning the state, those concerning the household, and those concerning marriage. This threefold division is clearly followed in pseudo-Peter's discussion of the Christian life. This discussion begins with a demand for submission to human governors (2:13–17), then exhorts slaves to be submissive even to hard and unjust masters (2:18–25), and asks Christian wives to submit themselves to their husbands, even when the latter are pagans and actively engaged against the Christian community by being disobedient to the word (3:1–6). While the passage does not contain an exhortation to masters, the admonitions to the wife are followed by a short exhortation to the husband (3:7).

Although the context of this household-code type of instruction is not that of cosmic reconciliation and heavenly enthronement as in Colossians, it is clearly connected with baptismal remembrance and instruction. The Christians are "born anew" by the incorruptible living word (1:23–25), they are elect and holy, they are the beloved who are called to an incorruptible living hope. As newborn babes they should "put off" all malice and vice (2:1), and live as "children of obedience" (1:14), so that they may "grow up to salvation" for they "have tasted the kindness of the Lord" (2:2f). As the spiritual temple, the priestly people of God, "they should be holy" just as God is holy who called them (1:14–16). They should cast all their anxieties on God, because it is God who cares for them (5:7).

As the royal priesthood they are a holy *politeuma*, a new people who have been "liberated from the futile ways inherited from your fathers" (1:18) through the death of Christ. Here the point of conflict between the Christian community and the surrounding society is named: they have left the ancestral customs and gods of their pagan households and turned to the "living stone," Jesus Christ. However, "as God's own people," they are now "exiles in the dispersion," strangers and immigrants. As such they are deeply alienated from their own society. They have to suffer various trials, are slandered, treated as criminals, and reviled. They are therefore exhorted not to give in to their fear, not to be afraid of those who may injure (3:13) or slander them (3:16). Nonetheless, knowing that they are called to

"God's eternal glory," they can have courage, for they will have to suffer only for a "little while" (1:6f, 5:10f) in order that their genuineness may be tested by fire.

It is obvious that these Christian communities of Asia Minor were a small and alienated minority group.[47] They represent an illegal religion that had disrupted the ancestral customs and religion of their patriarchal households.[48] Since no "masters" are addressed we can assume that the majority of their members were slaves of pagan masters and wives of pagan husbands. Because of their distinctive lifestyle and their heightened consciousness of election they were being persecuted. The writer of 1 Peter, seeking to encourage them in their trials, insists that their unjust sufferings because of Christ and their lifestyle "as God's own people" are necessary, and will last only for a "little while." At the same time he offers them a "strategy"[49] for survival in the midst of trials and persecutions. This strategy consists in "doing good" and proving themselves faithful "law-abiding" citizens; it presupposes that "what is good" is agreed upon by Christians as well as pagans and that Christian suffering is rooted in a pagan "misunderstanding," but not in a different societal-religious ethos.[50] The distinctiveness of Christian faith and religion is maintained only insofar as slaves and wives must be prepared to suffer for being Christians. However, for the sake of the Christian mission, they should seek to reduce suffering and tensions as much as possible by a lifestyle that is totally conformed to the customs and ethos of their pagan household and state.

The interpretational key to the household-code instructions is given in 2:12, which introduces the whole section:

> Beloved, I beseech you as aliens and exiles. . . . Maintain good conduct among the Gentiles so that in case they speak against you as wrongdoers [better, lawbreakers] they may see your good deeds [your law-abiding behavior as good citizens] and glorify God on the day of visitation. [2:11a, 12]

The author concludes the whole exhortation:

> Have no fear of them nor be troubled, but in your hearts reverence Christ as Lord. Always be prepared to make a defense (apology) to anyone who calls you to account for the hope that is in you, yet do it with gentleness and respect, and keep your conscience clear, so that when you are abused, those who revile your good behavior in Christ may be put to shame. For it is better to suffer for doing right [being a good Christian and citizen] if that should be God's will, than for doing wrong [i.e., breaking law and custom]. [3:14b–17]

It is apparent that the author conceives of the household code as a form of apologia for the Christian faith.[51] However, unlike Josephus or Philo who write such defenses for the attackers of the Jews, the author addresses Christians, who are powerless and without legal recourse, urging them to adapt to the *politeuma* of Rome and its ancestral customs. In this way, the author does not lessen the tension between the Christian community and the patriarchal society, since this tension is created precisely by the abandonment of the religion of the *paterfamilias*. The author wants to strengthen their rejection of the "old religion," but he does so by relinquishing the new freedom of those slaves and women who became members of the new priestly people.[52] He restricts it to "their hearts" for the sake of their own survival and that of the Christian minority group. A quite different strategy was chosen by the prophet-author of the book of Revelation for whom the emperor and Rome were the embodiment of the Antichrist. As an oppressive power Rome had to be resisted even at the risk of prison and death. Both authors wrote around the same time to Christians in Asia Minor.

While the author points to the example and suffering of Christ in his exhortation to the slaves, he appeals to the example of the holy women of the Old Testament in his admonition to the wives. Sara, who was the "mother" of proselytes, is held up in particular, because she was obedient and called Abraham "her lord."[53] The wives' submission and quiet behavior is a strategy for survival in this precarious situation ("let nothing terrify you") but it also has missionary interests at heart. By submitting to the order of domination, wives might win over their husbands to Christianity "without saying a word." In line with the ideals of the time, wives are not to instruct their husbands in the gospel and seek to convince them of their Christian hope, but are to counter their husbands' slanders with quiet behavior. It is not adornment, but the quietness of spirit seeking peace and harmony in submitting to their husbands as their lords which might convince the husbands that their wives are law-abiding and virtuous.[54] Through their behavior they will prove false the slanderous accusations against Christians.

The patriarchal pattern of submission, therefore, does not so much seek to put wives back into their proper patriarchal roles and places, but seeks to lessen the tension between the Christian community and the pagan patriarchal household. Especially the conversion of wives and slaves provoked such political tensions between the Christian movement and its pagan society. This conflict was a conflict of values and allegiances between the Christian community and the patriarchal family:

> Christianity like all evangelizing religions addressed its message to individuals—men, women, and children. The strategy from the Christian point of view was thus a vital and almost obvious one: to denigrate so far as possible the historic and still deeply rooted kinship tie and offer the community of Christians itself as the only real and true form of kinship[55]

The accusation of second-century pagan writers that Christianity destroys the household by attracting especially women, slaves, and young people can thus not just be pushed aside as unfounded slander but must be taken seriously. Nisbet points this out with respect to women.

> There is some ground in fact for regarding this religion during the first century in any event, as involved in a kind of women's liberation: from the powerful patriarchal and masculine orientation of the traditional family. To succeed in disengaging women from their family ties . . . it was necessary at one and the same time to denigrate the family and to proffer Christianity as itself a family—the highest of all types of families.[56]

It was generally accepted, as a matter of good civil order, that slaves as well as wives practice the religion of their masters or husbands and preserve the religious ancestral customs of the house. This general assumption of Greco-Roman society is expressed by Cicero:

> No one shall have gods to himself, either new gods or alien gods, unless recognized by the state. Privately they shall worship those gods whose worship they have duly received from their ancestors. . . . No sacrifices shall be performed by women at night. . . . Nor is the worship of the "lares" handed down by our ancestors, established in sight of farm and homestead, and shared by slaves as well as masters, to be rejected. Next, the "preservation of the rites of the family and of our ancestors" means preserving the religious rites which, we almost say, were handed down to us by the gods. [*Laws* II.7.19–27]

The conversion of women, slaves, and young people who belonged to the household of an unconverted *paterfamilias* already constituted a potential political offense against the patriarchal order. It could not but be considered an infringement of the political order as well, insofar as in antiquity the patriarchal order of the house was considered to be the paradigm for the state. The patriarchal *familia* was the nucleus of the state. Not enthusiasm but conversion of the subordinate members of the house who were supposed to share in the religion of the *paterfamilias* constituted a revolutionary subversive threat.

Judaism had been attacked for its infringement upon the religious patriarchal prerogatives of the *paterfamilias,* insofar as it admitted slaves and women of pagan households as godfearers and converts. How deeply the Romans resented the social disruption wrought by proselytism is evident in the following statement of Tacitus:

> For the worst rascals among other peoples, renouncing their ancestral religions, always kept sending tribute and contributions to Jerusalem. . . . Those who are converted to their ways follow the same practice [i.e., of hating other peoples, being immoral, adopting circumcision], and the earliest lesson they receive is to despise the gods, to disown their country, and to regard their parents, children and brothers as of little account. [*History* V.5]

In his defense against Apion, Josephus insists that it was not the Jews but the Greeks who had introduced new gods, for the Jewish customs were of greater antiquity. He completely supports the sentiment that one must observe ancestral customs:

> A wise man's duty is to be scrupulously faithful to the religious laws of his country, and to refrain from the abuse of those of others. [*Ag Ap* II.144]

In the context of such missionary apologetics, Josephus—and Philo as well—insists that Jewish households are properly ruled and ordered.

Whenever slaves or wives converted to Judaism, to the Isis cult, or to Christianity, the order of the household was endangered and with it, therefore, the political order of the state. The Isis cult, in particular, was considered a threat to Roman civil life because Isis was proclaimed as the one who makes women and men equal.[57] The Roman historian Dio Cassius transmits a speech in which Octavian calls on his soldiers "to maintain the renown of your forefathers, to preserve your own proud traditions, to take vengeance on those who are in revolt against us, to repel those who insult you, to conquer and rule all humanity, to allow no woman to make herself equal to a man."[58] The whole speech associates a preservation of the customs of the forefathers with opposition to the Isis cult and with the assertion that Isis reverses the proper relationships between men and women.[59]

I have argued that the pagan perception of Christians interfering with the patriarchal order of the house was not unfounded. Insofar as Christians accepted slaves and women from pagan households as converts and members, they clearly broke the ancestral laws. Their self-understanding as the new eschatological community, the new creation, the new humanity, in which the social-political stratifications of religion, class, slavery, and patriarchal marriage are abolished, and all are equal in Christ, was an alternative vision that clearly undermined the Greco-Roman patriarchal order. The Christian message was so attractive and convincing for women and slaves, precisely because it promised them liberation from the patriarchal order and gave them a new freedom in the community of equals.

That Christians were suspected of political subversion and of threatening the societal order and institutions of the patriarchal house comes again and again to the fore in pagan attacks against Christianity in the second and third century.[60] Even Jesus was accused of this. The variant reading of Luke 23:1ff, which is attested for the first time by Marcion in the second century, maintains that Jesus was indicted before Pilate because he was "leading astray both women and children."[61] The variant reading of Epiphanius elaborates: "He has turned our children and wives away from us for they are not bathed as we are nor do they purify themselves," that is, they do not observe the ritual laws of their ancestral Jewish religion. A passage in Acts, which has caused problems for exegetes, states that Paul and Silas were accused before the magistrates in Philippi because they had created a great disturbance in the city by advocating "customs . . . illegal for us Romans to adopt and follow" (16:21). This accusation is made by the owners of a slave-girl who was possessed by an oracular spirit, and had brought large profits to her owners by telling fortunes. Paul had healed her (16:18) and thus made her useless to her owners. By freeing the slave from her spiritual bondage, Paul interfered with the property rights and ancestral laws of the household.[62]

That Christian missionaries were accused of disturbing the Greco-Roman patriarchal order is especially emphasized in the apocryphal Acts, which were circulating in the communities of Asia Minor at the time when 1 Peter and the Pastoral Epistles were written. According to the *Acts of Paul and Thecla* Paul is accused of corrupting "all the women." Thecla, an upper-class woman of Iconium, renounces her roles of daughter, wife, mother, and mistress. It is for this she is sentenced to death, not her Christianity. Her own mother demanded from the governor: "Burn the lawless one. Burn her so that all the women who have been taught by this man may be afraid" (3.20.3–5).

Where the *Acts of Paul and Thecla* and other apocryphal Acts elaborate the disruption which the conversion of women wrought in pagan households, especially when it was connected with sexual asceticism, 1 Peter presupposes such a situation and seeks to remedy it. In doing so the author "spiritualizes" or "internalizes" the Christian calling as a purely religious calling that does not disrupt the established order of the house and state. Christian slaves and wives, by being submissive and obedient to their "lords," can prove that the slanders against Christians are unjustified. Christians are not enemies of the Roman political order, but they support it.[63]

Naturally this "defense" could not establish that Christians did *not* disrupt the Greco-Roman order of the partriarchal house and state, since, by abandoning the religion of their masters and husbands, they in fact *did* so. However, this strategy for survival gradually introduced the patriarchal-societal ethos of the time into the church. As a result, in the long run it replaced the genuine Christian vision of equality, by which women and slaves had been attracted to become Christians. However, whereas in pseudo-Peter this patriarchal order of domination does *not* apply to either Christian marriage or to the Christian community, the letter to the Ephesians interprets Christian marriage in light of it, and the Pastoral Epistles identify it with the structures of the Christian community.

Ephesians and the Household Code

Ephesians presents the "hope to which Christians are called" (1:18) as the gospel of peace (6:15).[64] Such universal peace was accomplished by Christ's victory over the powers of darkness, a victory which did away with the gulf between Jews and non-Jews. Forgiveness of sin means liberation from the spiritually evil heavenly powers and unification of the two into one "new third race" or into the one family of God. The divine mediator has healed the breach between the world above and the world below, Christ has reconciled Jews and gentiles to a new universal harmony and peace.[65]

The author writes to gentile Christians and reminds them, using Old Testament-Jewish and early Christian traditional materials, that they have received access to the one true God of Israel in Jesus Christ. They who have been sojourners and strangers have become fellow-citizens with the saints and angels. The dividing wall of the Temple, which is here projected into the whole cosmos and into the structure of the universe, is broken down, and a new unified humanity has come into existence in the church. Ephesians reinterprets the cosmic stress of Colossians in terms of ecclesiology. Christ is the head and source of peace for the church. His work as universal peacemaker is now to be carried out by the church, which is his *plērōma*, the sphere of his influence and the force-field of his peacemaking power. The church "embodies" the peace of Christ. Those who are baptized are a new creation (2:10), have put on the new human (4:24; cf. 4:13, the "perfect man"). They have risen with Christ and are seated with him above (2:6). By "grace they have been saved" (2:5c) and have been "sealed with the promised Holy Spirit, the "guarantor" of their "inheritance" (1:13). They are children of God (5:1, 8).

The universal peace of Christ must be manifest in the community of Jew and gentile Christians. They are admonished to "lead a life worthy of your calling to which you have been called" (4:1). They must be eager to preserve

> the unity of the spirit in the bond of peace. There is one body and one Spirit, . . . one Lord, one faith, one baptism, one God and Father of us all. [4:4ff]

The baptismal remembrance of 2:11–22 clearly refers to the pre-Pauline baptismal formula with its opposites, uncircumcision/circumcision. The author expresses in various ways the unification of Jews and gentiles through the death of Christ and their equality in the new community of those baptized into Christ's death and resurrection. Those who once were "far off" have "now been brought near in the blood of Christ" (2:13). Three times the author stresses in 2:14–18 that Christ has made "both one" (*ta amphotera hen*): v. 14 stresses that Christ "our peace" has abolished the enmity between Jews and gentiles; v. 15 names the result of this peacemaking: "That he might create in himself one new human being in place of the two," and v. 16 adds: "and might reconcile us *both* to God in *one* body"; v. 17 repeats again the expression that "those who were far off" and "those who were near" have received peace. Therefore, the author can sum up in v. 18: "For through him we *both* have access in *one* Spirit to the Father."[66] Therefore, the baptized are "members of the household of God" (2:19) which expands into a "holy temple in the Lord," in whom they are built up together as "a dwelling place of God in the Spirit." (2:21f).

The author applies this theological motif of peace and unification to the relationship of gentile and Jewish Christians in the community in order to insist on their unity, equality, and mutuality within the "household of God." He seeks to prevent gentile believers from regarding themselves as superior to Jewish Christians and to encourage them to mutual respect and support of each other. Although there are many similarities between 2:11–22 and 5:21–33 (the admonition to husband and wife), his perception of "making peace in Christ" is quite different here. Whereas wives and slaves are admonished to subordinate themselves and to obey with "fear and trembling," the author does not admonish Jews to subordinate themselves in order to preserve the "peace" of the community; but to live according to their calling. He resorts to a variety of Jewish Christian theologoumena to persuade the gentiles, who seem to be the powerful and decision-making members in the congregation, to preserve the "peace" to be manifested in the body of Christ.

That the author also has the baptismal formula in mind, when elaborating the traditional household code[67] in terms of the Christian community, is apparent from the statement in 6:8c that everyone, slave or free, will receive the same eschatological recompense from the Lord.[68] While the author insists on the mutuality, unity, and equality of uncircumcised and circumcised here and now, he maintains such equality for slaves and freeborn only for the eschatological future. Moreover, whereas it was uncertain whether the admonitions of Colossians applied to Christian relationships with pagans, and whereas the advice of 1 Peter clearly was directed to wives married to unbelievers and slaves living in pagan households, Ephesians applies the traditional rules for the household to relationships between Christian couples and Christian slaves and masters, *and thus to the Christian household itself*. That this household is seen in terms of a house church is likely from the introductory section to the traditional household code in 5:18–20, which speaks of the Spirit-filled worship of the Christians. Moreover the whole community is understood as the "household" (2:19), the family (3:15), the house (2:20) of God. The believers are children (5:1, 8; 1:5, sons) of God who have the guarantee of a glorious inheritance (1:4, 18), their father is God (3:14, 4:6; cf. 1:2, 3).

However, it is important to recognize that the author does not develop the patriarchal domination-subordination relationship in terms of the whole community. Although he speaks of those who are apostles, prophets, evangelists, pastors, and teachers for the "equipment of the saints" (4:12), he does not ask the saints to subordinate themselves to them nor does he say that they are the sign of unity. Neither does the author claim that the leaders represent God, the "father" of the household, nor that they are males acting in the name and place of Christ. The church does not, as J. Ernst maintains, receive here "in imitation of the ancient state organizations a social structure which regulates the concrete life in common."[69] Ephesians elaborates only that some have received these gifts and some have received others "for the upbuilding of the body of Christ." Its enumeration of ministries expands the Pauline catalogue to include evangelists and pastors, but does not restrict it to men.

While the Colossian code clearly was interested in the patriarchally appropriate behavior of slaves, the Ephesian code elaborates upon the relationship of wife and husband in patriarchal marriage.[70] In so doing, the author combines the traditional household code form with the church-body theology and Pauline bride-bridegroom notion found for the first time in 2 Cor 11:3. The relationship between Christ and the church, expressed in the metaphors of head and body as well as of bridegroom and bride,[71] becomes the paradigm for Christian marriage and vice versa. This theological paradigm reinforces the cultural-patriarchal pattern of subordination, insofar as the relationship between Christ and the church clearly is not a relationship between equals, since the church-bride is totally dependent and subject to her head[72] or bridegroom. Therefore, the general injunction for all members of the Christian community, "Be subject to one another in the fear of Christ," is clearly spelled out for the Christian wife as requiring submission and inequality.

As the church is subordinated to Christ, so the wife has to subject herself to her husband in everything. The phrase "in everything," which in the Colossian code was associated with the obedience of children and slaves, here underlines the subordinate position of the wife (v. 24). 5:22 insists that the submission of the wife to her husband is on a par with her religious submission to Christ, the Lord. The instruction to the wives thus clearly reinforces the patriarchal marriage pattern and justifies it christologically. The instructions to the wife are therefore summed up in the injunction to fear or to respect her husband (v. 33).

However, the patriarchal-societal code is theologically modified in the exhortation to the husband. The negative demand of Colossians that men are not to be harsh with their wives is not repeated here. Instead, the husbands are three times commanded to love their wives (5:25, 28, 33). Jesus' commandment, "to love your neighbor as yourself" (cf. Lev 19:18) is applied to the marriage relationship of the husband.[73] Moreover, the relationship of Christ to the church becomes the example for the husband. Christ's self-giving love for the church is to be the model for the love relationship of the husband with his wife. Patriarchal domination is thus radically questioned with reference to the paradigmatic love relationship of Christ to the church.

Nevertheless, it must be recognized that this christological modification of the husband's patriarchal position and duties does not have the power, theologically, to transform the patriarchal pattern of the household code, even though this might have been the intention of the author. Instead, Ephesians christologically cements the inferior position of the wife in the marriage relationship. One could say that the exhortations to the husbands spell out what it means to live a marriage relationship as a Christian, while those to the wives insist on the proper social behavior of women. The reason for this theological shortcoming might be the author's interest in clarifying the relationship between Christ and the church, whose unity is his primary concern in the rest of the letter. His interpretation of Gen 2:24 shows that this is the case. Although early Christian theology used this Old Testament text for understanding the marriage relationship, the author applies it primarily to the relationship of Christ and the church.[74]

Eph 5:21–33 thus participates in the trajectory of the patriarchal household-code tradition insofar as it takes over the household-code pattern and reasserts the submission of the wife to the husband as a religious Christian duty. At the same time, it modifies the patriarchal code by replacing patriarchal superordination and domination with the Christian command of love to be lived according to the example of Christ. On the whole, however, the author was not able to "Christianize" the code. The "gospel of peace" has transformed the relationship of gentiles and Jews, but not the social roles of wives and slaves within the household of God. On the contrary, the cultural-social structures of domination are theologized and thereby reinforced. However, it must not be overlooked that the code and its theological legitimation are not descriptive of the actual situation of women and slaves in the communities of Asia Minor. It is exhortative or prescriptive and seeks to establish a Christian behavior that is not yet realized in the life of the Christians in Asia Minor.

The Gnostic-Patristic Trajectory

The theological ideas of the unification of male and female as well as of human marriage and "couples" as paradigms for heavenly cosmic realities are developed even further and in a different direction in gnostic cosmological speculations, which might also have been inspired by the baptismal formula transmitted in Gal 3:28.

Whether or not Marcion can be called a gnostic is disputed.[75] He distinguished the alien God of Goodness, the Father of Jesus Christ, from the World God of Justice, who is the antithesis of the Good God. The Demiurge, or World God, created the cosmos and humankind, but the Good God is absolutely alien to all created things. Human creatures belong bodily and psychically to the World God. Christ came to save them from the World God and to make them children of the alien Good God. Since the Marcionites rejected the created world, they were devoted to rigorous asceticism, and by protesting against flesh and matter they demonstrated that they did not owe allegiance to the World God. Because procreation strengthens the sphere of the Demiurge, they did not marry and have children.

Severus, an associate of Marcion, taught "that woman is the work of Satan. . . . Hence those who consort in marriage fulfill the work of Satan."[76] Marcionism belongs to the type of gnosticism that starts from a dualism of two opposed principles. In this system femaleness belongs to the sphere of creation, whereas maleness stands for heavenly transcendent realities. In *The Gospel of the Egyptians* a saying of the savior is given: "I have come to destroy the works of the female, by the 'female' meaning lust, and by the 'works' birth and decay."[77]

The classic expression of this dualism is found in terms of male and female in the pseudo-Clementines: "The present world is female, as the mother bringing forth the souls of the children, but the world to come is male, as a father receiving his children."[78] Therefore, of the two types of prophets in the world, one type is the female, whose words accord entirely with the created world, and the other type is the male prophet who speaks for the coming higher world. In the encratite *Acts of Thomas* the "communion of the male" is a parallel expression to the "highest gift of grace," "Holy Spirit" or "the power of the Most High."[79] The categories "female and male," therefore, do not so much characterize actual women or men as denote opposite types of dualistic principles.

Like the Marcionites, the Carpocratians distinguish between the unbegotten Father and the God who gave the law.[80] Since they believe in the migration of the soul, they hold that they can be liberated from the body and from reincarnation not through asceticism but through libertinism. All things are indifferent, and nothing in the world is by nature evil. Not through obedience to laws, however, but only through faith and love are persons saved.[81] The Carpocratians appeal to Salome, Mary Magdalene, and Martha as the source and guarantors of their traditions. One of their teachers, Marcellina, represented their teaching in Rome in the middle of the second century and acquired many followers there.

The son of Carpocrates, Epiphanes, taught that the "righteousness of God is communion with equality."[82] Since God provided for all beings equally, no distinction should be made between "rich and poor, people and ruler, foolish and wise, female and male, free and slave."[83] Epiphanes thus espouses the same ideal as Paul (Gal 3:27f), but argues the fundamental equality of all, not on the basis of baptism but on the basis of creation. Therefore, his "fellowship with equality" extends not only to gender roles in the Christian community but also to sexuality and marriage. "In that God made all things in common for man and brought together the female with the male in common and united all the animals likewise he declared righteousness to be fellowship with equality."[84] The reflections of Epiphanes elaborate Gal 3:28 in terms of Plato's ideal state. They do so, however, from a male perspective insofar as all women seem to have been available for intercourse to all men before the institution of marriage, but not vice versa.

It was the evil Lawgiver God who introduced "mine and thine" and so promulgated private property rights and the institution of marriage. Since his law destroyed the fellowship of the Divine Law, in their liturgies the Carpocratians attempt to restore the Divine Law by uniting "as they will and with whom they will."[85] However, we do not know if this "love feast" of the Carpocratians was a ritual celebration of the basic equality between the sexes or whether they practiced intercourse indiscriminately, since the charge of fornication was a standard polemic of various religious groups against each other.[86]

Valentinianism belongs to that type of gnostic dualism which holds that maleness and femaleness are not antagonistic opposites, but complementary. This group placed the origin of darkness, evil, and dualism within the godhead itself "by means of a genealogy of personified divine states evolving from another, which describe the progressive darkening of the original Light in categories of guilt, error and failure."[87] Thus "the Valentinians did not identify the female with any absolute principle of evil, but rather with the fallible part of God, which became involved in the material world."[88] The Valentinian system begins with the dyad Bythos = Primal Cause and Sigē = Silence, who bring forth a couple, Nous and Truth. Although the Primal tetrad appears to consist of four different hypostases, Bythos and Sigē as well as Nous and Truth form one single male-female substance or entity. The second tetrad, Logos and Life and Man and Church, comes from the first tetrad and brings forth in turn ten and twelve aeons. The ten aeons in the female series have names which allude to the union between man and woman, whereas the names of the twelve aeons in the male series recall the Christian virtues. The divine Pleroma thus consists of a series of male-female aeons.

The last aeon, Sophia, plays the role of Cosmic Eve. Because of her ignorance and her desire to know the incomprehensible Father, she initiates a Fall in the Divine World that is the origin of the evil, visible world. Sophia is restored to the Pleroma, but her "abortion" cannot remain in the Pleroma. It is given form by Christ and the Holy Spirit and called Achamoth. Since Achamoth cannot enter the Pleroma, she falls into all sorts of distress. At her request the Savior, Jesus, is sent to give the "formation according to knowledge" and to release her from her passions. Achamoth can now give form to the Demiurge, who in due course fashions everything else. The Demiurge creates the human body first as incorporeal and later puts a skin over it, but without his knowledge Achamoth introduces spiritual "seeds" in some humans. Humanity, therefore, consists of three classes of beings: the hylics, or "fleshly" ones, the psychics, who have souls; and the pneumatics, who have the spiritual seed from the Mother or Achamoth. The female and the male element were originally united. They are reunited when the female element becomes male, and are then united with the angels and enter into the Pleroma. "Therefore it is said that the woman is changed into a man and the Church here below into angels."[89] It is clear that "male and female" are not simple gender distinctions, but mythological, archetypal realities.[90]

The gnosticism of Marcus, a disciple of Valentinus, is distinguished by the fact that he places another tetrad, called Unity, Oneness, Monad, and One, before the thirty aeons. The tetrad is also called "the inconceivable and nonmaterial Father, who is without paternity and who is neither male nor female."[91] He claims that the "spiritual man," formed in the image and likeness of God, was masculine-feminine.[92] The Marcosians seem to have celebrated the sacraments of the "bridal chamber" and of baptism. They baptized into "the name of the unknown Father of all things, into Truth, the Mother of all, into him who descended on Jesus, into union, into redemption, into the communion of the powers."[93]

The rite of the "bridal chamber" is related to New Testament bridal and marriage imagery.[94] The celebration of the "spiritual marriage" in the Marcosian rite was a prefiguration of the perfect eschatological marriage union. At the end of the world-process, Achamoth will enter the Pleroma and receive the Savior as her bridegroom. The perfected "spiritual seed" will then be given as brides to the angels. The "spiritual marriage after the image of the unions above" expresses in different terms what is meant by "becoming male."[95] Thus the Valentinians had a very positive image of the marriage union and took it as a symbol and type of salvation that restores the original androgynous unity of humanity. According to *The Gospel of Philip*,[96] a book which shows close affinities with the Marcosian teachings, when Eve was separated from Adam "death arose. When they reunite and he receives her to himself, death will be no more." Christ came in order to remove the separation and unite the male and female.[97]

Marcus is reported to have had great success with women, which his opponents ascribed to his sorcery and love potions. Irenaeus claims that Marcus deceived especially wealthy women of high rank in order to obtain their property and to abuse them physically. Such a woman was prepared "to be united with him in everything, in order that she, with him, might enter into the One."[98] It is apparent that Irenaeus no longer understood "the mystery of union" and the rite of the "bridal chamber" which was an "anticipation of the eschatological union between the spiritual gnostics and the angels." Such a misunderstanding was easily possible, since according to *The Gospel of Philip* the "holy kiss" was the center of the rite: "For the perfect conceive through a kiss and give birth. Because of this we also kiss another. We receive conception from the Grace (*Charis*) which is among us."[99] In the same *Gospel of Philip* Mary Magdalene is called the "consort of Christ" whom he loved "more than the disciples, and kissed her [mouth] often."[100] Since the Valentinian system knew three Christs and perceived the divine and the world in *syzygies* (couples), it is possible that Mary Magdalene was thought of as consort of the earthly Jesus, just as the Holy Spirit was the consort of the aeon Christ in the Pleroma, and Sophia was the consort of the Savior.

Gnosticism, we may conclude, employed the categories of "male" and "female," not to designate real women and men, but to name cosmic-religious principles or archetypes. Salvation in the radically dualistic gnostic systems requires the annihilation and destruction of the female or the "feminine principle." In the moderately dualistic systems, salvation means the reunification of the male and female principles in an androgynous or asexual unity. In gnosticism, the pneumatics, men and women, represent the female principle, while the male principle stands for the heavenly realms, Christ, God, and the Spirit. The female principle is secondary, since it stands for the part of the divine that became involved in the created world and history. Gnostic dualism shares in the patriarchal paradigm of Western culture.[101] It makes the first principle male, and defines femaleness relative to maleness. Maleness is the subject, the divine, the absolute; femaleness is the opposite or the complementary "other." Gnostic dualism reflects the chasm between the world and the divine, the body and the spiritual self. We do not know whether this dualism also divided men from women and whether, in the rite of "the bridal chamber," men represented the male and women the female archetype, since all gnostics understand themselves as "female."

In any case, here, as in Ephesians, earthly marriage becomes the paradigm for heavenly cosmic-divine unification. Like Ephesians the *Gospel of Philip* understands it in terms of its own patriarchal conceptuality.

> Whereas in this world the union is one of husband and wife—a case of strength complemented by weakness—in the aeon, the form of the union is different, although we refer to them by the same names."[102]

As with the union of Christ and the church in Ephesians, so here too "the bridal chamber" is a true mystery that is still hidden. "No one shall be able to see the bridegroom with the bride unless one becomes one." However, this mystery does not refer to social-ecclesial-marital relationships[103] but to the transformation of the full-fledged gnostic into a resurrected being:

> *Gos. Phil.*, fully confident in the efficacy of the image, the 'mirrored' bridal chamber, asserts a more optimistic view of world and man than one generally associates with Gnostic systems. The Creation as such might have originated, and persists still, in misunderstanding and ignorance. Nevertheless true believers know how to use the vehicles of this world in order to transcend it. This transcendence implies, essentially, a collapse of a dualistic worldview.[104]

But such a collapse of a dualistic world view happens for the individual soul of the gnostic only. It engenders a spiritual elitism and ecclesial dualism between the full-fledged gnostics who have received already "the perfection of the marriage" and the "psychics" or "Hebrews" who are not able to rise from the "psychic" to the "pneumatic" level of existence.[105] Whereas Ephesians promotes a marriage theology of subordination, the *Gospel of Philip* promotes the sacrament of "the bridal chamber" as a spiritual-symbolic means for individual perfection and psychological unification. Here "in this world" the wife represents "weakness" and must remain "subordinated in everything". The female principle is secondary to the male, not only on earth but also in heaven.

However, such cosmic-anthropological dualism is neither peculiar to gnosticism nor limited to it. R. Bear has convincingly shown that Philo of Alexandria uses the categories "male and female" in two different ways: on the one hand, Philo maintains that the rational human soul is closely related to the divine and does not participate in sexuality at all, while the human irrational soul that encompasses the human body participates in sexual male-female polarity. The categories male and female therefore apply to human mortality, not to the immortal part of humans created in the image of God. On the other hand, Philo uses the category male in order to denote the human soul, while he characterizes the irrational soul as female.[106] In this context male is always used in a highly positive fashion while female terminology and figures have pejorative connotations.

Human spiritual and moral development are understood as "becoming male" when the emphasis lies on human effort and *askesis*, while Philo speaks of "becoming a virgin" or "becoming one" in order to stress that true virtue is a free gift of God's grace. To become "male" or "to become a virgin" is to move beyond the sphere of sexual polarity, because the human rational soul created after the image of God is neither male nor female.

> The union of human beings that is made for the procreation of children, turns virgins into women. But when God begins to consort with the soul, He makes what before was a woman into a virgin again, for he takes away the degenerate and emasculate passions which made it womanish [*ethelyneto*] and plants instead the native growth of unpolluted virtues. Thus He will not talk with Sarah till she has ceased from all that is after the manner of women [Gen 18:11], and is ranked once more as a pure virgin. [*Cherubim* 50][107]

Although Philo's language of "male and female" shows close affinities to much of gnostic language and speculation, Philo's categories function within a limited dualism and do not signify two ultimate divine principles.

Patristic writers also assume a far-reaching anthropological dualism similar to that of some gnostic writers. Like Philo they refrain, however, from generalizing this anthropological dualism into an absolute cosmological dualism or divine duality. Instead, they stress that divine reality is monistic and that duality belongs to this world, to creation and the body. While some stress that in Christian marriage women and men are companions and siblings, and that both women and men have one creator, one origin, "one image of God, one law, one death and resurrection,"[108] the majority of the Fathers combine a theological monism with an anthropoligical-cosmic dualism. They stress that the reality of the divine is monistic and unitary but that sexual duality characterizes this world as earthly, bodily reality.[109]

Like Philo (and Aristotle) the Fathers consider man to be the paradigmatic human being and maleness to be symbolic of the divine. Whereas their philosophical and theological conceptuality assumes the natural inferiority of women and sees the feminine as symbolic of earthly, bodily, carnal reality, the logic of their Christian beliefs imposed on them a recognition of the fact that all the baptized are equal.[110] Their theological problem was: how can a Christian woman who was made inferior by nature, law, and the social-patriarchal order achieve in her life the Christian equality which belongs to her as a disciple of Christ? The Fathers answered this question by declaring that a Christian woman is no longer *woman*. While a female nonbeliever is defined by her physical sex, the believing woman "progresses" to the "perfect man," to the measure of the maturity of Christ [cf. Eph 4:13].[111]

The nonsexual monism of the divine pertains to the soul redeemed from the duality of bodily sexuality. The soul is equal and of the same essence in man and woman. Male and female are equal in divine likeness because on the level of the soul there is neither male nor female, but on the historical-creational level woman has to be subordinated to man. The anthropological corporeal duality of the sexes is subsequent to the fall and does not pertain to the original spiritual creation in the image of God. Therefore, the virgin or "single one" represents the original "spiritual, angelic" human being created in the image of God. Having progressed to "the perfect man," she ceases to be woman and can be called "man."

> This is a simple though far-reaching transformation of a New Testament concept. The equality of man and woman through baptism which Saint Paul expressed in the statement, "There is neither male nor female" has been severed from baptism and made an effect of the ascetic life. In their souls men and women are one and the same, though in their bodies they are not. Destined, however, to be restored in oneness and equality when the soul leaves the body, they may already learn to participate in the heavenly life. This participation offered to all believers, cannot be achieved without strenuous effort: it requires abstinence from marriage, reeducation of the senses, and an absolute avoidance of the ways of society.[112]

Since patristic writers see virginity as the true expression of Christian equality, they often very adroitly criticize patriarchal marriage and its oppressive effects on women. However, rather than transforming such patriarchal marriage in terms of Christian equality and freedom for women as well as men, they restrict such equality and freedom to those who remain free from the social-legal bondage of patriarchal marriage that is the result of the curse in paradise. Equality of women and men was claimed for only a small number of elite Christians who chose the lifestyle of the virgin and ascetic.[113] Jovinian, who maintained that baptism, not virginity, defines the true Christian, was condemned by Pope Siricius in 389/390 C.E. Jerome quotes him as having taught "that virgins, widows, and married women, once they have been washed in Christ, are of equal merit if they do not differ in their other works."[114]

Just as gnosticism transposed its cosmic-spiritual dualism into ecclesial-spiritual dualism and praxis, so did the patristic church. Not all the baptized, but only a spiritual ascetic elite could transcend earthly-bodily-sexual dualisms and progress to spiritual perfection. Although women were the weaker sex, as ascetics they could become "like men." Gnostic and patristic writers agree on this point. The theological and christological utilization of the patriarchal submission pattern leads to a dualistic ecclesial praxis: true religious women are no longer women but have progressed to the "perfect man," while Christian married women remain "women" and therefore have to suffer the "curse" of patriarchal marriage. Nevertheless, within the context of the patriarchal church even those women who had become like "males" could not exercise leadership functions because they were still women.[115] Since it was restricted to the soul, the discipleship of equals could neither transform patriarchal marriage nor prevent the formation of a patriarchal church and the elimination of women from its leadership. Gnostic as well as patristic dualisms are the ideological result of patriarchal reality and structures.

In the process, Gal 3:28 was not only modified in terms of the patriarchal household, either for missionary or theological reasons, but also "spiritualized" because the church and its leadership became patriarchalized. Such a patriarchalization of the church is not yet found in the first century. In discussing the household-code trajectory I have attempted to show that patriarchal household and family structures were not determinative for the house churches of the early Christian mission.

Moreover, "realized" or "enthusiastic" eschatology and cosmological speculation have engendered a Christian theological adaptation of the patriarchal pattern of submission. The widespread exegetical argument that enthusiastic theology, realized eschatology, or gnosticizing speculations are responsible for the Christian self-understanding expressed in Gal 3:28 cannot be proven. To the contrary, the praxis of coequal discipleship between slaves and masters, women and men, Jews and Greeks, Romans and barbarians, rich and poor, young and old brought the Christian community in tension with its social-political environment. This tension engendered by the alternative Christian vision of Gal 3:38, and not by "enthusiastic excesses," became the occasion for introducing the Greco-Roman patriarchal order into the house church. Colossians and Ephesians testify that realized eschatology, rooted in the dualism between this world and the world above, is responsible for developing a theological justification of the patriarchal order. The Pastoral Epistles allow us to trace the beginnings of patriarchalization not just of the Christian household but also of the church as "the house of God."

NOTES

1. For an extensive discussion of the question of Pauline authorship, see W. G. Kümmel, *Introduction to the New Testament* (Nashville: Abingdon, 1975), pp. 315–87, and other general introductions to the New Testament.

2. Cf. e.g. H. Goldstein, *Paulinische Gemeinde im Ersten Petrusbrief* (SBS 80; Stuttgart: Katholisches Bibelwerk, 1975).

3. See my "Discipleship and Patriarchy: Early Christian Ethos and Christian Ethics in a Feminist Perspective," in L. Rasmussen, ed., *Selected Papers, 1982: The American Society of Christian Ethics* (Waterloo, Ont.: Council on the Study of Religion, 1982), pp. 131–72, for a review of the literature.

4. For an extensive bibliography on Asia Minor and the churches in Asia Minor, see J. H. Elliott, *A Home for the Homeless: A Sociological Exegesis of 1 Peter* (Philadelphia: Fortress, 1981), pp. 88–90.

5. See my "Apokalypsis and Propheteia: The Book of Revelation in the Context of Early Christian Prophecy," in J. Lambrecht, ed., *L'Apocalypse johannique et l'Apocalyptique dans le Nouveau Testament* (BETL 53; Gembloux: Duculot, 1980; Leuven: University Press), p. 105–28.

6. See e.g. V. Schultze, *Altchristliche Städte und Landschaften: Kleinasien* (Gütersloh: Bertelsmann, 1922), especially pp. 1–62.

7. For the assumption that this house church belonged to the Christian community at Colossae, see E. Lohse, *Colossians and Philemon* (Hermeneia; Philadelphia: Fortress, 1971), p. 186.

8. See the discussion of the information on persons found in 2 Timothy in M. Dibelius and H. Conzelmann, *The Pastoral Epistles* (Philadelphia: Fortress, 1972), pp. 127ff.

9. See V. Corwin, *St. Ignatius and Christianity in Antioch* (New Haven: Yale University Press, 1960), pp. 16f.

10. See A. von Harnack, *Mission and Expansion of Christianity in the First Three Centuries* (New York: Putnam, 1908), 2.70.

11. R. M. Grant, "The Social Setting of Second-Century Christianity," in E. P. Sanders, ed., *Jewish and Christian Self-Definition* (London: SCM Press, 1980), 1.16–29:27f.

12. See the discussion in R. Schnackenburg, *Die Johannesbriefe* (HThKNT 13/3; Freiburg: Herder, 1963), pp. 306f.

13. See L. Swidler (*Biblical Affirmations of Woman* [Philadelphia: Westminster, 1977], pp. 315f.), who follows E. Gaugler, *Die Johannesbriefe* (Zurich: EVZ-Verlag, 1964), p. 283.

14. See my article "The Quest for the Johannine School: The Apocalypse and the Fourth Gospel," *NTS* 23 (1977) 402–27.

15. A. J. Malherbe, "The Inhospitality of Diotrephes," in J. Jervell and W. A. Meeks, eds., *God's Christ and His People: Studies in Honour of Nils Alstrup Dahl* (Oslo: Universitetsvorlaget, 1977), pp. 222–32:228f.

16. See P. Paris, *Quatenus Feminae Res Publicas in Asia Minore, Romanis Imperantibus, Attigerint* (Paris: Burdigale, 1891). For a critical evaluation of Paris, see O. Braunstein, *Die politische Wirksamkeit der griechischen Frau* (Leipzig: A. Hoffmann, 1911), pp. 64ff., who emphasizes that the civic-political role of women in Asia Minor was exceptional in the Hellenistic world.

17. Cf. L. Ross Taylor, "Artemis of Ephesus," in F. J. Foakes-Jackson, eds., *The Beginnings of Christianity* (New York: Macmillan, 1933), 5.251–56; B. Kötting, *Peregrinatio Religiosa* (Münster: Regensburg, 1950), pp. 32–57.

18. See my "Miracles, Mission and Apologetics," in E. Schüssler Fiorenza, ed., *Aspects of Religious Propaganda in Judaism and Early Christianity* (Notre Dame: University of Notre Dame Press, 1976), pp. 16–20.

19. See M. Stern, "The Jewish Diaspora," in S. Safrai and M. Stern, eds., *The Jewish People in the First Century* (Philadelphia: Fortress, 1974), 1.143–55.

20. A. T. Kraabel, *Judaism in Western Asia Minor under the Roman Empire, with a Preliminary Study of the Jewish Community at Sardis, Lydia* (Th. D. diss., Harvard University, 1968) pp. 42–50. See also S. E. Johnson, "Asia Minor and Early Christianity," in J. Neusner, ed., *Christianity, Judaism and Other Greco-Roman Cults* (Leiden: Brill, 1975), 2.77–145:98.

21. *CII* 741 (= *IG*, IV, 1452; Greek). For a discussion of this inscription, see B. J. Brooten, "Inscriptional Evidence for Women as Leaders in the Ancient Synagogue," *SBL Seminar Papers* 20 (1980), 1ff.

22. For a survey of NT writings, see R. Hamerton-Kelly, *God the Father: Theology and Patriarchy in the Teaching of Jesus* (Philadelphia: Fortress, 1979), pp. 82–99.

23. See Lohse, *Colossians and Philemon*, pp. 177–83, for a comparison of Colossians and Pauline theology; see also J. Lähnemann, *Der Kolosserbrief* (Gütersloh: Mohn, 1971), pp. 11–28, 153–82.

24. Lohse (*Colossians and Philemon*, pp. 142–47) argues that the series has been adopted from tradition. But whereas the tradition insists that the "new humanity" or "new creation" realized in the Christian community has "cut through distinctions of social position," Col understands the "putting on of the new human" in moral terms.

25. See especially W. A. Meeks, "In One Body: The Unity of Humankind in Colossians and Ephesians," in Jervell and Meeks, *God's Christ and His People*, pp. 209–21.

26. For the many attempts to identify the "opponents" of Colossians, see F. O. Francis and W. A. Meeks, eds., *Conflict at Colossae* (SBLSBS 4; Missoula, Mont.: Scholars Press, 1973).

27. However, Lohse (*Colossians and Philemon*, pp. 156f.) argues that this addition is not a "mere formal element. Rather the entire life, thought and conduct of believers is subordinated to the lordship of the Kyrios."

28. See J. E. Crouch, *The Origin and Intention of the Colossian Haustafel* (FRLANT 109: Göttingen: Vandenhoeck & Ruprecht, 1972), pp. 150f.

29. E. A. Judge, *The Social Pattern of Christian Groups* (London: Tyndale Press, 1960), pp. 60, 71.

30. See Crouch, *Origin and Intention*, p. 141.

31. For an excellent review of previous research on the *Haustafeln*, see Crouch, *Origin and Intention*, pp. 9–36, and his own conclusion on pp. 146–51; see also W. Schrage, "Zur Ethik der Neutestamentlichen Haustafeln," *NTS* 21 (1974/75) 1–22; W. Lillie, "The Pauline House-tables," 86 (1975) 179–83; E. Schweizer, "Die Weltlichkeit des Neuen Testaments: Die Haustafeln," in H. Doner, R. Hanhart, and R. Smend, eds., *Beiträge zur Alttestamentlichen Theologie: Festschrift für Walther Zimmerli* (Göttingen: Vandenhoeck & Ruprecht, 1977), pp. 397–413.

32. K. Thraede, "Zum historischen Hintergrund der 'Haustafeln' des NT," *JAC* Ergänzungsband 8 (1981) 359–68:365.

33. D. Lührmann, "Wo man nicht mehr Sklave und Freier ist: Überlegungen zur Struktur früchristlicher Gemeinden," *Wort und Deinst* 13 (1975) 53–83; idem, "Neutestamentliche Haustafeln und antike Ökonomie," *NTS* 27 (1981) 83–91.

34. D. L. Balch, *Let Wives Be Submissive: The Domestic Code in 1 Peter* (SBLM 26; Chico, Calif.: Scholars Press, 1981).

35. F. Wilhelm, "Die Oeconomica der Neupythagoreer Bryson, Kallikdratidas, Periktione, Phintys," *Rheinisches Museum* 70 (1915) 161–223:222.

36. Cf. especially S. Moller Okin, *Women in Western Political Thought* (Princeton: Princeton University Press, 1979), pp. 234–304.

37. For this whole section, see Okin, *Women in Western Political Thought*, pp. 15–96, on Plato and Aristotle; and Balch, *Let Wives Be Submissive*, pp. 33–38. For the translation of Aristotle's *Politics*, see H. Rackham (Loeb Classical Library; Cambridge, Mass.: Harvard University Press, 1926).

38. See e.g. K. E. Børresen, *Subordination and Equivalence: The Nature and Role of Women in Augustine and Thomas Aquinas* (Washington, D.C.: University Press of America, 1981).

39. D. L. Balch, "Household Ethical Codes in Peripatetic, Neopythagorean and Early Christian Moralists," *SBL Seminar Papers* 11 (1977) 397–404.

40. Crouch, *Origin and Intention*, pp. 81f.

41. Ibid., p. 83; see also D. L. Balch, "Josephus, *Against Apion* II.145–295," *SBL Seminar Papers* 9 (1975), 1.187–92.

42. Thraede, "Zum historischen Hintergrund," p. 364; see also his article "Gleichheit," in *RAC* 10 (1978) 122–64.

43. For this section, see K. Thraede, "Ärger mit der Freiheit," in G. Scharffenorth and K. Thraede, *Freunde in Christus werden . . ." Die Beziehung von Mann und Frau als Frage an Theologie und Kirche* (Gelnhausen: Burkardthaus-Verlag, 1977), pp. 59–62; and especially K. O'Brien Wicker, "First Century Marriage Ethics: A Comparative Study of the Household Codes and Plutarch's Conjugal Precepts," in J. W. Flanagan and A. W. Robinson, eds., *No Famine in the Land: Studies in Honor of John L. McKenzie* (Missoula, Mont.: Scholars Press, 1975), pp. 141–53.

44. See D. Balch, "Let Wives Be Submissive: The Domestic Code in 1 Peter" in its dissertation form (Ann Arbor: University Microfilms, 1974), p. 102.

45. Ibid., p. 104. For a warm and loving relationship between husband and wife, see especially the letters of Pliny the Younger to his wife Calpurnia; cf. M. F. Lefkowitz and M. Fant, eds., *Women in Greece and Rome* (Toronto: Samuel-Stevens, 1977), p. 184.

46. Besides Balch (*Let Wives Be Submissive*) and Elliott (*A Home for the Homeless*), see also K. H. Schelkle, *Die Petrusbriefe; Der Judasbrief* (HThKNT 13/2; Freiburg: Herder, 1961), pp. 68–98; L. Goppelt, *Der erste Petrusbrief* (Meyer K 12/1; Göttingen: Vandenhoeck & Ruprecht, 1978), pp. 155–226; N. Brox, *Der erste Petrusbrief* (EKKNT 21; Zurich: Benziger, 1979; Neukirchen-Vlnyn: Neukirchener Verlag, 1979), pp. 111–63.

47. See N. Brox, "Situation und Sprache der Minderheit im Ersten Petrusbrief," *Kairos* 19 (1977) 1–13.

48. Ca. one hundred years later, Tertullian still reflects this situation: "A wife who has become chaste is cast out by her husband now that he is relieved of his jealous suspicions of her. A son, now docile, is disowned by a father who was patient with him

in the past. A servant, now trustworthy, is banished from the sight of a master who was formerly indulgent. To the degree that one is reformed under the influence of the Name, he gives offense." (*Apology*, 3.4; [trans. Sr. E. J. Daly, C. S. J., *Fathers of the Church*, 1950]).

49. See C. F. Sleeper, "Political Responsibility According to 1 Peter," *NovT* 10 (1968) 270–86:284f.

50. See W. C. van Unnik, "The Teaching of Good Works in I Peter," *NTS* 1 (1954/55) 92–110; idem, "Die Rücksicht auf die Reaktion der Nicht-Christen als Motiv in der altchristlichen Paränese," in W. Eltester, ed., *Judentum, Urchristentum, Kirche* (BZNW 36; Berlin: Töpelmann, 1964), pp. 221–34.

51. The apologetic character of the household code is rightly stressed by Balch, whereas Elliott argues that the household code was adopted "for the sake of group solidarity and cohesion" (Elliott, *Home for the Homeless*, p. 111). "The household code also provided the means for stressing the social engagement and responsibilities *within* the sect, thereby to foster group solidarity" (p. 211). His arguments against Balch are not convincing, however, since Balch's thesis does not depend on its reliance upon Josephus' *Against Apion* (cf. p. 216).

52. For the discussion of this notion, see my book *Priester für Gott: Studien zum Herrschafts- und Priestermotiv in der Apokalypse* (NTAbh 7; Münster: Aschendorff, 1972), pp. 51–59.

53. See H. L. Strack and P. Billerbeck, *Kommentar zum Neuen Testament aus Talmud und Midrasch* (Munich: C. H. Beck, 1926), 3.764; and L. Ginzberg, *Legends of the Jews* (Philadelphia: Jewish Publication Society of America, 1913), 1.203.

54. Balch (*Let Wives Be Submissive*, pp. 95–105) has documented how much the whole section (3:1–7) is permeated by Greco-Roman patriarchal ethics.

55. R. A. Nisbet, *The Social Philosophers: Community and Conflict in Western Thought* (New York: T. Y. Crowell, 1973), p. 178.

56. Ibid., p. 178. Although Elliott refers to Nisbet, he overlooks Nisbet's stress on the conversion of *individuals*, which interrupted the patriarchal order of the Greco-Roman household. 1 Peter, unlike the Pastoral Epistles, does not insist on the patriarchal order for the Christian community, but only for household relationships.

57. *POxy.*, 1380.1.214–16. See also R. E. Witt, "Isis-Hellas," *Proceedings of the Cambridge Philological Society* 12 (1966) 62, for the assertion that by the time of Augustus the Isis cult was dominant: "It was an international religion. In the service of the Queen of the Whole Universe fellow slaves could band themselves together and feel free, coloured Africans could join with Romans, and women could claim the same power as men."

58. Dio Cassius *Roman History* 50.28.3; cf. Balch, *Let Wives Be Submissive*, pp. 70f.

59. Cf. S. Pomeroy, *Goddesses, Whores, Wives and Slaves* (New York: Schocken Books, 1975), pp. 223–25.

60. Cf. P. de Labriolle, *La réaction païenne* (Paris: L'Artisan du Livre, 1948), pp. 284f., 418f.; Jeanne-Marie Demarolle, "Les femmes chrétiennes vues par Porphyre," *JAC* 13 (1970) 42–47.

61. See K. Thraede, "Frau," *RAC* 8 (1970) 228.

62. For a somewhat different interpretative emphasis, see Y. Redalié, "Conversion or Liberation? Notes on Acts 16:11–40," in N. K. Gottwald and A. C. Wire, eds., *The Bible and Liberation: Political and Social Hermeneutics* (Berkeley: Radical Religion, 1976), pp. 102–8.

63. Thraede ("Zum historischen Hintergrund," pp. 363f.) has therefore correctly stressed that the household-code tradition of the NT supports the anti-egalitarian and conservative tendencies of Greco-Roman culture.

64. For bibliographies of Eph 5:15–6:9, see J. P. Sampley, *Ephesians, Colossians, 2 Thessalonians, The Pastoral Epistles* (Proclamation Commentaries; Philadelphia: Fortress, 1978), pp. 9–39; J. Gnilka, *Der Epheserbrief* (HThKNT 10/2; Freiburg: Herder, 1971), pp. 1–52 and the excursuses.

65. The unity of Christians was celebrated in baptism; cf. Meeks, "In One Body," pp. 214ff.

66. See D. C. Smith, "The Two Made One: Some Observations on Eph 2:14–18," *Ohio Journal of Religious Studies* 1 (1973) 34–54; H. Merklein, "Zur Tradition und Komposition von Eph 2:14–18," *Biblische Zeitschrift* 17 (1973) 79–109.

67. For the whole section (5:15–6:9), see Gnilka, *Epheserbrief*, pp. 264–303 (literature).

68. See especially Meeks, "In One Body," p. 216.

69. J. Ernst, "From the Local Community to the Great Church: Illustrated from the Church Patterns of Philippians and Ephesians," *Theology Bulletin* 6 (1976) 237–57:245.

70. For this whole section, cf. especially J. P. Sampley, *"And the Two Shall Become One Flesh": A Study of Traditions in Eph 5:21–33* (SNTSM 16; Cambridge: Cambridge University Press, 1971).

71. See R. Batey, "'Jewish Gnosticism' and the 'Hieros Gamos' of Eph.v.21–33," *NTS* 10 (1963) 121–27; idem, "The *Mia Sarx* Union of Christ and the Church, *NTS* 13 (1966/67) 270–81.

72. For the sovereign headship of Christ over all things, see G. E. Howard, "The Head/Body Metaphors of Ephesians," *NTS* 20 (1975) 350–56.

73. Cf. V. P. Furnish, *The Love Command in the New Testament* (Nashville: Abingdon, 1972), p. 123.

74. See Sampley, *"And the Two . . . ,"* pp. 94–102.

75. The standard work on Marcion is still A. von Harnack, *Marcion: Das Evangelium vom fremden Gott* (1924; reprint ed.; Darmstadt: Wissenschaftliche Buchgesellschaft, 1960).

76. Epiphanius *Panarion* 45.2.1; in the following section, the patristic quotations of gnostic leaders and their teachings are from W. Foerster, *A Selection of Gnostic Texts*, vol. 1, *Patristic Evidence*, trans. and ed., R. McL. Wilson (Oxford: Clarendon Press, 1972).

77. Clement of Alexandria *Stromateis* 3.63.

78. *The Pseudo-Clementine Homilies* 2.15.3.

79. *Acts of Thomas* 2.27; cf. Edgar Hennecke, *New Testament Apocrypha*, ed. W. Schneemelcher, trans. R. McL. Wilson (Philadelphia: Westminster, 1965), 2.456f.

80. Cf. H. Kraft, "Gab es einen Gnostiker Karpokrates?" *Theologische Zeitschrift* 8 (1952) 434–44. For patristic evidence, see W. Förster, *Gnosis: A Selection of Gnostic Texts*, trans. and ed. R. McL. Wilson (Oxford: Clarendon Press, 1972), pp. 34–37.

81. Irenaeus *Adversus haereses* 1.25.1–6.

82. Clement of Alexandria *Stromateis* 2.2.6.

83. Ibid., 2.2.6.1.

84. Ibid., 2.2.8.1.

85. Ibid., 2.2.10.1.

86. Such accusations were made by pagans and Jews against Christians in general, by patristic Christianity against Montanist and gnostic Christians and vice versa, but also by various gnostic groups against each other; see R. Haardt, *Gnosis: Character and Testimony* (Leiden: Brill, (1971), p. 69, n. 1.

87. H. Jonas, *The Gnostic Religion: The Message of the Alien God and the Beginnings of Christianity* (Boston: Beacon Press, 1963), p. 237.

88. R. A. Baer, *Philo's Use of the Categories Male and Female* (Leiden: Brill, 1970), p. 71.

89. Irenaeus *Adversus haereses* 1.23.3.

90. For the affinity of Jungian thought to this second type of gnostic dualism, see R. M. Stein, "Liberating the Feminine," in R. Tiffany Barnhouse and U. T. Holmes, eds., *Male and Female* (New York: Seabury, 1976), pp. 76–86; and A. Belford Ulanov, "Jung on Male and Female," ibid., pp. 197–210. For a feminist theological critique of this dualism, see R. Radford Ruether, *New Woman New Earth: Sexist Ideologies and Human Liberation* (New York: Seabury, 1975), pp. 151–59.

91. Irenaeus *Adversus haereses* 1.14.1.

92. Ibid., 1.18.2.

93. Ibid., 1.23.3.

94. Cf. R. M. Grant, "The Mystery of Marriage in the Gospel of Philip," *Vigiliae Christianae* 15 (1961) 129–40.

95. Irenaeus *Adversus haereses* 1.21.3.

96. For translations, see R. McL. Wilson, *The Gospel of Philip* (London: Mowbray, 1962); see also the discussion in W. A. Meeks, "The Image of the Androgyne: Some Uses of a Symbol in Earliest Christianity," *History of Religions* 13 (1974) 191–95, and the literature cited. The English translation used here is by W. Isenberg, "The Gospel of Philip," in J. M. Robinson, ed., *The Nag Hammadi Library* (San Francisco: Harper & Row, 1977), pp. 131–51 (hereafter cited as *NHL*).

97. 2.68.20–25; *NHL*, p. 141.

98. Irenaeus *Adversus haereses* 1.13.4.

99. Cf. Wilson, *The Gospel of Philip*, p. 31.

100. *Gospel of Philip* 2.63.30–35; *NHL*, p. 138.

101. E. H. Pagels (*The Gnostic Gospels* [New York: Random House, 1979], pp. 66f.) recognizes this but does not acknowledge its systemic implications. See also her "What Became of God the Mother? Conflicting Images of God in Early Christianity," *Signs* 2 (1976) 293–303.

102. *Gospel of Philip* 2.76.5–10; *NHL*, p. 145.

103. Cf. 2.82.1–5; *NHL*, p. 149: "If there is a hidden quality to the marriage of defilement, how much more is the undefiled marriage a true mystery!"

104. J. Jacobson Buckley, "A Cult Mystery in the Gospel of Philip," *JBL* 99 (1980) 569–81:581.

105. Cf. E. H. Pagels, "The Valentinian Claim to Esoteric Exegesis of Romans as Basis for Anthropological Theory," *Vigiliae Christianae* 26 (1972) 241–58.

106. Baer, *Philo's Use*, pp. 14–44.

107. Ibid., p. 51.

108. In the same *Homily 37 on Matthew*, Gregory Nazianzen condemns the civil law that permits a husband to be unfaithful but punishes the wife for unfaithfulness: "The law was made by men, and for that reason is directed against women." In contrast, divine law does not make a distinction between the sexes; cf. *PG* 36.289–92.

109. For Gregory of Nyssa, cf. R. R. Ruether, "Virginal Feminism in the Fathers of the Church," in *Religion and Sexism* (New York: Simon & Schuster, 1974), pp. 150–83: esp. 153–55.

110. For Augustine, see K. Thraede, "Augustin-Texte aus dem Themenkreis 'Frau', 'Gesellschaft', und 'Gleichheit'," *JAC* 22 (1979) 70–97.

111. See my book *Der vergessene Partner* (Düsseldorf: Patmos, 1964), pp. 68ff.

112. G. H. Tavard, *Woman in Christian Tradition* (Notre Dame: University of Notre Dame Press, 1973), pp. 77f.

113. J. A. McNamara, "Sexual Equality and the Cult of Virginity in Early Christian Thought," *Feminist Studies* 3 (1976) 145–58.

114. Jerome *Adversus Jovinianum* 1.3 (*PL* 23.224); cf. D. Callam, "Clerical Continence in the Fourth Century," *Theological Studies* 41 (1980) 3–50: esp. 8–24 for bibliography.

115. Cf. R. Gryson, *The Ministry of Women in the Early Church* (Collegeville, Minn.: Liturgical Press, 1976), p. 113.

Chapter 8

The Patriarchal Household of God and the Ekklēsia of Women

S tudies on the development of church offices and church orders, though numerous, are inconclusive.[1] Despite the work that has been done tracing the cultification and clericalization of Christian ministry into a hierarchical and monarchical institution capable of replacing the political structures of the Roman empire, scant attention has been paid to the patriarchalization of Christian ministry and church. Some studies of the social world of early Christianity assume that a patriarchal self-understanding and structure were integral to the Christian missionary movement in the urban centers of the Greco-Roman world, while others stress the egalitarian character of the Christian group. More recent arguments insist that the two structures and attitudes were present in the church from its very beginnings: an insistence on the religious equality of believers as sisters and brothers combined with a hierarchically ordered superiority of ministers vis-à-vis the Christian congregation.

> The equality of believers, regardless of all worldly distinctions that might persist outside the church, is one of the pervasive themes of early Christianity. . . . Yet we must also recognize that there was one group in early Christianity which stood above or outside the general equality: the ministry. Already in the New Testament period there was a sense in which the apostle was superior to other Christians, and in the second century, the distinction between clergy and laity acquired clearer definition.[2]

This argument, however, telescopes distinct organizational forms and ends up with a dualistic understanding of church and ministry. It presupposes that equality and egalitarian organizational structures exclude authority and leadership. It overlooks the fact that equality or egalitarian structures are characterized by what sociologists call role-interchangeability.[3] Organizational equality is sustained by shifting and alternating authority and leadership among members of a group, all of whom—in principle—have equal access to authority, leadership, and power. This was the case in the early Christian movement, insofar as all members of the community were Spirit-gifted people of God who had received the power and endowment of the Holy Spirit for the building up of the community. Different members of the community may receive different gifts and exercise different leadership functions, but in principle all members of the community had access to spiritual power and communal leadership roles. God's gift and election were not dependent upon one's religious background, societal role, or gender and race. The stress on apostleship in the Pauline letters arises because Paul's apostleship was being questioned by many, not because of any need to stress the superiority of the apostle over and against all other leadership roles.[4]

The early Christian missionary movement was not defined by the dichotomy between the religious equality of all members and the spiritual superiority of the apostle and other ministers. Any basic distinction between forms of leadership is primarily one between *local* and *translocal* leadership. Paul's problems with the community in Corinth arose in part from the fact that, as a missionary, Paul was not a permanent member of the Corinthian community.[5] The leadership of prophets and apostles was translocal and derived its legitimacy from the direct revelation and authority of the resurrected Lord.[6] The local leadership—heads of house churches, bishops, deacons, and elders—seems to have developed by analogy to the administrative offices of Greco-Roman private associations and Jewish synagogue organizations, and were dependent on the community. Whereas the administrative charisms functioned primarily within the context of the house churches and local communities, the leadership of apostles, missionaries, and prophets was not limited to a local community.

The shift which took place in the second century was not a shift from charismatic leadership to institutional consolidation, but from charismatic and communal authority to an authority vested in local officers, who—in time—absorb not only the teaching authority of the prophet and apostle but also the decision-making power of the community. This shift is, at the same time, a shift from alternating leadership accessible to all the baptized to patriarchal leadership restricted to male heads of households; it is a shift from house church to church as the "household of God."

Such a shift also entailed a transfer of authority and influence from wealthy members of the community to the administrative local officers of the church. Although the legal analogy between the early Christian community and private associations or clubs is debated, the social analogy between the two is, for the most part, accepted. A century ago E. Hatch argued that the *episkopos* and *diakonos* titles designate the administrative and outreach officers of the Christian association just as they do in Greco-Roman clubs.[7] The elders, in turn, represent a council or committee of officers whose membership is based on seniority and patriarchal status. These local offices of associations were not always permanent, and often depended upon election by the club or cult members. Very significant for the life of Greco-Roman private associations and clubs were rich donors or patrons. The Greco-Roman patronage system gave them influence and power over the members. Thus, insofar as they provided space and assistance—both legal and financial—to the Christian association, wealthy members of the Christian community—especially those who presided over a house church—had great influence and power in the church from its very beginnings. In 1 Cor 1:16 Paul refers to the household of Stephanas, the first converts in Achaia who "have devoted themselves to the service (*diakonia*) of the saints" (16:15). Therefore, Paul urges the members of the community to "subordinate" themselves to them and to every missionary co-worker and laborer" (16:16). Still, at the beginning of the second century, the author of 3 John censures Diotrephes, the head of a house church who had refused hospitality to the emissaries of the elder and agitated against the elder himself.[9] To the extent that the offices of bishop and deacon began to gain strength and influence at the end of the first century by tending to replace all other leadership functions, the influence of the wealthy members of the community was progressively curtailed and came under the control of the administrative offices. Now the rich are admonished to give generously to the church and to the poor, but the financial control of church funds shifts more and more into the hands of the bishop and the clergy.[10] In Greco-Roman associations

> the patron gave designated gifts: the inscriptions carefully record the terms of the gifts and the limited freedom of the club's officers to alter these terms. In the church system, by contrast, the exhortation was simply that the rich should *give*, leaving the role of administration entirely to the clergy.[11]

Such a division between wealthy laypeople and the clergy is not yet found in the New Testament writings, however. The shift from patronage to administrative office becomes visible only in the second century. It was to have far-reaching consequences for the leadership of women, since—in Greco-Roman society on the whole and in private associations in particular—wealth gave women great influence and authority. The ascendency of local officers thus generated three interlocking developments: (1) the patriarchalization of local church and leadership; (2) the merger of prophetic and apostolic leadership with the patriarchally defined office of bishop; and (3) the relegation of women's leadership to marginal positions and its restriction to the sphere of women.

The Patriarchalization of Church and Ministry

The three New Testament writings commonly called the Pastoral Epistles[12] are not letters in the strict sense. While 2 Timothy seems closest to a personal letter, 1 Timothy and Titus read more like official documents of instruction. Only the latter two contain instructions for different groups within the church. The time of the apostles is past. Only Paul, in whose name the epistles are written, is called an apostle. Timothy and Titus are evangelists and missionaries, co-workers and disciples of Paul but not apostles. Their function, and calling, is to protect and foster the true teachings of the tradition. They are to combat the proclamation of other teachings and instruct the community regarding "sound" or "good" teaching.

The Pastorals do not promulgate a church order[13] as such, with clear delineations of particular offices and functions, but are instructions on "how to behave in the household of God," the church. It is difficult, therefore, to delineate with any clarity the different groups to whom they are addressed. Moreover, it is unclear whether the apostolic commissioners Timothy and Titus are in charge of several churches, how large these churches are, and whether the local church still consists of house churches. What is clear, however, is that the church is now stratified according to "natural" age and gender divisions. Though still the new "family," it is clearly understood in terms of the patriarchal household.[14] The church is understood as the household of God (1 Tim 3:15), the "great house" (2 Tim 2:20) which contains many different vessels. Its manager or administrator is the overseer/bishop, who must be educated, without reproach, good, prudent, just, pious, the husband of one wife, and respected by those who do not belong to the community. He should not be a recent convert or seek dishonest gain, but should rather devote himself to hospitality. In short, the overseer/bishop should be a good *paterfamilias* who has proven capable of governing his own household well (1 Tim 3:2ff; Tit 1:7ff). Likewise, the elders/presbyters must have proved that, as heads of households, they are capable of taking care of the whole community.[15]

The subordinate members of the household must, in turn, subject themselves to the head of the house. Just as wives (Tit 2:5), children (1 Tim 3:4), and slaves (Tit 2:9) must be submissive within the household, so they must observe their subordinate role within the community. A wife/woman is to learn in all quietness and submission, as her status requires. She is not to teach or have authority over a husband/man, since this would violate the order of submission (1 Tim 2:10–15). Slaves are told to submit to their masters and not contradict them, while false teachers are accused of being insubordinate and of talking foolish things (Tit 1:10; 2:9). Just as slaves should not have contempt for their masters (1 Tim 6:2), so the whole community should not have contempt for their ministers (1 Tim 4:12; Tit 2:15). Just as slaves should be well pleasing to their masters, so Christians should be well pleasing to God, their Father (2 Tim 1:2). The overarching value—for the authors of the Pastoral Epistles—is obedience and submission to those in authority, so that the community—and especially its subordinate members—will be a credit to Christian teaching (Tit 2:10, in respect to slaves) and so that, as a result of their behavior, "God's word may not be blasphemed" (Tit 2:5, in respect to wives). Christians are good citizens, observing the patriarchal order of the household and praying "for emperors and all authorities," so that they are able "to lead a quiet and peaceful life in all piety and dignity" (1 Tim 2:1ff).

The Pastoral Epistles advocate the patriarchal order of submission for more than apologetic reasons, however. The Christian community, as the household of God, has become stratified according to the age/gender divisions of the patriarchal household. Ministry and leadership are dependent upon age/gender qualifications, not primarily upon one's spiritual or organizational resources or giftedness. This is often overlooked in exegetical discussions which seek to differentiate between injunctions for church leaders and those for individual age groups divided by gender. This kind of differentiation cannot be made because church leadership is based on the societal status distinctions of the patriarchal household. For example, the injunction of 1 Tim 5:1 does not address age groups distinct from groups of ministers, but addresses both as one and the same group:

> Do not rebuke an older man/presbyter (*presbuteros*) but admonish him as one would a father, younger men/deacons (*neōteroi*) as brothers, older women/presbyters (*presbuterai*) as mothers, younger women/deacons (*neōterai*) as sisters in all propriety.[16]

Thus the leadership of the community consists of male and female presbyters on the one hand, and male and female deacons on the other. A special group are the widows. These are either women who are husbandless or women who have been enrolled as "true widows." The overseer/bishop seems to have been chosen from among the presbyters and—as in other contemporary organizations—was primarily the presiding administrator in charge of the collection and distribution of church funds. In this task he was assisted by male and female deacons. The presbyterion was the administrative council or committee consisting of the esteemed male and female heads of households. Since only one overseer/bishop is mentioned in the Pastorals, it is likely that this office was rotated among the presbyters.[17] 1 Tim 5:17, therefore, makes a distinction between presbyters and presiding presbyters who govern well. They are to receive double compensation. Moreover, the function of a presiding presbyter seems to have been the same as that of the overseer/bishop, namely, instruction and teaching.

Women presbyters[18] who were heads of households and house churches, therefore, must have taken for granted that they were also eligible for the function of overseer/bishop. It is significant that the admonition to subordination and quiet behavior[19] in the worship assembly of the community is addressed to wealthy women. By prohibiting a woman from teaching and having authority over a man, the author—in the name of Paul—denies women any eligibility for the office of overseer/bishop. Leading women are still permitted to teach, but their teaching is now restricted to the instruction of other women.[20] Thus the injunctions of 1 Tim 2:11 and Tit 2:3–5 are not contradictory, but rather present two sides of the same patriarchal coin. Women presbyters are to be "priestly" in their conduct and prove themselves "good teachers,"[21] but their teaching is to be restricted to the instruction of other women.

In conclusion, the Pastorals seem to merge the leadership of wealthy patrons with that of the local officers of the Christian association. In doing so they stratify church leadership according to patriarchal status and seniority. Leadership in the community still consists of male and female heads of households, of male and female presbyters, of fathers and mothers, but their functions are defined and limited according to the status stratifications of the Greco-Roman household and society. The ascendency of the patronage system usurps the more democratic offices of the private association by incorporating the local elite into its own ranks. In so doing, the office of bishop and deacon become patriarchalized to the extent that they are modeled after the wealthy Greco-Roman household. This development is supported by the Jewish patriarchal organizational form of a governing council of elders comprising the heads of leading families. The leadership and behavior of women and slaves becomes restricted and defined according to the patriarchal standards of Greco-Roman society so that outsiders will not take offense at their insubordinate behavior.[22] The patriarchal order of the house, when applied to the order of the church, restricts the leadership of wealthy women and maintains the social exploitation of slave-women and men,[23] even within the Christian household community.[24]

The *First Epistle of Clement*,[25] which might have been written before the Pastorals, allows us to glimpse the community's involvement in the appointment and dismissal of local officers. The letter is written by the church of Rome to the church of Corinth because the latter had removed certain presbyters/bishops[26] from office. The author argues that they ought not to have done so because those officers had been appointed with the consent of the whole congregation and had performed a good job. Removal from office by the congregation, then, seems to have been the rule whenever the appointed leaders of the church failed to perform their office well. Moreover, the author acknowledges that the Spirit was poured out over all members of the community (2.2) and that the congregation must decide what is to be done (54.2). Thus it would appear that the author knows of an older order in which the local ministers of the church were appointed by and dependent upon the whole congregation. Nevertheless he labels the initiative of certain members of the community in deposing well-esteemed presbyters/bishops as insurrection and strife. He insinuates that the deposed officers can trace their office back to the apostles (44.2ff) and argues that their opponents should reconsider their intervention and recant their actions. He concedes that strife and dissension had existed in the community of Corinth in Paul's time, but argues that the earlier problem was a lesser sin because the Corinthians were "partisans of notable apostles and of those they endorsed" (47.4ff).

The key theological concept in 1 *Clement* is "order."[27] This order is conceived of as analogous to the military order of ranks, the levitical order of the Old Testament priesthood, and the patriarchal order of the house. The Corinthian male heads of households are praised for having kept this patriarchal order in the past (1.3), and are admonished to reinforce it once more in the present (21.6–9). This order is based on nature and rooted in creation. God, therefore, is called Father of eternity and Master of the universe "who disciplines us" (56.16). Those Corinthians, therefore, who are "responsible for the revolt must submit to the presbyters . . . be disciplined . . . learn obedience . . . and curb their tongues" (57.1f), so that they can hold a creditable, though insignificant, place in Christ's flock, the church. Those responsible for removing the highly esteemed elders are characterized as follows:

> And so "the dishonored" rose up "against those who were held in honor," those of no reputation against the notable, the stupid against the wise, "the young against their elders." [3.3]

By contrast with this sort of conduct, the observance of God's law and order by the Corinthians is expressed in the following praise:

> You obeyed your rulers and gave your elders the proper respect. You disciplined the minds of your young people in moderation and dignity. You instructed your women to do everything with a blameless and pure conscience. [1.3]

It is important to note that among the heroes praised for their "humility and obedience" and placed before the community as examples to imitate are women. Moreover, women are also among those who suffered as victims because of strife and rivalry. Among those who caused rivalry are singled out wives who became estranged from their husbands and "annulled the saying of our Father Adam, 'this is now bone of my bone and flesh of my flesh.' " (6.3) Those who are admonished to learn obedience and curb their tongue include, in addition to those who are leaders against the elders/bishops, women: "by their reticence let them show that their tongues are considerate. Let them grant their love (*agape*) not with partiality [cf. 1 Tim 5:21] but in a holy manner show equal love to all those who fear God" (21.7). Finally, when the author calls the insubordinate members to repentance, he mentions—among the examples of those who were "noble, large-hearted, and full of love" (54.1)—many women who, empowered by God's grace, have "performed deeds worthy of men." Though the author mentions no male examples by name, he mentions the names of two women: Judith, who, with the consent of the elders, saved her people by endangering her own life, and Esther, who is characterized as a "woman of perfect faith" and "humility." As such, she saved her people from annihilation (55.3–6). Thus it seems safe to conclude that among those who were "not highly esteemed" and had "no reputation" (according to the patriarchal values of the author), but who had assumed leadership in the community at Corinth, were, in addition to young people,[28] also women. Furthermore, these women were probably wealthy, if *agape* can be understood in a spiritual as well as economic sense. Rather than have their donations controlled by the elders/bishops[29]—who seem to have disagreed over how their funds were to be distributed—the women appear to have joined with those who removed the elders/bishops from office. This was a perfectly permissible procedure within the context of Greco-Roman private associations. Thus it was not the procedure for removal, but the insistence upon the patriarchal submission to authority, which was the innovation.[30] This is clear, since even the author of 1 *Clement* must concede that all have received the Spirit. Moreover, the author has no power to reenforce the patriarchal order and fails to appeal to any particular person or group who might have had the power to do so. Instead, he appeals to the good will of the insubordinate members and puts them under moral pressure.

While 1 *Clement* does not argue that bishops/presbyters are the representatives of God, the Father and Master, Ignatius of Antioch[31] does accomplish this theological move. As was the case in the Pastorals, Ignatius does not speak of bishops/overseers in the plural, but knows only of one bishop who is clearly distinguished from the deacons and presbyters. The bishop must become the primary focal point for the unity of the church.[32] He should govern the church assisted by deacons and supported by a council of elders. For Ignatius, however, the authority of the bishop, deacons, and elders is not derived from the apostles, from a chain of succession, or from a chain of tradition. Instead, the officers are the earthly type of a heavenly pattern.[33] In this pattern the bishop represents God, the presbyters are the apostles, and the deacons Christ himself (*Magn.* 6.1). The authority of the bishop is not derived from a historical-sociological connection with the apostles but from an archetypal relationship between the one God in heaven and God's representative or *typos* on earth.

Erik Peterson, in a widely known study, has pointed out that monotheism has often served to justify politically monarchical rulership: one God, one emperor, one empire! In an analogous fashion Ignatius stresses: one God, one bishop, one church. However, just as Augustus is more and more understood as *pater patriae*, so—for Ignatius—the bishop is the type of God, the Father. Though the bishop of the

Magnesians is very youthful, he is to be respected by them as fully as they respect "the authority of God the Father" (*Magn.* 3.1). The bishop presides "in God's place," while presbyters take the place of the apostolic council and deacons are "entrusted with the ministry of Christ who was with the Father from eternity" (6.1). Just as Jesus Christ did nothing without the Father so the members of the community are to do nothing without the bishop. The Magnesians are to defer to the bishop just as Jesus deferred to the Father.

The Ephesians are admonished not to resist the bishop so that they may be subject to God (*Eph.* 5.3). The Trallians are told to respect the deacons for "they represent Jesus Christ, just as the bishop has the role of the Father, and the presbyters are like God's council and an apostolic band" (*Trall.* 3.1). On the other hand, those who act apart from the bishop, presbyters, and deacons do not have a clear conscience (7.2). The presbyters, in particular, are admonished to "encourage the bishop in honor of the Father, Jesus Christ and the apostles" (12.2). In his *Letter to the Philadelphians*, Ignatius stresses that the bishop does not owe his ministry to himself, or to other people, but to "the love of God the Father, and the Lord Jesus Christ" (1.1). The Smyrnaeans are admonished to "follow the bishop as Jesus Christ did the Father (*Smyrn.* 8.1). What the bishop approves pleases God as well (8.2). Those who honor the bishop honor God, whereas those who act without the bishop serve the devil (9.1). Even though the bishop can also be likened to Jesus Christ, and all Christians have the stamp of the Father, the predominant archetypal relationship is that between the one bishop and the one God, the Father who is called bishop of everyone (*Magn.* 6.1). The church is the church of God the Father and the beloved Christ (*Smyrn.* praescr.). In short, the patriarchal order is theologically justified by Ignatius.[34] While *1 Clement* justifies the patriarchal order with respect to nature and creation, Ignatius legitimizes it theologically and christologically. Subordination and respect for the bishop, not the discipleship of coequals, are theologically developed.[35]

The Teaching Authority of the Bishop

The shift which takes place in the second century with respect to ecclesial authority and structure is more than a shift from local leadership based upon spiritual giftedness and economic resources to a patriarchal ascendency of the local officers of the Christian association. It is also a shift from translocal charismatic authority with its amalgamation of the apostolic and prophetic toward an understanding of authority vested in the local offices, especially the monarchical episcopacy. Whereas apostleship[36] was restricted to the first generation, prophecy could be, and was, claimed by the patriarchally defined episcopacy.

The authority of the apostle, prophet, teacher,[37] or missionary was based on the direct intervention of the Spirit and an experience of the resurrected Lord's presence. Revelation, preaching, and teaching were its primary functions. Although we have but scattered references to prophecy in the New Testament, these references testify to the ubiquity of this phenomenon in the early Christian movement. Prophets and prophecy[38] were found in every Christian center of the Greco-Roman world. Prophets evidently wielded great authority and influence in the first centuries as spokespersons for the resurrected Lord, illuminating the present situation of the community theologically.

Prophecy was not, however, restricted to a few men in the early Christian movement. Rather, it appears to have been a characteristic of the whole community. Christian conversion and baptism led persons into a community which was the dwelling place of the Holy Spirit. Within this community the gifts and endowments of the Spirit were experienced and actualized. The foundation of Christian prophetic gifts must be sought in the early church's belief that—as the Spirit-filled congregation—it was the eschatological community, the new creation. While the Q document sees Jesus and his followers as prophets and messengers of divine Sophia sent as her envoys to each generation, Acts understands the outpouring of the Spirit as the fulfillment of Joel's eschatological promise:

> And in the last days it shall be, God declares, that I will pour out my Spirit on all flesh and your sons and your daughters shall prophesy . . . and on my menservants and maidservants in those days I will pour out my Spirit and they shall prophesy. [2:17–18][39]

The members of the early Christian missionary movement understand themselves as *pneumatikoi*, Spirit-filled persons. According to the Pauline literature, speaking in tongues, visions, miracles, prophecy, as well as agape, mutuality, and solidarity, were actualizations of the creative life-power of the Spirit. Women as well as men received such prophetic gifts. As was the case in Judaism and in the Greco-Roman world, so also in early Christianity virginity[40] seems to have been associated with prophecy. *1 Clement* still knows that the Spirit is poured out on all Christians.

Early Christian prophecy shared the world experience common to the ancient Mediterranean civilization.[41] Many regions throughout the Greco-Roman world had oracles or prophets through whom the gods made known their will. One of the best-known examples is the oracle of Apollo at Delphi.[42] The Pythia or priestess of the oracle gave forth inspired utterances, which were then explained by official interpreters called *prophetai*. The ecstatic nature of an oracular utterance was often emphasized by divine madness. Wild dancing, unintelligible speech, and frenzied behavior characterized divine inspiration.[43]

This understanding of prophecy as ecstatic behavior and speech is also known by Jewish writers such as Josephus and Philo, the latter of whom describes his own prophetic experiences as follows:

> By divine possession I fell into rapture and became ignorant of everything, the place, the present, myself. . . .[44]

This kind of experience came suddenly upon people; it could not be induced. In the context of such an experience of rapture and ecstasy, a person is a mere instrument in the hands of God.

> A prophet utters nothing of his [her] own, but is the interpreter of the promptings of another in all that he [she] proclaims. . . . Reason has withdrawn from the citadel of the soul where has come to dwell the divine Spirit. . . .[45] The prophet even when he [she] seems to be speaking, is in truth quiescent; It is Another who uses his [her] vocal organs, tongues and mouth.[46]

In Philo's view the Old Testament prophets were this kind of instrument of God. Moses stands at the head of them, but prophecy was not confined to him because, in a certain sense, "all the Lord's people were prophets. It is to every fine and noble creature that prophecy belongs. No worthless person may become an interpreter of God."[47]

Not all prophets—Hebrew or Greek—were mad and frenzied in their ecstasis. But they all understood themselves as "mouthpieces of God" because their human minds were displaced by the divine Spirit. Therefore, they can speak in the first person singular: "I am the Alpha and the Omega" or "I am the Way and the Truth." In so doing they are not assuming divine prerogatives for themselves, but are uttering divine revelation in the direct voice. In the *Testament of Job*, a first-century Hellenistic writing, Job gives his wealth to his seven sons, while to his daughters he gives three beautiful girdles which come, not from this world, but from heaven. They symbolize the prophetic power which will enable them to see future and past, and to speak the language of angels and to sing a song to God and the praise of heavenly things.[48]

Early Christian prophecy included the element of ecstasy and of speaking in tongues, as Paul, Acts, Revelation, and Hermas document.[49] The prophet proclaimed: "Thus says the Holy Spirit." Paul's admonition in 1 Thessalonians,[50] "Do not quench the Spirit, do not despise prophesying" (5:19f), is almost identical to the phrase used to prohibit the stifling of prophetic inspiration by an oracle. His emphasis upon the intelligibility of prophecy in 1 Corinthians 14, however, shows that this ecstatic activity of prophets was already being regulated by redefining it as an intelligible gift to be used for the sake of building up the community. Thus it is primarily the agape relationship among Christians—and not merely ecstatic endowment—which manifests the power of the Spirit in their midst.

The question of how widespread prophecy was in the early Christian movement is difficult to answer. From Luke—and the apocryphal *Acts of Paul and Thecla*—we learn that the major early urban Christian centers—Jerusalem, Antioch, and Ephesus—included influential prophets who gave their oracles during the liturgy. Prophets were certainly present at Corinth and Thessalonica as well. Philip's four prophetic daughters lived in Caesarea, and are said to have moved later to Asia Minor. According to Ephesians, the universal cosmic church is built on the foundation of apostles and prophets (2:20). 1 Tim 4:14 suggests that the grace of leadership and office was imparted to Timothy through the word of a prophet at his ordination by the elders. In 1 Tim 4:1 the author explicitly proclaims a prophetic word of the Spirit in order to denounce his opponents as "false prophets."[51] The Revelation of John claims to be "the words of prophecy," and therefore calls its readers to "hear what the Spirit says."[52]

In addition to Revelation, the *Didache*—a church order probably written in Syria toward the end of the first century[53]—proves that prophets and prophecy continued to have authority. People were reluctant to exercise judgment on the prophets' words and revelations for fear of committing blasphemy against the Holy Spirit. The *Didache* cautions: "Do not test or examine any prophet who is speaking in the Spirit, for every sin shall be forgiven, but this sin shall not be forgiven" (11:7). The criterion for judging true prophecy was not, as in Paul, a charismatic discernment of the Spirit, but rather the prophet's behavior: "But not everyone who speaks in the Spirit is a prophet, except the one who has the behavior of the Lord" (11:8). Prophets are to be judged on the basis of whether they practice what they prophesy, how long they stay in one place, and whether or not they ask money in return for their prophecies. Similar criteria for judging behavior are to be found in Matthew and in the *Shepherd of Hermas*.

On the positive side, the *Didache* esteems the prophets highly. It instructs Christians to give them a share of all their possessions, because prophets have the same roles and rights as the Jewish high priests. Their prophesying and liturgical speaking may not be controlled. They are exempted from adhering to the given liturgical prayer in celebrating the eucharist. They are free to conduct the sacred meal and eucharistic thanksgiving "in the Spirit" (10:7). Only if there are not prophets present do the tithes go to the poor and the liturgical leadership to the local ministers. The Fourth Gospel asserts that the Paraclete was sent to all the disciples and its community understanding was therefore prophetic.[54] It is thus no accident that the Fourth Gospel contains very powerful stories about women disciples like Martha, Mary, and Mary of Magdala.

Even Ignatius of Antioch—who champions the local ministries of bishop, deacon, and elder—claims ecstatic prophecy for himself.[55] When he speaks to the church at Philadelphia, he writes, "I cried out while I was there with you, I spoke with a great voice—with God's own voice—Give heed to the bishop, the presbytery and the deacons." Since some of his hearers may have suspected his prophetic status, he asserts that it was not really he himself "but the Spirit was preaching and saying: do nothing without the bishop" (*Phld.* 7.1–2). Ignatius must appeal to prophetic authority in order to strengthen the role and influence of the episcopacy.

The *Shepherd of Hermas*, probably written at Rome in the mid-second century, documents the continuing importance of prophecy.[56] True prophets are meek and humble, give no answers to anyone when consulted, and do not speak of their own accord.

> When someone who has the Divine Spirit comes into the meeting of the righteous who have the faith of the Divine Spirit and intercession is made to God from the Assembly, then the angel of the prophetic spirit rests on the person and filled with the Holy Spirit the prophet speaks to the congregation as the Lord wills. [*Mandate* XI.9]

False prophets, however, are empty and have no power. They are talkative, live in great luxury, accept remuneration for prophesying, and—if not paid—will not prophesy.

In addition to the Montanists, other ascetic and gnostic groups stressed the authority of the Spirit, of prophets and ascetics over and against noncharismatic local officers. Clement testifies that the Valentinians maintained the earliest Christian traditions on prophecy:

> The Valentinians say that the spirit which each of the prophets received specially for his [her] ministry is poured out upon all in the church: Therefore the signs of the Spirit—healings and prophesyings are accomplished through the church.[57]

The bishop Irenaeus polemicizes against the followers of the Valentinian Marcus.[58] Despite the theological belief systems of this group, which contained gnostic elements, its church order and pneumatic self-understanding seem still similar to those found in 1 Corinthians and Acts. Thus it may be seen to preserve an original apostolic prophetic practice. In this group, every initiate was assumed to have received the direct inspiration of the Holy Spirit. Whenever the congregation met, its members drew lots—a traditional Jewish and early Christian practice used to divine the will of God. By means of these lots, they were designated variously for the role of the presbyter, for celebrating the eucharist as bishop, for reading and expounding the Scriptures, or for teaching or addressing the group as a prophet. All members—women and men—were eligible to act as bishop, presbyter, teacher and prophet. Because these functions changed from meeting to meeting, they never became the exclusive prerogative of particular members. The drawing of lots, and the communal character of Spirit-filled leadership, appears close to what we know about pneumatic worship in the early Christian movement. This practice, moreover, would explain why the New Testament never identifies a presider or leader at the eucharist, and why noncanonical writings understand the prophet as such a eucharistic leader.

Women were among the prophetic leaders of the Pauline communities.[59] Luke characterizes Mary[60] and Elizabeth, as well as Anna, as prophets. He mentions the four prophetic daughters of Philip (Acts 21:9), whose fame—according to Eusebius—was so great that the provinces of Asia derive their apostolic origin from them. Papias, their contemporary in Hierapolis, claims them as one of the living sources who told him the wonderful story about the raising to life of the wife of Manaen. He also "reproduced a story about a woman falsely accused before the Lord of many sins," but Eusebius does not tell us whether Papias heard this story, too, from the daughters of Philip. Women prophets are thus acknowledged as transmitters of apostolic tradition (*Ecc. Hist.* III.39.7–17).

John, the author of Revelation, knows of a woman who was a prophet-teacher and the head of a prophetic school[61] or house church in Thyatira. Her followers are characterized as her disciples with the technical term "children" (*tekna*), an expression found in 2 John for the "elect lady's" house-church members. The influence of this woman prophet seems to have been strong enough to counter that of John, who does not apply the title prophet to himself. It is important, however, to note that despite his attack on a particular woman prophet-teacher,[62] John does not discredit female prophecy as such. Asia Minor continued to recognize women prophets even into the second and third centuries. Thyatira later became a center of the Montanist movement.

In the second century, the Montanists attempted to legitimize their prophecy and apostolic origin by establishing a prophetic line of succession. They referred to an Asiatic prophet called Ammia, whose name was still highly respected at the end of the second century. The anti-Montanist Eusebius does not deny her that prophetic ministry, but claims her for the Catholics. He lists—in his succession of recognized prophets—Agabus, Judas, Silas, the daughters of Philip, Ammia in Philadelphia, Quadratus, and some others (*Eccl. Hist.* V.17). In the middle of the second century, Justin affirms that Christian men and women have charisms from the Spirit of God (*Dial c. Tryph.* 88). Irenaeus argues against the *Alogoi*—a group who denied the validity of prophecy—that Paul acknowledged prophetic women and men in the community (*Adv. Her.* III.11).

The *Acts of Paul* mentions women prophets like Theonoe, Stratonike, Eubulla, Phila, Artemilla, and Nympha. At Corinth a prophet by the name of Myrta encouraged Paul and the community not to lose heart because Paul has to go to Rome. "The Spirit came upon Myrta, so that she said. . . . 'Paul the servant of the Lord will save many in Rome and will nourish many with the word . . . that there will be great grace in Rome.' "[63] The context of the worship service indicates that she spoke in the eucharistic assembly. Early Christian prophecy was liturgical prophecy.

Maximilla and Priscilla (or Prisca) were the leading prophets in Montanism.[64] They were not just companions and followers of Montanus, but had equal spiritual gifts and leadership in the Montanist movement. Like Montanus, the woman prophets claimed that the Paraclete or Holy Spirit spoke directly to and through them. This claim was based on faith in the revelations given by the Holy Spirit to women and men in prophetic ecstasy. The movement expected a speedy coming of the Lord and showed a passionate contempt for this world by advocating sexual asceticism, fasting, and martyrdom.[65] The pronouncement of the first three prophets—Priscilla, Maximilla, and Montanus—were written down and gathered together as sacred documents, much as the words of the Old Testament prophets, the sayings of Jesus, and the letters of the apostles were.

The two best-known oracles of the Montanist prophets Priscilla and Maximilla are significant. When Priscilla was asleep, Christ—in the form of a female figure—appeared to her, "caused wisdom to sink into her breast and revealed to her that this was a holy place and here would Jerusalem descend out of heaven" (Epiph. *Her.* XLIII.1.3; XLVIII.14.1). After the death of Montanus, Maximilla became the leader of the movement. She was persecuted, and commissions were sent out to expose her as a fraud. Her opponents attempted to raise doubts about the genuineness of the movement by testing her spirits. Maximilla complained bitterly: "I am pursued like a wolf out of the sheepfold; I am no wolf: I am word and spirit and power" (Eus. *Eccl. Hist.* V.16.17). Since the Montanists' opponents could not refute the movement on doctrinal grounds, they attacked it by slandering its leading prophets. Charges of immorality and of abandoning their husbands were brought against the women. It was claimed that Montanist leaders committed suicide, and that, in their mysteries, they slaughtered children and mingled their blood in the sacrifices, charges originally made by pagans against all Christians. Thus, despite their basic doctrinal orthodoxy, the Montanists were reviled and finally driven out of the monepiscopal church.

The considerable body of anti-Montanist literature focuses its attack on the leadership of women in particular. Since Maximilla and Priscilla were proof that the Holy Spirit spoke through the female sex, the Montanists admitted women to church "offices." Didymus (*On the Trinity* III.41.3) maintains that the women prophets in Montanism taught and prophesied in the assembly of the community. Firmilian knows of a prophetess in Asia Minor who, in 235 C.E., converted many laypeople and clerics. She baptized and celebrated the eucharist (Cypr. *Ep.* 75.10). According to Origen "those disciples of women, who chose as their master Priscilla and Maximilla, not Christ, the spouse of the bride, appeal to the following women prophets: the daughters of Philip, Deborah, Mary—the sister of Aaron, Hulda, and Anna—the daughter of Phanuel" (*Fragm. on 1 Cor.* 74). Origen refutes this tradition by arguing that these women prophets did not speak in public or in the assemblies, but only in private. Finally, Epiphanius mentions a number of groups related to Montanism, among them the Cataphrygians who held Priscilla and Quintilla in great honor, calling them prophetesses. They pointed out that Eve was the first to eat from the tree of knowledge to justify the admission of women into the clergy. As precedent for their practice, they referred to Miriam, the sister of Aaron, to the four prophetic daughters of Philip and to Gal 3:28:

> Frequently a procession of seven virgins carrying torches and dressed in white, is seen entering their assemblies. Under the power of prophetic delirium, they lamented the miseries of the human conditions and surrendered themselves to noisy peniten-tial demonstrations, so that the assistants also cried with them. But this is not all—they had women bishops and presbyters, since as they said they did not discriminate with regard to sex, to be in accord with the statement of Paul: In Christ Jesus there is neither male nor female.[66]

The second and third centuries are characterized by the struggle of the prophetic and local ministry for authority in the church. It is not the canon—as Adolf Harnack believed—but the episcopal hierarchy which replaced early Christian prophecy. The final redaction of the *Didache* allows for the appointment of bishops and deacons when no prophets are found in the midst of the community "because they also minister to you the ministry of the prophets and teachers" (15:1). In the mid-second century, the Martyrdom of Polycarp calls him "a prophetic man," indicating that his prophetic leadership was more highly acclaimed than his function as local bishop. Similarly, toward the end of the second century, the bishop Melito of Sardis is charac-terized as a prophet who uttered ecstatic revelations. It seems, in the second century, that the gift of prophecy was claimed first to strengthen the authority of the local bishop, then it was occasionally assumed that the bishop possessed the gift of prophecy, and then finally the authority of the bishop came to replace that of the prophet.[67] In later centuries only the official hierarchy could claim to speak "with God's own voice."

Everything we know about the Montanist movement comes from very biased and often slanderous sources, since their own writings were ordered burned by an imperial edict in 398 C.E.. Hippolytus acknowledged that the doctrine of the Montanists and of the great church were the same, except for the Montanists' introduction of a stricter discipline. The competition between the emerging episcopal hierarchy and the traditional authority of the inspired prophet gener-ated a bitter struggle against not only the Montanist movement but also against other ascetic, ecstatic, or gnostic groups. The struggle against Montanism, however, indicates that what was at stake was not a doctrinal issue but a competition between radically different church structures and Christian self-understandings. The Montanists, as well as many other groups, stressed the authority of the Spirit, that is, the authority of the prophets or ascetics, over and against the authority of noncharismatic local officers.

> But this initial clash between the authority of Church officials who mediate the message of God from the past with the free spirit of new ongoing, and uncontrolled "revelations" was an instance of a fundamental type of conflict. The Montanist controversy illustrates one type of basic disagreement that has remained with us throughout history. The hierarchically controlled church is faced with the accusation that it has maintained order and continuity at the price of suppressing or at least restraining the spontaneity and effervescence of the Spirit.[68]

The fact that this kind of a shift took place was still recognized as late as the end of the fourth century. Ambrosiaster, a pseudonymous Latin work, acknowledges in a commentary on Ephesians that in the beginning all taught and baptized (*omnes docebant et omnes baptizabant*). Later, however, a different order was instituted for governing the church because it seemed an irrational, vulgar, and vile thing that all could do everything (. . . *coepit alio ordine et providentia gubernari ecclesia, quia, si omnes omnia possunt, irrationabile esset et vulgaris res vilissima videretur*) (*Ad Eph.* 4:11.12). By the mid-third century, the teaching authority of the bishop was so well developed that it seems to have become the rule. Now "the ability to transfer Christian teaching to paper either belonged to the bishop or pointed a man toward consecration as a bishop."[69] Whereas in Judaism and in other mystery cults, governance and teaching were not combined in one and the same office, the patristic bishop enjoyed a special authority in all doctrinal matters.

Even though the Christian missionary movement was a subsociety in the Greco-Roman world with an alternative vision and social structure, its gradual adaptation to the patriarchal order of Greco-Roman society robbed the church of its clear-cut social boundaries vis-à-vis its prevalent patriarchal cultural-religious norms and environment. While prophetic, ascetic, and gnostic Christianity established its social self-identity as spiritual-religious identity in terms of essence and lifestyle, patristic Christianity drew its social boundaries in terms of submission to the episcopacy, which controlled the doctrinal belief systems. The patristic boundaries no longer established Christian identity over and against its patriarchal society but over and against other Christian social and doctrinal systems.[70] The patriarchically defined authority of the monepiscopacy thus became the social symbolic center of unity for patristic Christianity. The teaching authority of the bishop is constitutive for the self-identity of the patristic church.[71] Patristic writers, therefore, insist that women cannot teach, have intellectual leadership, or write books.[72] Nevertheless, it took centuries to gradually eliminate or repress women's authority as official prophets and teachers in the church. This process was never quite accomplished, however, since—throughout the centuries—women have claimed mystic-prophetic teaching authority and have preached even to bishops and popes.[73]

The arguments against women's public teaching and prophesying were developed in a special way in the debate with various gnostic groups and with Montanism. Since women actually dared "to teach, to debate, to exorcise, to promise cures, probably even to baptize,"[74] their initiative was curbed more and more by the patriarchally oriented church. The *Apostolic Constitutions* of the fourth century declare categorically: "We do not permit our women to teach in the church, but only to pray and listen to those who teach."[75] Furthermore, they limit the functions of the deaconesses to keeping the doors and assisting "the presbyters in the baptism of women for reasons of decency." Thus Montanism, gnosticism, and the patristic church all appealed to apostolic revelation and tradition to justify their own church orders and theologies. Since the formation of the canon was still in flux some groups considered apocryphal writings as Holy Scripture, whereas others rejected some of the writings which have become "canonical" Scripture.

How much scriptural interpretation and legitimization served political functions for the church can be illustrated by the example of Mary of Magdala.[76] The canonical Gospels mention women such as Mary Magdalene and Salome as disciples of Jesus. Gnostic and other groups build on these traditions to claim the women disciples as apostolic authorities for the reception of revelation and secret teachings. Patristic Christianity, on the other hand, attempted to play down the significance of the women disciples and their leader Mary Magdalene and concentrated on apostolic figures like Peter and Paul or the twelve. The debate between various Christian groups on primacy in apostolic authority is reflected in various apocryphal texts which relate the competition between Peter and Mary Magdalene.

Mary Magdalene is mentioned in all four canonical Gospels as the primary witness to the Easter faith-event. However, Luke's Gospel already attempts to play down her role as primary witness by stressing that the resurrected Lord appeared to Peter on the one hand and by omitting a resurrection appearance to the women disciples. The third evangelist also stresses that "the words of the women seemed to the eleven an idle tale and they did not believe them (Luke 24:11). The *Epistola Apostolorum*, an apocryphal document of the second century, underlines the skepticism of the male disciples. In this version Mary Magdalene and Sara or Martha and Mary are sent to announce to the apostles that Jesus had risen. However, the apostles did not believe them, even when the Lord himself corroborates their witness. Only after they touch him do they know that "he has truly risen in the flesh."[77]

The *Sophia Jesu Christi* relates that the redeemer appears to the twelve and the seven women disciples who had followed him from Galilee to Jerusalem.[78] Among the women disciples only Mary Magdalene is singled out by name. The redeemer teaches them about salvation and his own and Sophia's nature. These teachings conclude with a statement typical of gnostic writings: "From that day on his disciples began to preach the Gospel of God, the eternal Father." Obviously, women are counted among those who preach the gospel. The *Gospel of Philip*[79] and the *Dialogue of the Redeemer* mention Mary Magdalene with two other Marys, whereas the *Gospel of the Egyptians* gives a prominent role to Salome. In the *Great Questions of Mary* Christ gives revelations and secret teachings to his privileged disciple Mary Magdalene, whereas the *Gospel of Thomas* alludes to the antagonism between Peter and Mary Magdalene, a theme more fully developed in the *Pistis Sophia* and in the *Gospel of Mary* (Magdalene).[80]

In the third-century writing *Pistis Sophia* Mary Magdalene and John have a prominent place among the other disciples.[81] Jesus himself stresses that these two will surpass all his disciples and all those "who shall receive mysteries of the ineffable." "They will be on my right and on my left and I am they and they are I." Other women disciples mentioned are Mary, the mother of Jesus, Salome, and Martha. Mary Magdalene asks thirty-nine out of forty-six questions and plays a major role in giving interpretation. Peter's hostility toward her is apparent throughout the whole work. He objects, "My Lord, we shall not be able to endure this woman, for she takes our opportunity and she has not let any of us speak, but talks all the time herself." Mary in turn complains that she hardly dares to interpret the revelations received, because Peter who "hates the female race" intimidates her so much. However, she is told that anyone who receives revelations and gnosis is obliged to speak, no matter whether it is a woman or a man. The argument between Peter and Mary Magdalene clearly reflects the debate in the early church on whether women are the legitimate transmitters of apostolic revelation and tradition.

This controversy is even more pronounced in the second-century *Gospel of Mary*.[82] At the end of the first part, Mary Magdalene exhorts the disciples to proclaim the gospel despite fear and anxiety. After the departure of Jesus the disciples are not willing to do so because they fear they might suffer the same fate as did their Lord. Mary Magdalene assures them that the Savior will protect them and that they should not be afraid because he has made them to be "men." The second part of the work begins with Peter asking Mary to share with them the revelation which she has received from the Savior who loved her more than all women. But Peter and Andrew react with unbelief when she tells them about a vision she has received. Peter articulates the objection of the male disciples: "Did he then speak privily with a woman rather than with us and not openly? Has he preferred her over and against us?" Mary is offended and insists, weeping, that she has not invented her visions nor lied about the Savior. Levi comes to her defense and rebukes Peter:

> Peter, thou hast ever been of hasty temper. Now I see thou dost exercise thyself against the woman like the adversaries. But if the Savior has made her worthy, who then art thou to reject her? Certainly the Savior knows her surely enough. Let us rather be ashamed, put on the perfect Man, as he has charged us, and proclaim the Gospel.[83]

This polemical dialogue reflects the opposition that Christian groups encountered when they appealed to the women disciples as scriptural precedents and apostolic figures. Those groups, accepting apostolic authority of women, in turn might have argued that anyone who rejects the traditions and revelations transmitted under the name of a woman disciple rejects the revelation of the Savior and fails to proclaim the gospel.[84] Those who claim the authority of Andrew and Peter and argue against the teaching authority of women because of their hate for the female race distort the true Christian message.

The arguments of the patriarchal opposition are found in various third- and fourth-century church orders. The *Didascalia Apostolorum* argues that women were not appointed to teach and to preach. It does, however, acknowledge that women were disciples of Jesus and refers to three of them by name: Mary Magdalene, Mary the daughter of James, and the "other" Mary. However, the Lord did not send them "to instruct the people" together with the male disciples. "For if it were required that women should teach, our Master himself would have commanded these to give instructions with us."[85] The document appeals, however, to the example of the women disciples when arguing for the ministry of the deaconesses.

The so-called *Apostolic Church Order* transmits a dialogue between male and female disciples on whether or not women can celebrate the eucharist.[86] The dialogue is very similar in form to that in the *Gospel of Mary*. However, here it is not just Peter and Andrew but also John, James, and Mary herself who object to the eucharistic ministry of women. Andrew raises the question as to whether the apostles should organize a special ministry for women. Peter points out that some steps in this direction have already been taken. He then poses the question whether the eucharistic ministry should be open to women. Peter objects because at the Last Supper Jesus did not permit any woman to *stand* with the apostles. This argument reflects the liturgical practice of a much later time, since according to the New Testament Jesus "*lay down* at table" with his disciples. Martha objects that this is not an argument against women's eucharistic ministry. Jesus did not allow women to stand with the men because Mary, who was earlier identified as Mary Magdalene, had laughed. Mary rejects this accusation of Martha and quotes a saying of Jesus against the eucharistic ministry of women: "The weak shall be saved through the strong"; that is, women through men and not vice versa. A woman herself is used here to provide the theological argument against women's ministry.

In a similar fashion the *Questions of Bartholomew*[87] have Mary, the mother of Jesus, argue that women should pray standing behind the men, because the Lord (actually Paul) said that the head of man is Christ but the head of woman is man. However, later Mary herself stands up and lifts up her hands in prayer. The *Dialogue Between a Montanist and an Orthodox*[88] highlights the debate around the ecclesial leadership of women, clearly indicating that it centers around questions of public teaching and intellectual theological leadership, even in the middle of the fourth century.

> *Montanist:* Why do you reject the holy women Maximilla and Priscilla, and say that women are not permitted to prophesy? Didn't Philip have four daughters who prophesied? And wasn't Deborah a prophetess? And didn't the Apostle say: "Every woman praying or prophesying with her head uncovered . . ."? If women are not permitted to prophesy, they are not permitted to pray either. But if they pray, let them also prophesy!

Orthodox: We do not reject the prophecies of women. Blessed Mary prophesied when she said: "Henceforth all generations shall call me blessed." And as you yourself say, Philip had daughters who prophesied, and Mary, the sister of Aaron, prophesied. But we do not permit women to speak in the assemblies, nor to have authority over men, to the point of writing books in their own name: since, such is, indeed, the implication for them of praying with uncovered head. . . . Wasn't Mary, the Mother of God, able to write books in her own name? To avoid dishonoring her head by placing herself above men, she did not do so.

Montanist: Do you say that to pray or to prophesy with uncovered head implies not to write books?

Orthodox: Perfectly.

Montanist: When Blessed Mary says: "Henceforth all generations shall call me blessed," does or doesn't she speak freely and openly?"

Orthodox: Since the Gospel is not written in her name, she has a veil in the Evangelist.

Montanist: You shouldn't take allegories for dogmas!

Orthodox: There is no doubt, indeed, that Saint Paul took allegories as confirmation of dogmas when he said: "Abraham had two wives; since these women are two covenants, he spoke in an allegorical sense." If the head covering is not to be understood allegorically, you must renounce allegorical interpretations in all cases. If there is a poor woman who cannot afford to cover her head, should she abstain from praying and prophesying?

Montanist: Do you think that it is possible to be so poor that a person couldn't have a head covering?

Orthodox: We have often known women who could not afford to cover their head. But since you do not admit that there are poor women who cannot afford to cover their head, what do you do about those who are being baptized? Shouldn't these women pray? And what do you say about men who frequently, on account of illness, cover their head? Are you going to prevent them also from praying and prophesying?

Montanist: When he is praying or prophesying, he must uncover his head.

Orthodox: Must we not pray without ceasing, or should we disdain the teaching of the Apostle, who says: "Pray without ceasing"? Do you advise a woman not to pray when she is being baptized?

Montanist: Is it because they have written books that you do not receive Priscilla and Maximilla?

Orthodox: It is not only for this reason, but also because they were false prophetesses, following their guide Montanus.

Montanist: Why do you think that they were false prophetesses?

Orthodox: Didn't they say the same thing as Montanus?

Montanist: Yes.

Orthodox: Well, Montanus has been convicted of saying things contrary to Holy Scripture. These two, therefore, must without doubt be rejected with him.[89]

Jerome probably used this dialogue in his response to Marcella, to whom a Montanist had presented arguments for the scripturally founded faith of the Montanist movement. Didymus the Blind, another late-fourth-century writer, also seems to derive his information from this source:

Scripture recognizes as prophetesses the four daughters of Philip, Deborah, Mary, the sister of Aaron, and Mary, the Mother of God, who said, as recorded in the Gospel: "Henceforth all women and all generations shall call me blessed." But in Scripture there are no books written in their name. On the contrary, the Apostle says in First Timothy: "I do not permit women to teach," and again in First Corinthians: "Every woman who prays or prophesies with uncovered head dishonors her head." He means that he does not permit a woman to write books impudently, on her own authority, nor to teach in the assemblies, because, by doing so, she offends her head, man: for "the head of woman is man, and the head of man is Christ." The reason for this silence imposed on woman is obvious: woman's teaching in the beginning caused considerable havoc to the human race; for the Apostle writes: "It is not the man who was deceived, but the woman."[90]

The injunction of the Pastorals that women not be allowed to teach and have authority over men is here understood as an apostolic prohibition against writing books on their own authority.

The Genderization of Ecclesial Office

Patriarchalization of the early Christian movement and ascendency of the monarchical episcopacy[91] not only made marginal or excluded women leaders in the early church but also segregated and restricted them to women's spheres, which gradually came under the control of the bishop. Nevertheless, it must be emphasized again that the writings suggesting this kind of patriarchal dynamic are *prescriptive* rather than *descriptive,* since the male clergy were often dependent upon wealthy and influential women even into late antiquity.[92] Ideological prescription and actual social reality do not always correspond.

The author of the Pastorals admonishes not the bishop but the apostolic delegate to regulate and control the "widows" within the community. Requirements for their enrollment into the ranks of widows are similar to those for bishops and deacons.[93] Just as the male leader must have proven himself a good *paterfamilias*, not newly converted to Christianity, and with a good reputation among outsiders, so the widow must show evidence of having been a good *materfamilias*, having brought up her children well and having been the wife of one husband. By contrast, though a bishop need not be unmarried and advanced in age, this requirement is set forth for the widow only. It seems, therefore, that widows had leadership positions similar to those of the bishop, but—because they were women—they were treated differently. This is obvious not only in the pay/honor they receive—which is only half of that of the teaching presbyter—but also in the conditions and requirements placed on them.

1 Tim 5:3–16[94] addresses four distinct problems: (1) the financial support of the widow; (2) the conditions and qualifications for being enrolled officially as a widow; (3) the question of young widows; and (4) the question of widows who are supported by a Christian woman.

The author asserts that only "true widows" deserve the support of the community. A true widow is a woman who is completely alone and has no surviving family. Thus the author redefines widowhood, not simply as the state of being without a husband, but as a state in which a woman has no family at all. Such widows place their hope in God and pray day and night. Interestingly enough, while insisting on the dependence of widows upon their families, the author attacks those widows who are well off and can afford a comfortable lifestyle. Widows who have a family to support them are not to be paid by the congregation but are to be taken care of by their children or relatives.[95] This is reiterated at the beginning and the end of this first section. No such provision is set forth with respect to male elders or bishops. Their remuneration depends not upon their family status but upon their ability to teach and govern the community well. They are to receive double the amount widows receive.

The requisites for official enrollment in the rank of widows are advanced age, a good record of family and household management, and works of service, hospitality, and assistance to those in need. Here again the requirements are similar to those for male officers. Just as the bishop is required to live in an impeccable marriage relationship and to govern his household and children well, so, too, for the widow. However, though the bishop need not be celibate while in office, the widow must be. There is some question whether the requirement that she must have raised children refers to her own children or to the raising of orphans who, according to the *Shepherd of Hermas*, seem to have been entrusted to the care of the community widows.[96] It seems more likely here, however, that the author is thinking of the widow's own children who are now grown up and are thus a testimony to her "good work" as *materfamilias*. Like the bishop, the widow must have practiced hospitality, which was very important for early Christians traveling from place to place. Unusual is the requirement that "she must have washed the feet of the saints," a duty usually performed by slaves or servants. Finally, she must have assisted those who were afflicted and in need, as well as devoted herself to doing good in every way.

Thus the widow to be enrolled must have shown irreproachable conduct as *materfamilias*, as well as a Christian, since "good deeds" characterize true Christian behavior in the Pastorals. However, whereas in the section pertaining to the bishop's qualifications, only elements pertaining to his *status* either as head of a household or as a proven Christian are considered, the widow to be enrolled is given a list of *duties* which she must have performed. Finally, the requirement that a widow to be enrolled must be sixty years old must be a new one introduced by the author, since he himself appears to know of "younger" widows, and both Ignatius and Tertullian testify to the phenomenon. The sixty-year requirement is not so much an *age* requirement as a *legal* requirement, since—according to Roman legislation—widows remaining unmarried should be fifty or sixty years of age, that is, past the childbearing years. That what is at stake here is a concern with legal requirements becomes clear when we analyze the polemics of the author against "younger widows."[97]

The apostolic delegate is ordered to reject "younger widows" because they might be tempted to remarry and thus break their promise to Christ. It seems that as long as being a congregational widow was understood as a ministry rather than a way of life women enrolled for a certain time but were free to marry again. The author seems to have a different understanding, however, since he sees widowhood as a celibate lifestyle, an innovation when we compare it with the requirements for male officers of the congregation. Although he attacks his opponents for rejecting marriage, he himself makes celibacy a precondition for enrollment as a congregational widow. The outcome of this is pseudo-Paul's insistence that younger women marry, bear children, and rule their households despite Paul's advice, "If the husband dies she is free to be married to whom she wishes, only in the Lord. But in my judgment she is happier if she remains as she is. And I think that I have the Spirit of God" (1 Cor 7:39f). 1 Tim 5:14 provides the key for this contradiction between Paul and pseudo-Paul. Younger women are to follow the societal and *legal* requirements for women of their age so that the Christian reputation will be preserved.[98] It is possible that these younger women were not "real widows," but unmarried women who were enrolled as "widows." Ignatius, in his *Letter to the Smyrnaeans*, greets "the houses of my brothers with their wives and children, and the virgins who are called 'widows'" (13.1). Tertullian was appalled by an Asian bishop who had placed a virgin under twenty years into the order of widows.[99] Thus the official status of unmarried women, especially young women, must have caused offense and created tensions with Greco-Roman society and was in the way of the patriarchal adaptation of the church.

It is not merely a civil apologetic interest, however, but something more which seems to be at work in the author's change of Pauline tradition.[100] It is said that such younger widows go from house to house, learn idleness, and become gossips and busybodies, "saying what they should not" (5:13). The author does not say what it was that the widows were saying during these home visits. However, he admonishes Timothy in 1:3ff to forbid certain people "to proclaim other teachings and to indulge in endless stories or myth." Some have deprived themselves of the purpose of good instruction by running after "foolish talk. They wish to be teachers of the law and do not know what they are saying, nor to what they are bearing witness" (1:6ff). The opponents' teaching is based on "deceitful preaching by liars" who "forbid marriage and demand abstinence from food" (1 Tim 4:2–4). Timothy is admonished to "reject the profane stories told by old women" (4:7). That the opponents had especially good relationships and success with women is stressed in 2 Tim 3:6–9: they make their way into households and persuade "idle" or "little" women, who are negatively labeled as "overwhelmed with sins and driven by all kinds of desires." These women learn and study constantly, "but they can never arrive at the truth."

Tit 1:1–14 claims that "foolish talkers and deceivers, especially those of the circumcision," ruin entire households by teaching what is not becoming for the sake of dishonest gain. The members of the community ought not to turn away from sound faith by accepting Jewish stories and injunctions of people who turn their back on the truth. Although exegetes have yet to agree on the nature of the opponents' teachings and their Judaizing tendencies, they nevertheless assume that these opponents are men. It is possible, however, that, among those opponent teachers, there were also women who were found among the young "widows." Apparently the author cannot prove that these young unmarried women taught anything heretical, but that their whole lifestyle corresponded to that taught by the opponent teachers. It is possible that these other teachers were from the same circles responsible for the apocryphal Acts,[101] especially the *Acts of Paul and Thecla*, or other encratite, ascetic groups who allowed women to teach and participate fully in the church's ministry.[102] Over and against them, the author stresses "good citizenship" as the major content of Christian praxis and genderizes ministerial functions by prohibiting women from teaching, making them responsible instead for "the good works" characteristic of Christian agape.

After having severely curtailed the numbers and influence of the "true widows," the author insists that widows who live in the house of a Christian woman ought not to be paid by the community as well. Thus it would appear that in the beginning of the second century unmarried Christian women were already living together in community. Such communities of women are well known from the third and fourth centuries, but this passage suggests their existence already at the beginning of the second. Ignatius, in his letter to Polycarp (4:1–5:2), mentions three distinct social groups: widows, slaves, and married people.

> Do not let the widows be neglected. After the Lord you must be their guardian. Nothing is to be done without your approval, and you must do nothing without God—as indeed is your practice. Stand firm. Meetings should be more frequent; seek out all individually.

Since, in his *Letter to the Smyrnaeans*, Ignatius puts "the households of married members" in parallel with the "virgins who are called widows" (13.1), we can surmise that these widows lived together in households. The households of Alce and Tavia might have been such house churches of widows. Apparently Polycarp was not, in Ignatius's opinion, paying sufficient attention to, or exercising enough control over, the widows. He is told that he should act as their guardian, which implies legal as well as administrative and personal control.

According to Roman marriage legislation, the wife remained in the power (*manus*) of her father, and was, after twenty-five, only subject to the formal supervision of a legal guardian (*tutor*) or lawyer. Since wealthy women could choose their guardian, such legal supervision was often minimal.[103] Roman women thus retained control of their own property and could divorce themselves from their husbands without too much difficulty. In the papyri, the Greek word used here, *frontistēs*,[104] refers to the guardian or trustee of women who could not represent themselves in law courts. The word can, moreover, connote the managerial administration of a household or association. In an inscription from Pamphylia, a *frontistēs* of the synagogue is mentioned. Whether the word implies the legal tutorship and administration of the widows' affairs, or is used here in a more generalized sense, in any case it enforces the control of the bishop over the widows, and seeks to curtail their independence. This is emphasized by the following injunctions: "nothing should be done without your approval" and "stand firm."

The next admonition—to hold meetings more frequently and to know all individually—gives us a clue as to the problem which Ignatius had in mind but does not spell out.[105] In his *Letter to the Smyrnaeans* he had been concerned with the behavior of some deviant, probably docetist, members of the community, who did not attend the eucharist of the bishop but baptized and did the agape without him. Since such meetings without the bishop are not mentioned in Ignatius's other letters, they seem to be typical for Smyrna (7:1; 8:2). Is it conceivable that certain widows were accustomed to holding the eucharist in their homes? If such is the case, Ignatius does not prohibit this activity or censure the widows. He only insists that nothing be done without the approval of the bishop, because only that eucharist is "valid which is celebrated either by the bishop or someone he authorizes" (8:1). It would appear that the call for more frequent meetings and for personal acquaintance with every member of the community, especially the widows, is Ignatius's way of strengthening the control and supervision of the bishop.

While the injunctions of the Pastorals genderize the local ministries, those of Ignatius place women's ministerial leadership under the strict control of the bishop. Such control seems not to be understood merely as spiritual supervision, but is conceived as well in terms of legal and economic control which curtails the independence of unmarried women in the church. In this context, however, it is not only widows, but also slave-women and married women who are told not to expect emancipation from the church. Slave-women should not expect to be bought free with church funds, while married women are told to be satisfied or content with their husbands. At the same time, the bishop is put in control over ascetics, as well as over those contracting marriage. While in Rome marriage was not a religious affair and ceremony, now it is to be contracted only with the approval of the bishop.[106]

In conclusion: The Pastorals as well as the letters of Ignatius give us some indication that the gradual patriarchalization of the church and its leadership also engendered the "church of women," that gathering of unmarried, independent women who seem to have formed their own house church and religious association. This was possible since religious associations or cults restricted to women were known in the ancient world.[107] Nevertheless, the gradually patriarchalized episcopacy sought, very early on, to control these women's associations socially, legally, and economically.[108] Whereas Ignatius sees the bishop in the role of the legal guardian, the Pastorals seek to restrict the numbers of women officially engaged and paid as ministers.

In so doing, the Pastorals generate a split between orthodox teaching and orthodox praxis, between proclamation and *diakonia*. A similar division was also observed in Acts 6ff, which reserves missionary preaching to the apostles and restricts the Hellenists to service at tables (*diakonein*). This division of ministerial work in Acts, however, is not yet genderized. By constrast, the Pastorals entrust right teaching and transmission of tradition to men, while they demand from women the "good works" of Christian orthopraxis. Moreover, they do not forbid women elders to teach, but they restrict their teaching to the instruction of women. Women elders are told to be "good teachers" and to instruct younger women, but they are not allowed to teach or have authority over men. The stress on patriarchal submission and order of the church engenders the genderization of Christian ministry. That other Christians of the time had a different perception of discipleship and ministry is obvious when we look at the primary Gospels, particularly Mark and John.

Women as Paradigms of True Discipleship

Where the post-Pauline writers seek to stabilize the socially volatile situation of coequal discipleship by insisting on patriarchal dominance and submission structures, not only for the household but also for the church, the original Gospel writers move to the other end of the social "balance" scale. They insist on altruistic behavior and service as the appropriate praxis and ethos of Christian leadership. As we have seen, egalitarian leadership, sociologically speaking, is "shifting" or "alternating" leadership. To stabilize shifting situations of alternating leadership and power, one can introduce either permanent status relationships of dominance and submission or those which call forth altruistic behavior that benefits the whole group.

Independent of each other the evangelists called Mark and John gathered traditional materials and stories about Jesus and his first followers and molded them into the Gospel form.[109] They did so not because of antiquarian or nostalgic interest in the past of Jesus' life, but because they believed that the resurrected Lord was, at that time, speaking to their communities in the words and deeds of Jesus of Nazareth.[110] Both Gospels emphasize service and love as the core of Jesus' ministry and as the central demand of discipleship. The Gospel of Mark was written at approximately the same time as Colossians, which marks the beginnings of the patriarchal household-code trajectory. The final redaction of the Gospel of John emerges at about the same time as the Pastorals and the letters of Ignatius, and might address the same communities in Asia Minor.[111] It is, therefore, significant that the first writers of Gospels articulate a very different ethos of Christian discipleship and community than that presented by the writers of the injunctions to patriarchal submission, although both address Christian communities in the last third of the first century.

The Gospel of Mark

The unknown Christian who brought the various traditions and stories about Jesus of Nazareth together into a coherent narrative structure did so in order to strengthen the faith and praxis of the Christian community to whom s/he writes. Though scholars differ in their assessment of the theological tendencies and the historical situation in Mark, most agree that "the Jesus tradition was appropriated in this gospel in such a manner as to bear directly on the needs, responsibilities, self-understanding, anxieties, conflicts and weaknesses that characterized their community in their time."[112] The kind of community to which Mark writes is mirrored in his/her picture of the disciples, their questions, reactions, and failures.

Discipleship in Mark is understood as a literal following of Jesus and of his example.[113] Mark's christological emphasis, however, is on the necessity of Jesus' suffering, execution, and death. True understanding of Jesus messiahship does not come through the experience of miracles or through his public preaching or private instructions, but only in and through "taking up the cross" and following him on the way of suffering and death.[114] The true meaning of Jesus is not perceived in his miracles or in his teaching with authority, then, but only in and through the experience of persecution and suffering for the gospel's sake.

Suffering is not an end in itself, however, but is the outcome of Jesus' life-praxis of solidarity with the social and religious outcasts of his society. The threefold announcement of Jesus' suffering in 8:22–10:52 is followed each time by the misunderstanding of the disciples and Jesus' call to discipleship as a "following" on the way to the cross. Just as rejection, suffering, and execution as a criminal are the outcome of the preaching and life-praxis of Jesus, so will they be the fate of the true disciple. In Mark's view, this is the crucial christological insight that determines both Jesus' ministry and Christian discipleship. This theology of death and suffering is developed for Christians who are being persecuted, handed over to sanhedrins, beaten in synagogues, and standing trial before kings and governors "for Jesus' sake." Such arrests and trials are occasions for "giving witness" and "preaching the gospel in the whole world," for testifying in the power of the Spirit. They are instigated by hatred for Christians, even by their closest relatives and friends: "Brother will betray brother to death, and the father his child; children will rise against their parents and have them put to death" (Mark 13:12). Thus the Markan Gospel situates the persecutions and sufferings of its community in the context of tensions within their own households.[115] While the writers of 1 Peter or the Pastorals seek to lessen these tensions by advocating adaptation to the dominant society and avoidance of giving offense, the Markan Jesus clearly states that giving offense and experiencing suffering must not be shunned. A true disciple of Jesus must expect suffering, hatred, and persecution.

The section on "true discipleship" (Mark 8:22–10:52) is introduced and concluded with miracle stories about the healing of blind persons. The second healing story emphasizes that faith has the power to save and to enable one to walk the road of suffering discipleship. Thus the blind man who is healed and can see again becomes the paradigm of Jesus' true disciple. These two healing stories frame the three predictions of Jesus' suffering, execution, and resurrection. All three follow the same literary pattern: after the prediction is pronounced (8:31; 9:31; 10:33f), a problem of misunderstanding occurs (8:32f; 9:32; 10:35–41), which in turn is followed by an instruction on the nature of true discipleship (8:34–38; 9:33–37; 10:42–45).

While the first instruction on true discipleship is addressed to all the disciples, the second and third specifically address the twelve and discuss their form of leadership. Whereas the first instruction is an invitation to follow Jesus in suffering and persecutions even to the point of jeopardizing one's life, the latter two address the question of leadership in the community. Both stress that the greatest, that is, the leaders in the community, must become the least, that is, the servants of all.[116] In the first section the paradigm for such leadership behavior is a child/slave who in antiquity was totally powerless and at the mercy of the *paterfamilias.* Unlike the post-Pauline texts which admonish slaves and children to obedience and submission, the Markan Jesus exhorts those who are first to accept fully such persons of low status and to become their servants.

However, just as the disciples—with Peter as their spokesperson—do not comprehend Jesus' announcements of the necessity of suffering and death, so they fail to understand his invitation to appropriate Christian leadership. The third call to suffering discipleship, therefore, makes the same point even more forcefully. The sons of Zebedee, James and John, ask for the places of glory and power in Jesus' empire. Jesus points out that they are not promised glory and power but suffering and persecution. He explicitly stresses that while pagan leadership is based on power and domination of others, among Christians such patriarchal relationships of dominance are prohibited. The leaders of the community must be servants of all and those who are preeminent must become slaves of all.[117]

Community leaders are not to take the position of rulers but rather that of slaves because Jesus gave his life for the liberation of many. His death is understood as a ransom, as money paid for the liberation of slaves. The text does not speak of liberation from sins but of making free citizens of many. Jesus' death—understood as the liberation of many people—prohibits any relationship of dominance and submission. Leaders and highly esteemed members of the community must become equal with the lowest and socially weakest members of the community by becoming their servants and slaves. Equality is to be achieved through altruism, through the placing of interests of others and of the community first.

Whereas post-Pauline writers advocate adaptation to their society in order to lessen tensions with that society and thus to minimize the suffering and persecution of Christians, the writer of Mark's Gospel insists on the necessity of suffering and makes it quite clear that such suffering must not be avoided, especially not by adapting the structures of Christian community and leadership to Greco-Roman structures of dominance and submission. Whereas the post-Pauline writers appropriate the power of the *paterfamilias* for the leadership of the community and appeal to Christ's example in order to advocate freely chosen submission and suffering for slaves, Mark's Gospel insists that genuine Christian leadership can only be exercised as freely chosen servanthood and slavery of those who claim greatness and precedence in the Christian community. Peter, however, together with the eleven, does not understand Jesus' teaching about his own suffering or that which characterizes true Christian leadership.

Scholars agree that Mark's portrayal of the leading male disciples is rather critical and almost negative.[118] Not only do they misunderstand Jesus and his mission, they also misconstrue his nature and identity. Finally, they betray, deny, and abandon him during the time of his arrest and execution. Despite Jesus' special instructions and severe reprimands, they fail to comprehend both Jesus' suffering messiahship and his call to suffering discipleship. While some exegetes attempt to soften the critical features of the Markan portrayal of the leading male disciples, others suggest that this redactional criticism aims at correcting a false christology on the part of Mark's "opponents" who understand Jesus either as a great miracle worker[119] or a political Messiah, but reject Jesus' teachings on suffering. Such a christology might have been advocated by the leadership of the church in Jerusalem, but Mark advocates for his community a different christology.[120]

Such a characterization of Mark's "opponents" in terms of a false christology fails to account sufficiently for the fact that the three predictions of Jesus' passion are not ends in themselves but climax in the call to suffering discipleship and domination-free leadership. What is at stake is right leadership. This interpretation is supported by the whole Markan context which addresses other problems of communal life and Christian praxis. The christological statements in this section on discipleship function theologically to undergird the Markan Jesus' insistence on suffering discipleship and ministerial service. Domination-free leadership in the community and being prepared to undergo sufferings and persecutions are interconnected.

The misunderstanding and incomprehension of suffering discipleship exemplified by the twelve turns into betrayal and denial in the passion narrative. Judas betrays Jesus, Peter denies him, and all the male disciples abandon him and flee into hiding. But while the circle of the twelve male disciples does not follow Jesus on his way to the cross for fear of risking their lives, the circle of women disciples exemplifies true discipleship.[121] Throughout the Gospel Mark distinguishes between the circle of the twelve and a wider circle of disciples who, as Jesus' "very own," have received the mystery of the "empire of God" (4:11). Though the twelve are identified as men, through the list of names taken over by Mark from tradition, the wider circle of disciples are not identified as males. That Mark's androcentric language functions as inclusive language becomes now apparent in the information that women disciples have followed Jesus from Galilee to Jerusalem, accompanied him on the way to the cross, and witnessed his death. Just as in the beginning of the Gospel Mark presents four leading male disciples who hear Jesus' call to discipleship, so at the end s/he presents four leading women disciples and mentions them by name. The four women disciples—Mary of Magdala, Mary, the daughter or wife of James the younger, the mother of Joses, and Salome—are preeminent among the women disciples who have followed Jesus, just as Peter, Andrew, James, and John are preeminent among the twelve. Though the twelve have forsaken Jesus, betrayed and denied him, the women disciples, by contrast, are found under the cross, risking their own lives and safety. That they are well aware of the danger of being arrested and executed as followers of a political insurrectionist crucified by the Romans is indicated in the remark that the women "were looking from afar."[122] They are thus characterized as Jesus' true "relatives."

Mark uses three verbs to characterize the discipleship of the women under the cross: They *followed* him in Galilee, they *ministered* to him, and they *"came up with him* to Jerusalem" (15:41). The verb *akolouthein* characterizes the call and decision for discipleship (1:18).[123] In 8:34 and 10:28 Jesus insists that following him meant "to take up the cross," that is, to accept the danger of being executed (8:34). In pointing out that the disciples have left everything and followed Jesus, Peter is told that their reward here is both the new familial community and persecution. The women are thus characterized as true disciples of Jesus who have left everything and have followed him on the way, even to its bitter end on the cross.

The second verb *diakonein* emphasizes that the women disciples have practiced the true leadership demanded of the followers of Jesus. We have seen that *diakonein* cannot be restricted to table service only, since *diakonia* summarizes the whole ministry of Jesus, who does not subordinate and enslave others in the manner of gentile rulers (10:42), but is the suffering servant who liberates and elevates them from servitude. Similarly, those who exercise leadership in the community must take the last place on the community's social scale and exercise their leadership as servitude. Like Peter's mother-in-law

(1:31), the women under the cross are characterized as those disciples who have understood and practiced true Christian leadership.[124]

The last verb *synanabainein* refers not only to the four leading women disciples but to all the women disciples who had followed Jesus from Galilee to Jerusalem. Interestingly enough, apart from this passage, this verb is found only in Acts 13:31 where it refers to those who had encountered the resurrected Lord and become his witnesses.

> And for many days he appeared to those who came up with him from Galilee to Jerusalem, who are now his witnesses to the people.

The women who have followed Jesus from Galilee to Jerusalem are thus characterized as apostolic witnesses. Whereas Acts presents the twelve as the foremost apostolic witnesses,[125] Mark characterizes as such the women disciples under the cross. They are also mentioned after Jesus has died and the way into the temple sanctuary has been opened to all. Together with the Roman centurion who—as witness of the suffering and death of Jesus—confesses him as the Son of God, the women disciples under the cross signify that the community of Mark, including its leadership, was open across social, religious, sexual, and ethnic lines. This community no longer acknowledges any cultic purity laws (cf. chaps. 5 and 7) and rejects for its own leadership the dominance-submission pattern prevalent in Greco-Roman society and apparently advocated by some leading Christian authorities.

A similar indirect polemic against the male disciples is also indicated in the beginning and end of the passion narrative. It is a woman who recognizes Jesus' suffering messiahship and, in a prophetic-sign action, anoints Jesus for his burial, while "some" of the disciples reprimand her. Further, it is a servant woman who challenges Peter to act on his promise not to betray Jesus. In doing so she unmasks and exposes him for what he is, a betrayer. Finally, two women, Mary of Magdala and Mary (the mother) of Joses, witness the place where Jesus was buried (15:47), and three women receive the news of his resurrection (16:1–8). Thus at the end of Mark's Gospel the women disciples emerge as examples of suffering discipleship and true leadership. They are the apostolic eye-witnesses of Jesus' death, burial, and resurrection.

Such a positive interpretation of the emerging women disciples at the end of Mark's Gospel, however, seems prohibited by 16:8, the last verse of the Gospel.[126] Here it seems that the evangelist introduces the women disciples in order to show that like the twelve the women disciples also failed the test of true discipleship. By adding v. 7 and 8b to a traditional resurrection account, Mark at first glance seems to expose the women as disobedient to the command of the youth or angel.[127] Theodore Weeden has therefore concluded that the twelve never received the news about the resurrection and thus were never rehabilitated in the eyes of the Markan community.[128] The Gospel seems to climax with the failure of the women disciples to announce the good news of the resurrection, with their disobedient flight and silent fear. If this is the case then the other disciples together with Peter and the twelve never heard the gospel of the resurrection.

However, such a reading of the Gospel's ending is not necessary. It overlooks the fact that the women disciples flee not from the angel and the resurrection news but from the tomb.[129] While all the disciples and the unknown young man flee at the arrest of Jesus, the women flee from the tomb that is empty. To be found at the tomb of someone executed was to risk being identified as his/her follower, and possibly even being arrested. The women's fear therefore was well founded.[130] The statement that they kept silent because of this fear of being apprehended and executed like Jesus does not imply that they did not obey the command of the angel, however. "Generalized instruction to keep silence does not prevent disclosure to a specified individual (or group). It simply relates to the 'public at large'."[131] For instance, in Mark 1:44 Jesus charges the healed leper: "See that you say nothing to anyone; but go show yourself to the priest. . . ." The command to be silent does not exclude the information that must be given to the priest. Similarly, the silence of the women vis-à-vis the general public does not exclude fulfilling the command to "go and tell the disciples and Peter," and communicating the resurrected Lord's message of his going ahead to Galilee where they shall see him. Mark 16:7 and 8b, therefore, are not to be related as command and disobedience of the command, but as command and obedience which brings the message to special designated persons but does not inform anyone else.

Despite the extraordinary fear for their lives the women disciples stood with Jesus in his suffering, sought to honor him in his death, and now become the proclaimers of his resurrection. They preserve the messianic identity of the crucified and resurrected Lord which is entrusted to the circle of the disciples. Despite their fear and flight the good news of the resurrection is carried on. The Markan community still experiences this fear of Mary Magdalene and the other women.[132]

Like Peter, the community is tempted to betray Jesus in order to avoid suffering. The community gathers in secrecy and in house churches. It knows that the revelation of Jesus' true identity as the suffering Messiah is given to his disciples but not to outsiders. It struggles to avoid the pattern of dominance and submission that characterizes its social-cultural environment. Those who are the farthest from the center of religious and political power, the slaves, the children, the gentiles, the women, become the paradigms of true discipleship.

The Gospel of John[133]

The Fourth Gospel is written some twenty to thirty years after Mark. Although it is an independent version of the Gospel form, it also can be divided into three sections: Jesus' public ministry (the book of signs: chaps. 1–12), a special section of instructions for his disciples (chaps. 13–17), and the passion and resurrection narrative (chaps. 18–20). Chapter 21 probably was added by a final redactor. While Mark's instructions on discipleship center primarily around the necessity of suffering messiahship and suffering discipleship,[134] the Johannine discipleship instructions focus on the motif of altruistic love and service, though this topic is also found in Mark's discipleship instructions.

Like the Markan church, the Johannine community experiences persecutions and difficulties.[135] The "world" not only hated and killed Jesus because of the revelation he had to give, it also hates Jesus' disciples who, like him, are witnesses before the world (15:27; 17:14). Jesus had revealed that God loves the world (3:16)—or in the words of 1 John that God is love (4:8).[136] Having shown his love by giving his life for his own, by making them "friends," Jesus asks them therefore to love each other. The disciples give witness to the world insofar as they love one another (13:34f). This love is at its greatest when they give their life for their friends (15:13), for in doing so they demonstrate that they are not "of this world," that is, that their life is defined not by the destructive powers of hate and death but by the life-giving power of God revealed in Jesus. As Jesus has loved them until the last second of his life, so the disciples are to love one another. In and through their love for each other they are called to give public witness to the life-giving power of God's love revealed in Jesus. By this *praxis of agape* all people will know that they are Jesus' disciples. Thus discipleship must be lived in service and love. It must be lived as a public witness which indicts the hate and death-dealing powers of "the world."[137] Although the Fourth Gospel is interested in a political apology vis-à-vis Roman political authorities, it does not advocate an adaptation of the community to Greco-Roman patriarchal power structures. It insists that Jesus' power and the community of friends called forth by him is not "of this world" of hate and death.

That the Johannine community is an alternative community clearly comes to the fore in Jesus' sign-action, washing his disciples feet. Whereas in the Pastorals the enrolled widows are required "to have washed the feet of the saints," in the Fourth Gospel this is Jesus' action of love to be followed by *all* his disciples.[138] Jesus' whole ministry and his revelation of God is summed up in this scene:

> Now before the feast of the Passover, when Jesus knew that his hour had come to depart out of this world to the Father, having loved his own who were in the world, he loved them to the end. [He] rose from supper, laid aside his garments, and girded himself with a towel. Then he poured water into a basin, and began to wash the disciples' feet, and to wipe them with the towel with which he was girded. . . . When he had washed their feet and taken his garments, and resumed his place, he said to them, "Do you know what I have done to you? You call me teacher and Lord; and you are right, for so I am. If then I, your Lord and teacher, have washed your feet, you also ought to wash one another's feet. For I have given you an example that you also should do as I have done to you. Truly, truly I say to you, a servant [or slave] is not greater than [his/her] master; nor is [s/he] who is sent greater than [s/he] who sent [him/her]. If you know these things, blessed are you if you do them. [13:1, 4–5, 12–17]

The act of the foot washing and Jesus' interpretation of it are interrupted by the misunderstanding and protest of Peter, who does not understand that the disciples are already clean and holy through the word that Jesus has spoken to them (15:3; 17:17). The purpose of the symbolic sign-action is not ritual cleansing but the completion of Jesus' revelation in his praxis of service and love. If Peter fails to receive the service of love he has no part in Jesus and his ministry.

If relationships of equality are characterized by shifting relationships of power and by alternating leadership open to every member of the community, then the Johannine Jesus advocates the exercise of leadership and power through alternating service and love among the disciples who are understood as a community of friends.[139] Therefore, the Fourth Gospel never stresses the special leadership of the twelve among the disciples, even though it knows of the circle of the twelve. All the members of the community have received the Spirit, are born anew (3:3–9), and have received the powers of the new creation. The resurrected Lord appears to all the disciples, not just to the twelve. All the disciples are the recipients of the same mission Jesus had (20:21), they all receive the Spirit (v.22), and they are all given the power to forgive sins (v.23). If Raymond E. Brown is correct in his assumption that the pre-Gospel narrative referred to the eleven,[140] then the fourth evangelist has changed the tradition deliberately to refer to all the disciples and not primarily to the twelve (cf. Matt 16:19; 18:18; 28:16–20). The Johannine community of friends understands itself primarily as a community of disciples. The Beloved Disciple is their apostolic authority and symbolic center. This community is constituted as the discipleship of equals by the love they have for one another.

The disciple whom Jesus loved[141] is historically not identified by name. He appears for the first time at the Last Supper, characterized as the hour "when Jesus having loved his own, now showed his love for them to the very end." The Johannine Jesus celebrates his Last Supper not just with the twelve but with all the disciples. The resurrected Lord appears to all the disciples, gives them his peace and entrusts them with his mission. By enlivening them with the Spirit he constitutes all of them as the new creation (cf. Gen 2:7) and empowers all of them to forgive sins, to bind and to loose (20:19–23). Therefore, the Johannine Jesus likens the "hour" of his exaltation on the cross and the time of the disciples' bereavement to the experience a pregnant women has before and after giving birth. Just as the woman experiences anxiety and sorrow in anticipation of the child's birth, so the disciples are sorrowful and afraid because of Jesus' departure. But just as the woman is glad and full of joy when the child is born, so the disciples will have peace and joy after their new life and future is revealed in Jesus' resurrection (16:20–22).

Though the term *disciple* is inclusive of the twelve and though the fourth evangelist knows of their leading role in the tradition, s/he nevertheless explicitly contrasts the Beloved Disciple with Peter. The Johannine community clearly regards the twelve and their spokesman Peter as belonging to Jesus' "own," but by contrasting the community's hero with Peter they implicitly maintain the superiority of their own form of discipleship over that of Petrine Christianity. Though Peter is rehabilitated in the redactional chapter 21, the bulk of the Gospel narrative points in the other direction. Under pressure he denies that he is "a disciple of Jesus" (18:17–25); at the Last Supper Peter depends on the Beloved Disciple for information (13:23–26); he is not found under the cross of Jesus the hour when the new community is born (19:26f); he is not the first to believe in the resurrection (20:2–10); and he does not recognize the resurrected Lord (21:7) as the Beloved Disciple does.

Thus Brown seems to be correct in his conclusion that the "Johannine Christians, represented by the Beloved Disciple, clearly regard themselves as closer to Jesus and more perceptive"[142] than the churches who claim Peter and the twelve as their apostolic authority. One of those Christians claiming the name and authority of Peter is the writer of the first letter of Peter, who insists on the submission of slaves and wives. The dispute between Johannine and Petrine Christianity seems not to have centered on christological issues but on questions of discipleship. Chapter 21 acknowledges Peter's pastoral leadership of nurture but only on the condition that he "loves" Jesus, that is, that he subscribes to the altruistic leadership advocated by the Johannine Jesus (21:15–19).[143]

The discipleship and leadership of the Johannine community is inclusive of women and men. Although the women mentioned in the Fourth Gospel are examples of discipleship for women as well as men, it is nevertheless astonishing that the evangelist gives women such a prominent place in the narrative.[144] S/he begins and ends Jesus' public ministry with a story about a woman, Mary, the mother of Jesus, and Mary of Bethany. Alongside the Pharisee Nicodemus s/he places the Samaritan woman; alongside the christological confession of Peter s/he places that of Martha. Four women and the Beloved Disciple stand under the cross of Jesus. Mary of Magdala is not only the first to witness the empty tomb but also the first to receive an appearence of the resurrected Lord. Thus at crucial points of the narrative women emerge as exemplary disciples and apostolic witnesses. Although the story about the woman caught in adultery is a later addition to the Gospel's text, the interpolator nevertheless had a fine sense for the dynamics of the narrative which places women at crucial points of development and confrontation.[145] That such a preeminence of women in the Johannine community and its apostolic tradition caused consternation among other Christians is expressed in 4:27f where the disciples are "shocked" that Jesus converses and reveals himself to a woman. The evangelist emphasizes, however, that the male disciples knew better than to openly question and challenge Jesus' egalitarian praxis.

Jesus' public ministry begins with a miracle at a wedding in Cana. The pre-Johannine story, which might have belonged to the miracle source taken over and redacted by the evangelist, stresses Mary's influence[146] as the mother of Jesus, since she intervenes for her friends to compel Jesus to work a miracle. The tensions in the text indicate that the evangelist has modified this traditional account by inserting v. 4: "woman, what have you to do with me? My hour has not yet come." Since we have no precedent in Jewish or Greco-Roman sources for a son to address his mother as "woman,"[147] the address distances Jesus from his biological mother and rejects any claims she might have on him because of her family relationship to him. At the same time, it places Mary of Nazareth at the same level as the Samaritan woman (4:21) and Mary of Magdala (20:13), both of whom were apostolic witnesses and exemplary disciples. Here Mary proves herself to be such. Despite the rebuff she admonishes the servants (*diakonoi*): "Do whatever he tells you." If the Johannine community acknowledged *diakonoi* as leading ministers of the community, then Mary's injunction has symbolic overtones for the readers of the Gospel. In the beginning of the gospel ministry the leaders of the community are admonished: "Do whatever he tells you." Further, it is stressed that this exhortation must be accepted not because it comes from Jesus' mother but because it is given by a woman disciple.

The revelatory dialogue of Jesus with the Samaritan woman progresses through misunderstandings to a greater perception of the revealer. The whole section climaxes in the confession of the Samaritans that Jesus is the "savior of the world." The dramatic dialogue is probably based on a missionary tradition that ascribed a primary role to a woman missionary in the conversion of the Samaritans.[148] Exegetes agree that the Johannine community had a strong influx of Samaritan converts who might have been catalysts for the development of the high christology of the Gospel.[149] The present Johannine community reaps the harvest made possible by the missionary endeavors of a woman who initiated the conversion of the Samaritan segment of the community. In the "interlude" about missionary work (4:31–38) Jesus uses the Pauline verb *kopian* to describe her missionary work, "I have sent you to reap what you have not labored for. Others have labored, and you have come in to enjoy the fruits of their labor" (4:38). Since the term is used here in a technical missionary sense, the woman is characterized as the representative of the Samaritan mission.

Missionary conversion is understood by way of analogy to the call to discipleship. Just as Andrew calls his brother Peter into the discipleship of Jesus by telling him "we have found the Messiah" (1:40–42), so the woman's testimony motivates the Samaritans to come to him (4:39). Just as Nathanael becomes a disciple because Jesus knew what he had done under the fig tree (1:46–49), so the woman becomes a witnessing disciple because "he told me all that I ever did" (4:29). In 17:20 it is stressed that Jesus prayed not only for the disciples but also for "those who believe in him through their word." Using almost the same words, 4:39 states that many Samaritans believed in him "because of the words of the woman who testified." However, they come to full faith because of the self-revelation of Jesus. The Johannine community in Samaria no longer bases its faith on the proclamation of the missionaries but on its own experience of the presence and revelation of Jesus.

Finally, it is significant to note the response of the woman to Jesus and the content of his revelation. Faith and revelation are the two motifs that dominate the dramatic narrative. How revelation and faith interact dialectically can be seen in the progress of the christological statements: Jew (v. 9), Lord (v. 11), greater than our father Jacob (v. 12), prophet (v. 19), salvation comes from the Jews (v. 22), Messiah (v. 25), I am (v. 26), *Christos* (vv. 25, 29), Savior of the world (v. 42). In addition to the major topic of mission, two additional themes are dealt with: the gift of the revealer—living water—and the worship of the new community.

The question of the fullness of life which the revealer gives and promises is elucidated throughout the Gospel. Wine, water, bread, light, truth, way, vine, door, word, are essential to human life because without them people perish. These images not only designate Jesus himself but, at the same time, his gifts for life, the living and life-giving divine powers that lead to eternal life as well. It is the Spirit who creates and sustains such life (cf. 3:8; 6:63). The life mediated through the Spirit

> is the great gift of salvation, representing an active and vital reality in persons so that the image of the source welling up unfailingly could also be applied to it.[150]

The second theme in the revelatory dialogue with the Samaritan woman is that of "worship in spirit and truth" (4:20–24). The central symbol of religious power for the Johannine community is no longer either the Temple in Jerusalem or the one at Gerizim. Already in 2:13–22 we learned that the risen Jesus' "body" is the place where God is to be worshiped, the true temple replacing the central Jewish/Samaritan symbol of religious power. For the Johannine community the time is now, when the true worshipers will worship the Father in Spirit and truth, because God is Spirit, the life-giving power to be adored. Such worship takes place in the community of believers who are born anew in the Spirit and are called to "do the truth" (3:21). It is the worship of those who are made holy through the word and for whom social-religious distinctions between Jews and Samaritans, women and men no longer have any validity.

Jesus' public ministry climaxes in the revelation that Jesus is the resurrection and the life (11:1–54).[151] Whereas in the original miracle source the raising of Lazarus stood at the center of the story, the evangelist has placed the dialogue and confession of Martha at the center of the whole account. Central to the dialogue with Martha is the revelatory saying of Jesus in 11:25f, "I am the resurrection and the life. . ." as well as Martha's response in v. 27: "Yes, Lord, I believe that you are the Christ, the son of God, who is coming into the world." As the raising of a dead person the raising of Lazarus is the greatest miracle and therefore the climax of the "signs" of Jesus. However the evangelist has not placed it at the end of Jesus' public ministry and the beginning of Jesus' passion because of its miraculous character, but rather to make it clear that Jesus who will be killed is in reality "the resurrection and the life." The miracle becomes a sign pointing to the true resurrection and everlasting life: to Jesus himself. Although believers may suffer human death, they have life in an ultimate sense. In faith, human life gains a new dimension that does not know ultimate death; and this new dimension of life, eternal life, is opened up through Jesus.

Martha, Mary, and Lazarus are characterized as Jesus' friends whom he loved (11:5). They are his true disciples and he is their "teacher." Martha, after receiving the revelation and expressing her faith in Jesus' word, goes and calls Mary (11:20), just as Andrew and Philip called Peter and Nathanael. As a "beloved disciple" of Jesus she is the spokeswoman for the messianic faith of the community. She confesses, however, her messianic faith not in response to the miracle but in response to Jesus' revelation and challenge: "Do you believe this?" Her confession parallels that of Peter (6:66–71), but is a christological confession in the fuller Johannine messianic sense: Jesus is the revealer who has come down from heaven. As such it has the full sense of the Petrine confession at Caesarea Philippi in the synoptics, especially in Matt 16:15–19. Thus Martha represents the full apostolic faith of the Johannine community, just as Peter did for the Matthean community. More importantly, her faith confession is repeated at the end of the Gospel in 20:31, where the evangelist expresses the goal of her/his writing of the Gospel: "but these are written that you may believe that Jesus is the Christ, the Son of God, and that believing you may have life in his name." If Robert Fortna is correct that this summary statement concluded the signs source,[152] then it might be possible to conjecture that the evangelist deliberately put these words of his/her source into the mouth of Martha as the climactic faith confession of a "beloved disciple" in order to identify her with the writer of the book. Such a suggestion is not inconceivable since we do not know who the writer of the Gospel was. On the other hand, such a conjecture can neither be proven nor disproven historically.

While Martha of Bethany is responsible for the primary articulation of the community's christological faith, Mary of Bethany articulates the right praxis of discipleship. She is explicitly characterized as a beloved disciple whom the teacher has specifically called. She had many followers among "the Jews" who came to believe in Jesus (11:45). Though in 11:1–54 Mary plays a subordinate role to that of Martha, in 12:1–8 she is the center of action.[153] The evangelist might have used a tradition which was similar to Luke 10:38–42, in addition to the Markan (Matthean) anointing story and the Lukan story of a great sinner who washed Jesus' feet with her tears and dried them with her hair. The meal is in Bethany. (In Mark it is at the house of Simon the Leper, whereas here no name of the host is given). That Martha served at table could be an allusion to Luke 10:40, but it is here seen much more positively. If Corell's suggestion is right that the only established office in the Johannine community was that of diakonos,[154] then Martha is characterized here as fulfilling such a ministry. In John, Mary and Martha are not seen in competition with each other, as is the case in Luke. They are characterized as the two ministers at a supper, which takes place on a Sunday evening, the day on which the early church celebrated the eucharist.

Mary's anointing of Jesus' feet resembles the anointing story of the synoptics, but in the Johannine tradition the woman is not left unnamed. However, the feature of her wiping away the anointment with her hair is awkward and draws our attention to it. Therefore, it is possible that this gesture points forward to the Last Supper of Jesus, where Jesus washes the disciples' feet[155] and dries them with a towel. Moreover, the centrality of Judas both in this scene and in the foot washing scene emphasizes an evangelistic intention to portray the true disciple Mary of Bethany as counterpart to the unfaithful disciple Judas Iscariot. Whereas according to Mark 14:4 "some" and according to Matt 26:8 "the disciples" object to the waste of precious oil, in John it is Judas who objects and he does so because of avarice. Thus not only the person of Judas but also the male objection to Mary's ministry of anointing is discredited. This is also emphasized by the harsh rebuke of Jesus: "Let her alone." If we take all these different aspects of the story into account, it is most likely that the evangelist is interested in portraying Mary of Bethany as the true disciple and minister in contrast to the betrayer who was one of the twelve. She anticipates Jesus' command to wash the feet of each other as a sign for the agape praxis of true discipleship. Both stories—the messianic confession of Martha and the anointing of Jesus' feet by Mary—point to the death and resurrection of Jesus, to his hour of glorification.

According to the Fourth Gospel, women—Jesus' mother, his mother's sister, Mary, the wife of Cleopas, and Mary Magdalene—and one male disciple stood by the cross of Jesus (19:25–27). Numerous studies of this scene have been written and a variety of symbolic meanings has been suggested.[156] The most likely meaning of the scene is probably indicated by the explicit statement that the mother of Jesus became a part of the Johannine community after the death and resurrection of Jesus. Interestingly enough, neither she nor the Beloved Disciple are mentioned by name. Here, as in chapter 2, she is addressed by the title "woman" and thus characterized as one of the apostolic women disciples. The scene then probably has a meaning similar to that of Mark 3:31–35, where the discipleship community of Jesus as the replacement for all ties and claims of the patriarchal family is also stressed. In Jesus' death the "new family" of disciples is constituted, thus making them brothers and sisters. The scene then seeks to communicate the same message given in the prologue: "He came to his own, and his own people received him not. But to all who received him, who believed in his name, he gave power to become children of God (1:11–12). The Beloved Disciple, then, represents the disciples of Jesus who, having left everything, now receive a "new familial community," houses, and brothers, and, sisters, and mothers, and children, and lands, and in the age to come "eternal life" (cf. Mark 10:29–30). The Johannine community seems to have an understanding similar to that of Mark, namely, that the "new familial community" will include "mothers" as well as brothers and sisters, but not fathers—because their father is God alone.

Finally, the scene might also contain some historical overtones. Though Jesus' mother is explicitly acknowledged as one of Jesus' "own" who are represented by the Beloved Disciple, Jesus' brothers are not so rehabilitated. Raymond Brown has suggested that the brothers of Jesus in the Gospel might represent Jewish Christians of inadequate faith (John 7:1–10). According to early Christian tradition

James, the brother of the Lord, had received a resurrection appearance (1 Cor 15:7), had served as leader of the Jerusalem church (cf. Gal 1:19; 2:9; Acts 15; 21:18), and had died as a martyr in the early 60s:

> This fits into the present discussion when it is remembered that James, the brother of the Lord, was followed during his life-time by a number of Jewish Christians in Jerusalem who were more conservative than Peter and Paul (Gal 2:12), and after his death he became the hero par excellence for the Jewish Christians of the second century who gradually separated from the "Great Church."[157]

If Brown's suggestion has some historical plausibility, then it must be pointed out that the fourth evangelist distinguishes between the male and female members of Jesus' family and therefore implicitly also between male and female Jewish Christians. Not only the mother of Jesus but also her sister are among the faithful followers of Jesus. Could it be possible that women members of the Jerusalem church were more open to Johannine Christianity, thus prompting the evangelist to insist that they have become a part of the community of the Beloved Disciple?

The last woman to appear in the Fourth Gospel is Mary Magdalene who was also mentioned as standing under the cross of Jesus. She not only discovers the empty tomb but is also the first to receive a resurrection appearance. Thus in a double sense she becomes the *apostola apostolorum*, the apostle of the apostles.[158] She calls Peter and the Beloved Disciple to the empty tomb and she is sent to the "new family" of Jesus to tell them that Jesus is ascending "to my Father and your Father, to my God and your God." In contrast to Mark 16:8 we are unambiguously told that Mary Magdalene went to the disciples and announced to them: "I have seen the Lord." She communicated the message to them which he had given to her. Thus she is the primary apostolic witness to the resurrection. Whereas Matthew, John, and the Markan appendix credit primacy of apostolic witness to Mary Magdalene, the Jewish Christian pre-Pauline confession in 1 Cor 15:3–6 and Luke claim that the resurrected Lord appeared first to Peter. Since the tradition of Mary Magdalene's primacy in apostolic witness challenged the Petrine tradition, it is remarkable that it has survived in two independent streams of the Gospel tradition. Moreover, later apocryphal writings—as we have seen—reflect the theological debate over the apostolic primacy of Mary Magdalene and Peter explicitly.

The story "in the garden" must not be psychologized. Mary is characterized not so much as the "great lover" of Jesus who is upset about his death for personal reasons, but rather as representative of the disciples' situation after the departure of Jesus. Her great sorrow is turned into joy as Jesus had promised in the farewell discourse. She is characterized as a faithful disciple in a threefold way.

First, Jesus addresses her as "woman" and asks: "whom do you seek?" The Greek verb *zētein* has a rich meaning for the Johannine community which probably knew its technical meaning of "to study" and "to engage in the activities of a disciple." According to Culpepper John 13:33–35 implies

> that even though the disciples could not "seek" Jesus success-
> fully before the resurrection, subsequently (in the Johannine
> school), by observing the new commandment and remembering
> the words of Jesus (15:20; 16:4), they were distinguished from the
> Jews and able to seek (and find) Jesus (the Word).[159]

Mary Magdalene is the disciple who, despite her sorrow, "seeks" Jesus and finds him.

Second, she recognizes Jesus at the moment when he calls her by name. In John 10, the discourse on the good shepherd, Jesus asserts: "I am the good shepherd; I know my own and my own know me" (10:14). The good shepherd "calls his own sheep by name and leads them out. When he has brought out all his own, he goes before them and the sheep follow him for they know his voice" (10:3–4). Just as the good shepherd lays down his life for his sheep, so Jesus loved his "own" to the end (13:1). Mary Magdalene is characterized as one of "his own" because Jesus calls her by name and she recognizes his voice.

Third, her response is that of the true disciple. She recognizes the resurrected Jesus as "teacher." As the faithful disciple who "seeks" the Lord-Sophia, Mary of Magdala becomes the primary apostolic witness to the resurrection. Like Mary of Nazareth, the nameless Samaritan woman, Martha, and Mary of Bethany (and perhaps the nameless adulteress who was not judged but saved by Jesus), she belongs to Jesus' very own disciples. Thus for the evangelist—who might have been a woman—these five women disciples are paradigms of women's apostolic discipleship as well as their leadership in the Johannine communities. As such they are not just paradigms of faithful discipleship to be imitated by women but by all those who belong to Jesus' "very own" familial community.

Conclusion

Most of our New Testament literature was written in the last third of the first century and addressed Christian communities of that time. These communities seem to have experienced tensions, troubles, and even persecutions from their Jewish as well as their gentile environment. Although the post-Pauline literature seeks to lessen these tensions between the Christian community and Greco-Roman society by adapting the alternative Christian missionary movement to the patriarchal structures and mores of their Greco-Roman society and culture, the primary Gospel writers insist that such sufferings and persecutions cannot be avoided. Whereas the authors of the Epistles appeal to the authority of Paul or Peter to legitimize their injunctions for submission and adaptation to Greco-Roman patriarchal structures, the writers of the primary Gospels appeal to Jesus himself to support their alternative stress on altruistic love and service, which is demanded not from the least and the slaves but from the leaders and the masters—and I might add, not only from the women but also from the men.

While—for apologetic reasons—the post-Pauline and post-Petrine writers seek to limit women's leadership roles in the Christian community to roles which are culturally and religiously acceptable, the evangelists called Mark and John highlight the alternative character of the Christian community, and therefore accord women apostolic and ministerial leadership. In historical retrospective the New Testament's sociological and theological stress on submission and patriarchal superordination has won out over its sociological and theological stress on altruistic love and ministerial service. Yet this "success" can not be justified theologically, since it cannot claim the authority of Jesus for its own Christian praxis. The writers of Mark and John have made it impossible for the Christian church to forget the invitation of Jesus to follow him on the way to the cross. Therefore, wherever the gospel is preached and heard, promulgated and read, what the women have done is not totally forgotten because the Gospel story remembers that the discipleship and apostolic leadership of women[160] are integral parts of Jesus' "alternative" praxis of *agape* and service. The "light shines in the darkness" of patriarchal repression and forgetfulness, and this "darkness has never overcome it."

NOTES

1. See especially E. Schweizer, *Church Order in the New Testament* (SBT 32; London: SCM Press, 1961); and E. Schillebeeckx, *Ministry: Leadership in the Community of Jesus*

Christ (New York: Crossroad, 1981), pp. 5–52. See also the review of NT literature in A. Lemaire, "The Ministries in the New Testament," *Biblical Theology Bulletin* 3 (1973) 133–66; and on the early church J. Mühlsteiger, "Zum Verfassungsrecht der Frühkirche," *Zeitschrift für Katholische Theologie* 99 (1977) 129–55, 257–85.

2. L. W. Countryman, "Christian Equality and the Early Catholic Episcopate," *Anglican Theological Review* 63 (1981) 115–38:115.

3. Cf. E. Boulding, *The Underside of History* (Boulder, Colo.: Westview Press, 1976), pp. 48–67.

4. See the excursus on "apostle" in H. D. Betz, *Galatians* (Hermeneia; Philadelphia: Fortress, 1979), pp. 74f. (bibliography); and D. Georgi, *Die Gegner des Paulus im 2. Korintherbrief* (WMANT 11; Neukirchen-Vluyn: Neukirchener Verlag, 1964).

5. Cf. W. Wiefel, "Die missionarische Eigenart des Paulus," *Kairos* 17 (1975) 218–31:224; B. Holmberg, *Paul and Power* (ConBNTS 11; Lund: Gleerup, 1978), pp. 72–95.

6. Cf. H. Kraft, "Die Anfänge des geistlichen Amtes," *Theologische Literaturzeitung* 100 (1975) 82–98.

7. E. Hatch, *The Organization of the Early Christian Churches* (Oxford: Rivington, 1881).

8. Cf. H. Conzelmann, *1 Corinthians* (Hermeneia; Philadelphia: Fortress, 1975, pp. 36, 298.

9. A. J. Malherbe, "The Inhospitality of Diotrephes," in J. Jervell and W. A. Meeks, eds., *God's Christ and His People: Studies in Honour of Nils Alstrup Dahl* (Oslo: Universitetsvorlaget, 1977, pp. 222–32.

10. Cf. H.-J. Drexhage, "Wirtschaft und Handel in den frühchristlichen Gemeinden," *Römische Quartalschrift* 76 (1981) 1–72.

11. L. W. Countryman, *The Rich Christian in the Church of the Early Empire: Contradictions and Accommodations* (New York: Edwin Mellen Press, 1980), p. 164.

12. Cf. the review in A. Lemaire, "Pastoral Epistles: Redaction and Theology," *Biblical Theology Bulletin* 2 (1972) 25–42.

13. H. W. Bartsch, *Die Anfänge urchristlicher Rechtsbildungen: Studien zu den Pastoralbriefen* (ThF 34; Hamburg: Herbert Reich Evangelischer Verlag, 1965); A. Sand, "Anfänge einer Koordinierung verschiedener Gemeindeordnungen nach den Pastoralbriefen," in J. Hainz, ed., *Kirche im Werden: Studien zum Thema Amt und Gemeinde im Neuen Testament* (Munich/Paderborn/Vienna: Schöningh, 1976), pp. 215–37; G. Lohfink, "Die Normativität der Amtsvorstellungen in den Pastoralbriefen," *Theologische Quartalschrift* 157 (1977) 93–106.

14. Cf. J. D. Quinn, "Ordination in the Pastoral Epistles," *Communio* 8 (1981) 358–69; but what he claims as "the tried virtues of Christian family" are those of the Greco-Roman patriarchal household.

15. For this whole section, see especially H. von Lips, *Glaube-Gemeinde-Amt: Zum Verständnis der Ordination in den Pastoralbriefen* (FRLANT 122; Göttingen: Vandenhoeck & Ruprecht, 1979), pp. 94–150. He points out that the precondition for the "bishop" is that he has proven himself to be a good *paterfamilias*; however, he is not the *paterfamilias* of the household of God, but only its steward. The Lord of the household is God (p. 147, with reference to 2 Tim 2:21).

16. For such an interpretation, see R. E. Brown, "Episkopē and Episkopos: The New Testament Evidence," *Theological Studies* 41 (1980) 322–38:335.

17. For a thorough discussion, see J. P. Meier, "Presbyteros in the Pastoral Epistles," *CBQ* 35 (1973) 323–45; but note that his distinction between the church in Ephesus (1 and 2 Tim) and that in Crete (Titus) is not widely accepted.

18. R. E. Brown ("Episkopē p. 335, n. 29) suggests that "Aquila and Prisca offer the example of a man and a woman in roles that might be considered presbyteral" because they are in charge of a house church and engage in teaching.

19. It must not be overlooked that the text does not speak about the "silence" of women but demands their "quiet" behavior, which is the ideal for all Christians (cf. 2:2); cf. L. Scanzoni and N. Hardesty, *All We're Meant To Be* (Waco, Tex.: Word, 1974), pp. 70f. For the affinity of this passage to 1 Pet 3:1–6, see D. L. Balch, *Let Wives Be Submissive: The Domestic Code in 1 Peter* (Chico, Calif.: Scholars Press, 1981), pp. 95–105.

20. See also J. M. Ford, "Biblical Material Relevant to the Ordination of Women," *Journal of Ecumenical Studies* 10 (1973) 669–94:683; she argues that the prohibition against women's teaching seeks to exclude them from the formal decision-making process, which was to be left to the bishop who had the chief teaching office. H. W. Williams ("Let the Women Learn in Silence," *Exp Tim* 16 (1904/5) 188f.) argues for the silence of women, whereas N. J. Hommes ("Let the Woman Be Silent in the Church," *Calvin Theological Journal* 4 (1969) 410–16:410f.) maintains that women were free to participate in the teaching and admonishing of women because these functions were not bound to an office but occurred in the meeting of the congregation (cf. Eph 5:19).

21. *Kalodidaskalous* is usually mistranslated as "they are to teach what is good (see e.g. the RSV or J. L. Houlden, *The Pastoral Epistles* [New York: Penguin Books, 1976], pp. 146, 148).

22. This apologetic-political context of the instructions for women must not be over-looked, since the whole section on "how one must behave in the household of God" begins with a call to prayer for "emperors and all authorities, so that we may be able to lead a quiet and peaceful life in all piety and dignity" (2:2).

23. Christian slaves seem to have insisted on being treated equally with their Christian masters "on the grounds that they were brothers (and sisters)" as well as "believers and beloved" (1 Tim 6:1–2; for these expressions, see especially Paul's letter to Philemon).

24. It must not be overlooked that 1 Tim 2:12–15 legitimizes the prohibition of women's leadership and their adaptation to Greco-Roman household patterns with reference to the Bible. Not only was Eve secondary in creation; she also was first to sin. Misogynist theology was generated because of the adaptation of the household of God to Greco-Roman patriarchal household structures.

25. See the introduction in C. C. Richardson, *Early Christian Fathers* (New York: Macmillan, 1970), pp. 33–42, for bibliography; O. Knoch, "Die Ausführungen des 1. Clemensbriefes über die kirchliche Verfassung im Spiegel der neueren Deutungen seit R. Sohm and A. Harnack," *Theologische Quartalschrift* 141 (1961) 385–407; K. Beyschlag, *Klemens Romanus und der Frühkatholizismus* (Tübingen: Mohr-Siebeck, 1966).

26. The nomenclature is not clear; cf. P. Stockmeier, "Bischofsamt und Kirchen-einheit bei den Apostolischen Vätern," *Trierer Theologische Zeitschrift* 73 (1964) 321–35: 328.

27. Cf. G. Deussen, "Weisen der Bischofswahl im 1. Clemensbrief und in der Didache," *Theologie und Glaube* 62 (1972) 125–35.

28. Countryman (*The Rich Christian*, p. 156) suggests that they were not only wealthy but also "recent converts" (*neoi*).

29. According to Justin Martyr (Second Century), the Sunday collection was given to the presiding officer of the church, who in turn was to use it "for all who are in need" (*Apologia* 77.6). Visitors, the poor, and the lower clergy thus became economically dependent on the *episkopos*.

30. However, H. von Campenhausen (*Ecclesiastical Authority and Spiritual Power in the Church of the First Three Centuries* [Palo Alto, Calif.: 1969]) argues that Clement understood himself not as an innovator but as a defender of the traditional order.

31. For a translation and commentary, see R. M. Grant, *The Apostolic Fathers*, vol. 4, *Ignatius of Antioch* (London: Thomas Nelson, 1966).

32. See also R. Padberg, "Das Amtsverständnis der Ignatius Briefe," *Theologie und Glaube* 62 (1972) 47–54.

33. For this whole section, see E. Dassmann, "Zur Entstehung des Monepiskopats," *JAC* 17 (1974) 74–90.

34. For an attempt at sociological analysis, see B. J. Malina, "The Social World Implied in the Letters to the Christian Bishop-Martyr (Named Ignatius of Antioch)," *SBL Seminar Papers* 14 (1978), 2.71–119: esp. 97ff.

35. But W. R. Schoedel ("Theological Norms and Social Perspectives in Ignatius of Antioch," in E. P. Sanders, ed., *Jewish and Christian Self-Definition* [London: SCM Press, 1980, 1.30–56:55] points out that "the threefold ministry promoted by Ignatius is still

more remarkable for its sense of solidarity with the community than for its emergence as a distinct segment of the group."

36. Cf. the literature in F. Hahn, "Der Apostolat im Urchristentum," *Kerygma und Dogma* 20 (1974) 54–77; and my article "The Apostleship of Women in Early Christianity," in L. and A. Swidler, eds., *Women Priests* (New York: Paulist Press, 1977), pp. 135–40.

37. H. Greeven, "Apostel, Lehrer, Vorsteher bei Paulus," *ZNW* 44 (1952/53) 1–43.

38. See my "Apokalypsis and Propheteia: The Book of Revelation in the Context of Early Christian Prophecy," in J. Lambrecht, ed., *L'Apocalypse johannique et l' Apocalyptique dans le Nouveau Testament* (BETL 53; Gembloux: Duculot, 1980; Leuven: University Press), pp. 105–28, for literature.

39. For Luke's redaction of the Joel material in Acts 2:17–21, see R. F. Zehnle, *Peter's Pentecost Discourse* (SBLM 15; Nashville: Abingdon, 1971), pp. 28–34, 125ff.

40. See the four virgin daughters of Philip and the interpretation of 1 Corinthians 11 and 14 on pp. 226–33 above.

41. For the following, see H. Krämer, R. Rendtorff, R. Meyer, and G. Friedrich, *"prophētēs,"* TDNT 6.781–861.

42. Ibid., pp. 786–89.

43. H. A. Guy, *New Testament Prophecy: Its Origins and Significance* (London: Epworth Press, 1947), pp. 119–42.

44. Philo *De migratione Abrahami* 34f.

45. *De specialibus legibus* 4.49; cf. also 4.343.

46. *Quis rerum divinarum haeres* 250.

47. Ibid., 258.

48. Chaps. 47–50. See G. W. E. Nickelsburg, *Jewish Literature Between the Bible and the Mishnah* (Philadelphia: Fortress, 1981), pp. 241–48; he suggests an origin among the Therapeutae of Egypt, and asserts that the bequest of Job's heavenly powers to his daughters and of his earthly possessions to his sons "ascribes a higher religious status to women than to men, surely a reversal of values in the contemporary world" (pp. 246f.).

49. Cf. N. Bonwetsch, "Die Prophetie im apostolischen und nachapostolischen Zeitalter," *Zeitschrift für Kirchliche Wissenschaft* 5 (1884) 408–24, 460–77; E. Cothenet, "Prophétisme et ministère d'après le Nouveau Testament," *Maison-Dieu* 107 (1972) 29–50; J. Panagopoulos, "Die urchristliche Prophetie: Ihr Charakter und ihre Funktion," in idem, *Prophetic Vocation in the New Testament* (NovTSup 45; Leiden: Brill, 1977), pp. 1–32.

50. B. Hennecken, *Verkündigung und Prophetie im 1. Thessalonicherbrief* (SBS 29; Stuttgart: Katholisches Bibelwerk, 1969), pp. 103–13.

51. N. Brox, *"Prophēteia* im ersten Timotheusbrief," *Biblische Zeitschrift* 20 (1976) 229–32.

52. Cf. my *Invitation to the Book of Revelation* (Garden City, N.Y.: Doubleday, Image Books, 1980).

53. But see J.-P. Audet (*La Didachè: Instructions des apôtres* [EtBib; Paris: Gabalda, 1958]), who dates the book between A.D. 50 and 70. For translations and introductions, see Richardson, *Early Christian Fathers*, pp. 171–79; and R. A. Kraft, *The Apostolic Fathers*, vol. 3, *The Didache and Barnabas* (New York: Thomas Nelson, 1965), pp. 57–77, 134–77.

54. Cf. G. Johnston, *The Spirit-Paraclete in the Gospel of John* (SNTSM 12; Cambridge: Cambridge University Press, 1970), pp. 119, 126.

55. See Grant, *Ignatius of Antioch*, pp. 104f.

56. Cf. J. Reiling, *Prophecy and the Church: A Study of the 11th Mandate* (NovTSup 37; Leiden: Brill, 1973), pp. 155–76.

57. *Excerpta ex Theodoto* 1.24.1.

58. *Adversus haereses* 1.13.1–6; see also E. Pagels, *The Gnostic Gospels*, (New York: Random House, 1979), pp. 41ff., with reference to Tertullian, *De praescriptione haereticorum* 41.

59. See especially A. Wire, "Pieces for a Mosaic of the Corinthian Women Prophets" (Paper delivered at the annual meeting of the Society of Biblical Literature, New York, 1979).

60. A. Grillmeier ("Maria Prophetin: Eine Studie zur patristischen Mariologie," *Revue des Études Augustiniennes* 11 [1956] 295–312) points out that the Fathers refer not to Acts 2 but to the Magnificat when characterizing Mary as a prophetess.

61. See my article "The Quest for the Johannine School: The Apocalypse and the Fourth Gospel," *NTS* 23 (1976/77) 402–27.

62. For a discussion of the relationship of this woman prophet to the Nicolaitans, see my article "Apocalyptic and Gnosis in the Book of Revelation and Paul," *JBL* 92 (1973) 565–81.

63. Edgar Hennecke, *New Testament Apocrypha*, ed. W. Schneemelcher, trans. R. McL. Wilson (Philadelphia: Westminster, 1965), 2.379f.

64. Cf. K. Aland, "Der Montanismus und die kleinasiatische Theologie," *ZNW* 46 (1955) 109–16; H. Kraft, "Die altkirchliche Prophetie und die Entstehung des Montanismus," *Theologische Zeitschrift* 11 (1955) 249–71; T. Barnes, "The Chronology of Montanism," *Journal of Theological Studies* 21 (1970) 403–7; P. de Labriolle, *La crise montaniste: Les sources de l'histoire du montanisme* (Paris, 1913).

65. The *Martyrdom of Perpetua*, which is written from a woman's point of view, exhibits pro-Montanist tendencies but contains no evidence for Perpetua's association with the movement. "Perpetua's depiction in the role of both male and female intimates the early Christians' conviction that when the prophetic spirit breathes where it will there is no sexual preference" (R. Rader, "The Martyrdom of Perpetua: A Protest Account of Third Century Christianity," in P. Wilson-Kastner et al., *A Lost Tradition: Women Writers of the Early Church* (Washington, D.C.: University Press of America 1981), p. 10).

66. Epiphanius *Panarion* 49.2–3; cf. J. K. Koyle, "The Fathers on Women and Women's Ordination," *Église et Théologie* 9 (1978) 51–101:77.

67. See especially J. L. Ash, "The Decline of Ecstatic Prophecy in the Early Church," *Theological Studies* 37 (1976) 227–52, for the following.

68. R. B. Enno, "Authority and Conflict in the Early Church," *Église et Théologie* 7 (1967) 41–60:47f.

69. L. W. Countryman, "The Intellectual Role of the Early Catholic Episcopate," *Church History* 48 (1979) 261–68:261.

70. G. Vallee ("Theological and Non-Theological Motives in Irenaeus' Refutation of the Gnostics," in Sanders, *Jewish and Christian Self-Definition*, 1.174–85) argues that "an authoritarian pattern was devised to meet heretical challenges, the essential feature of this pattern being the criterion of antiquity (apostolicity) and that of consent (majority)" (p. 185). In my opinion, though, it is not so much the rejection of dualism that characterizes this authoritarianism as its adaptation to Greco-Roman patriarchal authority. Cf. Dassmann, "Zur Entstehung des Monepiskopats," pp. 83ff.

71. See also H. Kraft, "Vom Ende der urchristlichen Prophetie," in Panagopoulos, *Prophetic Vocation*, pp. 162–85: esp. 176ff.

72. See P. de Labriolle, "'Mulieres in Ecclesia Taceant'. Un aspect de la lutte antimontaniste," *Bulletin d'Ancienne Littérature et d'Archéologie Chrétiennes* 1 (1911) 3–24, 103–22, 291–98.

73. Among others, Hildegard of Bingen and Catharine of Siena.

74. Tertullian *De praescriptione haereticorum* 41.5 (CCL 1.221.12–15).

75. *Apostolic Constitutions* 3.6.1–2 (ANF 7.427).

76. For later traditions on Mary Magdalene, see U. Holzmeister, "Die Magdalenenfrage in der kirchlichen Überlieferung," *Zeitschrift für Katholische Theologie* 46 (1922) 402–22, 556–84; P. Ketter, *The Magdalene Question* (Milwaukee; B. Rubl, 1935); H. Hansel, *Die Maria-Magdalena-Legende* (Greifswald: Dallmeyer, 1937); V. Saxer, "Les Saintes Marie Madeleine et Marie de Béthanie dans la tradition liturgique et homilétique orientale," *Revue des Sciences Religieuses* 32 (1958) 1–37; M. M. Malvern, *Venus in*

Sackcloth: The Magdalen's Origins and Metamorphoses (Carbondale: Southern Illinois University Press, 1975).

77. Hennecke and Schneemelcher, *New Testament Apocrypha*, 1.195ff.

78. Ibid., pp. 243–48; J. M. Robinson, *The Nag Hammadi Library* (San Francisco: Harper & Row, 1977), pp. 206–28 (hereafter cited as *NHL*).

79. For English translations of these writings, see *NHL*.

80. Cf. P. Perkins, "Peter in Gnostic Revelation," *SBL Seminar Papers* 8 (1974), 2.1–13; M. Mees, "Das Petrusbild nach ausserkanonischen Zeugnissen," *Zeitschrift für Religions- und Geistesgeschichte* 27 (1975) 193–205; C. Kaehler, "Zur Form- und Traditionsgeschichte von Matth. xvi. 17–19,"*NTS* 23 (1976) 36–58:54.

81. Hennecke and Schneemelcher, *New Testament Apocrypha*, 1.250–59.

82. Ibid., pp. 340–44; *NHL*, pp. 471–74.

83. Berlin Gnostic Codex 8502, 7.18.

84. *Gospel of Mary* 7.18, 20 insists that the apostles did not lay down "any other rule or other law beyond what the Savior said."

85. *Didascalia Apostolorum* 3.6.2 (ANF 7.427).

86. *The Ecclesiastical Canons of the Apostles* 24.1–28 (trans. J. P. Arendzen, "An Entire Syriac Text of the Apostolic Church Order," *Journal of Theological Studies* 3 [1902] 71).

87. Hennecke and Schneemelcher, *New Testament Apocrypha* 1.492f.

88. See G. Ficker, "Widerlegung eines Montanisten," *Zeitschrift für Kirchengeschichte* 26 (1905) 447–63.

89. R. Gryson, *The Ministry of Women in the Early Church*, trans. Jean Laporte and M. L. Hall (Collegeville, Minn.: Liturgical Press, 1976), pp. 75–77.

90. Didymus the Blind *On the Trinity* 3.41.3 (*PG* 39.988C–989A).

91. It is too simplified to state that opposition to Gnosticism and Montanism led to the exclusion of women from church leadership. See A. von Harnack, *Mission and Expansion of Christianity in the First Three Centuries* (New York: Putnam, 1908), 2.64; and F. Heiler, *Die Frau in den Religionen der Menschheit* (Berlin: de Gruyter, 1977), pp. 115f.

92. See e.g. the deaconess Olympias and her economic-political support for Chrysostom and other clergy. Cf. E. Clark, *Jerome, Chrysostom and Friends* (New York: Edwin Mellen Press, 1979), pp. 107–57, and her "Sexual Politics in the Writings of John Chrysostom," *Anglican Theological Review* 59 (1977) 3–20.

93. Cf. P. Trummer, "Einehe nach den Pastoralbriefen," *Biblica* 51 (1970) 473–77.

94. For this section, cf., the commentaries as well as J. Ernst, "Die Witwenregel des ersten Timotheusbriefes—ein Hinweis auf die biblischen Ursprünge des weiblichen Ordenswesens?" *Theologie und Glaube* 6 (1969) 433–45; G. Lohfink, "Weibliche Diakone im Neuen Testament?" *Diakonia* 11 (1980) 385–400; and especially O. Bangerter, *Frauen im Aufbruch: Die Geschichte der Frau in der alten Kirche* (Neukirchen-Vluyn: Neukirchener, 1971), pp. 39–64.

95. Cf. the inscription on a Christian tombstone from Rome: "To well-deserving Rigina, her daughter nicely made this stone. Rigina, mother, widow, who remained a widow sixty years and never burdened the church; an *univira* who lived eighty years, five months, twenty-six days" (Dessau, 1581). Cf. M. Lightman and W. Zeisel, "Univira: An Example of Continuity and Change in Roman Society," *Church History* 46 (1977) 19–32:27.

96. Hermas is told to write two books, one for Clement and the other for Grapte: "And Grapte shall exhort the widows and orphans; but in this city you shall read it yourself with the elders who are in charge of the church" (Hermas *Visions* 2.4.; trans. K. Lake, *Apostolic Fathers* [Loeb Classical Library; Cambridge, Mass.: Harvard University Press, 1913], 2.25).

97. For the following, see especially J. A. McNamara, "Wives and Widows in Early Christian Thought," *International Journal of Women's Studies* 2 (1979) 575–92: esp. 586ff. (literature).

98. Ibid., pp. 582ff.

99. *De virginibus velandis* 9.4A; cf. C. Stücklin, *Tertullian De Virginibus Velandis* (Europäische Hochschulschriften 23; Bern: H. Lang, 1974), pp. 184ff.

100. Cf. R. Karris, "The Background and Significance of the Polemic of the Pastoral Epistles," *JBL* 92 (1973) 549–64; L. T. Johnson, "II Timothy and the Polemic Against False Teachers: A Re-examination," *Journal of Religious Studies* 6 (1978/79) 1–26, with extensive bibliography.

101. D. MacDonald, "Virgins, Widows, and Paul in Second Century Asia Minor," *SBL Seminar Papers* 18 (1979), 1.169–84.

102. Cf. J. M. Ford, "A Note on Proto-Montanism in the Pastorals," *NTS* 17 (1970/71) 338–46.

103. Cf. J. P. V. D. Balsdon, *Roman Women: Their History and Habits* (London: Bodley Head, 1962), p. 45.

104. Cf. S. Applebaum, "The Organization of the Jewish Communities in the Diaspora," in S. Safrai and M. Stern, eds., *The Jewish People in the First Century*, 1.497; J. J. O'Rourke, "Roman Law and the Early Church," in Benko and J. J. Rourke, *The Catacombs and the Colosseum: The Roman Empire as the Setting of Primitive Christianity* (Valley Forge, Pa.: Judson Press, 1971), pp. 165–86: esp. 169, 183.

105. This suggestion was made by D. Hunter in "Widows, Slaves, and Celibates: Social Roles in Ignatius of Antioch" (Seminar paper, University of Notre Dame, Fall 1980).

106. According to Schoedel, this "puts in the hands of the clergy one of the most potent instruments of social control ("Theological Norms and Social Perspectives," p. 50).

107. R. MacMullen (*Roman Social Relations* [New Haven: Yale University Press, 1974], p. 179, n. 86) calls for a new study of such women's collegia.

108. That the social reality was often quite different comes to the fore in the following statement of Jerome: "The very clergy whose teachings and authority ought to inspire respect kiss these ladies on the forehead, and then stretch out their hand . . . . to receive a fee for their visit. The women meanwhile seeing that priests need their help are lifted up with pride. They know by experience what a husband's rule is like, and they prefer their liberty as widows. They call themselves chaste nuns and after a diversified dinner they dream apostles" (*Epistula* 22.16; trans. F. A. Wright, *The Selected Letters of St. Jerome* [Loeb Classical Library, London, 1933]). It must not be overlooked that, in contrast to later nuns, the women of the early church could control their property.

109. J. M. Robinson, "On the Gattung of Mark (and John)," in *Jesus and Man's Hope* (Pittsburgh: Theological Seminary, 1970), 1.99–129.

110. Cf. H. Koester, "One Jesus and Four Primitive Gospels," in J. M. Robinson and H. Koester, in *Trajectories Through Early Christianity* (Philadelphia: Fortress, 1971), pp. 158–231.

111. For a discussion of place, date, and author, see the introductions to the NT and the commentaries on Mark and John.

112. H. C. Kee, *Community of the New Age: Studies in Mark's Gospel* (Philadelphia: Westminster, 1977), p. 176.

113. Cf. E. Schweizer, "The Portrayal of the Life of Faith in the Gospel of Mark," *Interpretation* 32 (1978) 387–99.

114. P. J. Achtemeier, "Mark as Interpreter of the Jesus Traditions," *Interpretation* 32 (1978) 339–52.

115. The "house" in turn is the place where the "new family" of Jesus gathers and Jesus teaches, whereas the crowd is outside (cf. 4:11). Cf. M. Karnetzki, "Die Gegenwart des Freudenboten," *NTS* 23 (1976) 101–8:102.

116. For the whole section, cf. the discussion and literature in R. Pesch, *Das Markusevangelium* (HThKNT 2; Freiburg: Herder, 1977), 2.1–175.

117. Anitra B. Kolenkow ("Beyond Miracles, Suffering and Eschatology," in *SBL Seminar Papers* [1973], 2.155–202) argues that Mark subordinates the idea of suffering to that of service.

118. Cf. the discussion of this question in R. E. Brown, K. P. Donfried, and J. Reumann, eds., *Peter in the New Testament* (Minneapolis: Augsburg, 1973), pp. 57–73.

119. T. J. Weeden, *Mark: Traditions in Conflict* (Philadelphia: Fortress, 1971).

120. W. Kelber, *The Kindom in Mark* (Philadelphia: Fortress, 1974).

121. See now also W. Munro, "Women Disciples in Mark?" *CBQ* 44 (1982) 225–41, but with a different interpretative emphasis.

122. See also L. Schottroff, "Maria Magdalena und die Frauen am Grabe," *EvTh* 42 (1982) 3–25:6f.

123. To argue that the women are not characterized as disciples, but only came with Jesus to Jerusalem on a pilgrimage is eisegesis, since the text does not say so (contra E. Schweizer, "Scheidungsrecht der jüdischen Frau? Weibliche Jünger Jesu? *EvTh* 42 (1982) 297ff.).

124. Kee (*Community of the New Age*, p. 91) argues, however, that "women were given places within the community," but that it "cannot be inferred from these passages that women occupied the leading offices in the community of Mark"; rather, they performed "menial tasks."

125. Cf. E. Haenchen, *The Acts of the Apostles* (Philadelphia: Westminster, 1971), p. 411.

126. Munro ("Women Disciples," p. 235) argues that "the women are not put forward to take the place of or to discredit the twelve." Among the reasons given is that "Markan redaction silences the women at 16:8."

127. Cf. T. E. Boomershine, "Mark 16:8 and the Apostolic Commission," *JBL* 100 (1981) 225–39.

128. Weeden, *Mark: Traditions in Conflict*, p. 50.

129. H. Balz, *TDNT* 9.211.

130. J. Blinzler, *Der Prozess Jesu* (4th ed.; Regensburg: F. Pustet, 1969), p. 386.

131. D. Catchpole, "The Fearful Silence of the Women at the Tomb: A Study in Markan Theology," *Journal of Theology for Southern Africa* 18 (1977) 3–10:6.

132. Cf. also Schottroff, "Maria Magdalena," p. 21.

133. See the research review in R. Kysar, *The Fourth Evangelist and His Gospel: An Examination of Contemporary Scholarship* (Minneapolis: Augsburg, 1975); and J. M. Robinson, "The Johannine Trajectory," in Robinson and Koester, *Trajectories through Early Christianity*, pp. 232–68.

134. P. J. Achtemeier, *Mark* (Proclamation Commentaries; Philadelphia: Fortress, 1975).

135. Cf. J. L. Martin, *History and Theology in the Fourth Gospel* (2nd ed.; Nashville: Abingdon, 1979).

136. For the affinity between the Gospel and 1 John in this respect, see F. F. Segovia, *Love Relations in the Johannine Tradition* (SBL Diss. 58; Chico, Calif.: Scholars Press, 1982), with extensive bibliography.

137. Cf. W. A. Meeks, "The Man from Heaven in Johannine Sectarianism," *JBL* 19 (1972) 44–72; and Segovia, *Love Relations*, p. 212, for the understanding that the Johannine community is an "introversionist" sectarian group.

138. For a survey of scholarship on the footwashing narrative, see G. Richter, *Die Fusswaschung im Johannesevangelium* (Regensburg: F. Pustet, 1967); and Segovia, *Love Relations*, pp. 213–19.

139. G. W. MacRae, *Invitation to John* (Garden City, N.Y.: Doubleday, Image Books, 1978), p. 170.

140. R. E. Brown, *The Gospel According to John* (Anchor Bible 29a; Garden City, N.Y.: Doubleday, 1970) 2.1034.

141. For a review of and literature on the problem, see T. Lorenzen, *Der Lieblingsjünger im Johannesevangelium* (SBS 55; Stuttgart: Katholisches Bibelwerk, 1971); and R. Schnackenburg, *Das Johannesevangelium*, vol. 3 (HthKNT 4; Freiburg: Herder, 1975).

142. R. E. Brown, *The Community of the Beloved Disciple* (New York: Paulist Press, 1979), p. 84.

143. But according to F. Grady ("Recent Developments in Johannine Studies," *Bibli-*

cal Theology Bulletin 12 [1982] 54–58, "If the hierarchical and Petrine Church would accept the witness of the Beloved Disciple as emphasizing faith and love as the basis of Christianity, then the Johannine community would accept the need and fact of an established Church order" (p. 57).

144. Cf. R. E. Brown, "Roles of Women in the Fourth Gospel," *Theological Studies* 36 (1975) 688–89, reprinted in idem, *Community of the Beloved Disciple*, pp. 183–98; S. M. Schneiders, "Women in the Fourth Gospel and the Role of Women in the Contemporary Church," *Biblical Theology Bulletin* 12 (1982) 35–45.

145. For the history of exegesis, see U. Becker, *Jesus und die Ehebrecherin* (BZNW 28; Berlin: Töpelmann, 1963); J. D. M. Derrett, "Law in the New Testament: The Story of the Woman Taken in Adultery," 10 (1963/64) 1–26; and R. Schnackenburg, *The Gospel according to St. John* (New York: Seabury, 1980), 2.162–71.

146. The literature on Mary in the Fourth Gospel is extensive. For a concise review, see R. E. Brown et al., eds., *Mary in the New Testament* (Philadelphia: Fortress, 1978), pp. 179–218.

147. Ibid., p. 188.

148. R. Bultmann, *The Gospel of John* (Philadelphia: Westminster, 1971), pp. 175ff.

149. Brown, *Community of the Beloved Disciple*, pp. 34f.

150. R. Schnackenburg, *The Gospel according to St. John* (New York: Herder and Herder, 1968), 1.432. For the importance of "images" and wisdom motifs in the Fourth Gospel, see A. Yarbro Collins, "New Testament Perspectives: The Gospel of John," *JSOT* 22 (1982) 47–53 (this issue of the *JSOT* is entitled *The Effects of Women's Studies on Biblical Studies*).

151. For this whole section, see Schnackenburg, *Gospel according to John*, 2.316–61.

152. R. Fortna, *The Gospel of Signs* (SNTSM 11; Cambridge: Cambridge University Press, 1970), pp. 197f.

153. See the commentaries and especially E. E. Platt, "Ministry and Mary of Bethany," *Theology Today* 34 (1977) 29–39; W. Munro, "The Anointing in Mark 14:3–9 and John 12:1–8," *SBL Seminar Papers* 18 (1979), 1.127–30.

154. Cf. A. Corell, *Consummatum Est: Eschatology and Church in the Gospel of John* (London: SPCK, 1958), pp. 40ff.

155. "His feet" occurs twice. Cf. Schnackenburg, *Gospel according to John*, 2.372.

156. See Brown et al., *Mary in the NT*, pp. 206–18; and R. F. Collins, "Mary in the Fourth Gospel: A Decade of Johannine Studies," *Louvain Studies* 3 (1970) 99–142.

157. Brown, *Community of the Beloved Disciple*, p. 76.

158. E. Schüssler Fiorenza, "Mary Magdalene: Apostle to the Apostles," *UTS Journal*, April 1975, pp. 22ff. See also K. H. Schelkle, *Der Geist und die Braut: Frauen in der Bibel* (Düsseldorf: Patmos, 1977), pp. 151f.

159. R. A. Culpepper, *The Johannine School* (SBL Diss. 26; Missoula, Mont.: Scholars Press, 1975), p. 298.

160. For the interpretation of these women in Christian art, legend, and history, see especially E. Moltmann-Wendel, *The Women around Jesus: Reflections on Authentic Personhood*, trans. J. Bowden (New York: Crossroad, 1982).

Epilogue
Toward a Feminist Biblical Spirituality: The Ekklēsia of Women

In the first part of the book I have argued that only in and through a critical evaluative process of feminist hermeneutics can Scripture be used as a resource in the liberation struggle of women and other "subordinated" people. The vision and praxis of our foresisters who heard the call to coequal discipleship and who acted in the power of the Spirit must be allowed to become a transformative power that can open up a feminist future for women in biblical religion. We have, therefore, moved from a reading of androcentric texts to the reconstruction of the history of women in early Christianity. Such a reconstruction was attempted in the second and third parts. It remains to reflect on the spiritual implications of such a reconstruction.[1]

In *Women of Crisis* Jane and Robert Coles tell us about a maid who is rather ambivalent about the feminist aspirations of the middle-class woman she works for. Nevertheless, "in a moment of mixed faith and doubt," so they report, the maid expressed "that she would like to see 'her people' have a better day." And the Coles comment:

> We thought she was being "ethnic," we thought she was speaking of class and race, of neighborhoods and cities, of income levels and church affiliations or occupational status; but no she explained when we asked: her people were "all the women in the world." [p. 273]

The image and vision of the people of God, of my people, who are women, theologically sums up my own spiritual feminist experiences and that of my sisters who have celebrated our bonding in sisterhood for empowerment and reclaimed our baptismal call to the discipleship of equals. This image and self-understanding allows us to build a feminist movement not on the fringes of church but as the central embodiment and incarnation of the vision of church that lives in solidarity with the oppressed and the impoverished, the majority of whom are women and children dependent on women.

Ekklēsia—the term for church in the New Testament—is not so much a religious as a civil-political concept. It means the actual assembly of free citizens gathering for deciding their own spiritual-political affairs. Since women in a patriarchal church cannot decide their own theological-religious affairs and that of their own people— women—the *ekklēsia* of women is as much a future hope as it is a reality today. Yet we have begun to gather as the *ekklēsia* of women, as the people of God, to claim our own religious powers, to participate fully in the decision-making process of church, and to nurture each other as women Christians. Baptism is the sacrament that calls us into the discipleship of equals. No special vocation is given, no more "perfect" Christian lifestyle is possible. Commitment, accountability, and solidarity in the *ekklēsia* of women are the life-praxis of such a feminist Christian vocation. They are a central embodiment and incarnation of the vision of a "new church" in solidarity with the oppressed and the "least" of this world, the majority of whom are women and children dependent on women.

It is usually assumed that spirituality has something to do with the life of the "soul," prayer life and worship, meditation and mystical union, with the "waiting" for God's will to come to pass and the religious experience of the divine. In this understanding spirituality concentrates above all on prayer and meditation, on "spiritual" direction and Christ's indwelling in the soul, on ascetic and religious exercises as the precondition for progress on the spiritual journey of the soul from one level to another. In a similar fashion feminist spirituality can be occupied with meditation and incantations, spells and incense, womb chant and candle gazing, feminine symbols for the divine and trance induction. Such an understanding of spirituality, of religious rituals and exercises, is found in all religions and not limited to Christianity. Therefore, it does not capture the specific new vision of Jesus and the movement initiated by him.

The gospel is not a matter of the individual soul; it is the communal proclamation of the life-giving power of Spirit-Sophia and of God's vision of an alternative community and world. The experience of the Spirit's creative power releases us from the life-destroying powers of sin and sets us free to choose an alternative life for ourselves and for each other. The focal point of early Christian self-understanding was not a holy book or a cultic rite, not mystic experience and magic invocation, but a set of relationships: the experience of God's presence among one another and through one another. To embrace the gospel means to enter into a community, the one cannot be obtained without the other. The gospel calls into being the church as the discipleship of equals that is continually recreated in the power of the Spirit. Jesus' ministry, his healings and exorcisms, his promise to the poor and challenge to the rich, his breaking of religious law, and his table community with outcasts and sinners made experientially available God's new world, not, as we used to think, *within* us but *among* us. God's presence is found in the "midst of us" (Luke 17:21). The name of Jesus is Emmanuel, God with us. This is also the name of the God of Judith. The God of Jesus is divine Wisdom-Spirit whose power is gentle and whose yoke is light.

Like Jesus' own ministry, the ministry of the community called forth by Jesus, the messenger of divine wisdom, is not an end in itself. In the power of the Spirit the disciples are sent to do what he did: to feed the hungry, heal the sick, liberate the oppressed, and to announce the inbreaking of God's new world and humanity here and now. In every generation Divine Wisdom commissions prophets—women and men—and makes them friends and children of God. To embrace the gospel means to enter into a movement, to become a member of God's people who are on the road that stretches from Christ's death to Her return in glory. *Ekklēsia* expresses this dynamic reality of Christian community. It is not a local or static term, it is not even a religious expression; it means the *actual* gathering of people, the assembly of free citizens in a town, called together in order to decide matters affecting their own welfare.

In the Greek Old Testament *ekklēsia* means the "assembly of the people of Israel before God." In the New Testament *ekklēsia* comes through the agency of the Spirit to visible, tangible expression in and through the gathering of God's people around the table, eating together a meal, breaking the bread, and sharing the cup in memory of Christ's passion and resurrection. *Christian* spirituality means eating together, sharing together, drinking together, talking with each other, receiving each other, experiencing God's presence through each other, and, in doing so, proclaiming the gospel as God's alternative vision for everyone, especially for those who are poor, outcast, and battered. As long as women Christians are excluded from breaking the bread and deciding their own spiritual welfare and commitment, *ekklēsia* as the discipleship of equals is not realized and the power of the gospel is greatly diminished. The true spiritual person is according to Paul the one who *walks* in the Spirit, she who brings about this new world and family of God over and against the resistance and pull of all oppressive powers of this world's enslaving patriarchal structures.

A feminist Christian spirituality, therefore, calls us to gather together the *ekklēsia of women* who, in the angry power of the Spirit, are sent forth to feed, heal, and liberate our own people who are women. It unmasks and sets us free from the structural sin and alienation of sexism and propels us to become children and spokeswomen of God. It rejects the idolatrous worship of maleness and articulates the divine image in female human existence and language. It sets us free from the internalization of false altruism and self-sacrifice that is concerned with the welfare and work of men first to the detriment of our own and other women's welfare and calling. It enables us to live "for one another" and to experience the presence of God in the *ekklēsia* as the gathering of women. Those of us who have heard this calling respond by committing ourselves to the liberation struggle of women and all peoples, by being accountable to women and their future, and by nurturing solidarity within the *ekklēsia* of women. Commitment, accountability, and solidarity in community are the hallmarks of our calling and struggle.

Two major objections are usually raised at this point. The first is that the church of women does not share in the fullness of church. This is correct, but neither do exclusive male hierarchical assemblies. Women's religious communities have always existed within the Catholic tradition. They were generated as soon as the local church structures became patriarchal and hierarchical and therefore had to relegate women to subordinate roles or to eliminate them from church office altogether. The male hierarchical church in turn has always sought to control these communities by colonizing them through male theology, liturgy, law, and spirituality, but was never quite able to do so. By abolishing these religious communities of women the Protestant Reformation has strengthened patriarchal church structures and intensified male clerical control of Roman Catholic women's communities in modern times. In the past centuries, however, women founders and leaders of their people have arisen again and again who sought to gather communities of women free from clerical and monastic control. A Christian feminist spirituality claims these communities of women and their history as our heritage and history and seeks to transform them into the *ekklēsia* of women by claiming our own spiritual powers and gifts, by deciding our own welfare, by standing accountable for our decisions, in short, by rejecting the patriarchal structures of laywomen and nun-women, of laywomen and clergywomen, which deeply divide us along patriarchal lines.

The second objection made is the charge of "reverse sexism" and the appeal to "mutuality with men" whenever we gather together as the *ekklēsia* of women in Her name. However, such an objection does not face sufficiently the issues of patriarchal oppression and power. It looks too quickly for easy grace, having paid lip service to the structural sin of sexism. Do we call it "reverse imperialism" if the poor of South and Central America gather together as a people? Or do we call it "reverse colonialism" whenever Africans or Asians gather together as a people? We do not do so because we know too well that the coming together of those exploited does not spell the oppression of the rich or that the oppressed are gaining power over white men and Western nations, but that it means the political bonding of oppressed people in their struggle for economic and cultural survival. Why then do men feel threatened by the bonding of women in our struggle for liberation? Why then can churchmen not understand and accept that Christian women gather together for the sake of our spiritual survival as Christians and women persons? It is not over and against men that we gather together but in order to become *ekklēsia* before God, deciding matters affecting our own spiritual welfare and struggle. Because the spiritual colonialization of women by men has entailed our internalization of the male as divine, men have to relinquish their spiritual and religious control over women as well as over the church as the people of God, if mutuality should become a real possibility.

Women in turn have to reclaim their spiritual powers and to exorcise their possession by male idolatry before mutuality is possible. True, "the dream of a common language" belongs to God's alternative world of cohumanity in the power of the Spirit. Yet it can only become reality among the people of God, when male idolatry and its demonic structures are rejected in the confession of the structural and personal sin of sexism and when the fullness of *ekklēsia* becomes a possibility in a genuine conversion of individual persons and ecclesiastical structures. Not women, but churchmen exclude women from "breaking the bread and sharing the cup" in eucharistic table community.

Images have a great power in our lives. For almost two hundred years two biblical images have dominated the American women's movement in and outside of organized religion. The image of Eden-home determines today the arguments and appeals of the so-called Moral Majority, while that of the Exodus has inspired radical feminism, calling us to abandon the oppressive confines of home and church. The "cult of true womanhood" proclaims that the vocation of women is "homemaker." The fulfillment of her true nature and happiness consists in creating the home as a peaceful island in the sea of alienated society, as Eden-Paradise to which men can retreat from the exploitations and temptations of the work-world. Women must provide in the home a climate of peace and happiness, of self-sacrificing love and self-effacing gentility in order to "save the family." Therefore, feminine spiritual calling is superior to that of men. This praise of femininity conveniently overlooks that poor and unmarried women cannot afford to stay "at home"; it overlooks the violence done to women and children in the home, and it totally mistakes patriarchal dependency for Christian family.

The Exodus image on the other hand compels women to leave everything behind they treasure: loving community with men, shelter and happiness, children, nurturance and religion because all this has contributed to their oppression and exploitation in patriarchal family and church. Women have to move away from "the fleshpots" of patriarchal slavery and institution and live "in a new space and time." The image of the Exodus calls women to move out from the sanctity of the home, to leave the servitude of the patriarchal family, and to abandon the certitudes of patriarchal religion. The spirituality of Exodus, however, overlooks not only that the patriarchal oppression of "Egypt" is everywhere but also that God is present not just on the boundaries but also in the center, if God is "in the midst of us" wherever and whenever we struggle for liberation. These two biblical images—that of Eden and that of Exodus—place us before the alternatives: either to become Martha serving Jesus in the home or to become Miriam, the sister of Moses, leading her people into the desert. These images, however, do not lead us into the center of patriarchal society and church bringing about God's vision of cohumanity in our struggle and solidarity with each other.

The Roman Catholic variation of these alternative biblical images is the image of Martha, as laywoman, serving Jesus and the family in the home, and that of Mary, as nun-woman, leaving the world of family and sexuality and serving Jesus in "religious life" and patriarchally defined ecclesiastical orders. The dichotomy evoked by the images of Exodus and Eden becomes structurally expressed in a dichotomy of lifestyles: virgin-mother, religious-lay, spiritual-biological. Women's sexual or spiritual relationship with men or the lack of it becomes constitutive for their Christian vocation. The calendar of saints therefore marks women, but not men, as "virgins" when extolling their sanctity.

Rather than defining women's relationship to God by their sexual relationship to men and through the patriarchal structures of family and church, a feminist Christian spirituality defines women's relationship to God in and through the experience of being called into the discipleship of equals, the assembly of free citizens who decide their own spiritual welfare. The image of the *ekklēsia of women*, the gathering of women as a free and decision-making assembly of God's people, replaces the other biblical images mentioned: that of Eden-home, Exodus-world, and virgin-mother by integrating them with each other. It can however only do so if the structural-patriarchal dualisms in which these alternative images have their spiritual roots are overcome. The *ekklēsia of women* as the new model of church can only be sustained if we overcome the structural-patriarchal dualisms between Jewish and Christian women, laywomen and nun-women, homemakers and career women, between active and contemplative, between Protestant and Roman Catholic women, between married and single women, between physical and spiritual mothers, between heterosexual and lesbian women, between the church and the world, the sacral and the secular. However, we will overcome these dualisms only through and in solidarity with all women and in a catholic sisterhood that transcends all patriarchal ecclesiastical divisions. These patriarchal divisions and competitions among women must be transformed into a movement of women as the people of God. Feminist biblical spirituality must be incarnated in a historical movement of women struggling for liberation. It must be lived in prophetic commitment, compassionate solidarity, consistent resistance, affirmative celebration, and in grassroots organizations of the *ekklēsia of women.*

Such a movement of women as the people of God is truly ecumenical insofar not only as it has in common the experience of patriarchal ecclesiastical sexism but also as it has as its central integrative image the biblical image of God's people that is common to Jewish as well as to Christian religion. Moreover, it is distinctive but not separated from the so-called secular women's movements. Any struggle against the structural sin of sexism won for Episcopal, Jewish, or Mormon women benefits the liberation struggle of all women and vice versa. Solidarity in the struggle with poor women, third-world women, lesbian women, welfare mothers, or older and disabled women spells out our primary spiritual commitment and accountability.

Although most women's lives are defined by the birthing and upbringing of children, the feminist movement in biblical religion has not paid sufficient attention to the needs of children and of women with children. The movement of women as the people of God, therefore, must recover the meaning of religious initiation into the *ekklēsia*

of women. It can provide "godmothers" who become intimately involved with the upbringing and socialization of children and young
people. It must provide a feminist ecclesial community of adults that
models itself on the discipleship of equals and from which children
can receive their bodily and spiritual sustenance. Children are not
just the responsibility of mothers, not even just the responsibility of
both parents. Their rights are given into the care of all of us, not
because we are women but because they are our future.

Women as the *ekklēsia* of God have a continuous history that can
claim women in Judaism, as well as in the Jesus and the early Christian movements, as its roots and beginnings. This history of women
as the people of God must be exposed as a history of oppression as
well as a history of conversion and liberation. When I speak of the
ekklēsia of women, I have in mind women of the past and of the
present, women who have acted and still act in the power of the life-
giving Sophia-Spirit. Such an understanding of catholic sisterhood
that spans all ages, nations, and continents does not need to deny our
hurt and anger or to cover up the injustice and violence done to
women in the name of God and Christ. It, however, also does not
need to claim salvific powers for women and to narrow its understanding of sisterhood to those women who are the elect and the
holy. It does not expect salvation from women, because it knows that
women have also internalized the structural sin of sexism and therefore can act against their own spiritual interests and leaders. It calls us
to solidarity with all women of the present and the past. Such a
solidarity in sisterhood allows us to treasure and recover our heritage
as Christian women and as God's people. As Judy Chicago has
pointed out: "All the institutions of our culture seek to persuade us
that we are insignificant" by depriving us of our history and heritage.
"But our heritage is our power."

Finally, a feminist Christian spirituality is rooted in the *ekklēsia* of
women as the "body of Christ." Bodily existence is not detrimental or
peripheral to our spiritual becoming as the *ekklēsia* of women but
constitutive and central to it. Not the soul or the mind or the inner-
most Self but the body is the image and model for our being church.
How can we point to the eucharistic bread and say "this is my body"
as long as women's bodies are battered, raped, sterilized, mutilated,
prostituted, and used to male ends? How can we proclaim "mutuality
with men" in the body of Christ as long as men curtail and deny
reproductive freedom and moral agency to us? As in the past so still
today men fight their wars on the battlefields of our bodies, making
us the targets of their physical or spiritual violence. Therefore, the

ekklēsia of women must reclaim women's bodies as the "image and body of Christ." It must denounce all violence against women as sacrilege and maintain women's moral power and accountability to decide our own spiritual welfare, one that encompasses body and soul, heart and womb.

A feminist biblical spirituality must remain a critical and communal spirituality. As a critical spirituality it seeks not only to articulate the liberating experiences of women in biblical religion but also to keep alive the memory of our foresisters' struggles and sufferings in patriarchal religion. In tracing the vision and struggle of our foresisters in the first century I have attempted to show that women as the people of God, as the *ekklēsia* of women, can claim the apostolic tradition of our foresisters and the example of Jesus for their own feminist vision and praxis of coequal discipleship. A communal feminist biblical spirituality reclaims the *ekklēsia* of women as our own biblical heritage. I have, therefore, sought to understand early Christian history as the history of women and men. I have reconstructed Christian beginnings not only as the history of patriarchal male agency but also as the history of women's struggles for liberation. The history of patriarchal oppression must not be allowed to cancel out the history of the life, struggles, and leadership of women in biblical religion.

Commitment to the *ekklēsia* of women as the people of God is sustained in consistent resistance to all forms of patriarchal oppression and in political involvement in women's struggle for liberation and equality. Only when the *ekklēsia* of women is joined by all those in biblical religion who share the vision of the people of God as the discipleship of equals, only then is the gospel proclaimed in the whole world. Only then will we be able to adequately tell what our foresisters have done *in memory of her.* In breaking the bread and sharing the cup we proclaim not only the passion and resurrection of Christ but also celebrate that of women in biblical religion.

Notes

1. These reflections were worked out in the context of the "Women Moving Church Conference," sponsored by the Center of Concern, Washington, D.C., and appeared in the proceedings of this conference (*Women Moving Church,* ed. Diann Neu and Maria Riley [Washington, D.C.: Center of Concern, 1982]) in a more expanded form under the title "Gather Together in My Name . . . Toward a Christian Feminist Spirituality."